The Challenge of Postmodernism

· · · · · · · · · · · · · · · · · · · ·

An Evangelical Engagement

THE CHALLENGE of

A
BRIDGEPOINT
BOOK

BridgePoint,
the academic
imprint of
Victor Books, is
your connection
for the best in
serious reading
that integrates
the passion of
the heart with
the scholarship
of the mind.

POSTMODERNISM

An
Evangelical
Engagement

DAVID S. DOCKERY, Editor

A
BRIDGEPOINT
BOOK

Baker Books

A Division of Baker Book House Co.
Grand Rapids, Michigan 49516

Published 1997 by Baker Books
a division of Baker Book House Company
P.O. Box 6287, Grand Rapids, MI 49516-6287

BridgePoint Books is an imprint of Baker Book House Company.

First published 1995 by Victor Books, a division of Scripture Press Publications Inc., Wheaton, Illinois.

Printed in the United States of America

Library of Congress Cataloging-in-Publication Data

The challenge of postmodernism : an Evangelical engagement / by David S. Dockery, editor.
    p.   cm.
Includes bibliographical references and index.
ISBN 0-8010-2121-9
1. Theology—History—20th century. 2. Postmodernism—Religious aspects—Christianity. 3. Evangelicalism. I. Dockery, David S.
BT28.C42 1995
230'.046—dc20   95-1614

For information about academic books, resources for Christian leaders, and all new releases available from Baker Book House, visit our web site:
http://www.bakerbooks.com

DEDICATION

. . . .

To
Cindy Meredith,
Jane Jones, and
Dianne Teafatiller

and the entire staff of
The Southern Baptist Theological Seminary,
whose labors in the Lord
are sincerely and deeply appreciated.

CONTENTS

. . . .

The Challenge for Apologetics/Ministry

The Challenge for the Future

PREFACE

· ·

A new day has dawned. A new generation has come of age. The new generation is post-Christian, post-Enlightenment, and postmodern. The church is faced with a new challenge. The previous generation of church leaders responded to the rationalistic, atheistic challenge of the claim that there is no God. But for postmoderns the question is not "Is there a God?" but "Which God?" The secularized world of our day, with its pluralistic worldview, however, still expresses a need for God and a hunger for spirituality as evidenced by Douglas Coupland's secret cry in his book, *Life After God.* Following his 360-page chronicle of his search for meaning and things spiritual, Coupland concludes, "My secret is that I need God—that I am sick and can no longer make it alone."

With a common commitment to address the issues raised by the first post-Christian, postmodern generation, we have assembled this series of essays. *Postmodernism* is simultaneously a challenge to evangelical Christianity and a unique opportunity for theology and biblical interpretation, missions and ministry, education and evangelism. This volume seeks to engage these various issues from an evangelical perspective.

Several of the essays were presented at the 1994 spring Southeastern Region meeting of the Evangelical Theological Society, hosted by The Southern Baptist Theological Seminary in Louisville, Kentucky. Other contributions have been added to address the full breadth of these significant matters.

Postmodernism comes in several varieties and impacts all areas of life from philosophy and theology to art and architecture. The contributors wrestle with understanding postmodernism and thus seek to address this movement from diverse perspectives, with a common commitment to the Bible as God's truthful and authoritative word and to Jesus Christ as God's unique and ultimate revelation to humankind. The contributors include senior evangelical statesmen like Carl F.H. Henry and Thomas Oden to a cadre of both seasoned and young scholars and practitioners. We offer this work with the prayer that it might help the church come to grips with the changes and challenges facing us to reach a new generation for Christ.

This work would not have been possible without the labors and support of many people. I am grateful to Robert N. Hosack for his editorial guidance and vision for a book of this kind. I am deeply appreciative of the support provided by Jane Jones, Dianne Teafatiller, and particularly Cindy Meredith to bring this work to fruition. This volume would have been impossible without the loving support of my wife, Lanese, and my sons, Jonathan, Benjamin, and Timothy. For their help throughout the project and particularly for their assistance in constructing the index for this book I am grateful. To each of the contributors and those who provided assistance for them I offer my thanks. We offer this book with the prayer that it might be used for the good of the church to advance the kingdom of God.

Soli Deo Gloria
David S. Dockery
Advent, 1994

PART ONE
INTRODUCTION

. . . . 1 . .

The Challenge of Postmodernism

David S. Dockery

W e are experiencing enormous changes in our country and in our world. Leith Anderson, in his book *A Church for the 21st Century,* says these changes "promise to be greater than the invention of the printing press, greater than the Industrial Revolution."[1] Christians must be aware of changes of this significance and magnitude. As we move into the twenty-first century, a new way of viewing the world has emerged. The "modern" way of thinking, that dominated the nineteenth and twentieth centuries, has become obsolete. These modern ideas no longer seem relevant. The twenty-first century will be characterized as the "postmodern age." This postmodern world becomes the new challenge for the evangelical church.

Understanding the Terms

The term "postmodern" primarily refers to time rather than to a distinct ideology. Until the last two decades the Western world thought itself capable of arriving at truth in all arenas through scientific inquiry. We have not thought in postmodern terms. Many of us still consider ourselves to be living in the modern world. Yet that modern world has given way to postmodernity. Postmodernity de-

David S. Dockery is Vice President for Academic Administration, Dean of the School of Theology, and Associate Professor of New Testament Theology at The Southern Baptist Theological Seminary in Louisville, Kentucky.

scribes a dislocating human condition that is being experienced in these last years of the twentieth century. We say it is "dislocating" because it tends to throw people out of the worldviews they have traditionally held. It is a cultural event happening right now wherever people are educated in and acculturated to Western civilization. Postmodern times have introduced a new philosophy or a way of viewing the world described as "postmodernism." Postmodernism presents Christians with new challenges as well as rich opportunities for evangelistic witness. Postmodernism is a new set of assumptions about reality, which goes far beyond mere relativism.[2] It impacts our literature, our dress, our art, our architecture, our music, our sense of right and wrong, our self-identity, and our theology. Postmodernism tends to view human experience as incoherent, lacking absolutes in the area of truth and meaning.

Many postmodernists assume that either no rational structures exist or that we cannot know them. James Sire has characterized five aspects of postmodernism: (1) Things and events do not have intrinsic meaning. There is only continuous interpretation of the world. (2) Continuous examination of the world requires a contextual examination; we ourselves are a part of the context. (3) Interpretation depends not on the external text or its author, but on the relative viewpoint and particular values of the interpreter. (4) Language is not neutral, but relative and value-laden. (5) Language conveys ideology.[3]

While modernists' attacks on Christianity are losing their force, postmodernists are attacking Christianity on different grounds, based on Sire's five characteristics. We can see that the agenda has moved from that employed by modernists in this past century. For example, modernists would argue in a variety of ways that Christianity is not true. Postmodernists, on the other hand, would critique Christianity by claiming that Christians think they have the only truth. The claims of Christianity are rejected because of the appeal to absolute truth. Absolute truth claims will be dismissed by the postmodernist for being "intolerant" — trying to force one's beliefs onto other people. Postmodernists have genuinely given up on the idea of absolute truth, thus the church faces new challenges in proclaiming the Gospel to our contemporary world.

The Apostle Paul reminds us to "understand the present time" in which we live (cf. Rom. 13:11, NIV). Many Christians unfortunately, including theologians, are still battling modernism, unaware that the issues have changed. George Barna observes that "most Christians do not perceive the church to be in the midst of the most severe struggle it has faced in centuries."[4] If Christians are to minister effectively in the postmodern world and avoid its temptations, they must understand the times and the seasons in which they live.

The New Challenge

A new disillusioned generation, sometimes referred to as "Generation X"[5] or the "baby busters," is now growing up in a post-Christian America. They are the first generation to bring postmodern assumptions to all aspects of life. As a result they are the first generation in American history who face life with these new presuppositions.

This new generation can be characterized by chaos. They are children of divorce, with 50 percent coming from broken homes. According to the most recent statistics, every day 13 youth commit suicide, 16 are murdered, 1,000 become mothers, 100,000 bring guns to school, 2,200 drop out of school, 500 begin using drugs, 1,000 begin drinking alcohol, and hundreds are assaulted, robbed, or raped.[6]

These sobering realities have produced a generation pessimistic about its own chances for survival. How do we impact this contemporary generation with the saving Gospel of Jesus Christ? The distinctive nature of Generation X results from growing up amidst this postmodern worldview. Their primary assumption is that truth is not rational or objective. Truth is defined by each individual and the community of which he or she is a part. This generation tends to define the world through the eyes of MTV. The challenge for the church is to claim this postmodern context for Christ.[7]

Approaching the Postmodern World

The contributors to this book are united in their desire to claim the postmodern context for Jesus Christ. However, there are differences in how postmodernism is to be understood and approached. Different times and different contexts call for different approaches. No longer do we have the luxury of a fixed framework. Premodern and modern views of things agreed that knowledge is certain, objective, and obtainable. The modern world was characterized by scientific thinking and Common Sense philosophy. Premodern and modern periods agreed on the objectivity of reality. Despite differences regarding the status of this reality, there was at least an agreement that such reality existed independently of any individual apprehension of it.

Postmodernism not only differs from premodern and postmodern viewpoints, but has many different meanings within the movement itself. This should not be surprising considering the lack of objectivity within the arena of postmodernism. A variety of views lay claim to the title of postmodernism. That is the reason that some contributors to this volume see postmodernism as a negative challenge, while others see it as a positive opportunity. Thus, in many ways it is both the "best of times and the worst of times." Not only are there a variety of postmodern viewpoints in the areas of art, architecture, film, and music, but there are a number of postmodern theologies. Millard Erickson, following David Ray Griffin, has classified these by the degree of their radicalness. That is, classifications are based on the understanding of the change needed from the modern period. There are basically four approaches.[8]

(1) *Deconstructive postmodernism* maintains that an attempt to take an objective approach to the facts of experience leads to the paradoxical conclusion that such an objective approach is not possible. It represents a radical denial of the objectivity involved in foundationalism, according to which there are certain basic or foundational facts to which thought can appeal, and the aim of thought is to base reasoning on such foundational truths. Language does not refer to objective objects as its referents: words refer only to other words. Thus, the aim of interpretation is to deconstruct additional objects of thought and the traditional methods of the discipline. Criteria of internal consistency and coherence are devaluated and believed to be inapplicable.

(2) *Liberationist postmodernism* focuses more on the social and political form of the contemporary worldview rather than the philosophical foundation. It reacts against social structures and seeks to transform them. This approach often needs an adjective such as feminist, gay, black, third world, or political, to define what kind of liberation motif is at work. Although it does not reject the search for objective truth as emphatically as the deconstructive approach, liberationist postmodernism does not value consistency, coherence, or objective truth in the same way as did modernism.

(3) *Constructive postmodernism* attempts to revise or reconstruct the modern worldview. It rejects metaphysics as a valid building block while maintaining that the construction of a worldview is possible. Process thought often forms the building blocks for this constructive postmodern approach.

(4) *Conservative or restorationist postmodernism* suggests that there is much within the premodern and modern worldviews worth retaining. It often seeks to reconstruct theology by going beyond modernism, building on those elements while transcending others. It

is often accused of being merely a return to premodernism, but this is not really the case.[9] This view maintains that the modern world-view reflects certain basic changes in the world that cannot be ignored or disregarded.

It is because of these differences in understanding post-modernism that evangelical Christians sometimes see post-modernism as a threat while others view it as a welcomed opportunity. We recognize the need to reevaluate our reasoned responses and our rhetoric. The church must learn to retell the "old, old story" while maintaining the exclusive nature of the Gospel. And the church must recognize the need to offer Christianity as plausible before making a defense of its creditability. This means that people need to be convinced that the Christian faith might be true and might deserve a serious hearing before they can be convinced that it is true. Traditional apologetics and evangelism have focused on attempting to prove and persuade hearers of the reality of Christianity, suggesting that there is "evidence that demands a verdict." In order for the new postmodern generations to consider the plausibility of Christianity they must be convinced of its authenticity, as well as its community-building characteristics, before they will hear its truth claims. We are certainly in the midst of a profound transition, away from the premodern and modern world into unchartered waters. We must learn to make use of postmodern scholarship and to address the dilemmas that postmodernists are facing.[10]

The postmodern intellectual climate should theoretically make room for appropriating a new Christian confessionalism. Post-modernism boasts that it allows all groups to have a right to speak for themselves, in their own voice, and have that voice accepted as authentic. Surely this should include Christian communities, who share the same beliefs and the same theological language. If postmodernism is concerned to bring the marginal into the center then surely Christianity should receive a hearing for it has been consigned to the margins of the modern world. As Thomas Oden has observed, the church is one of the few institutions that is truly prepared for the postmodern world since it is global, multicultural, and multigenerational.[11]

The psalmist has raised the question: "When the foundations are being destroyed, what can the righteous do?" (Ps. 11:3) Certainly the foundations are shifting. While the world is changing rapidly, we hold on to the truth that "Jesus Christ is the same yesterday and today and forever" (Heb. 13:8). The evangelical church must accept the challenge of proclaiming the unchanging Gospel of our Lord Jesus Christ to and for this contemporary world. We offer this volume to help meet this challenge.

NOTES

1. Leith Anderson, *A Church for the 21st Century* (Minneapolis: Bethany, 1992), 17.

2. Gene Edward Veith, Jr., *Postmodern Times: A Christian Guide to Contemporary Thought and Culture* (Wheaton, Ill.: Crossway, 1994), 15–24.

3. James Sire, "Logocentricity and Postmodern Apologetic: On Being a Fool for Christ and an Idiot for Nobody" (Unpublished paper presented at the Wheaton Theology Conference, 7–8 April 1994).

4. George Barna, *The Frog in the Kettle: What Christians Need to Know About Life in the Year 2000* (Venture, Calif.: Regal, 1990), 123.

5. This description is taken from the title of the novel by Douglas Coupland, *Generation X: Tales for an Accelerated Culture* (New York: St. Martin's, 1991).

6. Andrés Tapia, "Reaching the First Post-Christian Generation," *Christianity Today,* 12 September 1994, 18–23.

7. Ibid. See also George Hunter, *How to Reach Secular People* (Nashville: Abingdon, 1992).

8. Millard J. Erickson, *Evangelical Interpretation* (Grand Rapids: Baker, 1993), 99–103; see David Ray Griffin, *Varieties of Postmodern Theology* (Albany, N.Y.: State Univ. of New York, 1989), 1–7.

9. See Thomas C. Oden, *After Modernity . . . What? An Agenda for Theology* (Grand Rapids: Zondervan/Academie, 1990).

10. The best evangelical responses to date to help us in this matter are: Gene Edward Veith, Jr., *Postmodern Times: A Christian Guide to Contemporary Thought and Culture* (Wheaton, Ill.: Crossway, 1994); and D.A. Carson, *The Gagging of God* (Grand Rapids: Zondervan, forthcoming).

11. Thomas C. Oden, *Two Worlds: Notes on the Death of Modernity in America and Russia* (Downers Grove, Ill.: InterVarsity, 1992), 54.

PART TWO
THE CHALLENGE FOR THEOLOGY

2

The Death of Modernity and Postmodern Evangelical Spirituality

Thomas C. Oden

As we turn toward the last years of the twentieth century, the tradition-oriented believer is trying to extract some sense out of what seems to be unprecedented mutations in the church and society. The reflections in this chapter are a personal "take" on emergent classic Christian spirituality within the current cultural theater.

Terminal Modernity

Explaining an Odd but Useful Phrase

By *spirituality* we intend to point to personal life in union with Christ — a relationship with the incarnate and risen Lord through the power of the Holy Spirit, where His death is our death, His resurrection our resurrection. This life expresses itself in praise to the Triune God through loving service to the neighbor.

Spirituality in the New Testament sense is not a moral program, not a set of rules, not a level of ethical achievement, not a philosophy, not a rhetoric, not an idea, not a strategy, not a theory of meditation, but rather simply *life lived in Christ.*

In speaking of evangelical spirituality we must point to an actual

Thomas C. Oden is Henry Anson Buttz Professor of Professor of Theology and Ethics at the Theological School and the Graduate School of Drew University in Madison, New Jersey.

ethos, a living history of a covenant community of worship, in which life in Christ is taken seriously and joyfully as creation's true center, a community in which a disciplined approach to life in the Spirit is informed by classic Christian Scripture study within a supportive community of prayer, and more specifically by the traditions of discipleship shaped by the heirs of Athanasius, Augustine, Luther, Cranmer, Calvin, Wesley, and revivalism.

By *postmodern,* we mean the course of actual history following the death of modernity. By *modernity* we mean the period, the ideology, and the malaise of the time from 1789 to 1989, from the Bastille to the Berlin Wall.

By *evangelical* we embrace all those who faithfully believe and joyfully receive the Gospel of God in Jesus Christ. In particular we are thinking of those who even today deliberately remain under the intentional discipline of ancient ecumenical consensual teaching and classic Lutheran, Calvinist, Baptist, or Wesleyan connections of spiritual formation, especially in their renewing phases, freely subject to classic Christian teaching, admonition, and guidance.

Does this rule out the millions of old-line Protestants who suffer almost total amnesia concerning evangelical teaching, except for a romanticized version of Luther at Worms or a triumphal Calvin as an urban renewalist or Wesley at Aldersgate with a touch of heartburn? Not altogether, since even they too continue to sing the hymns of the Christian tradition, pray its liturgy, and breathe in emergency oxygen from the aging, surviving communities of classic Protestant spiritual formation.

Does Postmodern Imply Anti-Modern?

In postmodern orthodoxy we are taking for granted the achievements of modernity, of modern methods of inquiry, modern procedures of searching scientifically for truth, and modern assumptions about a just democratic political order. The problem my young fogey friends experience is not that they are yet to be introduced to these agendas. They have already been through these agendas ad nauseum. They know what modernity is all about, appreciate its strengths and are aware of its weaknesses. What they instead are doing is not a rerun of modernity, but the rediscovery of classical Christianity within postmodernity.

That does not mean a simplistic, sentimental return to premodern methods as if the achievements of modernity were to be circumvented or short-circuited. Rather it is a rigorous, painstaking rebuilding from the crash of modernity using treasures old and new for moral formation and spiritual reconstruction. These young people have been hardened by modernity to use the methods of modern inquiry (the methods of psychological analysis, sociological, political, historical analysis, scientific and literary analysis) to detoxify the illusions of modernity.

The axiom of postmodern consciousness is not that modernity is corrupt, but that it is defunct, obsolete, passé, antiquated. This is why after-modern evangelical spirituality is not accurately defined as anti-modern. It is not merely a censorious, embittered, negative emotional reaction against modernity. That would mistake the postmodern orthodox premise entirely. Note carefully: *there is no reason to be opposed to something that is already dead.* A frustrated, anti-modern, angry, caustic, emotive reaction errs in overestimating the continuing resilience of terminal modernity and its capacity to regenerate itself intellectually.

If advocates of modernity still had intellectual and moral vitality or the ability to sustain fertile culture-creation, then the charge might be more plausible that postmodern paleo-orthodoxy is merely an acrid, moody attack upon modernity. The tone of this analysis is not anger but sadness, not outrage but pathos. Evangelical awareness of grace may feel poignancy and tenderness toward the death of modernity, but never anger. Animosity is the least fitting conceivable response to death. Anger would be entirely misplaced if it should be the case that the patient is moribund or deceased.

The period of mourning is soon to be over. It lasted long enough, and the survivors are called to be about living, persevering, and rebuilding.

What makes this evangelical consciousness "post" is the fact that it is no longer intimidated by the once dominant voices of "mod rot" — the putrifying phase of modern ideologies. Many Christians in the university have doubly paid their dues to modernity. Now they search for forgotten wisdoms long ruled out by the narrowly fixated dogmas of Enlightenment empiricism and idealism.

There is no way for us to reflect upon modernity except amid the collapse of modernity. There is no need for believers in grace to despair over the losses of modernity. There is no reason to fight something already dead. So we should not consider ourselves anti-modern. Rather, we celebrate the providence of God that works amid the world that must suffer and live amid the wreckage strewn in the pathway of once modern ideologies.

The Turning Point

Today we celebrate a turning point: evangelical piety, scholarship, and institutional life have in fact outlived the dissolution of modernity. Against all predictions of the secularizers, we are still around and vitally flourishing. Even if the general condition of popular congregational health is uncertain, there is an emerging resolve in the worldwide evangelical family to renew the familiar, *classic spiritual disciplines:*

- daily meditative study of the written Word;
- an earnest life of personal prayer — a daily order of praise, confession, pardon and petition for grace and using of the means of grace;
- mutual care of souls with intensive primary group accountability;
- an ordering of daily vocational life in which persons seek faithfully to walk by grace in the way of holiness — regardless of how the environing world interprets it.

We have already been through the illusions of modernity. Having been disillusioned by the illusions of modernity, young evangelicals are now engaged in an unpretentious, low-keyed, quiet endeavor to return to the spiritual disciplines that not only have profoundly shaped our history and common life, but have in fact enabled our survival of modernity. This emergent consciousness remains small in scale and modest in influence, and is still being chiefly advocated by what Wesley called "young, unknown, inconsiderable men,"[1] and we should add women. It should not be exaggerated as if it were already a world-historical spectacle that *Time* magazine will run a cover story on in the next decade. But it, nonetheless, is a palpable, observable event. It is actually happening: the reawakening of determined, ardent evangelical spirituality precisely amid the postmodern world.

It might be possible and perhaps edifying to speak in other ways of the postmodern recovery of classical Christianity through the restoration of Anglican spirituality, or the Eastern Orthodox tradition, or post-Soviet Russian Christianity. But in this present ecumenical environment it seems most fitting to focus primarily on current evangelical strains of the postmodern rediscovery of ancient ecumenical Christianity. The European and American old-line Reformed and Lutheran traditions have already had their go at theological renewal in the five decades of Reformed neo-orthodoxy of the period from

1920–1970. But those days were never celebrated heartily by other more marginalized American evangelicals or the heirs of the revivalist or sanctificationist traditions.

A 1979 commitment to a postmodern paleo-orthodox *agenda for theology* has by now extended into a continuing project of writing—a ponderous armload of printed matter. Those who read my *Pastoral Theology* or *Systematic Theology* will find themselves up to their nostrils in references to the Christian writers of the first millennium. Throughout this project lies a continuing zeal for unoriginality. Paul's admonition has been taken to heart: "But even if we or an angel from heaven should preach a gospel *other than* the one we preached to you, let him be *anathema!* As we had already said, so now I say again: If anybody is preaching to you a gospel other than what you accepted—other than what you received from the apostles— let him be *anathema!*" (Gal. 1:8-9, author's trans.) The apostles were testy with clever revisionists.

Modernity as a Time Span, an Ideological Spell, and a Moral Spinout

In previous investigations we have defined and discussed the elusive concept of modern consciousness more explicitly than here. Readers who wish a more deliberate rendering of the terms modernity, postmodernity, orthodoxy, and postmodern orthodoxy are referred to the methodological sections in each of three volumes of my *Systematic Theology,* to *After Modernity . . . What?* and to *Two Worlds: Notes on the Death of Modernity in America and Russia.*[2]

Modernity as a Time Span

The easiest way to identify the *time span* or epoch of modernity is as this precise 200-year period between 1789 and 1989, between the French Revolution and the collapse of Communism.

While admitting that no dating of any historical period is ever unchallengeable, this one seems to cry out for special recognition. It was announced with such a spectacular beginning point (the opening up and storming of the wall of the Bastille prison in Paris with all its egalitarian fervor). It closed with a precise moment of collapse (the literal fall of a highly symbolic visible concrete wall in Berlin that the entire world watched tumble). The end of modernity can be timed precisely to the exact hour, even instant, of the fall of that wall in Germany.

So what is modernity, defined as a linear duration of time? It has lasted at least from the beginning of the French Revolution to the end of the Russian Revolution—that is modernity in its simplest epochal definition. It is a story of two walls and what happened in between. Within the bounds of those two walls an ideology—modern empiricism and idealism—in 200 years has emerged, gained dominance, peaked, and receded.

Modernity as an Ideological Spell

Modernity as a worldview has come and gone in two swift centuries. But modernity is not merely a period or temporal duration but more so a mesmerizing, spellbinding vision of the human possibility that has held the human imagination in its grip. Hence Christians have experienced modernity as an *ideological spell,* a bewitching, profoundly tempting enchantment. This enchantment has held the Western intellectual tradition in its grip for 200 years. It is an enchantment which may appear before 1789 and may recur sporadically after 1989, but these two centuries have been the time of its ascendancy, hegemony, and death.

The enchantment of modernity is characterized by technological messianism, enlightenment idealism, quantifying empiricism, and the smug fantasy of inevitable historical progress. We have fooled ourselves on all counts.

While present in fragmented ways before the French Revolution, these values have since dominated modern times, especially among its knowledge elites—those who trade in knowledge—the university, the press, jurisprudence, science, and the communications industry. This worldview has been blatantly promoted and championed by the modern institutions of academia, media, and liberal ecclesia, with few exceptions. There the assumptions, methods, values, and ideology of the *French Enlightenment,* coupled with *German idealism* and *British empiricism,* were advertised, hyped, and peddled. These ideas have invaded and to some degree temporarily conquered many disciplines in academic communities, including those founded by evangelical educators (to name a few: Northwestern, Syracuse, Princeton, Baylor, Texas Christian, Dickinson, Oberlin, Wesleyan, Emory, Drew, and the University of Toronto, and the list could continue for two pages).

The spellbinding efficacy of this ideological spin on modernity had its ascendancy roughly within the bounds of the two-century epochal definition of modernity as a duration. We are narrowing down to the center of our target, which is a moral denouement.

Modernity as a Moral Spinout

The bull's-eye definition of terminally fragmenting modernity (picture the inmost target of three concentric circles) is as a disabling social malaise, a crash of the moral immune system, a collapse of virtue, a *moral spinout.* This is a sad fact of history in the last thirty years. Like the crash of a daredevil at a flying exhibition, we have in our time watched this tailspin and blazing crackup. In the '60s, '70s, and '80s we have personally witnessed the rapid dissolution of what at the beginning of those thirty years seemed to be a stable intellectual environment that we expected to last many centuries. We have watched to our horror the disintegration of this 200-year worldview, splintering in relentless disarray — the acute phase of rapidly deteriorating modernity.

The party is over for the hedonic sexual revolution of the period from the sexy '60s to the gay '90s. The party crasher is sexually transmitted diseases, with AIDS leading the way. We are now having to learn to live with the consequences of the sexual, interpersonal, and familial wreckage to which this narcissistic money-grubbing, lust-enslaved, porn-infested, abortive self-indulgence has led us. Its interpersonal fruits are friendlessness, disaffection, divorce, and the despairing substitution of sexual experimentation for intimacy.

Can There Be a Simple, Unpretentious Definition of Postmodernity?

Postmodernity in my meaning is simply that historical formation that will follow the era of spent modernity — the *time span* from 1789 to 1989 which characteristically embraced an Enlightenment worldview that cast an *ideological spell* over our times, now in grave *moral spinout.* If what is ending is rightly labeled modernity, then what is to follow its death can be reasonably designated postmodernity, or after-modern consciousness. We could call what is passing the era of the French Enlightenment, German idealism, and British empiricism, but those influences are just more complicated ways of saying modern consciousness.

If modernity is a period characterized by a worldview which is now concluding, then whatever it is that comes next in time can plausibly be called postmodernity.

We are pointing not to an ideological program, but rather to a simple succession — what comes next after modernity. "Post" simply means after, following upon, later than. So postmodernity in our meaning is nothing more or less enigmatic than *what follows modernity.*

Why "Postmodern"
Is a Prevailing Misnomer for Ultra-modernity

Experience teaches that when avant-garde academics bandy about the term "postmodern," it is usually more accurate to strike *post* and insert *ultra*. For guild scholars, postmodern typically means simply hypermodern, where the value assumptions of modernity are nostalgically recollected and ancient wisdoms compulsively disregarded. Meanwhile, the emergent actual postmodernity that is being suffered through outside the ivory tower is not yet grasped or rightly appraised by those in it.

We do not at all mean by postmodernity what many academics mean — deconstructionist literary criticism and relativistic nihilism — what we call ultra-modernity which despairingly thinks these modern patterns will reduplicate endlessly. Richard Rorty and Jacques Derrida are ultra-modern writers according to this definition, rather than postmodern. Though they think of themselves as at the end of modern consciousness, their philosophical commitments and value judgments show the very kind of relativism that characterizes ultra-modern despair.

It is amusing that the most common way of academically naming the despair of ultra-modernity is "postmodernity." What is named post is actually a desperate extension of despairing modernity which imagines by calling itself another name (postmodern), it can extend the ideology of modernity into the period following modernity. But in this semantical switch, simply by naming itself post it does not cease being ultra.

Shouldn't we just give up on the name postmodernity if this is the case? No, because it is an indispensably accurate descriptive term. But isn't the hypermodern use of the term postmodern too involuted to be useful? It is corrupted, but its corruptions can be corrected with reasonable discourse. Why relentlessly contend for using postmodern in a different way than most others? The answer requires a personal narrative: My use of the term "postmodern" began in 1969 (in the *Structure of Awareness*[.]) in seeking to describe spiritual wanderers searching for roots, before Derrida and Foucault popularized it, and just before the architectural world began to shanghai the idea. When philosophers and literary critics got around to using the term postmodern later in the '80s to be applied to what we are calling ultra-modernity, my thought was that the term was being misapplied then, and it still is now. One can still argue about what a word rightly should denote, even when one stands in a minority position. We do not insist on a paleo-orthodox definition of post-modernity merely out of defiance, but because of its descriptive value and its rhetorical utility. Anyone has a right to use a term, but those who spin and tilt it later have some responsibility to try to understand how others had explicated it earlier. We can defiantly sit on the term postmodern with a paleo-orthodox spin, not merely on the basis of squatters' rights, or intellectual property antecedent rights, but on the grounds that its earlier meaning is preferable to its later meaning, and logic of a Christian understanding of modern history requires it. The logic of modernity requires something to follow it, even when the myth of modernity lives in denial of that possibility. What follows it will be just as providential as that which preceded it.

Four Leading Motifs of Terminal Modernity

The spinout phase of late modernity is epitomized by four interrelated motifs:

1. The autonomous individualism of the iconoclastic tradition from Nietzsche through Dadaism to Hemingway and Sartre has now come down to gun battles between nine-year-old boys in ornate tennis shoes.

2. The narcissistic hedonic assertiveness of the tradition from Rousseau and Bentham through Shelley and Whitman to D.H. Lawrence and Madonna is entangling countless young minds in its seductive, sensualist net.

3. The reductive naturalism of the tradition from Hobbes and Hume through Freud to Skinner is proving to be a narrow new philosophical dogmatism that denies freedom and misunderstands human accountability.

4. The absolute moral relativism and modern chauvinism typified by Feuerbach, Dewey, Bultmann, and Fellini that imagines the developing ethos of late modernity is destined somehow to be the unquestioned cultural norm by which all subsequent cultural norms are to be judged, and on this premise presumes to judge all premodern norms, texts, and ideas. Modern chauvinism regards modernity as the intrinsically superior ethos by which all premodern views are harshly judged as primitive, mysogenist, or artless.

All of these are smelted with a vengeance in the historical utopianism of the revolutionary idealist tradition from Marx and Lenin to Castro and Pol Pot that is now in collapse from Azerbaijan to Angola. Travels in Leningrad the week they voted to change the city's name to St. Petersburg, and then later in Havana to witness the fiscal collapse after the sudden disintegration of Soviet economic patronage, have provided me frontline views in watching radical cultural transformations occur dramatically in these two quintessential modern social orders.

Anatomy of a Cataclysm

Now bring the microscope closer to observe in more explicit detail the structure and dynamics of these four fallen idols, four strains of terminal modernity now in final collapse or radical metamorphosis:

First, *autonomous individualism* makes an idol of the detached individual as self-sufficient, sovereign self. The trajectory of this idolatry leads to intergenerational conflict, sexual detachment, family decomposition, and societal havoc. The corporate nature of both sin and grace are misplaced. The lonely self is cut off from community. Personal life is damned to seek meaning alone. The cities, families, and politics of terminal modernity are now being forced to live with the embittered consequences of this idolatry.

Second, *narcissistic hedonism* makes an idol of one's sensuality, body, and immediate pleasures. Other considerations are demoted in relation to this central value: making "me" feel good now. There is nothing wrong with happiness for me now unless that happiness is burdensome to others, or abstracted as if disrelated to the Giver of all finite goods. The consequence is a tangible hell, an anticipatory real damnation, as best symbolized by the actual recent history of sexuality.

Narcissus was the beautiful youth in Greek mythology who pined away for love of his own reflection. Narcissism is excessive interest in one's own comfort and importance. Its result is moral numbness (*narke*), stupor. Hedonists were a sect of Greek philosophers that placed the highest happiness in gratification of natural desires. Hedonism holds that pleasure (*he done*) is the principle good and should be the aim of action. Narcissistic hedonism is that orientation to life that fixates upon my pleasure and regards that fixation as the best one can expect of the self.

That one person's narcissistic binge may turn into another's lifelong misery is evident from the shocking number of American babies still being born suffering from their mothers' drug addictions — currently averaging over 300,000 per year.

This hedonic idolatry looms in living color in the network tube in what is advertised as family entertainment, but which turns out to be fixated on sex and violence. The antidote is to turn the tube off the instant it undermines and offends moral sensibilities.

Third, through *reductive naturalism* terminal modernity has made an idol out of empirical observation so as to ignore any other — intuitive, personal, charismatic, ecstatic, prophetic, and any revelation-grounded — mode of knowing. It imagines that the only reliable form of knowing is found in laboratory experimentation and quantitative analysis. Under the tutelage of this ideology, sex has been reduced to orgasm, persons to bodies, psychology to stimuli, economics to planning mechanisms, and politics to machinery. These idolatries so generally characteristic of modernity are today everywhere in crisis.

Finally, by its *absolute moral relativism* terminal modernity makes an idol of witless, inexpensive moral toleration. It views all moral values as arbitrarily contingent upon the changing social and psychological determinants of human cultures. In asserting normlessness uncritically and absolutely, relativism has itself become a new absolute dogmatism. Challenging it is the one great heresy in modernity.

Terminal modernity is being forced to live with the disastrous social fallout of its own relativistic assumptions: moral anomie, the forgetfulness of final judgment beyond history, the reduction of all moral claims to a common denominator of mediocrity. These losses result from the arrogant dogma of absolute moral relativism. This ideology is absolutely intolerant of anyone asking about that One in relation to whom all relativities are themselves relative. It is to this One that Jews and Christians have prayed, confessed, and sung praise, and upon whom their best minds have reflected for millennia — the infinite One in relation to whom all finite relativities are relative.

Old-line liberal Protestant congregations and families have suffered more deeply than evangelical, pietistic, and orthodox communities from the pretense that all value judgments are equally legitimate — and that all ideas being born equal are interchangeably tolerable — since they are presumed to be exhaustively formed by social determinants, without any transcendent or eschatological or even moral reference.

These four patterns are woven together into an ideological predisposition that still sentimentally shapes the knowledge elites of the liberal Protestant ethos, especially its politicized bureaucracies and academic institutions, who remain largely unprepared to grasp either their own vulnerability amid this cultural demise or their own possibility within this decisive historical opportunity.

Those evangelically founded and once-funded institutions and universities who have most lusted to adapt snugly to terminal modernity now remain most behind the curve, desperately trailing the wave, and not up to speed amid the actual reversals of contemporary history. The liberal old-line Protestant knowledge elites (including media gatekeepers, savants, pundits, intellectuals, professors, and bureaucrats) are tardy in grasping the moral sensibilities that have long since been grasped by those being more intentionally reformed by classic evangelical disciplines. These old modernites are impotent, unfit to transmit values intergenerationally. Their intellectual center is gone. It no longer has the capacity to reproduce itself. The capacity to regenerate is essential to any living organism. None of these four ideologies have the wit or energy to produce and fruitfully nurture another generation.

Meanwhile those intentional communities who have maintained the disciplines of classic Christian spiritual formation are experienced precisely at doing this: transgenerational transmission of their tradition, not merely making babies but parenting them. The remnants of these ideologies will continue to have residual effects, perhaps for a few generations, but the heart and spirit is gone out from them. The mercy of God, according to the prophets, does not permit societal sin to last more than three or at most four generations. We now have a new historical situation. This we call postmodernity and regard it as an exceptional opportunity for evangelical apologetics.

Tempering the Hypothesis

We do well to check the temptation to exaggerate our hypothesis on the demise of modernity. It is best to state it modestly, even meekly: we are now entering into a historical phase in which the strengths of modern ideological motifs are rapidly diminishing, and whatever is to follow modernity is already taking embryonic form. Few can any longer pretend that these deteriorating forces have vitality except among certain protected elites, in some universities, in a few clusters of church leadership circles, and defensive bureaucracies.

The Marxist-Leninism of the Soviet era is now gone. The Freudian idealization of sexual liberation has found it easier to have babies than parent them morally. The children of the post-psychoanalytic culture are at peril. The truculence of Nietzchean nihilism has spread to the bloody banks of Cambodian rivers with a trail of genocide along the way. The modern chauvinism of once-confident Bultmannians is now moribund, since the modernity it expected never arrived.

These once-assured ideologies are now unmasked as having a dated vision of the human possibility. None have succeeded in fashioning a transmissible intergenerational culture. Since each has colluded to support the other, they are now falling synchronously down like dominoes: the command economies, the backfiring therapeutic experiments, the mythic fantasies of demythology, the interpersonal fragments and splinters of narcissism.

These are shattered chips of key terminal modern ideologies that are despairingly trying to drag themselves into the postmodern world. All four voices in this dismal quartet are quintessentially modern, not postmodern.

The transition into the world after modernity may last many decades. Few processes in history happen quickly and none irreversibly. Now we see only a deepening crisis. But out of it is coming a society less deeply enamored by the illusions of modernity.

The Liberated Dinosaur:
The Decelerated Learning Curve of Academia

Some may protest that just these values still characterize academia. Answer: the university indeed remains belatedly addicted to antiquated modern habits, even when less erudite sufferers from modernity have long ago learned to begin to kick its obsessions. Many university faculty members have proven to be slow learners on a decelerated learning curve when it comes to grasping the limits of modernity.

These values (fornicating hedonism, me-first individualism, reductive naturalism, and self-destructive nihilism) may seem to be still triumphant in the academy. But scratch the surface and you will recognize their precariousness. The heart is gone from the idyllic song of modern progress. It has become a dirge with a heavy, hard steel bass beat.

Narcissism in the form of sexual experimentation may seem to be much alive in the university with its freely distributed condoms, bisexual advocacy groups, and coed residential suites, but everyone in the dorm knows that the orgy is over for the sexual revolution. AIDS is a slow but sure teacher. The intellectual foundations of narcissistic hedonism are crumbling. We are living in a time in which we still have many popular remnants of expressions of unfettered free lust and sexual binging, yet they are spawning so many human failures and no-win situations that they cannot long be sustained.

Condoms will not fix the problem we have fornicated our ways into. Just at the point where the condom was thought to be a technological fix, a minuscule hole has been found in it yet big enough for a stealthy virus to pass through. The failure rate of condoms makes the illusions attached to them more dangerous than ever.

What About the Case Is Terminal?

Modern consciousness has not died in every sense, but in a specific sense. When we speak of the death of modernity, we do not mean the death of all popular expressions of modernity. They will continue to have proximate vitality for some decades while they are realizing that their moral and intellectual foundations have become dubious. What we are mainly referring to is the bellying up of the ideological foundation, the energizing spirit of modernity. The spirit has died, and what we have on our hands is little more than a cadaver, maybe still a little warm, all dressed up in a black leather jacket. All this assumes seeing history from a long view.

We are to the end of the rope of speculative historical criticism, each emergent generation of which has outdone its previous (Marxist, Weberian, feminist, formcritical, structuralist, deconstructionist, reader-response, etc.) conjectures. New Testament criticism has swung from the grossest extremes from Schweitzer to Bultmann to Käsemann and finally full circle back to Pannenberg and Walter Wink and Eta Linnemann and Gerhard Meyer and Peter Stuhlmacher.

If the Freudian, Bultmannian, Marxist, and Nietzschean projects are all functionally morose, then later stage modernity is dead. That is what is meant by the phrase "terminal modernity."

We do not mean all social location analysis is dead. Marx is often credited with teaching us, as if for the first time, to see our motivations from the viewpoint of our class interests. But for those families with the history of social theory, this sort of analysis is found abundantly in the classic Christian tradition, from John Chrysostom through John Wycliffe to William Wilberforce and F.D. Maurice. We do not have to give up that good and useful form of analysis merely because Marx made it a bad and reductive systematic principle that has caused untold suffering.

This is not to imply that Marx will have zero influence in the future, but certainly the history of Marxist experimentation has so many strikes against its recovery that it will take some generations of slow forgetting even to venture toward a marginal, sentimentalist revival. And we do not mean that Freud will have no influence, but the once awesome tide of the Freudian triumphalism has wholly subsided due primarily to its poor record of therapeutic outcomes.

NOTES

1. John Wesley, *Scriptural Christianity*, iv.11, 1:179.

2. See Thomas C. Oden, *The Living God: Systematic Theology, Volume 1* (San Francisco: Harper and Row, 1987); idem, *The Word of Life: Systematic Theology, Volume 2* (San Francisco: Harper and Row, 1989); idem, *Life in the Spirit: Systematic Theology, Volume 3* (San Francisco: HarperSanFrancisco, 1992); idem, *After Modernity . . . What? Agenda for Theology* (Grand Rapids: Zondervan/Academie, 1990); idem, *Two Worlds: Notes on the Death of Modernity in America & Russia* (Downers Grove, Ill.: InterVarsity, 1992).

3. Thomas C. Oden, *Structure of Awareness* (Nashville: Abingdon, 1969).

3

Postmodernism:
The New Spectre?[1]

Carl F.H. Henry

Some champions of the "modern mind" have long disparaged the "medieval mind" as the outgrown mentality of the past. In like manner, more and more contemporary scholars now abandon so-called modernity in the interest of a presumably post-modern era.

The modern worldview is "less and less seen as The Final Truth," comments David Ray Griffin and "is increasingly relativized to the status of one among many."[2] Richard Lints observes that "modern theology has been relativized by its own commitment to relativism. It is viewed as historically conditioned by its own sense of historical consciousness."[3]

Seen broadly, postmodernism — so William A. Beardslee remarks — is a movement beyond scientistic modernism, one that is breaking away from "the determinism of the modern worldview."[4] Postmodernism does not stop there, however, and it is, in fact, beginning to shape the face of American culture.

The intensity of "anti-modern sentiment" is seen in the widening use of the term "postmodern" to signal a sweeping move beyond all the intellectual past — ancient, medieval, or modern — into a supposedly new era. Whether postmodernism is already entrenched as a decisive historical turning time, or is merely an influential episodic

Carl F.H. Henry is Senior Research Professor at The Southern Baptist Theological Seminary in Louisville, Kentucky.

phenomenon, is no doubt still a matter of debate. The insistent revolt against Marxist socialism, Cartesian epistemology, Freudian psycho-analysis, and classic modernist theology signals a sea change. Frontier thinkers who focus on cognitive novelties tend to confer on postmodernism the status of a major irreversible movement.

Others would treat it as but one among many divergent options such as liberation theology, feminist theology, and ecological theology. Langdon Gilkey's warning that hasty judgment can be premature has continuing merit.[5]

Some theological observers nonetheless identify the death-of-God eruption of the 1960s, when even professedly Christian thinkers abandoned transcendent deity, meaning, and purpose, as a decisive turning point. The modern era was collapsing by its own undoing, they say. As secular humanism's social agenda became less and less compelling in a universe of impersonal processes and historical relativism, it began to empty into raw naturalism.

From Modernity to Postmodernity

In its present understanding as a cultural descriptive, the term postmodernism was apparently first used in an essay by John Cobb in 1964.[6] An orderly postmodernist succession is difficult to expound. For one reason or another it includes such diverse figures as Jacques Derrida, Richard Rorty, Michael Foucalt, Stanley Fish, David Tracy, George Lindbeck, David Ray Griffin, and others. Its lifeblood flows not from the churches but from academe, and it reflects the reigning paradigms of conflicting intellectual centers.

David Tracy finds in the shift from modernity to postmodernity a deepening basic commitment to "secular standards for knowledge and action initiated by the Enlightenment."[7] Might we not in that case readily identify unbridled naturalism (a deterioration of secular humanism) as a legitimate expression of postmodernism? Surely naturalism mirrors the radical Enlightenment's disavowal of both a supernaturally inspired revelatory authority and a divine providential teleology. It presumes, however, to explain the whole of reality through the quantifiable laws of mathematics and by quantum events. Even if philosophical naturalism declares all that exists to be transitory, and labels all metaphysical and moral affirmations as culture-conditioned and historically relative, it nonetheless affirms an externally given reality and sponsors a naturalistic worldview.

For all that, the naturalistic is now becoming nihilistic; secular humanism is yielding to crass naturalism devoid of humanitarianism, and this blatant naturalism is yielding in turn to nihilism. To be sure, dogmatic philosophical naturalism still holds sway for many. But increasing numbers of frontier exponents lean toward sheer subjectivism and nihility. They profess neither to know what reality is—for there is no objective reality or world—nor what any text actually says, because individual interpretation and not authorial intent alone makes sense. None of these radical and thoroughgoing champions of the new hermeneutic considers naturalism's control ideas to be objectively true.

Postmodernism, in any case, holds that the so-called world that emerged intellectually from the sixteenth century onward has come to an end at the close of our twentieth century as surely as the so-called medieval era early on had its day.

D.A. Carson distinguishes "deconstructive postmodernism" from less virulent forms. Not content to adopt only selective insights of the new hermeneutic, it expressly insists that no escape whatever remains from the hermeneutical circle. Not only is all meaning held to be subjectively bound up with the knower rather than with text, but words are declared to have still other words as their only referent. Texts are declared to be intrinsically incapable of conveying truth about some objective reality. One interpreter's meaning is as proper as another's, however incompatible these may be. There is no original or final textual meaning, no one way to interpret the Bible or any other text. Since contemporary critics emphasize that authorial intention may itself be flawed, some consider it merely preparatory to modern experiences shaping a new life perspective.[8]

The medieval era held that nature and history reflect God's immutable ordering of the cosmos. Its worldview elaborated a distinctive understanding of the nature and destiny of the human self in a meaningful and purposive universe created and ruled by God. It embraced a special view of truth and the good and of history and its finalities. The transcendent, omnipotent, and omniscient Creator has entrusted to humanity the revelatory good news of redemption proffered to sinful humankind in a universe of moral answerability and judgment.

The modern era sought to *liberate* humanity from this *fate* or existence in a God-ordered universe. Secular science promised a new freedom for humanity and progress for the planet. The intellectual order of the world was relocated in human reasoning. This control over nature and history would free humankind from life and a predetermined universe. The scientific consciousness eclipsed the past and humanity's productive powers promised advancement and final utopia. So fascinating was the scientific vision of reality that for twentieth-century intellectuals it became unnatural to imagine any other kind of world.

Modernist theology freed time of eternal boundaries and constraints and meshed it with evolutionary advance that devalued the past. It maximized individual liberty by loosing it from transcendent authority. It ignored the bearing of sin and sanctification upon the social order and assumed that history and society are moving toward a utopian climax. In contrast to supposedly objective scientific claims, it privatized religious commitment.

Modern men and women soon found themselves entrapped in what Joe Holland calls "a new, more powerful, and destructive technological fate" with unparalleled potentiality for demolition of humanity and the planet.[9] The twentieth-century — the century of scientific progress — brought with it, among other debacles, World War I, World War II, Marxist totalitarianism, Auschwitz, the increasing poisoning of the planet, and bare escape from international nuclear destruction. Despite boundless expectations from science, modernity with its militarism and rape of nature is seen by postmodernity as a threat to planetary life and survival.

Marxism displaced confidence in evolutionary progress by revolutionary eschatology. It promised to achieve the socialist utopia by force rather than by education and democratic legislation. Religion, which modernism viewed as a universally shared phenomenon, was now either deplored or state-controlled and ideally was transformed into an activity of secular science.

First modernity transferred to itself the attributes that had long characterized the traditional deity; then it emptied the present life "of all but utilitarian value." All reality was held to exist for the human self — a sovereign isolated self, it was thought, which could totally control the world. Meaning was to be found only in thisworldly history; salvation, redefined as economic and technological advance, had its locus in this life alone.

The modern view issued in speculative disavowal of the existence of a supernatural personal being; in short, it proclaimed the death of the God of the Bible. The loss of God carried with it the loss also of the inherited view of truth, of the self, of meaning and worth, and of history. Modernity sought at first to retain these correlated affirmations in a mediating way. Indeed, as Griffin notes, "the denial of God was often made in the name of the ultimacy of the human self, of historical progress, of truth and/or morality—ideas whose very meaning was implicitly subverted by the denial of God."[10] Modernity failed to see that its effort to magnify the self by eliminating God is literally self-defeating. Once the self related to God is dismissed, the traditional self too must be abandoned. The self's cancellation of the distinction between the *is* and the *ought* involved living "beyond good and evil." The modern self had brought humanity "to the brink of total destruction."[11]

The retirement of this modern self was therefore welcomed by postmodernity. Alongside its mounting criticisms of modernity, postmodernism has ventured a depth analysis of the collapsing modern lifeview and worldview. But while postmodernism seeks to displace and succeed the modern view, much of the diversity that characterized modern theology still carries over into postmodernism's postulations.

Two Alternatives

The emerging alternative seems broadly, as Griffin contends, to take either of two paths. We shall distinguish them as a hard core destructivist approach and a soft core constructivist approach. The destructivists, by their elimination of God, purpose, truth and meaning, the self, and of a real world, seek to demolish any and every worldview. The constructivists elaborate a postmodern worldview that correlates scientific, moral, aesthetic, and religious concerns with a corresponding world supportive of ecological, pacifist, and feminist emancipatory proposals.

Destructive Postmodernism

Destructive postmodernism endeavors to exegete the implication of the death of God. Instead of replacing the inherited deity by some more congenial divinity, perhaps even by a New Age metaphysical All of which we are parts, it dissolves deity entirely. Absolute relativism prevails; objective truth is intolerable and nonexistent. Not only is any transcendent center of reality disavowed, but the unrelieved flux that replaces it has no center. The loss of humans as creatures formed in the divine image implies at the same time the loss of the ontological self. The self is constituted solely of changing relationships. Since no fixed perspective remains, no objective reality exists that the self ideally approximates. The external world is an ongoing process, comprised of aimless and meaningless sequences and having no objective or goal.

In short, destructive postmodernism eliminates not only God but also freedom, purposive agency, the self, realism, truth, good and evil, and historical meaning. It holds that there are no shared values, no universally agreed facts. Objective truth is deprecated. The world is not rational. There is no truth outside us waiting to be discovered. The Renaissance, Reformation, and modern scientism are alike dismissed as merely subjective traditions. Cultural dialogue is a cosmic talk show: interpretation is king, and everyone sponsors his or her own.

Among the intellectual underpinnings that contributed to postmodernism, along with philosophical decontructionism and the new hermeneutic, Carson lists the governing assumptions of naturalism: forfeiture of the quest for certainty, of any exclusive methodology, of all forms of rational foundationalism, and of any ahistorical universality for truth. Deconstructionism strips reality and written texts of inherent meaning. It reduces language to but a social construct mirroring the interpreter's personal perspective. Consequently, every interpreter is free to handle the text selectively, that is, to deconstruct it, and to refashion favored segments into fresh readings that reflect one's own preferences without evident anchorage in the text.[12]

Constructive Postmodernism

By contrast, so-called constructive postmodernism disavows destructive postmodernism, as Griffin puts it, as "inconsistent and counterproductive."[13] Griffin contends that the premises of destructive postmodernism are merely presupposed in the very attempt to eliminate them. Constructive postmodernism emphasizes that even where shared truths or values are theoretically or verbally denied, a shared content nonetheless in practice remains quite common, and that "common sense notions" provide humanity with an escape from unrelieved relativism. Griffin includes among such notions the conviction that one has personal freedom, that the distinction between better and/or worse is necessary, that an outer world exists, and that interpretative ideas are true to the degree that they correspond to that independent world.[14] Griffin therefore insists that not all "inherited notions" so readily dismissed by destructive postmodernists are simply culture-conditioned beliefs; some, he contends, are "hard-core common sense notions which are presupposed by all cultures." "Until someone can think consistently without presupposing these ideas, we have every reason to assume that these notions are universally presupposed. . . . By taking the hard-core common sense notions as the ultimate criteria," says Griffin, "we can move toward a worldview in which inconsistency as well as inadequacy to the facts of experience can be progressively overcome."[15]

This constuctivist option is an effort to escape both destructivist postmodernity and the raw naturalism into which secular humanism is now emptying. Griffin aims to do so by resorting to the process philosophy of Alfred North Whitehead and his recent modern successors. To that extent he offers a variant of the philosophy of modernity, one that simultaneously compromises historic Christian theism unconvincingly. A universe in which the world is as necessary to God as God is to the universe cannot arrive at a significant doctrine of deity or of meaning and purpose or of truth and the self. The view is less coherent than the biblical doctrine of the *imago dei* as the explanatory context for culturally transcendent ideas and ideals.

Evaluating Postmodernism

Postmodernism trumpets a strenuous revolt both against the medieval mind and against modernity, although it revises rather than rejects some elements of the modern mind. The inconsistencies that destructivist and constructivist postmodernism ascribe each to the other, alongside their conflicting revision of different aspects of modernity, reflects a refusal to search through premodern philosophy and the long history of ideas for more comprehensive illumination on their discomfiting tensions.

Postmodernism affirms that it offers choice or freedom, whereas premodernism allegedly offered fate; postmodernism considers God objectively irrelevant whereas premodernism recognized God as sovereign Creator and Redeemer, the transcendent source of meaning and truth and of the good, and the chief end of life. Postmodernism abandons the quest for a coherently integrated science. "Intrinsic to the postmodern critique of modernity," says Lints, "is the rejection of the goal of a unified science and correspondingly of a unified theology.[16]

Postmodernism has notably impacted philosophy, including the philosophy of science, and almost every endeavor of Western intellectual thought. Not in literature and the arts only but even in law, history, anthropology, and sociology are students introduced to the views of Jacques Derrida and Stanley Fish. Postmodernism has not fully displaced modernism or naturalism; contemporary journals and reviews reflect a confusing variety of viewpoints. Yet the whole field of science is today conceded to be theory-laden, and frontier thinkers and writers increasingly insist that postmodernism has the cutting edge. In some circles postmodernism has in fact already become a cliché.

Marsden and Longfield write of the increasing marginalization of Christianity by the academy.[17] Marsden notes that whereas its principles once were the motive force of the leading schools of higher learning, Christianity in the more recent past has been despised by academe, and moreover that today the academy specially disdains viewpoints that promote objective truth and ideals.[18] The more radical postmodernists—or destructivists—repudiate not only transcendent, objective, and external authority, but reject subjective and internal authority as well. Both the supernatural authority of the medieval era and the scientific authority of the modern era are disowned. As Carson notes, truth disappears, dissolving in the mists of post-modernity.[19]

The philosophically pluralistic theories hold that objective truth is inaccessible and that meaning resides not in external reality or texts but in the interpreter. This has rearranged some of the priorities bearing not only on cultural decay but on evangelical evangelism also, for it sponsors relativism in a new form; nobody is any longer expected to give an objectively valid reason for whatever hope he or she retains.

Postmodernity approves pluralism as a necessary and desirable cultural and philosophical phenomenon. "Although the postmodernist hesitates to deny the validity of all religions," says Lints, "he hesitates also to assert the exclusive truth of but one religion." He affirms "the revisability of all beliefs."[20]

Students are sapped of evangelical faith not by classroom refutation of the logic of their metaphysical commitments, but by the emphasis that no objective truth exists and that all religion reflects a historically conditioned bias. Since multitudes nonetheless believe specific religious doctrines, religion can be declared an ineradicable and influential personal phenomenon. One may indeed cherish one's religion if it is subjectively helpful. But one must not expect that it makes a transcendent claim on others or that any intelligent person will affirm its public truth. A personal spiritual testimony may be psychologically informative, but it has no theological validity.

Religion is not thereby abolished; destruction of religion is declared a lost cause. But religion is marginalized and trivialized. It can coexist and flourish in a secular society, but at the cost of retaining only private cognitive significance, and is considered irrelevant to external institutions, corporate life, and cultural expression. The Bible, when adduced, is usually cited disapprovingly. Not only are its miracle-claims disallowed but its ethical and spiritual superiority also is disavowed and it is held supposedly to support male superiority, racism, and sexism. The authority of religious literature is said to lie in its life-altering power in the culturally pluralistic community. In place of an authoritatively inspired Scripture containing divine revelatory theological and ethical information, and in place of a modernist Bible mirroring elements of universal religious experience useful in constructing a global theological and ethical framework, we are offered a narrative whose essence is found not in distinctive doctrines but in its life-transforming function in a faith community. This emphasis is anticipated in David Kelsey's *The Uses of Scripture in Recent Theology* which elevates the use to which the Bible is devoted above the question of its objective truth.[21]

Few aspects of postmodernism reflect more confusion than its epistemology. Lints speaks of its "epistemic pragmatism."[22] The Enlightenment elevated human reason as the way of knowing. Failure to justify this confidence led to "the recognition of the dogmatic (and therefore irrational) character of the Enlightenment's belief in reason—a belief much closer to a fundamental act of faith than to a scientific and critical act of reason."[23] Logical positivism sought a foundation for human knowledge in natural science: only what is empirically verifiable can be meaningful or true. But this supposition was not only too limited, but was as radically self-destructive as it was of much else. The Enlightenment confidence in human reasoning was assailed also by sociologists who protested that humans do not usually think only in valid syllogisms nor can they be wholly objective since hidden presuppositions underlie all human affirmations. These contentions would not have surprised the medieval mind which, however, would not have developed them antisupernaturalistically.

The one epistemic premise shared by all postmodernists is their rejection of foundationalism, the belief that knowledge consists of sets of beliefs that rest assuredly on still other sets of beliefs and that the whole is supported by irreversible foundational beliefs. Some think a species of pragmatism is foundationalism's only hopeful replacement, and no one has promulgated pragmatism more aggressively than has Richard Rorty.

Griffin declares destructive postmodernism no less unacceptable and inadequate than modernism. He critiques the logical inconsistencies of destructive postmodernism, noting especially references to "consciousness itself and to a realm of reality beyond consciousness."[24] By contrast, Griffin espouses a constructive alternative that retains belief in a centered universe, in a centered self, and in a meaningful history, and which consistently preserves the practical importance of beliefs about freedom, good and evil, purpose, reality, and truth. But Griffin's confidence is misplaced that process philosophy, which defines reality in terms of both actuality and relationships, serves ideally as a mediating alternative.

In line with dipolar theism, Griffin repudiates the historic Christian doctrine of a divine omnipotence and omniscience that involves "supernatural infallible inspiration or revelation." Along with postmodernism he rejects a return to divine authority and does so in view of "the nonoverridable creativity" of creatures. That God knows truth does not mean, Griffin holds, that He presently or eternally knows the future, a doctrine which Griffin gratuitously dismisses along with "debilitating fatalism or complacent determinism." Postmodern theology, he insists, involves commitment not to a temporal divine creation but to "eternal process"; the world, he says, has no absolute beginning, history has no "middle," and there will be no preconceived cataclysmic divine end. Each finite experience seeks immediate and cumulative satisfaction; humanity's future relation to the Holy will not differ qualitatively from what is presently possible.[25]

Lints notes that postmodernists not only emphasize the chasm between modernity and postmodernity, but they retain also the earlier Enlightenment chasm between Scripture and the modern world.[26] Thereby they more fully extend current alienation from the Bible. While there is nonetheless some growing awareness of the ineradicable influence that Scripture and its tradition exert even upon those who revolt against it, postmodernists screen Scripture and related tradition through an anthropological grid that shuns authoritative doctrine. The historical-critical method of scriptural interpretation is subordinated to the interplay of the textual horizon with that of the contemporary interpreter. Lints comments that the basic methodological shift in the present era "has been a movement away from a detached, disinterested, scientific and critical theology toward a subjective reader-response, literary and critical theology.[27]

The interest of evangelicals in postmodernism lies specially in their mutual rejection of the modern mind. But some appeal to postmodernist critiques to reinforce their own criticism of a radical fringe's excessive dogmatism, forgetting for the moment that postmodernist premises are destructive of any and every world-and-life view, however logically ordered. Postmodernism cuts off from objective truth not only evangelicals, Catholics, and orthodox Jews, moreover, but the whole tradition of biblical studies. It is therefore no gain but a colossal loss for exponents of the Christian heritage to sport the term postmodern as if it were a high asset. Some evangelicals screen the new hermeneutic for significant elements that need not destroy objective meaning and truth, although in doing so they run the risk of forgetting that nothing that postmodernism affirms is to be taken as objective truth. To preclude the possibility of knowing objective truth in principle, as Carson emphasizes, excludes an eternal Gospel entrusted to the people of God.[28]

The contemporary call for renewed theological engagement, insofar as it issues from postmodernist circles, must not be hastily misunderstood as a plea for a revival of theology in its traditional role of expounding an authoritative and logically compelling view of God and the world. No real gain can be made for theology if nobody any longer knows "what counts as a reasoned argument."[29] Theology is a lost cause if it is disengaged from the pursuit of universal truth.

While it may be inexcusable to ascribe some objective truth to postmodernism which denies objective truth in principle, the Christian may nonetheless identify such elements on his or her own principles.

Interpretation should stand in dialogic interaction with the text, so that critical conversation engages both text and interpreter. But whether and to what extent textual truth is actually distilled from this encounter divides postmoderns. Some of them question whether critical conversation with the biblical text is really possible, or whether this elevates the interpreter to a privileged platform that exempts one from distortion. Others are little concerned with belief-systems and focus on the consequences of critical dialogue for community life and practice. The range of postmodern theological interpretation thus accommodates diverse interpretations that stretch from Barth to Bultmann and beyond. Yet postmodern theologians routinely consider both themselves and their expositions Christian, despite their personal defection from historic Christianity and their insistence that the biblical heritage must be viewed through highly divergent lenses. Lints speaks of their desire that "a responsible theological community will provide plausible theological warrants for its proposals while also recognizing the culture-dependency of those warrants."[30]

An increasing number of generally evangelical theologians have called for the formulation of a "postmodern orthodoxy," among them Thomas Oden, Richard Lints, D.A. Carson, and Clark Pinnock. Evangelicals, says Lints, must engage "in a form of criticism founded not on the autonomy of human reason (as in theological liberalism), nor on the historical conditionedness of human reason (as in postmodern theology), but on the normative stance of revelation in the face of sin and unbelief of all varieties, even evangelical forms."[31] Since not a few evangelicals have themselves fallen victim to modern culture, the postmodern critique of modernity might in some respects encourage concessive evangelicals to be more resistant of the spirit of the age. Yet, as Lints warns, the fact that postmodernism retains much of the Protestant liberal perspective and even does so more radically, could be as much a liability as an asset. Its disenchantment with Western culture seems frequently to imply equal or greater enthusiasm for non-Western culture.

The collapse of optimism over a supposedly evolving socialist utopia, where pacifism would ultimately replace military conflict and liberal ideals would reign universally, nurtured doubt among disenchanted modernists over whether any one religion or set of cultural norms should be absolutized. Ertswhile lingering remnants of belief in divine providence, retained in modernist secularizations of the kingdom of God, are now emptying into doubts about the ultimate victory of good and evil and, moreover, about whether these two can even be confidently distinguished. The recollection of Auschwitz; wars in Vietnam, Iraq, Bosnia, and Rwanda; and the stalemating of both national and international responses, has encouraged moderns to view history as a purposeless sequence of events.

Hans Blumenberg has assailed the view that the modern era only modified and secularized the Hebrew-Christian conception of a divine Creator and Judge and its related eschatological worldview, so that its emphasis on progress merely distorted the coming of the kingdom of God.[32] Blumenberg shuns entirely any teleological view that sees present history in relation to a final goal. He contends for the discontinuity and newness of the modern age which he considers an epoch with its own foundations. A species of history thus arises exempt from universal truth and moral absolutes.

Lints stresses that for Christians the faithful representation of divine revelation holds priority over fidelity to the reigning methodological procedures and to community approbation. He welcomes especially as points of useful dialogue not only the postmodern critique of modernity, but additionally also its conception of the discipline of theology, its commitment to pluralism and liberation, and its use of the Bible.[33] A profound biblical critique of contemporary culture, he observes, could surface concerns common to postmodernity and to Christianity.

Carson holds that although confessional Christianity cannot wholly embrace either modernity or postmodernity, yet it must learn certain lessons from both. He decries the hubris that attributes perfect knowledge to humans, and affirms the need to recognize that all human knowledge is in some ways culture-bound and that all interpreters have a cultural location. Yet Carson would be first to concede and insist that these premises ultimately have scriptural legitimation.[34]

Human beliefs are indeed shaped in part by language, culture, and community. That is not all that is to be said, however. Carson has observed that in the realm of knowing, we join the experts of deconstructionism and of the new hermeneutic in insisting on human finiteness: but more, we go further and insist on human sinfulness. The noetic effects of sin are so severe that we culpably distort the data brought to us by our senses to make it fit into self-serving grids.[35]

If postmodernism assails the modernist hubris, it exhibits on its own part an even worse display. The sheer dogmatism of postmodernists, comments Oden, "is evidence that they are ultramodern, not postmodern."[36] Following Carson we can describe postmodernism as awesomely God-defying. Christians have no reason to treat postmodernism as if it were final or objective truth.

Yet Christians are called upon to confront the critical consequences of current theories. Carson specifies some models of textual approach that glean the best from the new hermeneutic, but do not destroy all possibility of absolute truth.[37] Cultural baggage can be removed from the text and from the interpreter without forfeiting objective truth, as Anthony C. Thiselton indicates.[38] Our lack of exhaustive knowledge does not condemn us to intellectual futility. The interpretive community—the nurturing community of faith—plays an important but not necessarily a determinative or decisive role in individual understanding. A Christian's comprehension of the Bible is not likely to be exhaustive, and the interpretive community's contribution can be rewarding rather than destructive. But the determinative difference is made by the sovereign omniscient God who speaks intelligibly and verbally. The Bible is not only a hermeneutical tool but the locus of authority, and its main focus is on the meta-narrative.

As a public discipline, Lints stresses, Christian theology is subject to appropriate tests. He emphasizes that the Bible records events that occurred "on the field of observable history."[39] In a quite sweeping judgment, Lints complains that over the past century evangelical theologians have wholly neglected the public aspects, and that evangelical apologists and theologians for the past fifty years have been mostly in hibernation. It serves evangelical realities better, however, when its cumulative assets are not so stridently overlooked. Yet it is the case, nonetheless, that much of popular evangelical theology and apologetics yielded finally to the Enlightenment demand that theological conclusions be validated on non-theological grounds, including the empirical appeal to design in nature to validate divine creation and preservation.

The evangelical theological conversation, while first and foremost with God, says Lints, should engage "the church, the academy, and the world."[40] Whereas the postmodern theologian is driven by the conviction of universally salvific religion, the evangelical is driven by the Christian conviction of redemptive exclusivism. Evangelical initiative in dialogue has currently been captured by historians and social scientists, including George Marsden, Nathan Hatch, Mark Noll, Robert Wuthnow, and James Davison Hunter, who have indicated ways in which Western culture soon adversely influenced evangelicals who set out to change it. Many evangelicals readily assumed an identity of the white middle-class values of self-esteem, technology, and prosperity, with those of the Bible. The postmodern critique can perhaps contribute to a more nuanced appraisal of this cultural indebtedness. Lints also protests a tendency among some evangelical theologians to present the Christian position as embracing a variety of options, for example, regarding baptism. The alternatives then reflect cultural circumstances and are really achieved independently of biblical testimony. Such ecumenical dilution downplays the importance of revelatory truth.

Lints explores postmodern's disinterest in a supernatural framework for criticizing secular society. Criticism of sensate modern life in a temporal context focused on the present can hardly, within the central ideas of relativity and transiency, ensure a meaningful or worthwhile existence. Postmodernists, we are told, assume a value-laden context that easily mirrors only the predispositions of academia. The concept of God may be retained, but the deity is recharacterized.

Moreover, say Lints, postmoderns affirm a "dynamic" theory of truth. They welcome religious pluralism as an enrichment of our moral vision. The underlying supposition, Lints holds, is that all religions are "fundamentally rooted in culture," so that no privileged access to truth anywhere exists.[41] But in that case, says Lints, even this supposed truth is subject to doubt. More importantly, the postmodern claim of universal culture-conditioning requires a fundamental reappraisal of the notion of divine revelation since its transcultural character is denied. Lints agrees that cultural aspects are involved in Christianity and other religions, but this does not exclude God's revelatory activity. Lints does not here elaborate, but he critiques the postmodern use of language theory that marginalizes questions of historical factuality and verbal revelation in the Scripture with the aim of adding imaginative new meanings.[42]

Conclusion

In summary, there are a number of claims that postmodernism rejects that modernism championed: there is the boundless truth that science assures personal freedom and human progress; the absolutizing of the scientific worldview; the belief that human reason and power control nature and history; the enthronement of Marxist socialism as the catalyst of a socio-political utopia; the reduction of values to utility; the ultimacy of the human self; the possibility of a coherently integrated science; and a universally shared religious experience despite doctrinal diversity.

Postmodernism retains a number of elements that characterized modernism: the rejection of transcendent deity and of miracle and the disavowal of supernatural revelation and of absolute truth, fixed meaning, and purpose. It repudiates all external, objective, transcendent authority, scientific authority also, and the mainly functional authority of religious literature, the Bible included, in its life-transforming role in a believing community.

Among postmodernists we have distinguished both a cold- blooded and warm-hearted view, or what we have called destructivist and constructivist views.

The destructivists eliminate God, purpose, truth, and meaning, the self, and a real world. They presume the death of God and with it the death of morality and the eclipse of truth. Absolute relativism prevails. No room whatever remains for objective reason; all existence is gripped by unrelieved process. The self is a purely relational sensate phenomenon. There is no freedom amid a realm of perpetual change having no fixed center. The world is meaningless and aim-

less; history has no goal. There is no good or evil, there are no
shared values. Not only are all transcendent authority and all scientific authority disavowed, but all internal and subjective authority
claims are rejected as well.

The constructivists propose a worldview that supports eco-
logical/pacifist/feminist concerns. They seek to escape nihilistic existence by relating to constants, whether in terms of unbridled naturalism or of dipolar theism, a retrograde form of Christianity. They
insist that humanity shares at least some values and truths, in practice if not theoretically. Whereas the unrelieved relativism of
destructivists relativizes even destructivism, constructivism insists
that a real world exists and makes room for freedom and for distinctions of truth and morality. Not all beliefs are simply culture-conditioned.

This contrast of hard-core and soft-core postmodernism involves
differences reflected also by the division of philosophical naturalism
into a declining secular humanism that supports a social agenda, and
a raw naturalism, which allows no exceptions in its insistence that all
scientific, moral, and cognitive claims are culture-conditioned and
historically relative.

Is there any need, however, to credit postmodernism with certain
philosophical influences that derive instead from biblical revelation,
and which a vigorous evangelicalism ought to appropriate whatever
may be the momentarily prevailing or contending religious movements? Has not evangelical Christianity repeatedly insisted that the
scientific worldview is inadequate and revisable, and that the scientific method is not the supreme way of knowing the ultimate world?
And does not the biblical doctrine of the *imago dei,* grounded in
divine creation, flawed by sin yet reinforced by revelation and sanctification, more consistently explain the debate over shared truths,
values, and facts than does constructivist postmodernism? Is it not
confusing to credit postmodernism, as Lints does, with potentially
encouraging evangelicals to stimulate the functional use of the Bible
in the life of the church or to shape a more sensitive social critique?

Must we not criticize both Protestant liberalism and postmodernity for their misconception of the God-ordered medieval world
as a sphere of deterministic fate, the one in the context of omnipotent divinity, and the other in the context of scientific mechanism?
Does postmodernism any more than modernism offer real freedom?
Is it justifiable to view modern science as a planetary threat only,
when the Christian view of nature spawned it and can in fact channel

it into a larger service of the good? Must we bow to postmodernity's insistence on pluralism as an inescapable cultural phenomenon and on the tentativity of all beliefs? Is not the identification of the present cultural situation in terms of postmodernity itself premature? Do not both its conflicting components and the prospect of still other emerging contributions to the movement of contemporary thought call for caution in making preemptive claims for postmodernism?

The emphasis of postmodernity that human beings are not motivated simply by logic but by volitional and emotional considerations also, and possibly mostly so, is not surprising to Christian theists. The deflective role of dubious presuppositions and of aberrant desire in human decision are important emphases in Christian theology. But not for a moment do they obscure the important role of appropriate evidence and of logical consistency. Much as Griffin critiques destruction postmodernism as logically defective, as indeed it is, his resort to process theology in order to expound a more acceptable alternative suffers from the same cognitive malady: the internal inconsistencies of the Whiteheadian view have long limited its credibility. Yet the destructive alternative is self-relativizing and, moreover, it involves the loss of the meaning and worth of distinctively human survival.

The collapse of modernity and the instability of postmodernity are a call to reach temporally behind them both to probe again the superiority of the Great Tradition. The problem of intelligible definition haunts postmodernism. Without some shared ideas its proponents cannot even communicate their radical negations. There is much to be said, moreover, for viewing the contemporary flux of ideas instead in terms of a spectacular decline of secular humanism to the abyss of raw naturalism.

Brook Thomas comments in his work devoted to *The New Historicism and Other Old-Fashioned Topics* that "postmodernism suggests that the pastness of the new. . . . The modern is described as postmodern and that which is considered behind us is referred to as the modern age. . . . 'Post' implies a belatedness, an age in which everything has already occurred." Postmodernism questions "the assumptions of self-consciously modern ages, especially the Enlightenment and its belief in progress and rationality."[43]

There is no good reason for allowing such semantic ambiguity to become the dominant discourse. The failed enterprise of modernity left unfulfilled its promise of enlightenment and emancipation. But the medieval heritage is not nearly as discredited as its current critics would have us believe. The root of evil is found neither in modernity nor in postmodernity and surely not in premodernity. It is found in humanity's disavowal of the living God of the ages who towers above the many gods of this age. It may well be that in the end postmodernity will prove to be better characterized in eschatological terms of prefinality. In any event, modernity's heady dismissal of the Christian heritage as sealed firmly in the past, through its identification in terms of the "middle ages," has now positioned modernity in the same unenviable role, and with more propriety.

NOTES

1. This chapter was delivered as a keynote address on 14 March 1995 at Westminster Theological Seminary, Philadelphia, Pa., opening the Contemporary Issues Conference on Apologetics, marking the 100th anniversary of the birth of Cornelius Van Til.

2. David Ray Griffin, ed., *Varieties of Postmodern Theology* (Albany: State Univ. of New York, 1989), xi.

3. Richard Lints, *The Fabric of Theology* (Grand Rapids: Eerdmans, 1993), 196.

4. William A. Beardslee, "Christ in the Modern Age," in *Varieties of Postmodern Theology*, 64.

5. Cf. Langdon Gilkey, "Theology for a Time of Trouble," in *Theology in Transition*, ed. James Wall (New York: Crossroad, 1981), 31.

6. However, in 1960 Dick Jellema authored a series of four essays in *Christianity Today* magazine charting the "rise of the post-modern mind." He noted that the post-modern mind was departing from a "patterned reality" and affirmed a "self that creates whatever value and meaning there is" in a context of an "impenetrable and awesome. . . . Unpattern." See *Christianity Today*, 9 May 1960, 23 May 1960, 6 June 1960, and 20 June 1960.

7. David Tracy, *Blessed Rage for Order: The New Pluralism in Theology* (New York: Seabury, 1978), 8.

8. See D.A. Carson, *The Gagging of God* (Grand Rapids: Zondervan, forthcoming).

9. Joe Holland, "The Postmodern Paradigm and Contemporary Catholicism," in *Varieties of Postmodern Theology*, 11.

10. Griffin, "Postmodern Theology and A/Theology," in *Varieties of Postmodern Theology*, 31.

11. Ibid.

12. See Carson, *Gagging of God*.

13. Griffin, "Postmodern Theology and A/Theology," 52.

14. Ibid., 36.

15. Ibid., 57–58.

16. Lints, *Fabric of Theology*, 199.

17. See George M. Marsden and Bradley J. Longfield, eds., *The Secularization of the Academy* (New York: Oxford Univ. Press, 1994).

18. See George M. Marsden, *The Soul of the American University* (New York: Oxford Univ. Press, 1994).

19. See Carson, *Gagging of God*.

20. Lints, *The Fabric of Theology,* 206.

21. See David Kelsey, *The Uses of Scripture in Recent Theology* (Philadelphia: Fortress, 1975).

22. Lints, *Fabric of Theology,* 218.

23. Ibid.

24. Griffin, "Postmodern Theology and A/Theology," 50.

25. Ibid.

26. Lints, *Fabric of Theology,* 222.

27. Ibid., 197.

28. See Carson, *Gagging of God.*

29. William C. Placher, "Revealed to Reason: Theology as a 'Normal Science,' " *Christian Century,* 1 February 1992, 195.

30. Lints, *Fabric of Theology,* 233.

31. Ibid., 238.

32. See Hans Blumenberg, *The Legitimacy of the Modern Age* (Cambridge: MIT Press, 1983).

33. Lints, *Fabric of Theology,* 235.

34. See Carson, *Gagging of God.*

35. See Carson's discussion in chapter 3 of *The Gagging of God.*

36. Thomas C. Oden, *After Modernity . . . What? Agenda for Theology* (Grand Rapids: Zondervan, 1990), 77.

37. See Carson, *Gagging of God.*

38. Anthony C. Thiselton, *The Two Horizons: New Testament Hermeneutics and Philosophical Description* (Grand Rapids: Eerdmans, 1980), 314–16.

39. Lints, *Fabric of Theology,* 238.

40. Ibid., 239.

41. Ibid., 246.

42. Ibid., 249.

43. Brook Thomas, *The New Historicism and Other Old-Fashioned Topics* (Princeton: Princeton Univ. Press, 1991), 25.

4

Disorientations in Christian Belief: The Problem of De-traditionalization in the Postmodern Context

Kurt A. Richardson

Culturally, we still consider ourselves quite modern but something about the modernist tradition has died such that, like the eclecticism of recent architecture, we find ourselves between pillar and post of old and new forms. Much of this death is due to the conflict over intellectual leadership, its politicization, and the shaming of earlier cultural traditions.[1] As a broadly artistic movement, this very fluid "postmodern" culture will likely prove to be a silver-aged formlessness between forms; *anti*-art that becomes *ante*-art. For the time being it is "axiomatically incompatible with maturity, permanence, and any aspiration toward *monumentality*," the intention to make a lasting contribution to cultural treasures and tradition.[2] Heightened awareness of the significance of public life and its own fluctuating nature is at the heart of the North American struggle in the postmodern situation. Primary to this public life are the "background" cultures of the universities and the churches. Given this heightened awareness, we should not be surprised by their politicization.[3] One dominant strategy to counter this has been to propose a dereligionizing of Christianity á la Bonhoeffer (rooted in Kierkegaard). Another began with separatisms of evangelicals from the mainline (the repository of the Protestant traditions), the independent evangelical church and parachurch movements with primi-

Kurt A. Richardson is Assistant Professor of Theology at Southeastern Baptist Theological Seminary in Wake Forest, North Carolina.

tivist claims about recovering New Testament Christianity today, and still another, that the transformations of modernity have nothing to do with Christian experience. In the midst of these processes substantive losses of tradition in faith and theology have gone unabated.

Our purpose in this chapter is to investigate some of the leading characteristics of this lost Christian tradition and to consider the crisis of North American Christianity from this larger point of view. One branch of current sociological research is devoted to identifying the causes and characteristics of "de-traditionalization" in society. From this research perspective, de-traditionalization is often seen as coterminous with secularization, the loss of religiousness in society. For Christian traditionalists and their national church heritage the classic *extra ecclesia nullam salus* has been emptied of a great deal of its public meaning.[4] We do not have the space here to trace the multitude of significant losses of tradition, certainly to the extent that David Wells has.[5] Although we may have some serious concerns about what appears to be Wells' anti-modernity, his *No Place for Truth: Or, Whatever Happened to Evangelical Theology?* is a valuable tour of de-traditionalization. But one must also look at some ways in which there emerges an unavoidable re-traditionalizing process where, for better or worse, Christian faith employs the weakness of its contemporary position for the progress of the Gospel. The statement by H.G. Gadamer bears keeping in mind here.

> In our continually manifested attitude to the past, the main feature is not, at any rate, a distancing and freeing of ourselves from what has been transmitted. Rather, we stand always within tradition, and this is no objectifying process, i.e., we do not conceive of what tradition says as something other, something alien. It is always part of us, a model or exemplar, a recognition of ourselves which our later historical judgment would hardly see as a kind of knowledge, but as the simplest preservation of tradition.[6]

The question for us is, have we lost confidence in our will to preserve tradition or have we lost the process altogether?

Here we have selected the category of tradition as an aperture through which to view that which is meant by the term "postmodern." The supposition taken here is that tradition is an inevitable by-product of human life and society. Just as Enlightenment modernity was characterized by a wholesale breaking free of traditional conventions, pluralistic postmodernism is a wholesale breaking free of the conventions of modernism. By way of considering the two-sided question above, we will set out below some leading questions from recent inquiry into the phenomena of de-traditionalization. These are drawn extensively from the research presented at a conference at the Centre for the Study of Cultural Values, Furness College, Lancaster University (1983).

What Is De-traditionalization?

Many of us have grown up so accustomed to the individualistic indulgences afforded by our open society that we are rather out of touch with tradition itself. We like to speak about traditional beliefs and values, but with each passing decade of our present deconstructive century, our world has become less and less guided by sets of conventions or rules to regulate social and cultural life. Sociological research identifies a number of sources of tradition: the laws of divine revelation and authority, the absolutist claims of secular authority in ancient empire or medieval state, or simply the rules of the close-knit life of the village. Habits of behavior stem from these rules which are imbibed through the community process, are not up for questioning or discussion, and rule out any question of authority residing in particular individuals. All that persons do must be evaluated according to the standards of the tradition.

In de-traditionalization the capacity of tradition to constrain the behavior of individuals by authority and through conventional behaviors, is in view. The most significant characteristic of the decline of tradition for the individual is the rise of "reflexive" experience: one's being faced with ever increasing sets of alternative norms, ends, means, and legitimations. De-traditionalization stands for the decline of a preset, natural order. The natural comes to be seen as fluid, adaptive, contingent, and even disorder itself. The only apparent alternative for many is an individualistic response requiring the creation of orders: political, aesthetic, legal, social, and even moral. Without traditional foundations and the voice of authority, the self assumes responsibility to ground itself by itself. A new kind of order is founded upon individual creativity and self-legitimation which we have come to call "modernity." But now at the end of at least three generations, modernity and its crisis of authority can be more clearly seen for what it is: the loss of tradition. Universalizing criticism which so early spawned the rise of the individual autonomous experience and thereby produced its own tradition is itself undergoing detraditionalization in the advanced stages of this process. This fact exposes the character of the postmodern and postliberal trends in Christian belief and theology: reconstruction of viable Christian tradition will be a reflexively creative process, but probably rules out the possibility of ever experiencing a naturalness of authority again.

What Are the Leading Responses to De-traditionalization?

The focus here is on four intellectual responses: (1) positive assessment of the increasing reflexivity as an intensified condition and thus postmodern. Issues of democratization of public, economic, and social life, equal opportunity of the sexes, heightening of individual responsibility, risk-taking in the entrepreneurial, information-intensive characteristics, including ecological concern and consciousness are all positive and determinative by-products of the de-traditionalizing situation.

(2) Fundamental criticizing of the order-giving reflexive self, in view of the flux and contingencies of situations in life, a Nietzschean *amor fati*. Here there is a giving in to complexity, contradiction, difference, and allegory in the midst of relations rather than any reality to its discursive ordering. De-traditionalizing must go further, and yet it is also aggravating the problem of illegitimate authority external to the self. This position represents radical opposition to all authority and an embracing of principal relativism.

(3) Qualified affirmation of de-traditionalization can also be found but with the sense that it has gone too far. Here some form of Heideggarian naturalism is favored and is anti-discursive through the triadic *bauen, wohnen, denken* of the vernacular. Here there is a rejection of reflexivity, not in order to embrace contingency, but to develop new habits of life or habitus. A longing for simplicity, nature, a kind of primitivism where the social, outer, and inner worlds are renaturalized.

(4) Finally, there is a fundamental questioning whether de-traditionalization is occurring at all. There is opposition to the distinction made between the traditional and the modern by seeking historical examples of reflexivity in traditional societies. The claim is made that reflexivity exists as much in traditional societies as in modern ones. Further, rather than de-traditionalizing, there is and has been continually a process of re-traditionalizing so that modern society is just as "grouped" and "gridded" as traditional societies. Indeed, it is most surprisingly claimed that certain adaptiveness and

flexibility has always been present in traditional societies such that much pluralism could be found there as well. Thus, modern and postmodern cultural, political, and religious forms are said to constitute new traditions beyond the old which they have supplanted.

What Approaches Are Used to Describe De-traditionalization?

Discourse, hermeneutics, and identity, aesthetics, memory, and meaning, and cultures of nature, all represent varieties of approach to engagement with the tendencies of the postmodern situation. Here we only have space to deal with those issues which impact the self, ethics, and religion as a context and a resource for doing theology. Here questions about the impact of ideologies of the authoritative self, markets, consumers, globalization, pluralism, and secularity upon religion and the reconstitution of tradition are at the fore. Is it possible to say that pluralism actually strengthens religion? We come also to note that the real limits of liberalizing of Christianity exist whereby it ceases to exist. Can religion be called a consumer value? What are emerging differences between the ethics of the self and of liberal ideals?

For evangelical belief and theology the whole matter of de-traditionalization perhaps catches us somewhat off guard. We may refer to "tradition" particularly in public debate about proper forms of family life, values, and morals. Fewer of us speak directly about theological, and more specifically doctrinal, tradition because of our separatist or parachurch background and context. Although the evangelical tradition was not caught up in the anti-dogmatic spirit of the Enlightenment and modernistic bias influencing theology, it did develop a doctrinal minimalizing and unintended de-traditionalizing move of its own known in the twentieth century as inter- or non-denominationalism. This goes directly back to the conflicts of the seventeenth century between Protestant and Catholic and others and the development of an irenic tradition. The irenic tradition filtered its way into the dogmatic minimalism of pietism, revivalism, and the separatistic movements which spawned modern evangelicalism. Except for the distinctly confessional and conservative communions who have gradually affiliated or at least cooperated with the larger evangelical movement, there continues this non-tradition of doctrinal minimalism, which at times is indistinct from anti-dogmatic positions, other than their outright indifference.

But doctrinal tradition does not touch upon the issue of de-traditionalization at its core. Doctrine is the product of the interpreting church offering up a faithful summary of its core beliefs which are to be taught faithfully wherever and whenever that church bears witness to Christ and His lordship. Much broader and deeper than this, there is a depth dimension to tradition which correlates with faithful living in the Christian community of church. It seems that much of the cultural loss which thoughtful evangelicals feel was not embodied simply in recent forms of Christian living and therefore proper only to evangelicals. The study of Christian history, particularly Protestant history and its contributions to the best of Western cultural traditions, is what they have in mind: art, science, literature, and political freedoms, and even prerogatives.

Examples of De-traditionalization

If evangelical theology is to properly respond to the postmodern dilemma of de-traditionalization it must first of all get a hold of examples which exemplify this process. We are now calling de-traditionalization a dilemma because the critical attitude which once focused upon the abandonment of pre-modern traditions has now turned in upon itself to abandon its own modern traditions of universality and selfhood. Here we will lay out a number of issues and then press on to a proposal of a theological agenda with the hope that it can contribute insight toward solutions and re-traditionalizing for the sake of Christian life and thought.

The rising predominance of the categories of health and sickness and the ideal of the self overcoming the old categories of traditional convention: metaphysics, morality, tradition, and past memory, often come into view. Here the abiding influence of Friedrich Nietzsche as prophet of postmodernity in his work *The Genealogy of Morals* (1956) might be referred to where nothing short of nihilism is embraced, in view of the fading away of so much tradition. In his overall work, Nietzsche is preoccupied with the self-awareness required of the philosopher who must lay out possible futures, as it were, of the impact of his thought. His readers must ask, was he brilliant? Do his books have destiny and with whom? As these kinds of queries are entertained, the mutual destruction of the entire philosophical project is secured. The ideal of an ongoing tradition is fundamentally disturbed. Another major theme for him is the transmission of authority from the destruction of old laws to the willful construction of new laws. The comic nature of this fluid yet powerful state of affairs in modern life is emphasized and is further reason for affirming nihilism. The sickness of the situation predominates, however, not the vast array of choices.

The only way to recover one's health then is to embrace the situation through the will to power and the serving and responsibility of the self. In the work itself, Nietzsche is obsessed with the "slave morality" of a decadent Christian civilization that would not and could not live up to its own tradition. Of course this had already been exposed over a generation earlier by Søren Kierkegaard from his deeply personal Christian perspective. The same rage over tolerating the intolerable created resentment or envy and the leveling mediocrity of social life was acutely displayed in his work.[7] The modern tradition of cultural Christianity found its two most incisive critics in these men, mostly in that they recognized the de-traditionalizing/re-traditionalizing process to be as unhealthy as it was. The former saw the corruption as endemic to Christianity and the latter as just that, the degredation of the true and pure original.

Further, the aspect of health has an altogether other way of becoming prioritized, radically contributing to de-traditionalization. Virtually the entire measure of classic theology and the record of Christian belief is one out of which the hope of a healthy life rested entirely with God. For the vast majority, health was not at all secure, and life served as the backdrop for preparing for eternity. Indeed, like the wretched Jorge in Umberto Eco's *The Name of the Rose* who sought to eliminate comedy, many of the preachers of past Christian eras sought the elimination of the hope of health to better prepare their hearers for a health beyond present sickness.

This situation, however, has radically changed. The persistent modern situation enjoins a tremendous individualism and responsibility upon everyone to maintain good health, indeed, a modicum of trimness, for success in the labor market. No longer a bestowment of God, health is a task and duty, and runs great risk over its neglect. The *sozai* of the earthly has a very compelling way of making health almost salvific and intensifying the individualism of our society and churches. Health becomes a tremendously powerful ideological tool for no one can argue against it. Health becomes an ultimate value against all established traditions, particularly in the case of gene technology. Expectations have radically changed as well whereby nature itself is inadequate before a new ought of change and improvement toward a healthier and better "you."

The issue of political health is one which provides an extremely rich resource for understanding the process of de- and re-traditionalizing. Baptists, for example, are acutely aware of the necessity of religious freedom in the traditional Christian state where, in every case, Baptist and other nonconformists or orthodox sects were traditionally excluded and marginalized. In fact, we can rightly say that religious freedom is the keystone of all the other freedom necessary for an open society. But with this freedom, there arises, in terms of the prior Christian tradition of the national church, which united the sacred and the secular, the centering of the secular within society for, in a very real sense, irreligion and secularity predominate among the majority of individuals when they consciously exercise the right to dissociate themselves from religious communities.

This issue becomes particularly touchy in cases that national Christianity and civil religion once saw as a religious crime, as in blasphemy. The inability to enforce blasphemy laws under the conditions of religious freedom effectively led to the right of an individual to blaspheme under certain very broadly construed, or even all, circumstances under the protection of the freedom of speech. It is questionable if there could ever be a law founded upon the claim that some sort of blasphemy constituted "fighting words."

The tradition of Christian education is also one that is fraught with paradoxes. Martin Marty, Mark Noll, and lately George Marsden have helped our understanding here greatly. As we investigate the de-traditionalizing and therefore secularizing of the Christian college or university a rather surprising pattern emerges, played out dozens of times over. After the school achieves a modicum of stability and then a reputation for its high standards of education, it becomes attractive not only to members of its close-knit church or denominational constituency, but also to students from other traditions. The curriculum which has confessional theology at its core and representing the faithful interpretation of the denomination is not at first seen as an impediment by these outsiders. But in the course of time, as the numbers of other Christian groups grow, pastoral representatives of these students insist upon alternative dogmatics courses for students out of their traditions. This leads to nearly interminable haggling over the curriculum and how it can be tailored to suit these "outsider" interests. Most often, in the effort to maintain the unity of the student body, an unexpected option is offered: to drop the teaching of dogmatics altogether and replace it with a course containing so-called essentials of Christianity. Of course, no one winds up being pleased with these events, and the church leadership on all sides becomes unalterably disenchanted with the institution. At this point, conflict management becomes long overdue.

In the meantime, standards of research continue to rise as does the demand for free inquiry, pedagogy which carefully initiates naive Christian students to critical research falters, and the conflict over any distinctive Christian identity becomes the mother of all battles. Finally, the administration and trustees, weary of the bickering, develop a self-perpetuating form of governance and separate from the denomination. With a lack of ability to direct an institution of Christian higher learning, the worst case scenario is being played out over and over again. Thus plays out the tragic process of becoming worldly at the hands of the godly, for the fateful step took place at the point when doctrinal tradition was abandoned and nothing representative of Christian practice was put in its place.

In the open society, created by the fundamental right of religious freedom, the freedom of conscience becomes almost unavoidably constructive with very little from the religious community to bind it from above or beside. The evangelical Christian is enjoined to "make Christ Lord," but the self-reflexivity of practically every aspect of this attempt makes this person's experience and testimony thoroughly impregnated with autonomous intentions and private judgments. In this case, a surprising form of deconstruction enters into our picture. Given the autonomous embracing of tradition making Jesus Lord — and self-direction — adoption of private judgment, self-directed deconstruction, and reconstruction occurs as the form of Christian life. Much of this is in evidence in the work of James Davison Hunter and many denominational surveys. The great problem here is that beliefs which are only properly public and pervasive become constricted and privatized. The traditional beliefs are no longer the bases for faith for the believer. Everything spiritual is based upon the partial and brief encounter. Simply put, religious identity is now a fragmentary phenomena.

Scholarly inquiry and the critique of tradition has proved helpful and even redemptive, especially in cases where tradition empowered the worst of human prejudices.[8] But how do we avoid a stance where, "The end of inquiry is . . . perpetually deferred?"[9] The reconstituting of tradition is occurring unavoidably all the time. This is the case even while operative reality of cultural criticism continues and indeed shows no sign of exhausting itself. So much of the historical is laden with shame, indefensible events based upon traditions embodying prejudice and justifying real evil. On the other hand, part of the function of tradition is to record how coping with evil has taken place on a realistic basis. And in the case of the Christian tradition is the matter of how evil events are affected by commitments to the mercy, grace, and forbearance of God embodied in the church. The reconstructive and re-traditionalizing process is, relatively speaking, only in its early stages. The expurgation of the repellent and shameful is always up for negotiation, whether it be in degrees of racism, cultural imperialism, or nonintervention during the Holocaust and other genocidal acts. But as of yet, this process of reconstituting tradition is very imperfect due to the realities of privatized faith and individualistic spiritualities inculcated in many evangelical sermons and books.

Given the privatized and individualistic condition of our experience, Jean-Luc Nancy's *The Inoperative Community* might be considered. Concern for community and its loss, Nancy declares, is conspicuously Christian. But the community to him must be construed only in terms of a copresence of autonomous selves and is therefore really fully post-Christian. Somewhat better is Robert Wuthnow's *Christianity in the Twenty-First Century,* which lays out, almost uniquely, values contributing toward healthy forms of church community.[10] He admits not only the difficulty of finding community, but that this difficulty is increasing. This is exacerbated by the increasing instability of two traditional community builders: the family and the church denomination. In fact, the proliferation of new denominations has done little to contribute to the overall increasing perception of their irrelevancy. Wuthnow specifically calls for the resacralization of everyday life, so omni-directional, so rich, and so concerned with all the aspects of life that pour into healthy living in community. But this is weak medicine in view of the diversity of Christian interpretations and community structures and clusterings.[11] The diversity, at times so competitive and at others so divisive, suggests to many, at least subliminally, a kind of relativism about Christianity's truth claims in general.

Evangelical Agenda for Re-traditionalizing the Community of Believers

We must recognize the postmodern for what it is: a movement embodying irresponsibility in any and every form. Postmodern mentality is simply to disconnect and then aggressively reconnect at ill-advised political moments. In many ways the postmodern should no longer exist, for it has close ties with cold war East Berlin, it is like the non sequiturs of comedy, but, without closure, becoming an interminable sick joke. In many ways it is the continuing counterculture radicalized, but now unashamedly superficial and schizophrenic as a way of preferred being. If art was conceived to imitate life, the postmodern is a misendeavor of life seeking to imitate art. As such, it is hedonistic, highly unstable, celebrative of degradation as the true colors of the avante-garde impulse and thus ultimately suicidal. Having said this, however, one must not imagine that the postmodern is simply confined to the cultural elites. The postmodern has eminently popular forms illustrated in the so-called *Panic Encyclopedia*, where even a kind of spirituality is found in the "panic God" of former televangelist Jim Bakker. The common thread running through the popularist postmodern then is the awareness that "in America, you have to be excessive to be successful."[12] The deconstructive response to historic Christianity has been to assume a Nietzschean abandonment of all standards in an attempt to minimize the destructiveness of human relations. The lostness of this viewpoint has not escaped minimalists of the atheistic kind who, curiously, enter in to do combat with the deconstructionists at this very point.[13]

Further, we must recognize that the postmodern is another name for our cultural crisis and possesses an excruciating difficulty with looking back. Nevertheless Eco, in his *Travels in Hyper-Reality*, relays something helpful: in our day, like the Middle Ages, a rigorous and yet new juxtaposing of old and new must take place requiring "new methods of adjustment" through the "constant retranslation and reuse" of the classic heritage.[14] We must also be extremely careful to guard against the temptation consigning the postmodern disorientation to a liberal celebration. Hitler himself was the avantgarde's greatest enemy and the object of his liquidation efforts. The autonomous irresponsibility of the right can be just as insidious as anything from the left. This is not, however, an advocacy of middle ground or mediating positions in theology or culture. Rather, it is a recognition that the lordship of Christ stands over and against all ideological positions, judges them, and calls the church to stand apart and to minister unto from entirely different bases.

Conclusion: Six Proposals for Reform

1. *Recovery of the ideal of reform.* Reform must come now in a consciously constructive sense, emphasizing both the sovereignty of God and the authority granted to the church to construct new institutions which embody its mission. Like criticism in the academic realm, reform has become part of the Christian tradition itself. Christians are those who reform themselves. Through repentance, a

regrounding in Scripture as supreme over tradition, it serves as the basis for the recovering and renewing of Christian tradition.[15]

2. *Recovery of a community-based discipleship.* In every age of the church there is a particular error or weakness which plagues it. There are certainly many signs of Christian presence still within North America, but the impact upon Western culture is light. The doctrine of the church is in need of "special honor" today. Baptists, for example, are unalterably committed to a believers' church doctrine, and one that is congregationally based in terms of a shared authority under Christ. Curiously, some of the healthiest examples of the Christian church show forth just these identifying marks. Every doctrine of the church entails every other evangelical doctrine. Recovery and renewal here will have an enriching effect on the general vitality of theology. Only upon the firm conviction that the vitality of everything truly Christian is realized in the life of the church will the complex of challenges and calling reach their proper engagement.

3. *Recovery of the Gospel as the heart of Scripture and the prioritizing center of the community.* The seemingly perennial harangue over biblical minutiae diverts the community of Christ from its mission in the world: to announce salvation to all nations. A thoroughgoing reestablishment of this singular reason for existence as Christians, as churches, is required for prioritizing the rest of life. Whether this is done through the renewal of worship, theology, or discipleship, the Word of Christ in both its particular and universal dimensions must be held as the only source of renewal. Only in this way can Christianity truly take up its singular mission before the plurality of religions and ultimate claims in the world. Christianity's agenda is its message which simultaneously embodies its mission. All other intellectual and cultural agendas pale in significance to this one. Surprisingly perhaps, we may discover that demonstration of the unique truthfulness of the Christian message will take place from this very standpoint.[16]

4. *Recovery of confessional theology.* Cognizant of the truth that a surfeit of orthodoxy produces skepticism, the bond of fellowship within the church is in large part encapsulated in its covenantal and normative confessions of faith. Confessions always, above all, are to symbolize the act of truly confessing Christ as Lord both *intra* and *extra ecclesia.* Confessing, convenanting, and normativity all characterize true confessional theology. Without this complex, rooted in Scripture, what we teach the next generation of Christians, both inside and outside our particular denomination, about orthodoxy and

orthopraxy will fall further into decline.[17] But this is also a spiritual (i.e., realized under the lordship of the Holy Spirit) process and condition. A renewing combination of the objective and subjective poles of Christian faith in inseparable relation are in view. As such, theological reflection and confessional statement are never held at an academic distance or used in an authoritarian way. Instead, they will be valid representations of the truth of the living God and the reality of His lordship. This "combinational" perspective has always been true of the best in the Christian theological tradition.[18]

5. *Recovery of the irenic impulse.* Based upon a recognition of the longing for a recovered vitality of Christianity, there are fellow believers throughout the diversity of denominations who need our collaboration under the singular lordship of Christ. Whether this is post-liberal or post-fundamentalist, the bitter heritage of elitism and separationism must be abandoned. In addition, a global perspective of the church — the incomparable international network of Christians — will require a determined commitment to the irenic principle of dwelling at peace with those who stand under the lordship of Christ and His commission to the church. Teachers within the churches of Jesus Christ need to understand the difference between denominational distinctives and sectarian antipathies and recover the ability to unite on practical bases when essential doctrinal agreement is present.

6. *Recovery of the Christian intellectual tradition.* This is a most important link between evangelical faith and constructive re-traditionalization. The cosmic dimensions of the saving economy of God places before the church the imperative of taking every thought captive unto Christ and of showing how all the treasures of wisdom and knowledge are to be most truly found in Him. Fresh expressions of the relationship between faith and knowledge need to come forth.[19] There is no question of recovering traditional forms of Christian life predicated on the heritage of the national churches. The grounding ideologies behind this heritage are today untenable. Nevertheless, as Jacob Neusner has recently reminded us, Christianity is inherently configured to establish truth-claims in some way on a universal or global basis. Only through the intellectual enterprise can Christianity reformulate and represent its rationale for such a sweeping claim. It is destined to do so, and the challenge before evangelicals is to take up this destiny in a noble spirit of service and intellectual honesty under Christ in the forging of new forms of Christian civilization.

NOTES

1. Karlis Racevskis, *Postmodernism and the Search for Enlightenment* (Charlottesville, Va.: Univ. Press of Virginia, 1993), 101–2.

2. Nicholas Zurbrugg, *The Parameters of Postmodernism* (Carbondale, Ill.: Southern Illinois Univ. Press, 1993), 1–3.

3. John Rawls, *Political Liberalism* (New York: Columbia Univ. Press, 1973), 215.

4. Ibid., 138.

5. Cf. David Wells, *No Place for Truth: Or, Whatever Happened to Evangelical Theology?* (Grand Rapids: Eerdmans, 1993).

6. Hans Georg Gadamer, *Truth and Method,* trans. Garrett Barden and John Cumming (New York: Crossroad, 1985), 250.

7. Roger Poole, *Kierkegaard: The Indirect Communication* (Charlottesville, Va.: Univ. Press of Virginia, 1993), 227–28.

8. Cf. Rene Girard, *The Scapegoat* (Baltimore: Johns Hopkins Univ. Press, 1986).

9. Michael Krausz, *Rightness and Reason* (Ithaca, N.Y.: Cornell Univ. Press, 1993), 47.

10. Cf. Robert Wuthnow, *Christianity in the Twenty-first Century: Reflections on the Challenges Ahead* (New York: Oxford Univ. Press, 1993), 88–93.

11. Robert Wuthnow, *Rediscovering the Sacred: Perspectives on Religion in Contemporary Society* (Grand Rapids: Eerdmans, 1992), 9–35.

12. Zurbrugg, *Parameters of Postmodernism,* 143.

13. Jerome A. Stone, *The Minimalist Vision of Transcendence* (Albany, N.Y.: State Univ. of New York, 1992), 210–24.

14. Umberto Eco, *Travels in Hyper-Reality,* trans. William Weaver (London: Picador, 1987), 65.

15. James Leo Garrett, Jr., *Systematic Theology,* vol. 1 (Grand Rapids: Eerdmans, 1990), 179–81.

16. Wolfhart Pannenberg, *Systematic Theology,* vol. 1, trans. Geoffrey Bromiley (Grand Rapids: Eerdmans, 1991), 172–87.

17. Robert W. Jenson, *Unbaptized God: The Basic Flow in Ecumenical Theology* (Minneapolis: Augsburg/Fortess, 1992), 1–17.

18. Ingolf U. Dalferth, *Kombinatorische Theologie: Probleme Theologischer Rationalitat* (Freiburgh: Herder, 1991), 99–100.

19. Cf. Robert P. Scharlemann, *The Reason of Following: Christology and the Ecstatic* (Chicago: Univ. of Chicago Press, 1991), 69–77.

5

The Integrity of the Evangelical Tradition and the Challenge of the Postmodern Paradigm

R. Albert Mohler, Jr.

"A spectre is roaming throughout Europe: the Postmodern." *Le Monde,* 1983

There is a spectre haunting classical Christianity, that of postmodernism. This assertion is intended as a warning rather than a threat, but it is a warning specifically addressed to American evangelicals.

Evangelicals, attracted to the vague but seductive notion of postmodernity as a breakdown of secular modernity, are in danger of romancing modernity's latest stage of representation and development, and thus risk forfeiting the integrity of the evangelical truth claim, and the Gospel itself. Under the guise of postmodernism, theological and philosophical variants have been welcomed within the evangelical tent, incorporated into the evangelical mind, and celebrated simultaneously as victory over the legions of modernity and as liberation from the bondage of the older evangelicalism. Nothing less than the integrity of evangelical Christianity is at stake.

What Is Postmodernism?

Postmodernism, whatever it is, now enjoys that most rare and enviable status of the almost universally acknowledged (though vaguely

R. Albert Mohler, Jr. is President of The Southern Baptist Theological Seminary in Louisville, Kentucky.

defined) cultural phenomenon. It is celebrated, debated, analyzed and, as a term of fairly recent vintage, radically over-employed.[1]

"Everyone begins the discussion of postmodernism by asking what the word could possibly mean,"[2] stated John McGowan, and yet, many seem to use the word without the slightest concern for its possible or actual meanings. There should be no embarrassment in asking such a foundational question as the definition of the term.

The word has a contested and controverted genealogy. Michael Kohler has traced the word to 1934, when Frederico de Oniz coined *postmodernismo.*[3] But the most significant early use of the term is probably that of Arnold Toynbee, who in 1939 suggested that the modern age had ended in 1914, and that the era which emerged out of the ruins of the shattering experience of the first world war should be described as "Post-Modern."[4]

Toynbee's focus on World War I should not be minimized. That cataclysmic event was the watershed of a new but unformed consciousness in the West. The war and its horrors brought to an end liberalism's promise of inevitable progress and determined optimism. The tragedy of the war and the ruin of supposedly civilized cultures both occasioned the reality and fostered the hope for a new way of understanding the world.[5]

Is postmodernism a coherent concept, or is it a phenomenon of popular intellectual culture — a term to be employed as a code word for the contemporary and avant-garde? Hans Bertens asks whether the phenomenon of postmodernism actually exists, "no matter how many critics have put their lives on the line for its defense."[6]

As currently applied, the term is an umbrella concept covering styles, movements, shifts, and approaches in the fields of art, history, architecture, literature, political science, economics, and philosophy — not to mention theology. Several of its leading theorists argue, in keeping with the diffusion, that there is not one postmodernism, but many. Hans Bertens states the obvious when he observes that "postmodernism is not a monolithic phenomenon."[7]

The term is imprecise, irregular, and malleable, but also highly marketable. It is inserted into book titles, advertising slogans, and academic course descriptions with abandon.

Furthermore, the term has been championed by and associated with some of the greatest enemies of intelligibility visible on the current scene. Few, if any, theorists have exceeded the influence of the French post-structuralist Jean-Francois Lyotard, who offered the following definition.

The postmodern would be that which, in the modern, puts forward the unpresentable in presentation itself; that which denies itself the solace of good forms, the consensus of a taste which would make it possible to share collectively the nostalgia for the unattainable; that which searches for new presentations, not in order to enjoy them but in order to impart a stronger sense of the unpresentable.[8]

Those seeking after a definition of postmodernism are not likely to find much assistance from such an unintelligible offering. But Lyotard is hardly alone. Marxist literary critic Terry Eagleton exceeds even Lyotard in his suggestion that

there is, perhaps, a degree of consensus that the typical post-modern artifact is playful, self-ironizing and even schizoid; and that it reacts to the austere autonomy of high modernism by impudently embracing the language of commerce and the commodity. Its stance towards cultural tradition is one of irreverent pastiche, and its cultural depthlessness undermines all metaphysical solemnities, sometimes by the brutal aesthetics of squalor and shock.[9]

This is, at best, what Alvin Kernan has identified as "ideology as aesthetics."[10] At worst it is a prime example of what C.S. Lewis labeled "verbicide." In any event, the definitions above reveal more about the current sophomoric fads in modern art and literary criticism than about the meaning of postmodernism.

Gladly, there are yet some theorists who will speak candidly and directly to the issue of definition. Michael Kohler offers this clarification.

Despite persisting controversies as to what constitutes the characteristic traits of the new area, the term "postmodern" is now generally applied to all cultural phenomena which have emerged since the second world war and are indicative of a change in sensibility and attitude, making the present age "post the modern."[11]

Clearly, the term is intended to mark a break with modernity and the modern age, however that is dated. But the larger issue is epistemological. Walter Truett Anderson tells the story of the three umpires. The first, representing the pre-modern perspective, explains his method as "There's balls and there's strikes, and I call 'em the way they are." The second, a modernist, asserts "I call 'em the way I see 'em." The third umpire, a postmodernist, claims "they ain't nothin' until I call 'em."[12]

Lyotard, professor of philosophy at the University of Paris at Vincennes, has emerged as the most formative defining force in the postmodern movement. In *The Postmodern Condition: A Report on Knowledge*,[13] Lyotard sets the context of postmodernism within the cultural and ideological crisis of Western civilization. This crisis involves virtually all cognitive issues, from ontology to epistemology.

Rejecting Jurgen Habermas' concept of a legitimation crisis, Lyotard asserts that the problem is more accurately described as a "crisis of narratives." Postmodernism, argues Lyotard, is "the state of our culture following the transformations which, since the end of the twentieth century, have altered the game rules for science, literature, and the arts."[14] He acknowledges that this crisis of narratives is a religious crisis as well.[15]

How is this new postmodern age to be distinguished from modernity? Lyotard suggests that the modern age is the age of the meta-discourses, the meta-narratives, which seek to undergird and to explain the nature of the universe, the origin of meaning, and the various enterprises and schemes of modernity. These enterprises include science itself, which Lyotard notes is usually hostile to narratives, for judged by "scientific" terms, "the majority of them prove to be fables."[16]

But even science is required in the age of modernity to supply its own narratives in order to legitimate itself. So, what is the modern? As Lyotard explains:

> I will use the term *modern* to designate any science that legitimates itself with reference to a metadiscourse of this kind, making an explicit appeal to some grand narrative, such as the dialectic of Spirit, the hermeneutics of meaning, the emancipation of the rational or working subject, or the creation of wealth.[17]

Thus all grand narratives, ranging from the unified field theory and Hegel's dialecticism to the Christian Gospel, are declared modern, and therefore dead, though vestigial reminders of the narratives still remain. The meta-narratives themselves are, Lyotard insists, untenable and dead.

What does this mean? Put bluntly, Lyotard's conception of post-modernism is based upon the assumption that modernity's rationalizing and totalizing gestalt and worldview have passed from the scene. Confidence in rationality has itself been deconstructed.

Lyotard's most pointed definition sets the issue clearly: "Simplifying to the extreme, I define *postmodern* as incredulity toward metanarratives."[18] How did this happen? As Lyotard describes:

> The narrative function is losing its great functors, its great hero, its great dangers, its great voyages, its great goal. It is being disbursed in clouds of narrative language elements— narrative, but also denotative, prescriptive, and so on. Conveyed within each cloud are pragmatic valencies specific to each kind. Each of us lives at the intersection of many of these. However, we do not necessarily establish stable language combinations, and the properties of the ones we do establish are not necessarily communicable.[19]

This is a classic defining statement of postmodernism. According to this worldview, universal truth claims are impossible. All discourse is particular, limited, and insular, and it inevitably breaks down into the competing language games operating among different communities of meaning.[20]

All that remains is *les petites histoires,* the little stories. As theorist Ihab Hassan describes these, the surviving narratives are

> paratactical, paradoxical narratives meant to open the structures of knowledge as of politics to language games, to imaginative reconstitutions that permit us either a new breakthrough or a change in the rules of the game itself.[21]

This is a decidedly political statement. The grand narratives of modernity (and those, such as Christianity, which predated modernity), are to be broken down into fragmented and truncated mininarratives, which function as language games for discrete communities and interest groups.

The issue of postmodernism lays open a major breech in European high culture of the post-World War II era. In particular, it occasioned the conflict between Habermas and Lyotard over the character of postmodernity. Habermas sees postmodernism as the repudiation and end of what he has described as "the modernist project." Postmodernism, according to Habermas, is "a farewell to modernity as a return to the premodern."[22] As he warns, "I think that instead of giving up modernity and its project as a lost cause, we should learn from the mistakes of those extravagant programs which have tried to negate modernity."[23]

Habermas sees the modernist project as liberation from Western culture's oppressive misuse of power. From his vantage point, postmodernism appears as an anti-modernist regression, not a step into the future — and certainly not the answer to the legitimation crisis. Habermas celebrates the meta-narratives of liberation and the extension of modernity.

But Lyotard celebrates precisely what Habermas decries. For Lyotard, the death of the meta-narratives is itself liberation. All that remains are the petit narratives, inherently perspectival and political.

In the end, Lyotard has asked the right question. Where, after the demise of the meta-narratives, does legitimacy reside? The very notion of legitimacy is itself contested among the postmodernists and their counter theorists such as Habermas. Here, Habermas breaks decisively with the postmodernists, for the postmodernists have debased any claim to legitimacy or to legitimating discourse. No legitimating transcendent remains, whether it be ideological, historical, or merely political. In this important sense, all postmodernisms which reject any objective moral referent inevitably slide into deconstructionism of some variety. Deconstructionism is the only logical option left after the demise of the meta-narratives. This progression explains much of what has happened in the fields of literature, art, history, and politics in recent years.

At this point the example of Michel Foucault is instructive. One of the most celebrated figures of postmodernism for the last twenty years, Foucault was himself a period piece of the Paris intelligentsia.[24] His deconstruction of the moral tradition was demonstrated to the observing world by his own radically "liberated" homosexual lifestyle, his extended arguments for pederasty, and his experimentation with hallucinogenic drugs.[25]

In Foucault, the Enlightenment project reaches its dead-end. Evident here is a shift from the radical subjectivism of the Enlightenment's left wing to the absolute deconstruction of meaning when radical subjectivism reaches its conclusion. Foucault's famous notion of the "death of the author" is perhaps the clearest rejection of any objective meaning. Communal understandings are undermined and subverted. All that remains is the task of ideological and moral genealogy, a task Foucault believed was left unfinished with the death of Nietzsche.

Foucault was determined to complete, or at least to extend, the Nietzschian project. His works were an eccentric attempt to trace a genealogy of knowledge and power. His linkage of knowledge and power is rooted in his argument that knowledge is always derived from power, and that the possession of knowledge inevitably leads to greater misuses of power. Sex, he argued, was the most significant intersection of knowledge and power, and was thus the limit of human experience. The "heterotopia" Foucault sought was sexual in nature.

This notion explains not only Foucault's ideological construct, but his biography as well. His category of "limit experience" was linked to his call for "polymorphous perversity."[26] Foucault thus serves as a fitting symbol of modernity's revolt against the moral order, buttressing E. Michael Jones' description of modernity as "rationalized sexual misbehavior."[27] His effort to localize the search for meaning in the sexual act was an effort at moral rationalization. His "death of the author" removed all moral absolutes, and nothing was left in the debris but absolute moral relativism and the deconstruction of meaning. Postmodernism would produce heterotopia.

A Postmodern Turn in Theology?

As Lyotard acknowledged, the postmodern condition represents a religious crisis: the deconstruction of meaning and moral order and the demise of the meta-narratives—all this was an ax laid to the trunk of the Christian tradition. Foucault's notion of the death of the author sets the challenge clearly, for according to the Christian doctrine of revelation, the ultimate author is God Himself.

If postmodernism is a theological movement in response to modernity, where did it begin? Following Toynbee's argument, World War I would be the decisive turning point. The towering figure of Karl Barth thus intrudes upon the scene. Barth's experience of World War I and its antecedent events in Germany did indeed lead him to repudiate much of the modern experiment.

Barth had come to adulthood and to the German academic culture at the pinnacle of modernity's optimism. But his observation of the events leading to the war were devastating to Barth. In particular, the fact that ninety-three German university professors and other intellectuals signed an infamous declaration supporting the war policy of Kaiser Wilhelm II and Chancellor Bethmann-Hollweg was devastating to Barth, then a pastor in Safenwil, Switzerland.

Barth's realization that his professors could so quickly and publicly support the German war policy caused him to question their theological systems as well. In his words, "For me it was almost worse than the violation of Belgian neutrality. And to my dismay, among the signatories I discovered the names of almost all my German teachers. . . ."[28] Further, "It was like the twilight of the gods when I saw the reaction of Harnack, Hermann, Rade, Eucken and company to the new situation."[29] The conclusion was, to Barth, inescapable. As he reflected, "a whole world of exegesis, ethics, dogmatics and preaching, which I had hitherto held to be essentially trustworthy, was shaken to the foundations, and with it, all the other writings of the German theologians."[30]

Barth's theology, often characterized as "neo-orthodoxy," was a self-conscious rejection of the liberal German theology and of its philosophical antecedents. It was, however, not as thorough a rejection of the German tradition of critical philosophy as Barth himself thought. Barth did reject the tradition of Harnack, Hermann, and Troeltsch, but he remained embedded within the structures of modern thought, including the categories of critical philosophy. He was, in the end, more successful in opposing Harnack than Kant.

How should we then characterize Barth? Is his theological system and his *Church Dogmatics* essentially pre-modern, modern, or is it a postmodern model of theological engagement? There is no evidence to support a pre-modern reading of Barth. His thought is inherently rooted within the structures of the Enlightenment, even to the extent of the vestigial remnants of dialectical thought in his doctrine of the Word. On the other hand, Barth did often express himself in terms which appeared to be pre-modern in substance.

Yet, Barth is not genuinely postmodern. He was too far removed from the ideological consciousness and cultural crises of the late twentieth century to understand the postmodern paradigm. As Thomas Oden suggests, Barth "never entered empathetically enough into the ideological categories of modernity or the ethos of the late stages of deteriorating modernity."[31] This, by extension, Oden applies to neo-orthodoxy as a movement, which "by no fault of its own, did not live deep enough into the outrageous decline of the twentieth century to behold the precipitous moral deterioration of modernity."[32]

A very different reading of Barth is offered by Hans Küng, Barth's former student. Küng argues for the use of postmodernism as a "heuristic concept." Karl Barth, Küng argues, was the initiator of the postmodern paradigm in theology.

After rejecting both Roman Catholic and liberal neo-Protestant theologies, Barth initiated a postmodern paradigm in theology. As Küng explains:

> This means two things: First, I would like to make it clear to Barth's despisers that Karl Barth really is an initiator, indeed the *main initiator* of a "postmodern" paradigm which had already begun to set in back then. But, second, I would say to uncritical admirers of Barth that Karl Barth is *only* an *initiator* and not the perfecter of such a paradigm.[33]

According to Küng, Barth shifted from a vigorous embrace of liberal theology to status as "the harshest critic of that enlightened-modern paradigm."[34] Thus,

> in the end Barth became *the chief initiator of a postmodern paradigm in theology* in the following way: In the many-layered crisis of the whole existing order it had become completely clear to him that Christianity can in no way be reduced to a critically graspable historical phenomenon of the past and a largely moral inner experience of the present.[35]

Nevertheless, though Barth carried out what Küng described as "an Enlightenment of the Enlightenment,"[36] he was not to pioneer the realization of a truly postmodern paradigm. Barth remained only an initiator, argued Küng, "because he reverted to a backward shift," not completely uncritical, but in the end too conservative for Küng's postmodern paradigm. The fact that Barth retained and restated the doctrine of the Trinity and affirmed such teachings as the Virgin Birth, Christ's descent into hell, and Christ's ascension, Küng found to be a reversion to a premodern paradigm and, in themselves, quite "remarkable."[37]

A similar reading of Barth as the initiator of a postmodern or post-Enlightenment paradigm was offered by evangelical theologian Bernard Ramm. Barth, asserted Ramm, serves as "a paradigm for writing theology in the twentieth century."[38] Ramm identified a crisis in evangelical theology and called for a new paradigm.

> The critical issue is whether evangelical theology needs a new paradigm in theology or not. If an evangelical feels that the Enlightenment and modern learning have ushered in a new cultural epoch, which in turn has precipitated into existence a new and radical set of issues for evangelical theology, then such

a person will feel the need for a new paradigm. If an evangelical feels that the Enlightenment is but one more chapter in the history of unbelief, then he or she will not feel that a new paradigm is necessary.[39]

Ramm did perceive such a crisis, and he called for a new evangelical engagement with the Enlightenment. But it is not at all clear that Ramm took into full consideration the actual nature of the postmodern challenge. Even by the time Ramm released *After Fundamentalism,* the most radical wing of the Enlightenment was testing the theoretical waters of deconstructionism. His optimistic reading of Karl Barth and his underestimation of the postmodern challenge to the Christian truth claim underscore the difficulty of assessing Barth out of his own historical circumstance and the danger of minimizing the radical nature of many postmodern theorists.

In the end, Barth may be best characterized as an *anti-modern modernist.* He did recognize many of the fatal conceits of liberal theology and critical philosophy. He clearly recognized the dangers of the older liberalism and the proposals of Rudolph Bultmann and Paul Tillich. He was gravely concerned about the course of modern theology, and he mourned the ascent of figures such as John A.T. Robinson. He had drawn deeply from the classical sources of Christian theology, including Holy Scripture. He was not reluctant to draw from the classical traditions of the Fathers, the medieval theologians, the Reformers, the Protestant Scholastics, and the older evangelical theologies.

Nevertheless, Barth did not embrace classical orthodoxy, and his revisions of the dogmatic structure denied Barth and his followers any stable foundation or defenses against the acids of modernity. He deserves full credit for his critique of the prevailing liberal theology. But he is not a postmodern model for evangelical theology. What the postmodernists find most attractive in Barth, the evangelicals may find most dangerous.

The most properly identified postmodern theological models would include Küng himself, whose ecumenical theology supplements the older liberal theology with liberation strains; David Tracy, whose revisionist model is deeply rooted and consistently conversant with postmodern epistemology and hermeneutics;[40] and David Ray Griffin, whose process-oriented postmodern theology is nothing less than a total revision of theism.[41]

The most influential postmodern experiment in the United States may well be that of the so-called "New Yale School." With leading characters such as George Lindbeck, David Kelsey, and the late Hans Frei, the movement is also associated with Yale Old Testament scholar Brevard Childs. Foundational to this school is the claim that a new epistemological situation represents a new post-Enlightenment challenge to the Christian truth claim and to our understanding of Scripture and doctrine.

With links to the anthropology of Clifford Geertz and the Wittgensteinian notion of "language games," the main thrust of this movement is to shift the basis of Christian theology away from a propositional claim based upon an objective and universal revelation, to a self-consciously local and particular narrative claim rooted in a specific cultural-linguistic system. Thus, the universal truth claim of Christianity is reduced to a culture-specific system of shared meaning.

Virtually all of the variants on the contemporary theological scene wish to claim the postmodern mantle. These would include the various liberation theologies, the theologies of representation[42] (including feminist theology, black theology, Latino theology, and the Asian theologies), narrative theology, and the other models dominant in the academy.

Diogenes Allen has identified four streams of postmodern theology: the confessional stream represented by Karl Barth, the existentialist-hermeneutical stream, theological deconstruction, and process theology.[43] Allen sees the emergence of the postmodern moment as a new opportunity for theology, and a new openness for faith. The situation of the Christian church "is not far better than it has been in modern times because our intellectual culture is at a turning point."[44] He continues:

A massive intellectual revolution is taking place that is perhaps as great as that which marked off the modern world from the Middle Ages. The foundations of the modern world are collapsing, and we are entering a postmodern world. The principles forged during the Enlightenment . . . are crumbling.[45]

Modernity, argues Allen, was inherently resistant and hostile to Christian truth. Postmodernity, however, represents a new opening, and Allen laments that Christian theology has been slow to seize the moment. "Christian theology," he remarked, "has yet to become postmodern."[46]

Allen seeks a via media between Enlightenment skepticism and premodern dogmatism. "Theologians," he asserts, "no longer need to labor within the tight, asphyxiating little world of the Enlightenment or to become premodern."[47]

Nevertheless, these have never been the alternatives. Allen ignores the contributions of evangelical theologians who refused to accept this characterization of the challenge. Allen attempts to remove the offense of Christian truth claims without taking on the direct claims of relativity among the cultured despisers. Evangelicals cannot be satisfied with this posture, since it limits the universality and objectivity of the Christian truth-claim.[48]

Postmodernism and the Evangelical Tradition

Stanley Grenz's Revisioning of Evangelical Theology

Among evangelicals championing the postmodern moment is Stanley Grenz, professor of theology and ethics at Carey Hall/Regent College in Vancouver, British Columbia. Grenz agrees with Allen that the break between the modern and postmodern worlds may rival in historical significance the shift from the Middle Ages to modernity. "Fundamentally," he argues, "postmodernism is an intellectual orientation that is critical and seeks to move beyond the philosophical tenets of the Enlightenment, which lie at the foundation of the now dying modern mindset."[49] As such, the new intellectual era calls for "nothing less than a rebirth of theological reflection among evangelicals."[50]

With echoes of Ramm's proposals in *After Fundamentalism,* Grenz seeks to define the theological identity of evangelicalism in contrast to fundamentalism. He identifies a "postfundamentalist shift" in movement from a "creed-based" identity toward a "spirituality-based" identity. In terms of the basic structure of theology, he calls for the shift from a "solely propositional paradigm." As he argues:

> Evangelical theologians ought to move away from conceiving their task as merely to discover divinely disclosed truth understood as the single, unified doctrinal system purportedly lodged within the pages of the Bible and waiting to be categorized and systematized. Although to some degree systematization does belong to our overarching program, our task is not simply the explication of this one, true scriptural system of doctrine. Rather, it has a distinctively practical intent.[51]

Grenz views the propositional paradigm as passing from the scene and a focus on doctrine giving way to an emphasis upon spirituality. This shift from doctrine to spirituality is the defining motif of Grenz's vision of a reoriented evangelical theology. As he traces the shift:

> In recent years we have begun to shift the focus of our attention away from doctrine with its focus on propositional truth in favor of a renewed interest in what constitutes the uniquely evangelical vision of spirituality. Corresponding to this trend is a growing attempt to reformulate our evangelical self-consciousness away from the creed-based conception of the recent past toward an understanding based on the piety that lies deep in the broader evangelical heritage.[52]

Evangelical theologians, Grenz insists, should not focus too intently upon doctrine and issues of propositional truth, but upon the spiritual vision of the community, instead.

According to Grenz, the very task of theology must be redirected.

> The contemporary situation demands that we as evangelicals not view theology merely as the restatement of a body of propositional truths, as important as doctrine is. Rather, theology is a practical discipline oriented primarily toward the believing community.[53]

How are truth claims to be addressed and evaluated, if at all? Grenz allows that situation "does not necessarily prevent theologians from raising the truth question."[54] As he explains:

> Because faith is linked to a conceptual framework, our participation in a community of faith carries a claim to truth, even if that claim be merely implicit. By its very nature, the conceptual framework of a faith community claims to represent in some form the truth about the world and the divine reality its members have come to know and experience.[55]

And yet, the truth question is ill defined in Grenz's proposal. Truth is, for Grenz, inherently communal and it is not an autonomous discipline. According to Grenz:

To the extent that it embodies the conceptual framework of a faith community, therefore, theology necessarily engages in the quest for truth. It enters into a conversation with other disciplines of human knowledge with the goal of setting forth a Christian worldview that coheres with what we know about human experience in the world. To this end, theology seeks to understand the human person and the world as existing in relationship to the reality of God, and in so doing to fashion a fuller vision of God and God's purposes in the world.[56]

Thus, theology must conduct a "conversation" with the other disciplines, and the theological framework must "cohere" with human experience. But what about Scripture? Should we understand the Bible as did the older evangelical tradition, complete with a defense of its authority and purpose? Seeking to avoid any charge of foundationalism, Grenz answers in the negative, suggesting that efforts to establish the role of Scripture in Christian theology are "ultimately unnecessary."[57] Further,

in engaging in the theological task, we may simply assume the authority of the Bible on the basis of the integral relation of theology to the faith community. Because the Bible is the universally acknowledged book of the Christian church, the biblical message functions as the central norm for the systematic articulation of the faith of that community. Consequently, the divine nature of Scripture or its status vis-a-vis revelation need not be demonstrated in the prolegomenon to theology. *Sufficient for launching the systematic-theological enterprise is the nature of theology itself as reflection on community faith. And sufficient for the employment of the Bible in this task is its status as the book of the community.*[58]

That is to say, evangelicals should reformulate their doctrines in less propositional and more pietistic constructs, and the authority of Scripture is to be assumed by the Christian community, not asserted and defended before the larger world.

In the end, Grenz's "revisioning" of evangelical theology amounts to a total revision of the evangelical tradition. The doctrine of revelation, which has functioned most often as a foundational doctrine and the epistemological fulcrum for the theological task, is now to be shifted to an interior discussion within the theological system.

Biblical authority—however defined and articulated—is to be assumed, for it is "the book of the community."[59]

In the end, Grenz's proposal is similar to those of Lindbeck, Kelsey, and others of the New Yale School.[60] The universality of the Christian truth claim is either minimized or, depending on one's reading, denied. In any event, the abdication of the universal truth claim and the retreat into the notion of truth as communal, defined within a given cultural-linguistic system, is a massive concession fatal to any evangelical theology.[61]

Grenz argues that "evangelical theologians tend to misunderstand the social nature of theological discourse."[62] This may be a fair critique, but it is not a license to redefine the truth content of evangelical theology in terms of that social discourse.

It is precisely at the doctrine of Scripture that Grenz's proposal is most dangerous—and yet most attractive to those seeking a retreat into a "postmodern" evangelicalism. By arguing that evangelicals should simply "assume" the authority of the Bible because we can establish an "integral relation" between theology and the Christian community, and by asserting that the Bible is the church's "universally acknowledged book," Grenz offers evangelicals a convenient way out of the pattern of debates and controversies over the inerrancy and inspiration of Scripture. Nevertheless, Scripture has been displaced as the foundation of Christian theology, and it must stand beside communal Christian experience. At root, Grenz's argument is more anthropological and phenomenological than theological.

Though he directs evangelicals toward a renewed appreciation for narrative within the Christian community, he has effectively forfeited the historic Christian claim to the universal truthfulness of the church's meta-narrative, drawn from the Scripture.

Grenz is a creative thinker, well described as postmodern in approach and worldview. The issue for evangelicalism is whether his proposal will produce a genuinely evangelical theology. Given its concessions to postmodernity's skepticism and localizing tendencies, in the end it cannot result in a genuinely evangelical system.[63]

Thomas Oden's "Postcritical" Theology

Quite a different approach is taken by Thomas Oden, whose biography traces a trajectory from modernity to postmodernity. In 1979, his *Agenda for Theology: Recovering Christian Roots* served as both theological critique and personal confession.[64] By his own testimony, Oden came to a postmodern position after his extended commitment to modernity. In fact, he describes himself in his earlier period as a "movement theologian" who was marked by "a diarrhea of religious accommodation."[65]

Oden traces a progression of theological fads and movements he followed until finally coming to the shattering conclusion that he had subverted the faith he had sought to modernize. In reflection, "The shocker is not merely that I rode so many bandwagons, but that I thought I was doing Christian teaching a marvelous favor by it and at times considered this accommodation the very substance of the Christian teaching office."[66]

With courage and conviction rarely matched in theological autobiography, Oden honestly faces the crumbling ruins of modernity and counts the cost. He is chastened by his knowledge that

> we have seen the language of Christianity tamed by the civil religionists, neatly pruned by the logical positivists, "dehistoricized" by the existentialists, "deabsolutized" by the process theologians, naturalized by behaviorists, sentimentalized by the situation ethicists, made into chemistry by the drug-oriented spiritualists, secularized by the "death of God" partisans, politicized by social activists, and set free from all bonds by the sexual liberationists.[67]

Having repudiated modernity, Oden now does not seek to be contemporary, but neither does he deny the challenge of the Enlightenment and the modern age. Oden represents a model of postmodern theology in the sense that he is confessing and defending classical Christian theology — that is, orthodoxy — amidst the collapse of modernity.

The 1979 edition of *Agenda for Theology* employed the term "postmodern," but Oden laments that in recent years, the term "has been pounced upon and taken captive by the followers of certain Continental writers . . . who just about ruined the term for any useful purposes."[68] Oden now prefers the term "postcritical" to describe his own posture.

Without embarrassment, Oden calls for the embrace of classical Christianity, and he noted with approval that "the sons and daughters of modernity are rediscovering the neglected beauty of classical Christian teaching."[69] He continued: "It is a moment of joy, of beholding anew what had been nearly forgotten, of hugging a lost child."[70]

Modern theology's courtship with modernity will, Oden seems confident, eventually come to an end. Modernity is falling — a victim of its own excesses and indulgences. As Oden reflects, "The philosophical center of modernity is no dark secret. It is a narcissistic hedonism that assumes that moral value is reducible to now feelings and sensory experience."[71]

Looking over the postmodern terrain, Oden sees an evangelistic opportunity in modernity's demise. Thus, Christian theology must redirect itself to a new agenda.

> The agenda for theology at the end of the twentieth century, following the steady deterioration of a hundred years and the disaster of the last few decades, is to begin to prepare the postmodern Christian community for its third millennium by returning again to the careful study and respectful following of the central traditions of classical Christian exegesis.[72]

Though to the modern mind, the Christian tradition seemed destined to fall victim to the onslaughts of modernity, it was instead modernity which crumbled, though its demise is not yet fully apparent. Nevertheless, evangelicals risk disaster by arguing or assuming that modernity is a stage through which Western culture has passed. Here, Oden may overstate the current moment in the history of Western culture.

Conclusion:
Evangelicals and the Postmodern Challenge

The main contours of modernity remain powerful forces in the contemporary worldview. It is the foundations of modernity which have crumbled, but the superstructure appears intact with regard to many of modernity's most formidable challenges to Christian truth. Though the crumbling foundations are certain to doom the structure above, evangelicals will risk disaster by employing a naïveté which underestimates the extended reach of modernity's corrosive ideological solvents. The modern worldview still prevails in the mass media, the formative educational institutions, and the popular Western consciousness. Modern assumptions still frame the thinking of most North Americans and Europeans — and it is still a powerful missionary movement around the globe.

Postmodern philosophy is generally limited in reach to the elite academic circles common to the ideological left and the so-called

"New Class" of post-World War II intellectuals in the knowledge industry. It is not yet formative in the worldviews of most individuals in mass culture.

And yet, something significant and enduring has occurred in the Western mind. Modernity is giving way to something new — something *post-the-modern*. But the so-called "death of the meta-narrative," the demise of the grand explanatory theory or universal truth, ensures that postmodernism will not be a single, unified reality.

In one respect, postmodernism may well represent a new evangelistic moment; an opportunity to transcend the corrosive elements of the older modern ideologies and to restate Christian truth in terms faithful to the biblical revelation and the Christian tradition, and yet addressed to a new consciousness.

Nevertheless, the false promise of postmodernism as the repudiation of modernity's radical skepticism is evident in the degeneration of so many postmodernists into deconstructionism and nihilism. Among evangelicals, postmodernism has been the occasion for much fuzzy and slippery thinking. Some evangelicals have been too hasty in embracing what are presented as postmodern alternatives to prevailing options. There is much that the Christian worldview and postmodernism can share in common, including a proper skepticism toward the cherished secular meta-narratives of progress moral perfectability, technological advance, and economic determinism. But Christians must not be unaware that the postmodern incredulity toward meta-narratives extends to the Christian truth claim as well. Postmodernism's ardent denial of absolute truth extends to the truth of the Gospel. On the altar of pluralism will be sacrificed the exclusive claims of Christianity, as well as the hegemonistic pretensions of modernity.

At this stage of the development of postmodernism, it would appear that the movement is the latest representation of modernity. As Karl Marx warned, the condition of modernity means that "all that is solid melts into air." That should serve as sufficient warning, for nothing less than our fidelity to the substance of the Christian faith is at stake. Postmodernism will establish the contours of the twenty-first century mind. Evangelicals will do well to measure this emerging worldview inch by inch.

NOTES

1. If modern-day theologians were prohibited from using the terms "postmodern" and "paradigm," some might well be unable to communicate. Nevertheless, since both terms appear in the title of my chapter, I must offer a sincere mea culpa.

2. John McGowan, *Postmodernism and Its Critics* (Ithaca, N.Y.: Cornell Univ. Press, 1991), viii.

3. Michael Kohler, " 'Postmodernismus': Ein begriffsgeschichtlicher Uberblick," *Americkastudien* 22 (1977): 8–18, cited in Hans Bertens, "The Postmodern *Weltanschauung* and Its Relation to Modernism: An Introductory Survey," in *A Postmodern Reader*, ed. Joseph Natoli and Linda Hutcheon (Albany, N.Y.: State Univ. of New York Press, 1993), 25.

4. Thomas Docherty, "Postmodernism: An Introduction," in *Postmodernism: A Reader*, ed. Thomas Docherty (New York: Columbia Univ. Press, 1993), 1–2.

5. The very different experiences of the war remembered by the United States, on the one hand, and by the European nations, on the other, explain in part why so many of the critical, existential, and deconstructive schools of thought emerged in Europe prior to their emergence in the United States. By the end of the war, the United States was recognized as the rising world power and the glories of the European civilizations were either smoldering ruins or relics of a faded past.

6. Bertens, "Postmodern *Weltanschauung* and Its Relation to Modernism," in Natoli and Hutcheon, *Postmodernism*, 1.

7. Ibid., 26. Accordingly, Bertens characterizes his own approach as "pluralist" postmodernism.

8. Jean-Francois Lyotard, "Answering the Question: What Is Postmodernism?" in Docherty, *Postmodernism: A Reader*, 46.

9. Cited in David Harvey, *The Condition of Postmodernity* (Oxford: Blackwell, 1990), 8.

10. Alvin Kernan, *The Death of Literature* (New Haven, Conn.: Yale Univ. Press, 1990), 11.

11. Kohler, "Postmodernismus," in Docherty, *Postmodernism*, 42.

12. Walter Truett Anderson, *Reality Isn't What It Used to Be* (New York: Harper and Row, 1990), 75.

13. Jean-Francois Lyotard, *The Postmodern Condition: A Report on Knowledge*, trans. Geoff Bennington and Brian Massumi, in *Theory and History of Literature*, vol. 10 (Minneapolis: Univ. of Minnesota Press, 1984).

14. Lyotard, *Postmodern Condition*, xxiii.

15. Ibid., 6.

16. Ibid., xxiii.

17. Ibid.

18. Ibid., xxiv.

19. Ibid.

20. Of course, the very notion of community is suspect, given this epistemology. Communal meaning can quickly devolve into an oxymoron.

21. Ihab Hassan, in Natoli and Hutcheon, *Postmodern Reader*, 51.

22. Cited in Hans Küng, *Theology for the Third Millennium: An Ecumenical View*, trans. Peter Heinegg (New York: Doubleday, 1987), 6.

23. Jurgen Habermas, "Modernity versus Postmodernity," *New German Critique* 22 (1981): 3–14. Republished in Natoli and Hutcheon, *Postmodern Reader*, 91–104.

24. See James Miller, *The Passion of Michel Foucault* (New York: Simon and Schuster, 1993); and Didier Eribon, *Michel Foucault*, trans. Betsey Wing (Cambridge: Harvard Univ. Press, 1991).

25. For Foucault's theory of sexuality, see his *The History of Sexuality,* vol. 1, "An Introduction," trans. Robert Hurley (New York: Vintage, 1978) and *The History of Sexuality,* vol. 2, "The Use of Pleasure," trans. Robert Hurley (New York: Vintage, 1985).

26. This attention to Foucault's personal life is not a diversion from the focus on postmodern theory. His philosophical writings were, as he admitted, an extended apologetic for his lifestyle, which included death from AIDS after experimentation in San Francisco's violent homosexual subculture. As he once remarked, "In a sense, all the rest of my life I've been trying to do intellectual things that would attract beautiful boys" (From an interview with Edmund White, 12 March 1990, cited in Miller, *Passion of Michel Foucault,* 56.). The truth of Foucault's lifestyle is considered off-limits to many within the academy, but the truth will not be separated from his theory. As Weaver long ago observed, ideas have consequences; see Richard Weaver, *Ideas Have Consequences* (Chicago: Univ. of Chicago Press, 1948).

27. E. Michael Jones, *Degenerate Moderns: Modernity as Rationalized Sexual Misbehavior* (San Francisco: Ignatius, 1993).

28. Eberhard Busch, *Karl Barth: His Life from Letters and Autobiographical Texts,* trans. John Bowden (Philadelphia: Fortress, 1976), 81.

29. Ibid.

30. Ibid.

31. Thomas C. Oden, *After Modernity . . . What? Agenda for Theology* (Grand Rapids: Zondervan/Academie, 1990), 65.

32. Ibid., 63–64.

33. Küng, 271.

34. Ibid., 272.

35. Ibid., 273.

36. Ibid., 274.

37. Ibid., 275–76. A similar argument is found in Hans Küng, *Great Christian Thinkers,* trans. John Bowden (New York: Continuum, 1994), 185–212.

38. Bernard Ramm, *After Fundamentalism: The Future of Evangelical Theology* (San Francisco: Harper and Row, 1983), 28.

39. Ibid., 25–26.

40. See David Tracy, *Blessed Rage for Order: The New Pluralism in Theology* (New York: Seabury, 1978); idem, *The Analogical Imagination: Christian Theology and the Culture of Pluralism* (New York: Crossroad, 1981); idem, *Plurality and Ambiguity: Hermeneutics, Religion, Hope* (San Francisco: Harper and Row, 1987).

41. See David Ray Griffin, *God and Religion in the Postmodern World: Essays in Postmodern Theology* (Albany, N.Y.: State Univ. of New York Press, 1989); and David Ray Griffin, William A. Beardslee, and Joe Holland, *Varieties of Postmodern Theology* (Albany, N.Y.: State Univ. of New York Press, 1989).

42. I identify these as the "theologies of representation" because that is how they function both internally and externally. Each seeks representation and exhibits a political agenda based upon either gender or ethnic uniqueness.

43. Diogenes Allen, *Christian Belief in a Postmodern World: The Full Wealth of Conviction* (Louisville: Westminster/John Knox, 1989).

44. Ibid., 2.

45. Ibid.

46. Ibid., 6.

47. Ibid., 7.

48. This is the inherent problem with many current critiques of foundationalism (or what is popularly identified as foundationalism). Such critiques, now not uncommon among some evangelical academics, eventuate in an abdication of all claims to universality, objectivity, historicity, and metaphysics. In the name of pluralism, many are tempted to surrender what is essential to Christianity, while yet claiming allegiance to these "doctrines" as if they were symbols in tribal discourse. The proper critique of foundationalism should be directed to the root issue, the unhealthy dependence of Christian theology upon any philosophical system. The opposite danger is philosophical naïveté.

49. Stanley J. Grenz, *Revisioning Evangelical Theology: A Fresh Agenda for the 21st Century* (Downers Grove, Ill.: InterVarsity, 1993), 15.

50. Ibid., 17.

51. Ibid., 88.

52. Ibid., 56–57.

53. Ibid., 79.

54. Ibid. On this point Grenz cites the contribution of Michael Polanyi.

55. Ibid.

56. Ibid.

57. Ibid., 94.

58. Ibid. Emphasis mine.

59. This is precisely the path followed by Grenz in his systematic theology. See Stanley J. Grenz, *Theology for the Community of God* (Nashville: Broadman and Holman, 1994).

60. See George A. Lindbeck, *The Nature of Doctrine: Religion and Theology in a Postliberal Age* (Philadelphia: Westminster, 1984); and David H. Kelsey, *The Uses of Scripture in Recent Theology* (Philadelphia: Fortress, 1975). See also Mark I. Wallace, *The Second Naivete: Barth, Ricoeur, and the New Yale Theology,* Studies in American Biblical Hermeneutics (Macon, Ga.: Mercer Univ. Press, 1990).

61. According to Lindbeck, et al., the truth of a theological statement is not dependent upon its correspondence to an objective external reality (historical or otherwise), but it is linked to the legitimacy of the statement's function in expressing and ordering the life of the community. It is, as Paul Holmer argued, a matter of grammar.

62. Grenz, *Revisioning Evangelical Theology,* 73.

63. This is partly due to the severe and artificial distinctions Grenz employs as he establishes his categories (e.g., piety vs. propositionalism and creed-based vs. narrative).

64. Thomas C. Oden, *Agenda for Theology: Recovering Christian Roots* (San Francisco: Harper and Row, 1979). Later revised and republished as *After Modernity . . . What?*

65. Oden, *After Modernity,* 28.

66. Ibid.

67. Ibid., 24.

68. Ibid., 11. Specifically, among the "certain Continental writers," Oden lists Lyotard, Foucault, and Derrida, among others.

69. Ibid., 14.

70. Ibid.

71. Ibid., 31.

72. Ibid., 34. This is the agenda followed by Oden in his systematic theology, written after his turn from modern theology. See Thomas C. Oden, *The Living God: Systematic Theology, Volume One* (San Francisco: Harper and Row, 1987); idem, *The Word of Life: Systematic Theology, Volume Two* (San Francisco: Harper and Row, 1989); idem, *Life in the Spirit: Systematic Theology, Volume Three* (San Francisco: HarperSanFrancisco, 1992).

6

Star Trek and the Next Generation: Postmodernism and the Future of Evangelical Theology

Stanley J. Grenz

The camera slowly focuses on a futuristic spacecraft against the background of distant galaxies. The narrator's voice proudly recites the guiding dictum: "Space—the final frontier. These are the voyages of the Starship *Enterprise*. Its continuing mission—to explore strange new worlds, to seek out new life and new civilizations, to boldly go where no one has gone before." With these words begins another episode of the popular television series, "Star Trek: The Next Generation," which recently completed its final regular season.

In many ways "The Next Generation" is simply an updated version of the earlier "Star Trek" series placed in a future era, after the resolution of some of the galactic political difficulties that plagued the universe of the previous space voyagers. Yet, sometime after Jean-Luc Picard's new breed of explorers took over the command of the redesigned *Enterprise* from Captain Kirk's crew, the creators of the series discovered that the world of their audience was in the midst of a subtle paradigm shift: Modernity was giving birth to postmodernity. As a result, "The Next Generation" became a reflection—perhaps even a molder—of the worldview of the emerging generation.

The shifts heralded by the newer "Star Trek" carry far-reaching implications for evangelical theology.

Stanley J. Grenz is Pioneer MacDonald Professor of Baptist Heritage and Theology at Carey Hall/Regent College in Vancouver, British Columbia.

The Movement from Modernity to Postmodernity

Many social observers agree that the Western world is in the midst of change. In fact, we are apparently experiencing a cultural shift which rivals the innovations that marked the birth of modernity out of the decay of the Middle Ages—the transition to the postmodern era. Of course, transitional eras are exceedingly difficult to describe and assess. Nor is it fully evident what will characterize the emerging epoch.[1] Nevertheless, we see signs that monumental changes are engulfing all aspects of contemporary culture.

The term "postmodern" came into use already in the 1930s as the designation for certain developments in the arts.[2] Later it denoted a new style of architecture. But not until the 1970s did post-modernism gain widespread attention, first as the label for theories expounded in university English and philosophy departments and eventually as the description for a broader cultural phenomenon.

Whatever else it might be, as the name suggests, postmodernism is the quest to move beyond modernism. Specifically, it is a rejection of the modern mind-set, but under the conditions of modernity. Therefore, to understand postmodern thinking we must view it in the context of the modern world which gave it birth and against which it is reacting.

1. The Modern Mind

Many historians place the birth of the modern era with the dawn of the Enlightenment which followed the Thirty Years War. The stage, however, was set earlier—in the Renaissance, which elevated humankind to the center of reality. Characteristic of the new outlook was Francis Bacon's vision of humans exercising power over nature by means of the discovery of nature's secrets.

Building on the Renaissance, the Enlightenment elevated the individual self to the center of the world.[3] The French philosopher René Descartes laid the philosophical foundation for the modern edifice with his focus on doubt. This led him to conclude that the thinking self is the first truth which doubt could not deny. (Hence, his reappropriation of Augustine's dictum, *Cogito ergo sum.*) In so doing, Descartes defined human nature as a thinking substance and the human person as an autonomous rational subject. The British physicist Isaac Newton later provided the scientific framework for modernity. He pictured the physical world as a machine whose laws and regularity could be discerned by the human mind. The modern human, therefore, is Descartes' autonomous, rational substance encountering Newton's mechanistic world.

The postulates of the thinking self and the mechanistic universe opened the way for the explosion of knowledge under the banner of what Jurgen Habermas called the "Enlightenment project." The goal of the human intellectual quest became that of unlocking the secrets of the universe, in order to master nature for human benefit and create a better world. This quest led to the modernity characteristic of the twentieth century—bringing rational management to life and seeking to improve the quality of life through technology.[4]

At the intellectual foundation of the Enlightenment project are certain epistemological assumptions. Specifically, the modern mind assumes that knowledge is certain, objective,[5] and good, and that such knowledge is obtainable, at least theoretically.

The demand for certain knowledge sets the modern inquirer in search of a method of demonstrating the essential correctness of philosophic, scientific, religious, moral, and political doctrines.[6] The Enlightenment method places the many aspects of reality under the scrutiny and criterion of reason,[7] resulting in an unchallenged faith in our rational capabilities.

Enlightenment knowledge is not only certain (and hence rational), it is also objective. The assumption of objectivity leads to a claim to dispassionate knowledge. The modern knower professes to stand apart from being a conditioned participant and to be able to view the world as an unconditioned observer,[8] that is, to peer at the world from a vantage point outside the flux of history. The pursuit for dispassionate knowledge divides the scientific project into separate disciplines[9] and elevates the specialist, the neutral observer who has gained expertise in a limited field of endeavor.

In addition to being certain and objective, Enlightenment knowledge is inherently good. For this reason, the modern scientist assumes that the discovery of knowledge is a self-evident, unchallengeable axiom. The assumption of the inherent goodness of knowledge also means that the Enlightenment outlook is optimistic. Progress is inevitable, for science coupled with the power of education will eventually free us from out of vulnerability to nature, as well as from all social bondage.

Enlightenment optimism, coupled with the focus on reason, elevates human freedom. Suspect are all benefits that seem to curtail autonomy or to be based on some external authority, rather than reason (and experience). The Enlightenment project understands freedom largely in individual terms. In fact, the modern ideal elevates the autonomous self, the self-determining subject who exists outside of tradition or community.[10]

Like modern science fiction in general, the original "Star Trek" series encapsulates many aspects of the Enlightenment project and of late modernity. The crew of the *Enterprise* included persons of various nationalities working together for the common benefit of humankind. They were the epitome of the modern universalist anthropology. The message was obvious: we are all human. As humans we must overcome our differences and join forces in order to complete our mandate, the quest for certain, objective knowledge of the entire universe of which space looms as "the final frontier."

The hero of the old "Star Trek" was Mr. Spock. Although he was the only crew member who came from another planet (Vulcan), his partially alien status actually served as a transcendent human ideal. Spock was the ideal Enlightenment man, completely rational and without emotion (or with his emotions in check). Repeatedly, his dispassionate rationality provided the calculative key necessary to solve the problems encountered by the *Enterprise.* According to the creators of "Star Trek," in the end our problems are rational and, therefore, they require rational expertise.

Postmodernism represents a rejection of the Enlightenment project and the foundational assumptions upon which it was built.

2. The Postmodern Mind

Modernity has been under attack since Friedrich Nietzsche (1844–1900) lobbed the first volley in the late nineteenth century. But the full-scale frontal assault did not begin until the 1970s. The immediate impulse for the dismantling of the Enlightenment project came from the rise of deconstruction as a literary theory, which influenced a new movement in philosophy.

Deconstruction arose in response to a theory in literature called "structuralism." Structuralists theorized that cultures develop literary documents — texts — in an attempt to provide structures of meaning by means of which people can make sense out of the meaninglessness of their experience. Literature, therefore, provides categories whereby we can organize and understand our experience of reality. Further, all societies and cultures possess a common, invariant structure.[11]

The deconstructionists (or post-structuralists) rejected the tenets of structuralism. Meaning is not inherent in a text itself, they argued, but emerges only as the interpreter enters into dialogue with the text.[12] Consequently, the meaning of a text is dependent on the perspective of the one who enters into dialogue with it, so that there are as many interpretations of a text as readers (or readings).

Postmodern philosophers applied the theories of the literary deconstructionists to the world as a whole. Just as the meaning of a text is dependent on the reader, so also reality can be "read" differently depending on the perspectives of the knowing selves that encounter it. This means that there is no one meaning of the world, no transcendent center to reality as a whole.

On the basis of ideas such as these, the French philosopher Jacques Derrida called for the destruction of "onto theology" (the attempt to set forth ontological descriptions of reality) as well as the "metaphysics of presence" (the idea that a transcendent something is present in reality).[13] Because nothing transcendent inheres in reality, all that emerges in the knowing process is the perspective of the self who interprets reality.

Michel Foucault added a moral twist to Derrida's call. Every interpretation is put forward by those in power, he theorized. Because "knowledge" is always the result of the use of power,[14] to name something is to exercise power and hence to do violence to what is named. And social institutions do violence by imposing their own understanding on the centerless flux of experience. Thus, in contrast to Bacon who sought knowledge in order to gain power over nature, Foucault claimed that every assertion of knowledge is an act of power.

Richard Rorty, in turn, jettisoned the classic conception of truth as either the mind or language mirroring nature. Truth is established neither by the correspondence of an assertion with objective reality or by the internal coherence of the assertions themselves. Rorty argued that we should simply disband the search for truth and be content with interpretation. Hence, he proposed to replace classic "systematic philosophy" with "edifying philosophy" which "aims at continuing a conversation rather than at discovering truth."[15]

The work of Derrida, Foucault, and Rorty reflect what seems to have become the central dictum of all of postmodern philosophy: "All is difference." This view sweeps away the "uni" of the "universe" sought by the Enlightenment project, the quest for a unified grasp of objective reality. The world has no center, only differing viewpoints and perspectives. In fact, even the concept of "world" itself presupposes an objective unity or a coherent whole that does not exist "out there." In the end, the postmodern world becomes merely an arena of dueling texts.

Although philosophers such as Derrida, Foucault, and Rorty have been influential on university campuses, they are only a part of a larger shift in thinking reflected in Western cultures. What unifies the otherwise diverse strands of postmodernism is questioning of the central assumptions of the Enlightenment epistemology.

In the postmodern world, people are no longer convinced that knowledge is inherently good. In eschewing the Enlightenment myth of inevitable progress, postmodernism replaces the optimism of the last century with a gnawing pessimism. It is simply not the case that "each and every day in each and every way we are getting better and better." For the first time in many years, members of the emerging generation do not share the conviction of their parents that we will solve the enormous problems of the planet or that their economic situation will surpass that of their parents. They know that life on the earth is fragile, and the continued existence of humankind is dependent on a new attitude which replaces the image of conquest with cooperation.

The new emphasis on wholism is related to the postmodern rejection of the second Enlightenment assumption, namely, that truth is certain and hence purely rational. The postmodern mind refuses to limit truth to its rational dimension and thus dethrones the human intellect as the arbiter of truth. Because truth is nonrational there are other ways of knowing, including through the emotions and the institution.

Finally, the postmodern mind no longer accepts the Enlightenment belief that knowledge is objective. Knowledge cannot be merely objective, because the postmodern model of the world does not see the universe as mechanistic and dualistic, but historical, relational, and personal. The world is not simply an objective given that is "out there," waiting to be discovered and known. Instead it is relative, indeterminate, and participatory.

In rejecting the modern assumption of the objectivity of knowledge, the postmodern mind likewise dismisses the Enlightenment ideal of the dispassionate, autonomous knower. Knowledge is not eternal and culturally neutral. Nor is it waiting to be discovered by scientists who bring their rational talents to the giveness of the world. Rather, knowledge is historically and culturally implicated, and consequently, our knowledge is always incomplete.

The postmodern worldview operates with a community based understanding of truth. Not only the specific truths we accept, but even our understanding of truth, are a function of the community in which we participate. This, in turn, leads to a new conception of the relativity of truth. Not only is there no absolute truth, more significantly, truth is relative to the community in which we participate. With this in view, the postmodern thinker has given up the Enlightenment quest for the one, universal, supracultural, timeless truth. In its place, truth is what fits within a specific community; truth consists in the ground rules that facilitate the well-being of the community in which one participates.

The postmodern perspective is reflected in the second "Star Trek" series, "The Next Generation." The humans who made up the crew of the original Enterprise are now joined by humanoid life forms from other parts of the universe. This change represents the broader universality of postmodernity: humankind is no longer the only advanced intelligence, for evolution has been operative throughout the cosmos. More importantly, the understanding of the quest for knowledge has changed. Humankind is not capable of completing the mandate alone, nor does the burden of the quest fall to humans alone. Hence, the crew of the *Enterprise* symbolizes the "new ecology" of humankind in partnership with the universe. Their mission is no longer "to boldly go where no man has gone before," but "where no *one* has gone before."

In "The Next Generation," Data replaces Spock. In a sense, Data is Spock, the fully rational thinker capable of superhuman intellectual feats. Despite his seemingly perfect intellect, rather than being the transcendent human ideal Spock embodies, he is an android—a subhuman machine. His desire is not only to understand what it means to be human, but also to become human. However, he lacks certain necessary aspects of humanness, including a sense of humor, emotion, and the ability to dream (at least until he learns that his maker programmed dreaming into his circuitry).

Although Data often provides valuable assistance in dealing with problems, he is only one of several who contribute to finding solutions. In addition to the master of rationality, the *Enterprise* crew includes persons skilled in the affective and intuitive dimensions of human life. Especially prominent is Counselor Troi, a woman gifted with the ability to perceive the hidden feelings of others.[16]

The new voyages of the *Enterprise* lead its variegated crew into a postmodern universe. In this new world, time is no longer simply linear, appearance is not necessarily reality, and the rational is not always to be trusted.

In contrast to the older series, which in typical modern fashion generally ignores questions of God and religious belief, the postmodern world of "The Next Generation" also includes the supernatural, embodied in the strange character "Q." Yet its picture of the divine is not simply that of traditional Christian theology. Although possessing the classical attributes of divine power (such as omniscience), the godlike being "Q" is morally ambiguous, displaying both benevolence and a bent toward cynicism and self-gratification.

Postmodernity and Evangelical Theology

As George Marsden correctly concludes, in some sense evangelicalism — with its focus on scientific thinking, the empirical approach, and common sense — is a child of early modernity.[17] The emerging generation, however, has been nurtured in a context shaped less by commitment to the Enlightenment project embodied in "Star Trek" than by the postmodern vision of Rorty and "Star Trek: The Next Generation." Consequently, the transition from the modern to the postmodern era poses a grave challenge to the church in its mission to the next generation and to evangelical theologians, whose task is to decipher the implications of postmodernism for the Gospel.

1. Evangelicalism and the Postmodern Critique of Modernity

Evangelicals facing the postmodern context will likely recoil from certain theories proposed by Derrida and Rorty. Their rejection of the Enlightenment project goes too far, for it leads to a skepticism that seems to undermine the Christian conception of truth. Having assumed that reality is not a unified whole, these philosophers have given up the quest for a universal, ultimate truth, leaving us only with our conflicting interpretations. And in the absence of any absolute criterion, all human interpretations are equally valid because all are equally invalid (in fact, as adjectives describing interpretations, "valid" and "invalid" become meaningless terms). At best these interpretations can only be judged according to pragmatic standards. Postmodern skepticism leaves us in a world characterized by a never-ending struggle among competing interpretations, reminiscent of Hobbes' war of all against all.

Evangelical theology cannot acquiesce to the radical skepticism of postmodernism. In contrast to the postmodern philosophers, we believe that there is a unifying center to reality and that this center has appeared in Jesus of Nazareth. Until the eschaton we may witness the struggle among conflicting interpretations of reality. But although all interpretations are in some sense invalid, they are not all equally invalid. On the basis of the Incarnation, evangelicals assert that conflicting interpretations can be evaluated according to a criterion which in some sense transcends them all and that the Christian worldview is superior to all other claimants.

As necessary as it is, however, we dare not allow our cautious stance toward the radical skepticism of Derrida and Rorty to blind us to the significance of the broader postmodern phenomenon. On the contrary, we ought to find ourselves in fundamental agreement with the postmodern critique of the modern mind[18] and its underlying Enlightenment epistemology.

Postmodernism questions the Enlightenment assumption that knowledge is certain and that the criterion for certainty rests with our human rational capabilities. In a similar manner, many evangelicals have continually argued that the rational, scientific method is not the sole measure of truth, for aspects of truth lie beyond reason and cannot be fathomed by reason. As the old pietists declared, "the heart has reasons which the head cannot understand."

Similarly, evangelicals can commend the postmodern questioning of the Enlightenment assumption that knowledge is objective and hence dispassionate. We simply cannot stand outside the historical process or gain universal, culturally neutral knowledge as unconditioned specialists, for we are conditioned participants in our historical and cultural context. Postmodern epistemologists seem to echo Augustine as they assert that our personal convictions and commitments not only color our search for knowledge, they also facilitate the process of understanding.

Likewise, evangelicals can applaud the postmodern rejection of the Enlightenment assumption that knowledge is inherently good. Events of the twentieth century bear poignant witness that the knowledge explosion cannot guarantee utopia, for technological advances not only bring the possibility of good but also the potential for evil. Evangelicals understand the theological reality that necessitates this critique: the human problem is not merely ignorance, but also a misdirected will.

2. Contours of a Postmodern Evangelical Theology

The ongoing mandate of the church means that we are called to proclaim the Gospel to the next generation and to live it out in the midst of a culture that is increasingly postmodern in its thinking.

This mandate challenges evangelical theologians to assist the church by exploring how we can embody the Gospel in the categories of our emerging social context. The postmodern rejection of the Enlightenment epistemology suggests several contours that ought to shape a future evangelical theology.

First, an authentic postmodern evangelical theology must be post-individual.

One of the great gains of modernity has been the elevation of the individual human person, indicative of modernity. We must always keep in view the biblical focus on the God who is concerned about each person, the individual as personally responsible to God, and a salvation message that is directed to every human being. The lessons of totalitarianism remind us that we must continually stand against the tyranny of the collective in all its various forms.

While maintaining the individual focus of the Bible, however, we must shake ourselves loose of the radical individualism that characterizes the modern mind-set. We must affirm with postmodernism that knowledge — including knowledge of God — is not merely objective, not simply discovered by the neutral knowing self.

Here we can learn from contemporary communitarian scholars who have joined the postmodern assault on the modern epistemological fortress. In place of the modern paradigm with its focus on the self-reflective, autonomous subject and the modern ideal of the self-determining self who exists outside any tradition or community, they offer a constructive alternative: the individual within community.

Community is integral to the process of knowing, communitarians argue, for crucial to the knowing process is a cognitive framework mediated to the individual by the community in which he or she participates. Similarly, the community of participation is crucial to identity formation. A sense of personal identity develops through the telling of a personal narrative[19] which is always embedded in the story of the communities in which we participate.[20] The community mediates to its members a transcending story which includes traditions of virtue, common good, and ultimate meaning.[21] Rather than requiring a neutral, objective stance, therefore, knowing occurs within a community and the position of personal commitment that presence in a community entails.

Evangelical theologians must take seriously the discoveries of contemporary communitarians,[22] insofar as they are in a sense echoing a great biblical theme, namely, that the goal of God's program is the establishment of community in the highest sense. Instead of elevating the individual to the center, therefore, postmodern evangelicals must carve out a theology that integrates the human person into community, acknowledging as well the importance of the believing community and our presence within it to our knowledge of God. In short, in our theologizing we must take seriously the reality of community as the context in which the individual is necessarily embedded.

In addition to being post-individual, a postmodern evangelical theology must be post-rational.

Another significant gain of the Enlightenment has been the elevation of reason. Consequently, a postmodern evangelical theology dare not become anti-intellectual. Yet it must embody the biblical understanding that the cognitive dimension does not exhaust either the human person, reality as a whole, or the truth of God. Nor can we continue to collapse truth into the categories of rational certainty that typify modernity. Rather, our theology must give place to the concept of "mystery" — not as an irrational aspect alongside the rational, but as a reminder of the fundamentally nonrational or suprarational reality of God. This means that while remaining reasonable, our theology must jettison the unwarranted rationalistic bent of all modern theologies.

Central to this task is the rethinking of the function of theological propositions. We must continue to acknowledge the fundamental importance of rational discourse, of course, and hence of propositions. Yet, our theology cannot remain fixated on the propositionalist approach of the older evangelical theologies, which viewed Christian truth simply as correct doctrine.

In their attempt to replace the individualistic foundational rationalism of modern Western thinking with an understanding of knowledge and belief that views them as socially and linguistically constituted,[23] postmodern social theorists provide helpful assistance in understanding the role of propositions. At the heart of being a Christian is a personal encounter with God in Christ which shapes and molds us and which unites us with the community of believers. On the basis of this encounter, we seek to bring into an understandable whole the diverse strands of our personal lives and the incorporation of our lives in that of the faith community by appeal to categories such as "sin" and "grace," "alienation" and "reconciliation," "helplessness" and "divine power," "having been lost" but "now being saved." It is in this context of making sense out of life by means of recounting the story of a transformative religious experience that theological propositions find their importance. No experience occurs in a vacuum; no transformation comes to us apart from an interpretation facilitated by the concepts — the "web of belief" — we bring to it. On the contrary, experience and interpretive concepts are reciprocally related. Our concepts facilitate the experiences we have in life; at the same time, our experiences determine the interpretive concepts we employ to speak about our lives.

So also the encounter with God in Christ is both facilitated by, and expresses itself in theological categories which are propositional in nature. These categories which form the cradle for this experience, in turn, constitute the grid by means of which we now view all of life.

A post-rational evangelical theology will be "wholistic." The Enlightenment project was built on the division of reality into the dualism of mind and matter, which was expressed anthropologically through the distinction between soul and body. Evangelicals imbued with the Enlightenment outlook are concerned about saving souls, with at best a secondary concern for bodies which, however, has no eternal theological importance. If we would minister in the postmodern world, we must realize that the human person is a unified whole, and the Gospel must exercise an impact on humans in their entirety. This does not mean merely giving greater place to human emotion or the affective aspects of life alongside the rational, but integrating the emotional-affective, as well as the bodily-sensual, with the intellectual-rational within the one human person. In other words, we must be willing to acknowledge the "Counselor Troi" in each of us.

But postmodern evangelical wholism must go beyond putting together the soul and body torn asunder in the Enlightenment. In a post-individualist theology, the human person will also be put back into the social and environmental context which forms and nourishes us. We must not merely speak of the human person in isolation, but also as the person-in-relationship. Our anthropology must take seriously that our identity includes being in relationship to nature, in relationship with others, in relationship with God and, in this manner, in relationship with ourselves.

Finally, a postmodern evangelical theology must be focused on spirituality.

A final gain of the Enlightenment was the quest for knowledge, which was viewed as good. Indeed, knowledge is *a* good, and hence evangelical theology is concerned to discover the truth of God. Consequently, the goal of theologizing includes right thinking, acknowledging that right beliefs or correct doctrine are important. However, our goal can never merely be the amassing of a wealth of knowledge for its own sake. Nor should we be under any illusion that the possession of knowledge — even theological knowledge — is inherently good (1 Cor. 8:1). Knowledge is only good when it facilitates a good result, specifically, when it fosters spirituality in the knower.

A theology that is "focused on spirituality," therefore, views itself as immensely practical. In the postmodern world we must reappropriate the older pietist discovery that a "right heart" takes primacy over a "right head." Theology must take its lodging in the heart, for it is concerned with the transformation of not only the intellectual commitments, but also the character and the life of the believer (as well as of the faith community).

To this end, a theology that is "focused on spirituality" fostersa proper ordering of activism and quietism. No longer can we follow the modern outlook which looks to overt activity, conduct, or specific decisions as the sole measure of spirituality. Rather, the postmodern world correctly understands that activism must be born from inner resource. Theology, in turn, contributes to this inner resource, for it seeks to clarify the foundational belief structure which shapes our responses to the situations of life and which structure is reflected in the acts we choose to do.

Conclusion

Our society is in the throes of a monumental transition, the movement from modernity to postmodernity. The emerging generation — those who were raised on "Star Trek: The Next Generation" — is already imbued with many aspects of the postmodern mind. Confronted by this new context, we dare not fall into the trap of wistfully longing for a return to the modernity that gave evangelicalism its birth — indeed, we simply cannot turn back the clock — for we are not called to minister in the past, but in the contemporary context, influenced as it is by postmodern ideas.

Postmodernism does pose dangers. Nevertheless, it would be ironic and tragic if evangelicals ended up being the last defenders of the now dying modernity. Rather, imbued with the vision of God's program for His world, we must claim the new postmodern context for Christ by embodying the Christian faith in ways that the new generation can understand. In short, under the banner of the cross, we must "boldly go where no one has gone before."

NOTES

1. Some thinkers have boldly sought to set forth the new postmodern mood, but these often tend to be projections of the author's own sympathies. For example, McFague includes among the postmodern assumptions "a greater appreciation for nature, a recognition of the importance of language to human existence, a chastened admiration for technology, an acceptance of the challenge that other religions present to the Judeo-Christian tradition, an apocalyptic sensibility, a sense of the displacement of the white, Western male and the rise of those dispossessed due to gender, race, or class, perhaps most significantly, a growing awareness of the radical interdependence of life at all levels and in every imaginable way" (Sallie McFague, *Metaphorical Theology* [Philadelphia: Fortress, 1982], x–xi).

2. Craig Van Gelder, "Postmodernism as an Emerging Worldview," *Calvin Theological Journal* 26/2 (1991): 412.

3. For a short discussion of the Enlightenment period and its impact on Christian theology, see Stanley J. Grenz and Roger E. Olson, *Twentieth Century Theology: God and the World in a Transitional Age* (Downers Grove, Ill.: InterVarsity, 1992).

4. Van Gelder, "Postmodernism and an Emerging Worldview," 413.

5. James M. Kee, " 'Postmodern' Thinking and the Status of the Religions," *Religion and Literature* 22/2-3 (Summer-Autumn 1990), 49.

6. Richard Luecke, "The Oral, the Local and the Timely," *Christian Century*, 3 October 1990, 875.

7. Klaus Hedwig, "The Philosophical Presuppositions of Postmodernity," *Communio* 17 (Summer 1990): 168.

8. Merold Westphal, "The Ostrich and the Boogeyman: Placing Postmodernism," *Christian Scholars Review* 20/2 (December 1990): 115.

9. Ted Peters, "Toward Postmodern Theology," *Dialog* 24 (Summer 1985): 221.

10. At first, the Enlightenment project appeared as the friend of religion, offering to place beliefs on the more sure footing of human reason. Later thinkers, however, no longer accepted the understanding of God and the world salvaged earlier. This new skepticism led to the atheistic-materialistic worldview of late modernity. Specifically, the ideas of Descartes and Newton undergirded a dichotomy between body and soul and posited an absolute gulf between the human soul and the rest of creation. Late moderns found it difficult to conceive of God's action in this dualistic world (*deus ex machina*). As the problem of interaction between soul and body led to the conclusion that the mind is an epiphenomenon, a by-product of the brain, thinkers also eliminated the human soul, viewing it as the unsubstantiated "ghost in the machine." See, David Ray Griffin, *God and Religion in the Postmodern World: Essays in Postmodern Theology* (Albany, N.Y.: State Univ. of New York Press, 1989), 21–23, 54–56.

11. W.L. Reese, "Structuralism," *Dictionary of Philosophy and Religion* (Atlantic Highlands, N.J.: Humanities, 1980), 553.

12. This proposal is often credited to Gadamer. See, for example, Hans-Georg Gadamer, *Truth and Method,* trans. Garrett Barden and John Cumming (New York: Crossroad, 1984), 261.

13. Jacques Derrida, *Of Grammatology,* trans. Gayatri Chakravorty Spivak (Baltimore: Johns Hopkins Univ. Press, 1976), 50.

14. Michel Foucault, "Truth and Power," in *Power/Knowledge: Selected Interviews and Other Writings 1972–1977,* ed. Colin Gordon (New York: Pantheon, 1980), 133.

15. Richard Rorty, *Philosophy and the Mirror of Nature* (Princeton, N.J.: Univ. of Princeton Press, 1979), 393.

16. Women are not stereotyped into affective roles, however, for the ship's medical doctor is also a woman.

17. George M. Marsden, "Evangelical, History and Modernity," in *Evangelicalism and Modern America,* ed. George M. Marsden (Grand Rapids: Eerdmans, 1984), 98.

18. Several evangelicals have recently expressed sympathy for postmodernism. See, for example, Jonathan Ingleby, "Two Cheers for Postmodernism," *Third Way* 15/4 (May 1992): 25.

19. Robert Bellah, et al., *Habits of the Heart: Individualism and Commitment in American Life* (Berkeley: Univ. of California Press, 1985), 81.

20. See, for example, Alisdair MacIntyre, *After Virtue,* 2nd ed. (Notre Dame, Ind.: Univ. of Notre Dame Press, 1984), 221.

21. E.g., George A. Lindbeck, "Confession and Community: An Israel-like View of the Church," *Christian Century,* 9 May 1990, 495.

22. See, for example, Daniel A. Helminiak, "Human Solidarity and Collective Union in Christ," *Anglican Theological Review* 70/1 (January 1988): 37.

23. This opinion was recently articulated by Lindbeck, "Confession and Community," 495.

7

Jerry H. Gill's Postmodern Philosophy of Religion: An Evangelical Option?

Robert A. Weathers

The Philistines thought they had Samson neutralized. They had him trussed to the pillars of the temple, and they reveled in their traditional festivities within the very structure that contained him. But when his power returned, the pillars of the temple weakened as he pushed, and eventually, by wrecking the structure's most critical supports, he destroyed the edifice that confined him.

Modernity is crumbling from the strain of Western culture's discontent with the Enlightenment paradigms. Like a captive whose power has returned, postmodernism is wrecking the edifice meant to confine it. Its models, previously submissive to the self-assurance of modernity, are now flexing their muscles and emerging from the dust of modernity's crumbling edifice. Modernity is giving way to postmodernity.

Central to the shift from modernism to postmodernism is the rejection of ontological and epistemological dichotomies characteristic of the critical philosophies of Descartes and Kant. These dualisms were the foundations for Western philosophical models, and they are suffering from the strain of post-critical thinkers who are attempting to dispense with these dichotomies.

In theology, many postmodernists are constructing models that

Robert A. Weathers is Director of Ministry at the Dudley Shoals Baptist Church in Granite Falls, North Carolina.

exhibit extensive revisions of evangelical or Reformation paradigms. As a result, evangelicals risk philosophical myopia when faced with postmodernism, thinking that all postmodern paradigms are either liberal or deconstructivist. Unlike liberalism, however, postmodernism is a theological context more than it is a movement. Deconstructivism is one extreme response to modernism within the postmodern context.

Postmodernism is far easier to describe than to define. Whereas modernists hailed individuality, technology, Western imperialism, atomism, and reductionism, postmodernists advocate participation in every level of the human community, human creativity and imagination, pluralism, and holism. Instead of focusing on the cognitive dimensions of communication, postmodernists stress the symbols, metaphors, and stories that give continuity to the human family. Whereas modernists jettisoned philosophical and theological stances that did not fall within the confines of rational exploration, postmodernists seek to meld the link broken by Kant and Descartes between the imminent and the transcendent.[1]

But when so much postmodern theological activity seems so destructive, what options are available for evangelicals doing theology in the postmodern context? Can evangelicals be involved in the postmodern context without compromising distinctives of the biblical faith and Reformation theology? While most postmodernists offer few options for evangelicals to consider, some thinkers within the evangelical tradition are drafting more balanced postmodern approaches. Evangelicals searching for a viable option would benefit from analyzing these efforts. Such analyses serve as reflective self-studies and assist in pointing out the strengths and weaknesses of the evangelical position as it stands within the postmodern context. By this evangelicals may polish their strengths and fortify their weaknesses.

The work of Jerry H. Gill provides an opportunity to study one option. Evangelicals who are familiar with the work of Gill are most often acquainted with his writings in the area of language, linguistic analysis, and hermeneutics. He is regarded as an important scholar for Wittgensteinian studies within the evangelical tradition, and his remarks on language analysis are considered by many to reflect an evangelical stance.[2] Yet, his views on language compose only one category within a broader, more complex philosophical blueprint that he has been drafting throughout thirty years of writing. In order to satisfactorily understand his beliefs in a particular theological category, his entire system should be examined to identify how his beliefs in that category issue out of his system. In turn, his developing system can be best understood in the context of his academic life, from which germinated his postmodern concerns.

Who Is Jerry H. Gill?
The Growth of a Postmodern Thinker[3]

Born in 1933 in Bellingham, Washington, Jerry Gill was converted to Christianity through the influence of the "Young Life" program in his high school. Gill began studying religion and philosophy at Westmont College, a conservative Christian liberal arts institution. While at Westmont, he decided to enter the teaching ministry. He graduated in 1957 and began graduate studies at the University of Washington, where he earned a master of arts in philosophy, and went from there to New York Theological Seminary, receiving his master of divinity in 1960. With the completion of his seminary education, he began his teaching ministry at Seattle Pacific College, where he taught until 1964. With a desire to further his education, he left Seattle Pacific and traveled to Durham, North Carolina, where he began doctoral studies at Duke University.

Gill reports that the work of the late E.J. Carnell of Fuller Theological Seminary influenced his early thought. During the years that he taught at Seattle Pacific, however, Gill struggled with the challenge that logical empiricism posed for the meaningfulness of religious language. In his effort to find viable solutions to these philosophical issues, he was assisted by the works of John Hick, particularly *Faith and Knowledge,* and Ian Ramsey's *Religious Language and Models* and *Mystery.* Furthermore, at Duke University he studied with William Poteat, and for one semester at Oxford he studied with Ian Ramsey and Gilbert Ryle. He subsequently wrote his dissertation on the thought of Ramsey, which he completed to graduate with his doctor of philosophy in 1966.[4]

In his early studies, Gill grappled with the works of erudite evangelicals. In addition to Carnell, he points to Bernard Ramm and James Orr as among those who shaped the early stages of his philosophy of religion. Since that time, however, he attributes greater influence over his philosophical development to such thinkers as Ramsey, Wittgenstein, Hick, H. Richard Niebuhr, Alfred North Whitehead, Karl Marx, Michael Polanyi, Maurice Merleau-Ponty, and Nelson Goodman.

To these thinkers Gill has looked for assistance in his ongoing desire to bridge the gap between subject and object that has characterized Western thought. In its place he wishes to substitute a philosophy of religion built from an integrative and holistic epistemology, an effort which he describes as reconstructive.[5] Gill believes that his present teaching position at The College of Saint Rose in Albany, New York, affords him the freedom necessary to develop this approach to philosophy.[6]

Gill's biography portrays a thinker in transition, shifting from the rationalistic objectivism of modernity to a holistic epistemology that disdains the subject-object dichotomy. This shift is similarly demonstrated in his Christian stance, which has moved from a fundamentalist evangelical posture to his present theological leaning, one that he categorizes as "left-wing evangelical."[7] Respecting this shift means that one cannot require of Gill's philosophy a conservatism that is not resident within it. Nevertheless, a study of Gill's postmodern blueprint provides an opportunity to engage a like-minded thinker who has strived for decades to build a constructive and comprehensive postmodern philosophy of the Christian religion. Evangelicals should scrutinize his work as a postmodern method within their own tradition, giving them an opportunity to criticize and complement that method while learning to bridge the gap from modernity to postmodernity.

Gill's Postmodern Project: Wrecking and Rebuilding Ontology and Epistemology

Realms vs. Dimensions

Gill maintains that the purpose of his philosophy of religion is "to construct a synthesis" of the premodern or traditional and the modern models in ontology and epistemology "that will take us beyond them both while preserving their undeniable contributions."[8] For him, this is a "reconstructive" effort toward eliminating the fact-value, subject-object dichotomy of modernism. He is driven in his project by the belief that Western modernists have proven themselves incapable of breaking free from the dichotomies that bind their models to the Kantian heritage. He wants to recover the transcendence that was lost in modern epistemology with the exclusion of the divine from the realm of human knowledge.[9] Therefore, he attempts to dismantle the structures of modern thought before he erects a new edifice, one built "upon a more holistic base."[10] The footings for this structure, however, cannot be premodern or classical assumptions, a move which he considers "naive."[11]

The naiveté he perceives is the failure to recognize the weaknesses inherent in the ontological assumptions of the premodern and modern eras. Gill teaches that the errors in human conceptions of experience, meaning, and knowledge that characterize premodernism and modernism, and that led to the exclusion of transcendence from serious epistemological discussion, have their roots in the ontological posture of the period. He labels this posture "realmism," a model of reality that portrays the natural and spiritual realms as distinct and distinguishable. In this model, God exists in complete distinction from the natural order.[12] As a result, while both the premodern and the modern thinkers conceived of reality in realms, the shift from the premodern to the modern era occurred at the point where the vertical picture of realms was discarded in favor of the horizontal picture. Epistemology thereby supplanted metaphysics as the concern of philosophy and theology.[13] Those who affirm two realms and those who deny a transcendent realm agree on the fundamental principle that "experienced reality *must* be understood in terms of realms."[14]

Gill extends his rejection of a dichotomous picture or reality to the theological assertion that the natural and the supernatural may be cleanly divided. He believes that this traditional bifurcation results in two erroneous impressions: first, that one has only these two choices for conceiving reality and, second, that intangible reality exists and is explicable independently of tangible reality.[15] For premodernists, this view led to the misconception that divine activity in the natural realm came in the form of an intrusion or invasion. The belief that miracles were necessary as proofs of the activity of the divine demonstrates this misconception.[16]

The first step toward building a post-critical and postmodern philosophy of religion, Gill argues, is to disassemble this confining structure and the epistemology that it generated. From the wreckage one may reconstruct an ontology free of the bifurcation of modernity.

Gill's most fundamental concept, on which he builds his overall system, is that reality exists not in realms, but in dimensions. He believes that this distinction is a rudimentary difference between critical and post-critical philosophy. He originates his reconstruction from the empiricist insistence that one's experience of reality determines the nature of that reality for the knower.[17] In turn, one gains knowledge of that reality through experience, so that the dimensional model of reality, the experience of that reality, and the knowledge of that reality are indivisibly intertwined. Reality, he says, can only be understood as *"experienced reality,* doing away with the notion that it exists independently of our participation in it."[18]

According to Gill, in a dimensional model reality is understood

> as composed of a number of simultaneously interpenetrating
> dimensions rather than as separate levels or domains. More-
> over, these dimensions are experienced as *mediated* in and
> through one another rather than being juxtaposed to each
> other.[19]

So reality does not exist in stratified levels, but it is multidimensional and is experienced in a complex hierarchy. Through this hierarchical pattern humanity's experience of reality merges with that
reality. "It is this sort of hierarchical pattern," Gill writes, "that
characterizes our experience of reality as dimensional."[20] At this
junction the importance of the concept of mediation for Gill's picture
of reality becomes clear. The concept of mediation is the cornerstone
Gill lays into an elaborate reconstruction of ontology and epistemology after he has pushed away the erroneous assumptions of modernism. He describes reality as mediated within its own interpenetrating
hierarchies, and in turn people experience reality and have knowledge of it because it is mediated to humanity within the concurrent
dimensions. He writes:

> Not only do various dimensions of reality interpenetrate and
> mediate one another, but they are arranged in a mediational
> hierarchy according to their varying degrees of richness and
> comprehensiveness. The level of meaning of any given di-
> mension emerges out of those levels that ground and mediate
> it in such a manner as to both depend upon and transcend
> them.[21]

By "richness" Gill refers to the complexity and significance of
the pattern by which the mediated dimensions emerge out of each
other, and by "comprehensiveness" he refers to the "wider and
wider inclusiveness" of this same pattern of emergence.[22]

He thereby believes that his model "provides us a way to retain
transcendence as a viable concept" while avoiding the liabilities of
reductionism and without resorting to traditional dualism.[23] If he is
right, his model opens the way toward salvaging transcendence from
the discarded wreckage of the Enlightenment. He argues that his
model offers an alternative description of reality that exhibits how a

"transcendent or divine dimension of reality might be active in human experience without being reducible to the other dimensions constituting that experience."[24] Gill contends that "the [Kantian] gap itself is a result of the realm model and collapses when the dimensional model is introduced."[25] Yet, here is where Gill's project weakens, for, despite his claim to the contrary, it is reductionistic. The Divine is reduced to a divine dimension, which in turn is reduced to the physical dimensions, a weakness that infects the viability of his entire proposal.

Gill's hierarchical model ensconces the physical dimension in the lowest position. As the hierarchy moves upward the religious or transcendent emerges as the highest dimension, slightly preceded by or often identified with the moral dimension. The superiority of the transcendent dimension is evident in that it shapes the way people understand the other dimensions. Nevertheless, an asymmetrical relationship exists between those dimensions that are mediated and those by which they mediated. "In other words," Gill explains, "the former not only include and rely upon the latter, but in a sense they are controlled by them as well."[26] For instance, the physical dimension sets boundary conditions for the transcendent dimension. This claim is a significant, but subtle, ontological twist that influences Gill's whole system. Whatever shape the transcendent dimension may take, it is limited to the activity of persons as embodied agents. In addition, the dimensions are symbiotically and relationally ordered, whereby "the various aspects constituting any given dimension of significance exist in a pattern of mutual interdependence wherein the reality of each is a function of its relationship to the other."[27] In particular, the divine transcendent reality "interpenetrates the other dimensions at all points, is mediated in and through them *so as to be both transcendent and immanent.*[28] The Divine, then, must function within the confines of the mediating dimensions of the natural order.

Gill believes that it is the advantage of his model to provide a better alternative for understanding divine revelation, instead of conceiving it as an intrusion by the Divine into the natural realm.[29] Yet, he undermines his postmodern project by eliminating the one dualism that Christian theology cannot afford to lose — the Creator/creature distinction. In his effort to free reality from the realm model of modernism, Gill has in turn shackled God to His creation. By his unique natural theology he equates transcendence with the Transcendent One, both of which are absorbed in his model into the immanent reality which mediates knowledge of the intangible reality. To be effective, Gill must clearly distinguish between the transcendence that God enjoys as Creator over His creation and the transcendence that His creatures experience in reality. In his ontology, transcendence (intangible reality) and immanence (tangible reality) are integrated.[30] How is intangible human reality equivalent to, or analogous to, the transcendence of God?

God in a Multidimensional Reality

Gill has not written extensively on the nature of God because he is primarily concerned to describe the epistemological status of humanity and the reception of knowledge of the transcendent dimension. So, in his natural theology, his description of God is based on and filtered through his multidimensional picture of reality. Against theologians who model God according to specific attributes, he models God by using the Incarnation as the primary paradigm.

For Gill, the incarnation of Christ demonstrates how people receive mediated knowledge of God. The incarnation of Christ reveals the central motifs of God's character, and the most important feature of God's character revealed in Christ is His activity in the world.[31] Gill correctly observes that the biblical God interacts, interrelates, and communicates with humanity, and He initiates divine action on behalf of humanity. By this God reveals that His love, enfleshed in Christ, is His primary characteristic. Knowledge of God may be mediated to humanity not only through the incarnation of Christ but also through other dimensions of the world as God interacts with the world as an active, personal agent.[32]

Against the Calvinistic stress on the sovereignty of God, Gill stresses the scriptural emphasis on the love of God. He teaches that, in order to achieve His higher purposes, God created human beings with the capacity to love and to trust, and then "God also chose a self-limitation, *setting aside total control of the world.*"[33] "God's power," he writes, "does not lie in being able to control the outcome of every situation but in the *quality* of God's involvement *in* every situation."[34]

So Gill wants to retain the biblical image of the personal God, but he allows that God to function only within the hierarchies of the multidimensional reality. The result is an odd picture of a deity who has created the universe, relinquished control of it, and at the same time manages to reveal himself through the dimensions of its reality. This deity has chosen to set aside "total control" of the world, and yet He is immanent in it.

Jerry Gill is not a process theologian, and he does not advocate that position. But his model of God more closely resembles process philosophy's God of two natures, one primordial and complete and the other consequent and incomplete, than it does biblical theology.[35] He has constructed a dualistic God in his effort to avoid a dualistic view of revelation. An active, intruding God, which he equates with the realm model that he wishes to abandon, will not fit his mediational scheme. Instead, by His choice to be immanent, his God is virtually ineffective in the natural world. In His self-limitation, this God functions interdependently with the creation.[36] He is a God of persuasion, not of action.

Inferential Knowledge vs. Tacit Knowledge

Continuing from his incarnational motif, Gill relies on a paradigm of participation for his epistemology. From the phenomenologists, he borrows the concept of a person as being-in-the-world who interacts with his or her world holistically, through the simultaneous effects and interpretations of the senses.[37] From this description of a person, Gill theorizes that knowledge arises from one's participation in the interpenetrating dimensions of reality. "Knowledge," he writes, "flows out of relationship."[38] Therefore, reality, the experience of that reality, and one's knowledge of that reality become inseparably intertwined.

How does the act of knowing take place within his model of a multidimensional reality? Gill makes it clear that the modernist epistemology will not work with his reconstructed ontology, for it severs the activity of cognition from the participating of the knower in her world. He argues that the concept of transcendence was jettisoned from modern epistemology "on the basis of an overly narrow understanding of what cognition involves."[39] To replace the foundationalist epistemology of modernism, which held the concept of knowledge received by inference as its core belief, "what is needed is an epistemology in which the body is not viewed simply as a conduit between the external world and the mind."[40] "Whatever is known," he writes, "participates in a variety of dimensions at the same time."[41] Any epistemology that ignores this truth, as though the knower functions with only one avenue of perception at a time, is inadequate.

Suppose one grants to Gill the fact of a multidimensional reality and then adds to it the belief that all knowledge is mediated through those interpenetrating dimensions. Still, how does a person, at the most practical level, actually receive knowledge from the more comprehensive and richer dimensions through which transcendence is mediated? To answer this, Gill bolsters his model with the epistemology of Michael Polanyi, a scientist and philosopher who has had a lasting impact on postmodernists.

Polanyi teaches that intangibles, such as problems, "possess a deeper reality" than tangibles.[42] In his post-critical epistemology he shifts the axis of epistemology from the naive objectivism of modernists to an emphasis on the participation of the knower in the act of knowing.[43] He inaugurates his post-critical epistemology by asserting "the fact that *we can know more than we can tell.*"[44] All human knowledge, therefore, is "fundamentally tacit" rather than explicit.

In the tacit dimension the knower integrates particular clues into holistic meaning. The knower may not be able to offer an explanation of how he arrived at his knowledge, but he is entirely involved in the achievement of that knowledge. Hence, the individual's bodily involvement in the reception of knowledge is a crucial element of Polanyi's approach.[45] Tacit knowing is an experience of attending *from* something *to* something else, achieving an integration and interiorization of particulars, as one indwells and dwells in reality. Polanyi thereby advances that tacit knowledge is primary to explicit knowledge.

Also, in the tacit dimension, Polanyi distinguishes between two kinds of awareness: the subsidiary and the focal. Subsidiary awareness applies to those objects or activities which are "not watched in themselves" but of which we are "intensely aware." They are not "objects of our attention, but instruments of it."[46] Focal awareness, however, applies to those objects or activities which are the direct objects of our attention. Within this realm of awareness, people are aware of their bodies subsidiarily, as objects external to their bodies become points of focal awareness. This act of integration makes tools, such as a hammer, part of the human person. Such tools are assimilated "as part of our own existence," Polanyi writes. "We accept them existentially by dwelling in them."[47]

Gill adopts Polanyi's assertion that the knower and the known are integrally bound together, and that knowledge arises by the knower's participation in a given context. He declares, "There can be no knower apart from the act of knowing and that which is known, and there can be no known apart from being known by a knower."[48] He dismisses the modernist notion that the reception of knowledge is a static, objective experience, in which the knower passively receives the knowledge of the known by inference. Instead, he writes, one should think of the knowing process "as a dynamic, contextual relationship in which the factors and dimensions constituting the knower and the known are subject to a good deal of fluctuation."[49]

Gill believes that Polanyi's reflection that "we can know more than we can tell" is true and can be best understood in a mediational, multidimensional reality.[50] He acknowledges the importance of the distinction between focal and subsidiary awareness, and he believes that the mediational model is substantiated by these poles of awareness.[51]

Furthermore, a mediational epistemology surpasses the modernist view of knowledge acquisition as passive and inferential reception. While both models offer a "from-to" structure of understanding, the inferential model viewed knowledge as a result of reasoning from premises inductively or deductively toward a conclusion. By contrast, in the mediational model one attends from subsidiary, contextual factors to focal factors. Therefore, in Gill's view, the mediational structure of awareness is logically prior to the inferential.[52] Gill admits that the distinction between focal and subsidiary awareness is relative because of the model's reliance on contextuality. That is, what is subsidiary awareness in one context may be focal in another. Nevertheless, he denies that this perspective leads to relativism by virtue of its adherence to contextualization.[53] Gill summarizes that "the major epistemological point to be drawn from this distinction is that not only is cognitive awareness exclusively a function of contextual significance, it is a function of a continuum between focal and subsidiary awareness as well."[54]

Gill, therefore, replaces the pillar of modernist epistemology — the assumption of objectivity and passivity in the reception of knowledge — with his stress on the involvement in the act of knowing. Tacit knowledge results from the integration of the poles of subsidiary awareness and bodily activity.[55]

Though he acknowledges that every form of knowledge combines both tacit and explicit elements, Gill confidently asserts the precedence of the tacit dimension over the explicit. He argues that every context in which cognitive significance is present contains both tacit and explicit factors. These factors act like poles for cognitive integration, and

> the interaction between those factors of which the subject is focally aware and the conceptual response gives rise to explicit knowledge. . . . The interaction between those factors of which the subject is subsidiarily aware and the more nonverbal, bodily response gives rise to tacit knowledge.[56]

Explicit knowledge, therefore, arises primarily from focal awareness and is characterized by analytic clarity and both deductive and inductive reasoning. Tacit knowledge, on the other hand, is characterized by the employment of skills, patterns of behavior, and what one can show but not explain. Tacit awareness is not only a legitimate form of knowledge, but in fact it precedes explicit awareness because it consists of those undergirding truths which the person knows but cannot express.[57] The further one moves up the mediational hierarchy, the less explicit one may be about the specific truths he or she understands. "In short," Gill writes, "as not all words can be defined, so not all words can be explicated."[58] Therefore, it naturally follows that knowledge of the transcendent is the most inexplicable kind of knowledge.

Because subsidiary awareness and bodily activity interact to yield tacit knowledge, and the tacit dimension is typified by physical skill and bodily awareness, the embodied character of human experience is a vital part of Gill's epistemology. "It should be obvious," he writes, "that the vast majority of human behavior is an inextricable mixture of both verbal and bodily activity."[59] Humans understand physical reality only because they are themselves embodied in it. For instance, "we understand the notion of *causation* . . . because we exist as active, casual *agents*."[60] Furthermore, the "synaesthetic" embodied experience of humanity means that, against atomism, humans "encounter reality as holistic, integrated beings who interact with the world in and through all the dimensions of bodily existence simultaneously."[61]

Gill returns to the incarnation of Christ as an ideal of the correlative concepts of participation, embodiment, and contextualization in the reception of knowledge through experience. In this event God's interaction with humanity was contextual and required not merely God's involvement but, in fact, God's *bodily* involvement. Through this activity of God humans could know the divine in and through the physical dimensions of reality, rather than by God's direct manifestation of Himself. Gill emphasizes that an incarnational model demonstrates that knowing is the result of the actions of an agent, an activity in itself, and not the passive reception of knowledge. The agent participates actively with the reality he or she knows and is incapable of knowledge apart from that participation.[62] The knower, then, is established as the central figure in Gill's postmodern structure. His philosophy of religion is a human-centered, empirical, natural theology.

How Does It Work?
Mediation in Revelation, Art, Language

In actual practice, how does one utilize Gill's model in crucial philosophical and theological categories? Applying his model to such categories is like standing walls upright within the edifice he has constructed — they show the viability and the parameters of his project.

Mediation and Revelation

First, having eliminated the possibility of viewing revelation as an intrusion of the divine into the natural realm, how does a multidimensional reality account for the concept of revelation? Gill argues that the mediational approach to knowledge of the transcendent solves the difficulty of finding a way to ground theological understanding in the concrete dimension of human experience. The concept of revelation, he writes, "is greatly enhanced when it is seen as mediational in structure, rather than as direct and immediate on the one hand or as indirect and inferential on the other hand."[63] Instead of communication from another realm which transcends the other dimensions of life, revelation should be pictured as an awareness of another dimension of reality being mediated through the more familiar ones.[64]

Revelation, then, provides tacit knowledge of God when one responds to the religious dimension as it is encountered through interaction with one's community, history, and private context. A faith commitment to God, therefore, is not so much conceptual as it is experiential and tacit.[65] Here Gill's natural theology dominates his thinking. He clearly regards his view of mediated revelation as synonymous with a proper understanding of general revelation. "By means of his relation to the natural and moral dimensions of reality, each person is in a position to become aware of the religious dimension," he writes.[66] He contrasts this view of history's relationship to God's revelation with the traditional and modern views. In the former, he sees the emphasis on the facts of Jesus' life to support the fact-value dichotomy, while the latter view supports it by emphasizing value in history. Both sides of this modernist dichotomy are eliminated when one accepts that revelation is mediated through history. Gill believes that some theologians succeeding Barth and Bultmann now advance this perspective as they see history as the arena of mediated revelation. For instance, although Gill might reject Wolfhart Pannenberg's scientific approach to theology (because of its ties to Enlightenment rationalism), he commends the German theologian for his teaching that revelation is mediated through history.[67]

Mediation and Art

Aesthetic experience provides Gill with his most intriguing illustration for his model. He has written an unpublished monograph on Catholic novelist Flannery O'Connor that is a challenging addition to his developing thought, and he has applied his ideas to the work of filmmaker Ingmar Bergman. Furthermore, he is an avid sculptor, so many of his ideas about reality and mediation originated from his own experience in the arts.[68] If his model is a functionally viable option, this viability is demonstrated in aesthetic experience more than any other sphere of philosophy.

For Gill, aesthetic experience exemplifies the mediational, multidimensional nature of reality and experience. He observes that, although one may experience motion in a painting or sadness in a piece of music, neither motion nor sadness can actually be seen or heard in the physical properties that make up the work of art. How, then, do people experience these intangible qualities when interacting with works of art?[69]

Gill says that previous attempts to explain this phenomenon fail by accounting for the experience only after it has occurred. "They do not explain our experience of such qualities as *experienced.*" As an alternative he finds it

> far more helpful to say that the dimension of experienced reality that we term the "aesthetic" is encountered in and through the physical dimension, that it is *mediated* by it. . . . Motion and sadness are reasonably said to be *in* the painting or piece of music, respectively, without being isolatable from the sensory particulars thereof.[70]

Therefore, the intangible elements of reality are experienced mediationally through the tangible elements of the work of art. The aesthetic experience, then, is a holistic experience, not fragmented, reductionistic, or dichotomized.[71] A person participates in more than a single aspect of experience at a time.

Therefore, Gill argues, the tacit dimension is clearly evident in aesthetic awareness and even "lies at the heart of the artistic experience."[72] The aesthetic experience is an epistemological experience for which one has no exact explanation. Though indeed cognitive, aesthetic judgments are beyond articulation. How, then, does one justify a work of art? Gill repeats that the incarnational quality of participation remains the key for understanding mediated meaning in reality. Aesthetic judgment or experience is the meaning found in the work of art, which is justified by the artist's participation in the medium. The artist and the medium interact as mutual bodies in a given context. No result or meaning can be achieved outside the confines allowed by the medium and the context, through which meaning is mediated.[73]

Yet, as significant as this application may be, what remains absent is an explanation of how one's emotional response to a work of art may differ or be analogous to the transcendence that God enjoys as a Creator separate from His creation.[74] Aesthetic awareness closely resembles religious awareness. God, however, cannot be absorbed into either experience without the loss of the biblical picture of a personal God. More than resulting in knowledge, an experience of the Divine evokes worship of God as its object. Mediation may work as a model for understanding the aesthetic experience to transcendence, but it does not necessarily follow that it can serve as anything more than a good illustration of what one's experience with God may be like.

Mediation and Language

Finally, turning to the area in which evangelicals know Gill best, Gill integrates his philosophy of language into his mediational model. In fact, Gill insists that language plays a constitutional role in human embodied existence. "It is my contention," he writes, "that the structure of reality is mediated through experience, and that experience itself is mediated through language."[75]

Not surprisingly, Gill rejects the modernist contention that language identifies, names, and pictures actual states of affairs. Philosophers and theologians using this representational view of language always assumed that they could talk about reality, truth, and value without explicitly considering the medium through which these discussions took place. With the rise of logical positivism, however, this philosophy of language was catapulted into an extreme atomism, and knowledge about the transcendent realm and meaningful dialogue about metaphysic, theology, and ethics were eliminated at the outset.[76] Existentialists did not choose a better course, for they simply moved to the opposite extreme of the fact-value dichotomy, and taught that thought, language, and knowledge were primarily poetical and symbolic.[77]

As with most postmodern thinkers, Gill contends that the later work of Wittgenstein terminated the viability of the picture theory of language. The focus of discussion shifted from viewing the meaning of language as resident in the words to an understanding that meaning exists in the people who use the words. For Gill, in his later work Wittgenstein returned to theologians the capability to talk about transcendence. The meaning of utterances is mediated through one's context by the embodied character of linguistic activity. Rather than expressing the reality that people observe, "language *mediates* and largely *constitutes* our world."[78] In this model, "mediated meaning is at once transcendent of and dependent on that by which it is mediated." Therefore, full articulation is not essential for communication to take place. Instead,

> full articulation and precision are replaced as ideals by *adequate* articulation and *significant* precision. . . . Therefore, the fundamental structure of linguistic communication is itself an example of the reality of mediated transcendence.[79]

But in practice, how might one rescue discussion of the transcendent from the junk heap of the meaningless, onto which it was dumped by modernist thinkers? What mode of speech best communicates the richer dimensions of a multidimensional reality? Gill believes that metaphoric speech, and religious metaphor in particular, exhibits the qualities needed in religious discourse. Unlike analogy or simile, "metaphor does not parallel or compare; rather it mediates the richer in and through the less rich."[80] Metaphoric speech utilizes the complexity of a multidimensional reality and, therefore, is the most appropriate for religious expression in a postmodern context. "That which exists in mediated relationship and is known tacitly," he teaches, "can only be given expression by means of speech which suggests and 'shows' more than it says directly."[81]

Has any thinker arrived at a model for religious discourse that accounts for this type of expression and returns the transcendent to theological discussion? Gill points to Ian Ramsey's disclosure-commitment model as an appropriate paradigm for the postmodern context. Like Gill, Ramsey views the mystery of the transcendent as known through the empirical in a movement from tacit, inexplicable awareness, to explicit, logical, and volitional description and commitment, and then to further levels of commitment that are inexplicable in propositional terms. In much the same way that Gill teaches that knowledge of the transcendent is mediated through any level of humanity's multidimensional reality, Ramsey's empiricism allows that *any* situation may give rise to a disclosure of the transcendent.[82] Talk of this transcendent is possible through a qualifier-model paradigm of language, in which a phrase, such as "infinitely wise," is understood in its context of use. The first word is a qualifier that is understood by the second, the model. The meaning of the first word, then, is mediated by the second; that which is inexplicable is understood by that which can be explicated. By this model, Gill is satisfied that the transcendent has been returned to religious discourse.

Conclusion

Jerry Gill certainly offers one of the most ambitious efforts of any thinker within the Christian tradition to respond to the challenges of postmodernism. Is his model an option for evangelicals in the postmodern theological climate? Three questions provide a useful framework for an appraisal of his postmodern project.

Gill's Postmodernism

The first question is the most basic, and therefore the most easily overlooked. *Is Jerry Gill's philosophy of religion indeed* post*modern?* Yes, in at least two respects Gill's reconstruction project is unquestionably postmodern. First, he surmounts the boundaries of modernism, so in the most literal sense his work is *post*modern. Second, and more importantly, he attacks the assumptions of the modern era. He targets the dualistic mind-set of the modernists and shatters the epistemological presuppositions that fortify it. He replaces it with a reconstructed system that is holistic and that stresses participation in epistemology. By these two ingredients it is plainly postmodern. Furthermore, he makes this replacement without falling into the trap of postmodern deconstructionism that disallows any constructive analysis of truth claims. He stretches beyond the confines of existentialism and rationalism, and he circumvents *some* popular theological shanties, such as liberationism. Even with the slips he makes into popular revisionist theologies, he is not merely reactionary, but he accomplishes his proposal to be reconstructive and remains within the parameters of the Christian tradition.

In fact, Gill's system renews the credibility of Christian apologetics in a community of theological modernists.[83] In particular, theologians within the academic community who contend for humanity's ability to know the transcendent may receive an injection of fortitude from Gill's efforts. He addresses those who have eliminated knowledge of the transcendent as a serious option, and by doing so on their own terms he returns theology to its residence in metaphysical dialogue. His work stands an invitation to modernists and postmodernists alike to reconsider the Christian faith as an option not to be eliminated simply on modernist philosophical assumptions.[84]

When interpreters question humanity's ability to know the Divine, and not the more specific argument for the nature of God, his method is a useful response. He underscores the biblical perspective that facts point toward reality and that God's acts in history render evidence of His qualities which would be hidden except for His revelation. For this reason, the distinction between tacit and explicit knowing is helpful for Christian apologists who argue that "faith seeks understanding," because this distinction demonstrates that the Christian faith can, in fact, integrate the various detached aspects of reality left by the modernist worldview.[85] Nevertheless, though Gill rightly asserts that the biblical worldview is the one that can properly integrate all of reality, his system still suffers from the loss of the first requirement, a God who can *act* on that reality to provide integration.

Also, Gill's brand of postmodernism helps evangelicals remember that the Christian life is not lived in a vacuum. One's context must be taken seriously in both the project of theology and the living of viable faith. Faith is an embodied characteristic of Christianity. He helpfully stresses the metaphors and symbols that give continuity to humanity and human language. Not all human communication is cognitive, as one is reminded by Gill's stress on the metaphorical. In turn, however, Gill must remember that the primacy of metaphor does not exclude the significance of explicative, cognitive language. Further, his stress on the tacit dimension is a reminder that God may determine to *demonstrate* His character as often as *explicate* it. Indeed, a great deal occurs in one's relationship with God which words cannot seem to express. And, Gill is right, as the concept of the tacit dimension reminds us, people learn best by participation, the way the Spirit of God often chooses to teach His people the hardest lessons of faith.

Gill's Methodology

The second question for appraisal necessarily follows the first: *Though his system may be postmodern, is Jerry Gill's method valid?* In the final analysis, his epistemology remains more plausible than the ontology it generates. Although he affirms the biblical picture of God as a loving, active agent, one is unable to ascertain *how that God* can actually function within Gill's system. Further, in the last analysis,

Gill does not follow through with his proposal to construct a synthesis of modernism and premodernism that preserves the best offerings of both eras. Instead, he scuttles the contributions of both and thereby constructs a model that ignores their contributions in favor of materials borrowed from revisionist theologies.

If all knowledge is mediated, then it is all secondhand. No knowledge of the Divine can be immediate, so how does one know that he is in fact experiencing the divine and not simply a response to the mediating object, symbol, or person? Mediated knowledge must be distinguished from the agents of mediation. In Gill's empiricism, reality and the mediated knowledge of that reality are so closely associated that an individual would not be able to know what reality he or she was experiencing, that of divine transcendence or of some natural occurrence. The person so actively constitutes the experience as to disallow the experience any real credibility. One could virtually claim that any experience, from a headache to a theophany, was an experience of transcendence.[86] With Alister McGrath, evangelicals affirm that all experience must be interpreted within the confines of a previously established interpretive sytsem.[87] One cannot let the experience give its own interpretation. Every experience is an experience *of* something. The biblical picture is that only a Source that transcends context and time can offer that interpretation, and the interpretation is mediated through Christ.

Again, Gill cannot have transcendence and at the same time fuse all transcendence and immanence by mediation. The transcendent is distinguishable if one keeps a necessary dualism between immanence and transcendence. He defends his system against this accusation based on his argument for the Incarnation as the primary paradigm of his ontology. He asks the interpreter to envision a give-and-take relationship between the searching mind and the reality it knows. In so doing, he admonishes, one can distinguish between relationality and identity. If he were advocating the identity of the knower and the known, he claims, that would simply be mysticism.[88]

While Gill retains some essentials of the biblical picture of God in Christ, his description is still too vague to justify him against a charge of pantheism. He strives to preserve two positions at once. When speaking of God, he keeps the formal distinctions between God and the world sympathetic with the biblical picture of the Creator/creature relationship. Nevertheless, when he begins to speak of humanity's reception of knowledge as mediationally received the distinction disappears. He therefore makes an unnecessary elimination in the practice of his model, for in the biblical view God's activity is mediated while the Creator/creature dualism remains intact.

William Dean's analysis of American empiricism provides insights for appraising Gill's method. Dean examines the empiricism that has developed through the Whiteheadian school of philosophical theology, which he places within the tradition of North American liberalism. In this tradition, the experience of the religious person is the first and most basic authority. Therefore, Dean refers to the philosophical posture of the movement as "empirical liberalism."[89]

Although Gill is not, in fact, advancing process philosophy as a solution to the dichotomy between immanence and transcendence, his ontology locates him closer to Dean's description of American empiricism than to American evangelicalism. One must maintain the crucial distinction between the Divine dwelling within history as opposed to revealing Himself through history. Gill wants to teach God's revelation *through* history as he affirms the biblical picture of God, but his rejection of realmism will not allow him to actually use this picture in his epistemology. In a mediational epistemology, God dwells within history.

The Whiteheadian empiricism collapses all dualisms of spirit and matter as it exalts the single reality of experience. By comparison, Gill argues that his model

> enables us to speak of the transcendent *within* our experience rather than beyond, above, or other than it. The traditional dichotomy between the natural and the supernatural can be set aside.[90]

The experience of humanity becomes the center, and thereby the norm, in Gill's philosophy of religion.

Furthermore, Gill contextualizes truth, and thereby relativizes truth. Religious adequacy is preferable to certainty, and the embodied participation of the knower eventually decides what is truth for the context at hand. He raises experience to the status of a norm for metaphysical truth. Although he takes seriously the holistic nature of human experience and existence, he confuses the discovery of knowledge by one confronted with the God who reveals Himself with the participation of the knower in daily living that results from that knowledge. His contextualization is so complete he loses the mystery of revelation potentially offered in the tacit dimension. No faith dimension is retained outside the natural sphere, neither rationally nor intuitively. Here Gill is wrong, for a faith commitment must be cognitive as well as intuitive, through a mediated experience that is "distinctively personal."[91] How can Gill avoid the conclusion that transcendence is a characterizing factor in all beings and reality? Participation, not historical reality, becomes the guiding principle of truth, thus allowing each individual only his or her corner of participation for a knowledge of truth.

One is left wondering how Gill's God can, in fact, reveal Himself. By the time God has infiltrated and passed through the multiple mediating dimensions necessary to become knowledge through human experience, what is the content of His revelation? Gill overlooks this evident evacuation of any real content from his model for revelation. He does not grasp that *what* is revealed is just as important as the fact that the Transcendent can reveal and humans can know that revelation.[92] The ultimate dualism, between Creator and creature, cannot be, and need not be, eliminated.[93]

Gill has become so concerned with the fact of one's knowledge of the Divine that he has lost sight of the significance of the nature of God. In his compulsion to wreck the spatial metaphors of realmism, he has housed his God within a similar spatial perspective. Even for Jerry Gill, *where* God is has replaced in prominence *who* God is. The consequent immanentalism that he proposes, like similar models, forfeits revelation's mystical quality by detaching it from the glory and grace of the God who reveals by His own choice. The God who mediates revelation of Himself through the immanent cannot be reduced to the mediating dimensions. The biblical God is not a "divine dimension." One is no better off claiming that the physical dimension sets "boundary conditions" for the activity of God. This simply reduces God to an impotent agent.

Many theologians in the evangelical household have argued that the concept of a God who intrudes upon humanity from outside the natural realm does not eliminate the possibility that revelation is mediated as well as immediate. It is simply unnecessary to make the radical adjustment that Gill has made to accommodate the possibility of religious knowledge. In fact, the picture of God as an intrusive deity accentuates the particularity of the incarnation of Christ. Yet, Gill's approach, contrary to his overarching desire, makes God the object of empirical knowledge by cordoning Him within the natural world. His anthropology also suffers from this adjustment. Sin cannot be a personal affront to a God that has lost His personal status. Instead, sin becomes an affront only to the natural order. In the final analysis, Gill's ontology contributes to the immanentalist approaches so prevalent in theology today.

Gill's Philosophy of Religion

The third and final question useful for reviewing Gill's work has actually served as the focus for this entire study of his work: *Is Jerry Gill's postmodern philosophy of religion an adequate option for evangelicals?*

Evangelicals constructing models within the climate of postmodern theology are "postmodern evangelicals." This terminology properly places evangelicals within a postmodern context. The climate for the communication of evangelical distinctives has changed, not the distinctives themselves. Such terminology also accentuates the truth that evangelicals are among the most "postmodern" of all theologians without surrendering to the postmodernists' liquidation of truth. Evangelical theology does not have to be

> "post-modern" in order to be a responsible option in the post-modern world. Awareness of the post-modern context, however, is indispensable.[94]

By contrast, the term "evangelical postmodernists" might signify a revisionist subgroup within the evangelical culture and betrays some accommodation to postmodernist theologies. In the final analysis, Gill is in this latter grouping. Three facts extracted from this study of his work support this contention.

First, Gill falls prey to the fallacy that what is new is inherently better. In theology this is a particularly hazardous stance to take, for by it he relinquishes the traditions of the past as unworthy of proper consideration because they rely on dualisms that he would rather terminate. This is the first judgment on his part with which evangelicals cannot agree. Properly done, a postmodern evangelical methodology should involve a "conversation in which the Christian heritage of understanding, which is called tradition, is given a place alongside the headscratchings of today. . . ."[95]

Postmodern evangelical theologians should retain the foundations and exterior edifice necessary to continue allegiance with the theological orthodoxy of their past, as well as remain confident and attentive to the thoughts of other traditions as they test future theological constructions. At the same time, evangelicals can learn from postmodernists that the time has come to depart from the stalwart rationalism that characterized much of early evangelicalism after modernism and that tended to exact a definitive, albeit artificial, separation between theory and practice. One finds no such separation in the biblical picture of knowledge and reality.

Second, in his effort to clean the modernist house of dust of the Enlightenment, Gill has swept out the essential nuggets of a biblical faith. At this most current juncture of his project he is moving into the household of revisionism to the extent that his work is beginning to resemble modernist subjectivism more than postmodern evangelicalism. His primary weakness remains the inability to retain the distinctive relationship that the God of the Bible enjoys with His creation. In fact, mediation is part of that picture, so it is not necessary to remodel God in order to retain it. Evangelical interpreters agree that one's knowledge of the truth is mediated through experience with the particulars of reality. This safeguards against attributing too much authority to the experience itself.[96] One's understanding of that experience as an experience of the Divine is guided by an objective authority, such as Scripture, that demonstrates the characteristics of the Creator for His creatures. This dualism is not tied to modernism's philosophical models, so it is not necessary to eliminate it.

Finally, despite his incorporation of the tacit dimension and his emphasis on participation, Gill's epistemology lacks an adequate assessment of the role of the individual knowledge in the reception of knowledge. Assuming that all religious knowledge is universally available, he does not explore the possibility that a personal experience with God may be required for full knowledge of God. In fact, one must ask whether, in Gill's model, a personal experience with the Divine is even possible. Christian faith does not issue from a universal experience of transcendence, but from an individual's response to a personal God.

Gill's work lacks serious biblical exegesis, and his consideration of personal experience suffers most for this lack.[97] How can his model account for biblical displays of human encounters with God that assume both an intrusion of God into the natural realm as well as an individual response to that intrusion? Paul's encounter with Christ on the Damascus road exemplifies this illustration and should be addressed by Gill. As it is, however, he simply ignores these references in Scripture in favor of his unique natural theology.

An evangelical engagement of the postmodern challenge should extend beyond strict rationalistic rejections of aberrant theologies toward the construction of a viable response to modernism that accounts for the essential elements developed in premodernism. Gill's work gives impetus for evangelicals to build that response from the materials available within their own tradition. But, if one learns anything from Gill's reconstruction it is the frightening ease with which one may discard the more essential of those materials, even if unintentionally. Evangelicals building on postmodern soil do not need to eliminate essential pillars in an effort to accommodate colleagues reveling in new ideas. When too much accommodation is allowed, the foundations start to crack. The challenge for evangelicals in the postmodern context is to realize, build upon, and maintain with integrity the foundation that is the substance of their own tradition—the biblical faith.

NOTES

1. Pivotal thinkers in theology's shift from modernism to postmodernism include Kierkegaard, Heidegger, Kuhn, Nietzsche, and Wittgenstein. See Diogenes Allen, *Christian Belief in a Postmodern World: The Full Wealth of Conviction* (Louisville: Westminster/John Knox, 1989), passim; Wolfhart Pannenberg, *Metaphysics and the Idea of God*, trans. Philip Clayton (Grand Rapids: Eerdmans, 1990), chap. 1, passim; Diogenes Allen, *Philosophy for Understanding Theology* (Atlanta: John Knox, 1985), 250–56; Thomas Kuhn, *The Structure of Scientific Revolutions* (Chicago: Univ. of Chicago Press, 1962), passim; Henry Ruf, "The Origin of the Debate over Ontotheology and Deconstruction in the Texts of Wittgenstein and Derrida," in *Religion, Ontotheology, and Deconstruction*, ed. Henry Ruf (New York: Paragon, 1989), passim; Nancy Murphy and James W. McClendon, Jr., "Distinguishing Modern and Postmodern Theologies," *Modern Theology* 5 (April 1989): passim. Examples of efforts to evaluate modern theologies and to formulate postmodern theologies include the liberationist model of Harvey Cox, *Religion in the Secular City: Toward a Postmodern Theology* (New York: Simon and Schuster, 1984), passim; the proposal of H. Smith to return to a premodern, primordial philosophy for post-criticalism, as he demonstrates in *Beyond the Post-Modern Mind* (New York: Crossroad, 1982), 32–91, 132–38; and ethicist Gibson Winter's reliance on the metaphors of dwelling and creativity to replace the technological paradigms of modernism in his *Liberation Creation: Foundations of Religious Social Ethics* (New York: Crossroad, 1981), ix–10.

2. See Norman Geisler and Winfried Corduan, *Philosophy of Religion*, 2nd ed. (Grand Rapids: Baker, 1988), 229–331, 288–90; Millard J. Erickson, *Christian Theology* (Grand Rapids: Baker, 1983–85), 135; J.P. Newport, *Life's Ultimate Questions: A Contemporary Philosophy of Religion* (Waco, Texas: Word, 1989), 102; and R.A. Christian, "Wittgenstein Wittgensteinians, and the Epistemological Status of Religious Belief" (Ph.D. diss., Univ. of Pennsylvania, 1981), 400–410. In fact, in more than thirty years of writing, the only major article that Gill has published in the conservative evangelical magazine *Christianity Today* is one in which he evaluated contemporary views of theological language. The article is reprinted as J.H. Gill, "The Mean-

ing of Religious Language," in *Readings in Christian Theology: Vol. 1, The Living God,* ed. Millard J. Erickson (Grand Rapids: Baker, 1973), 105–13.

3. Unless otherwise indicated, the following biographical sketch is taken from J.H. Gill in a letter to the author, 13 April 1992; J.H. Gill, "Children of God, What a Pity! Reflections on Christian Maturity," manuscript photocopy (N.p., n.d.), 1–3; and from *Contemporary Authors,* New Revision Series, vol. 12, ed. L. Metger (Detroit: Gale Research Tower, 1984), 202. Where these sources conflict, the correspondence with the author is considered definitive.

4. A revision of Gill's dissertation was later published as J.H. Gill, *Ian Ramsey: To Speak Responsibly of God,* Contemporary Religious Thinkers Series, ed. Hywel D. Lewis (London: George Allen and Unwin, 1976).

5. J.H. Gill, "Shaping and Being Shaped," *Christian Century,* July 1975, 686.

6. Jerry Gill prefers to characterize himself as a teacher, rather than a writer or a scholar. His writings have been produced in his "spare time." J.H. Gill, telephone interview by author, 26 May 1993.

7. Letter to author, 13 April 1992.

8. J.H. Gill, *Mediated Transcendence: A Postmodern Reflection* (Macon, Ga.: Mercer Univ. Press, 1989), 11.

9. Ibid., 1–2.

10. J.H. Gill, *The Possibility of Religious Knowledge* (Grand Rapids: Eerdmans, 1971), 87.

11. J.H. Gill, *On Knowing God* (Philadelphia: Westminster, 1981), 14. Gill described modernists as "pioneers" who "strove to set knowledge free from the restrictions imposed by the medieval practice of thinking *within* certain established theological and philosophical ideas" (p. 42). Cf. Thomas C. Oden, *After Modernity . . . What? Agenda for Theology* (Grand Rapids: Zondervan, 1990), 15–16, 21.

12. J.H. Gill, "Transcendence: An Incarnational Model," *Encounter* 39 (Winter 1978): 41.

13. Gill, *Mediated Transcendence,* 7; idem, *Metaphilosophy: An Introduction* (Lanham, Md.: Univ. Press of America, 1982), 25.

14. Gill, *On Knowing God,* 29. Emphasis Gill's.

15. J.H. Gill, *Faith in Dialogue: A Christian Apologetic* (Waco, Texas: Word, 1985), 36; idem, "The Orphic Voice: Language, Reality, and Faith," *Encounter* 42 (Summer 1981): 237.

16. Gill, *On Knowing God,* 117–18.

17. Ibid., 75.

18. Gill, *Faith in Dialogue,* 116. Emphasis Gill's.

19. Gill, *Mediated Transcendence,* 20. Emphasis Gill's.

20. Ibid., 24.

21. Ibid.

22. Ibid., 26.

23. Ibid., 25.

24. Ibid., 26.

25. Gill, "Transcendence," 41.

26. Gill, *Mediated Transcendence,* 27.

27. Ibid., 40.

28. Gill, *On Knowing God,* 119. Emphasis added.

29. J.H. Gill, "The Tacit Structure of Religious Knowing," in *Logical Analysis*

and Contemporary Theism, ed. John Donnelly (New York: Fordham University Press, 1972), 259.

30. Gill, *Mediated Transcendence,* 35–36.

31. J.H. Gill, *Toward Theology* (Lanham, Md.: Univ. Press of America, 1982), 85.

32. Ibid., 85–89.

33. Ibid., 92. Emphasis added.

34. Ibid., 93. Emphasis Gill's.

35. See John P. Newport, "Representative Contemporary Approaches to the Use of Philosophy in Christian Thought," *Review and Expositor* 82 (Fall 1985): 512.

36. Cf. Stanley J. Grenz and Roger E. Olson, *20th Century Theology: God and the World in a Transitional Age* (Downers Grove, Ill.: InterVarsity, 1992), 137–42.

37. Gill, *On Knowing God,* 72–73.

38. Ibid., 74–75.

39. Gill, *Mediated Transcendence,* 50.

40. Mari Sorri and J.H. Gill, *A Post-Modern Epistemology: Language, Truth, and Body, Problems in Contemporary Philosophy,* vol. 19 (Lewiston, N.Y.: Mellen, 1989), 116.

41. Gill, *Mediated Transcendence,* 50–51.

42. Michael Polanyi, *The Tacit Dimension* (Garden City, N.Y.: Doubleday, 1966), 32–33.

43. Michael Polanyi, *Personal Knowledge: Towards a Post-Critical Philosophy* (Chicago: Univ. of Chicago Press, 1958), 15–17.

44. Polanyi, *The Tacit Dimension,* 4.

45. Ibid., 4–7, 15; idem, *Knowing and Being,* ed. Marjorie Grene (Chicago: Univ. of Chicago Press, 1969), 133.

46. Polanyi, *Personal Knowledge,* 55.

47. Ibid., 59.

48. Gill, *On Knowing God,* 74.

49. Gill, *Mediated Transcendence,* 51.

50. J.H. Gill, "Reasons of the Heart: A Polanyian Reflection," *Religious Studies* 14 (June 1978): 143. Gill usually quotes Polanyi with a slight, but insignificant, variation on Polanyi's words: "We know more than we can say."

51. Ibid., 144.

52. J.H. Gill, "On Seeing through a Glass, Darkly," *Christian Scholar's Review* 5 (1976): 267; idem, "Reasons of the Heart," 147; idem, "Tacit Knowing and Religious Belief," *International Journal for Philosophy of Religion* 6 (Summer 1975): 80.

53. Cf. J.H. Gill, "The Case for Tacit Knowledge," *Southern Journal of Philosophy* 9 (Spring 1971): 58; idem, *Mediated Transcendence,* 53; idem, "The Tacit Structure of Religious Knowing," 253.

54. Gill, *Mediated Transcendence,* 54.

55. Ibid., 55.

56. Ibid., 56.

57. Gill, "Tacit Knowing and Religious Belief," 80–81; idem, "Mysticism and Mediation," *Faith and Philosophy* 1 (January 1984): 177; idem, *Mediated Transcendence,* 57.

58. Gill, *Mediated Transcendence,* 57.

59. Gill, "The Case for Tacit Knowledge," 50.

60. Ibid., 64. Emphasis Gill's.

61. Ibid.

62. Gill, *On Knowing God*, 126–27; idem, *Learning to Learn: Toward a Philosophy of Education* (Atlantic Highlands, New Jersey: Humanities, 1993), 48.

63. Gill, "On Seeing through a Glass," 269.

64. Gill, *Possibility of Religious Knowledge*, 173.

65. Gill, "Tacit Structure of Religious Knowing," 269; idem, *Mediated Transcendence*, 146–49; idem, *Faith in Dialogue*, 135.

66. Gill, *Possibility of Religious Knowledge*, 174.

67. Ibid., 174–76.

68. J.H. Gill, *Art and Incarnation* (unpublished manuscript, n.d.); idem, *Flannery O'Connor: Faith and Fiction* (unpublished manuscript, n.d.); idem, "Posing as an Artist as an Old Man: An Interdisciplinary Encounter," *Christian Scholar's Review* 8 (1978): 47; idem, "Shaping and Being Shaped," *Christian Century*, July 1975, 687–88; idem, "On Knowing the Dancer from the Dance," *Journal of Aesthetics and Art Criticism* 34 (Winter 1975): 132–33; idem, *Ingmar Bergman and the Search for Meaning* (Grand Rapids: Eerdmans, 1969); idem, "Of Snakeskins and Wineskins: Art and Religion in the Work of Ingmar Bergman," *Encounter* 37 (Spring 1976): passim.

69. Gill, *Mediated Transcendence*, 32.

70. Ibid. Emphasis Gill's.

71. Gill, *Art and Incarnation*, 52.

72. Gill, "Posing as an Artist," 50.

73. Gill, "Posing as an Artist," 50; idem, *Faith in Dialogue*, 151–52.

74. Y. Woodfin, *With All Your Mind: A Christian Philosophy* (Nashville: Abingdon, 1980), 124–28.

75. Gill, *The Possibility of Religious Knowledge*, 92.

76. Gill, *Faith in Dialogue*, 119–21; idem, *Mediated Transcendence*, 112.

77. Gill, *Possibility of Religious Knowledge*, 97–98.

78. Gill, *Mediated Transcendence*, 115. Emphasis Gill's.

79. Ibid., 116. Emphasis Gill's.

80. J.H. Gill, "The Orphic Voice: Language, Reality, and Faith," *Encounter* 42 (Summer 1981): 237.

81. J.H. Gill, *Wittgenstein and Metaphor* (Lanham, Md.: Univ. Press of America, 1981), 197.

82. Gill, *Ian Ramsey*, 59; I.T. Ramsey, "Talking about God: Models Ancient and Modern," in *Christian Empiricism: Ian Ramsey*, ed. J.H. Gill (Grand Rapids: Eerdmans, 1974), 130.

83. Alister E. McGrath, in "The Challenge of Pluralism for the Contemporary Church," *Journal of the Evangelical Theological Society* 35 (September 1992): 365, rightly remarks that apologetics is "the area of theology that is most sensitive to" postmodern developments because in the postmodern context "all claims to truth are equally valid."

84. Philip LeMasters, review of *Faith in Dialogue: A Christian Apologetic* and *Mediated Transcendence: A Postmodern Reflection*, by Jerry H. Gill, in *Perspectives in Religious Studies* 17 (Fall 1990): 270. Pannenberg, in *Metaphysics and the Idea of God*, xiii, 3–21, defends enterprising thinkers whose models strive toward a responsible relationship between theology and philosophy. He insists that "a theological doctrine of God that lacks metaphysics as its discussion partner falls into either a kerygmatic

subjectivism or a thoroughgoing demythologization." (p. 6).

85. Cf. Newport, *Life's Ultimate Questions,* 428–36.

86. Cf. Anthony N. Perovich, Jr., "Mysticism or Mediation: A Response to Gill," *Faith and Philosophy* 2 (April 1985): 180–81.

87. Alister E. McGrath, "The Christian Church's Response to Pluralism," *Journal of the Evangelical Theological Society* 35 (December 1992): 493; idem, *The Genesis of Doctrine: A Study in the Foundations of Doctrinal Criticism* (Cambridge: Blackwell, 1990), 66–72.

88. Gill, *Faith in Dialogue,* 134.

89. William Dean, *American Religious Empiricism,* SUNY Series in Religious Studies, ed. R.C. Neville (Albany, N.Y.: State Univ. of New York Press, 1986), 5–6, 8.

90. Gill, *Mediated Transcendence* 154. Emphasis Gill's. Cf. Dean, *American Religious Empiricism,* 50.

91. As Woodfin, *With All Your Mind,* 27, affirms. Gill clearly believes that a faith commitment is necessary for one's Christian maturity, but his empiricism does not require faith for the knowledge of God. See Gill, "Children of God," 4.

92. Interestingly, as a young scholar Jerry Gill chided Paul Tillich for a similar error. See J.H. Gill, "Paul Tillich's Religious Epistemology," *Religious Studies* 3 (April 1968): 485.

93. The Apostle Paul explicitly offers this position in his apologetic to the Areopagus on Mars Hill. See Acts 17:22-31.

94. M.C. Parsons, "Making Sense of What We Read: The Place of Biblical Hermeneutics," *Southwestern Journal of Theology* 35 (Summer 1993): 17.

95. J.I. Packer, "Is Systematic Theology a Mirage? An Introductory Discussion," in *Doing Theology in Today's World: Essays in Honor of Kenneth S. Kantzer,* ed., J.D. Woodbridge and T.E. McComiskey (Grand Rapids: Zondervan, 1991), 23.

96. John P. Newport, *What Is Christian Doctrine?* Layman's Library of Christian Doctrine, vol. 1 (Nashville: Broadman, 1984), 32.

97. As an example, Gill continually employs 1 Cor. 13:12a, that we "see through a glass, darkly," to support his epistemological assumptions. Whereas he is correct that in this text Paul is making a basic epistemological assertion, and that Christ is indeed the "glass" through which believers interpret reality, this is not an appropriate text to support this contention. In his use of this text he makes three errors, all a result of a faulty use of context. The first error generates the other two. First, Gill does not put the verse in context of the entire chapter. As a result, he misuses the text to refer directly to Christ when, in fact, Paul's concern is the spiritual life of a believer in whom the Spirit of God is incarnate. Therefore, although Christ's incarnation is an appropriate paradigm for understanding the Spirit in the believer, this text is primarily about believers and only secondarily about Christ. Finally, third, Gill does not address the latter half of the verse, in which Paul is clearly accounting for a completion of the believer's knowledge at the eschaton or in heaven, not in the present age. Cf. C.K. Barrett, *A Commentary on the First Epistle to the Corinthians,* Harper's New Testament Commentaries, ed. H. Chadwick (San Francisco: Harper and Row, 1968), 306–8; W.H. Mare, *1 Corinthians,* in *The Expositors' Bible Commentary,* vol. 10, ed. Frank E. Gaebelein (Grand Rapids; Zondervan, 1976), 269–70.

PART THREE
THE CHALLENGE FOR HERMENEUTICS

8

Postholes, Postmodernism, and the Prophets: Toward a Textlinguistic Paradigm

E. Ray Clendenen

F rom the hubris of modernity we have moved to the subjectivity and uncertainty of postmodernism. We travel in the foggy world of postmodernism and, like Lot, remain there as resident aliens, unable to extricate ourselves.

Students introduced to Heisenberg's uncertainty principle learn that it is impossible to measure subatomic particles without altering those particles. But it is not until later that they likely realize its impact on daily life, that real human objectivity, the ability to observe dispassionately from the outside, is an illusion. Part of the human condition of finiteness is that observation is always from the inside. Like trying to photograph a room, we can never see the whole at once. There is an infinite number of perspectives on reality, but we can only have one at a time. Only God has genuine objectivity. Only He can see things as they really are in their totality.

No longer can we think of a text as a transparent window through which one may naively observe the author's mind and the reality of the world beyond. Nevertheless, unlike some we affirm here that there is a real world of the text and that while our perspective is limited there is in fact something there and we can see it, however imperfectly. In answer to Stanley Fish's question, "Is there a text in this class or is it just us?"[1] we affirm that there is definitely a text.

E. Ray Clendenen is Academic Editor at Broadman and Holman Publishers in Nashville, Tennessee.

Reading is a process of interaction between reader, text, author, and world. It is a process in which a text affords the reader a series of distant glimpses of the author's intentions and world as they are manifest in the world of the text.[2] The reader continually attempts on the basis of his or her own worldview—one's knowledge, experience, and perspective—to piece the glimpses together into a meaningful picture of the world of the text. This involves continually examining and reexamining the glimpses for coherence not only with themselves but also with the author's world as it is known and with the reader's own world, repeatedly revising and rearranging the picture and, to a lesser extent, both consciously and unconsciously revising the reader's worldview.

A native of the postmodern world, for whom distinctions and boundaries have collapsed, would reject a dichotomy between reader and text and also the expectation of a coherent picture.[3] But stubbornly maintaining that readers and writers are shackled and blinded by their own worldviews so that messages cannot be conveyed and worldviews cannot be transformed runs counter to experience and reason, as well as to Christian faith.[4] Particularly does an evangelical view of revelation, of conversion, and even of discipleship demand that we view the Bible as communication from human authors and ultimately from the divine author (cf. 2 Peter 1:20-21). And if our understanding of deity means anything, that means that the messages of the biblical texts are comprehensible, authoritative, and transforming.

Acceptance of the Gospel necessitates acknowledgment that the biblical texts, while not transparent or panoramic windows on reality, are nevertheless at least tinted peepholes designed ultimately by God to afford glimpses from different angles (cf. Heb. 1:1) which together can be constructed into a true, however incomplete, picture of all of reality we need in order to know God and to please Him with our lives.[5] If the Bible is only a mirror by which we can see nothing but ourselves, then continuing to claim that it is in any sense authoritative for the church is the real bibliolatry of which fundamentalism has been so often accused.

At any rate, the biblical author's world is accessible through the world of the text, and that fact motivates us to investigate the text with every available tool, expecting those "transforming effects" that Anthony Thiselton discusses.[6] Now that we understand that interpretation is a process of interaction between the reader and the text in which the text does things to the reader, perhaps we can better understand the biblical assertion that the Word of God is active, sharper than a two-edged sword (Heb. 4:12; cf. Jer. 1:10). This approach, Thiselton says, "provides a welcome corrective to more antiquarian and purely informational approaches."[7] We must reject, however, the radical view that despairs of meaning in the text and equates the effect of a text with its meaning. The meaning of a text resides in the connection between the author's intentions and the author's world on the one hand and the text on the other. In the case of a biblical text it is frequently possible to extend the authorial intentions and world beyond the human author by means of the canonical context, while affirming that the divine author's intentions and world include those of the human author. This is analogous to saying that the meaning of a historical event (e.g., the crowning of Pippin the Short of France in A.D. 751[8]) can be far greater than its immediate participants and observers realize when seen in the larger context of its historical effects.

Howard Hendricks has warned his students against "posthole thinking," continuing to dig for biblical understanding in the same hole. He advocates "lateral thinking," digging in many holes. In its iconoclastic emphasis, postmodernist hermeneutics also opposes "posthole thinking." While interpretative models or paradigms are necessary to the reading process, we must recognize that they are but tentative constructions needing constant revision. If traditions of interpretation are allowed to become frozen and authoritative in themselves, they can obstruct our view of the text.[9] We need new perspectives to keep us from being isolated from the text. New tools can help destabilize our thinking and afford us this new perspective. The interdisciplinary field of textlinguistics is such a tool, working together with sociolinguistics[10] and speech act theory[11] to transform "biblical reading from routine and predictable processes to more creative and productive ones."[12]

Our goal is to explain and demonstrate the usefulness of a textlinguistic model of interpretation for the Old Testament prophets by treating them as hortatory discourses. One of the reasons for this interest is the desire, whenever possible, to avoid in interpretations nebulous appeals to *context* and explanations of grammatical variation simply as *emphasis*. While such statements may not be wrong, they are insufficient, and interpreters should aim at precision. The primary questions to be considered here are (1) What is hortatory discourse and how does it work? and (2) How does this relate to what the prophets were doing?[13]

Relationship between Prophecy
and Hortatory Discourse[14]

Old Testament prophecy refers to Old Testament literature written or delivered by individuals designated or recognized as "prophets." The explicit purpose of such literature is to affect behavior through encouragement and warning.

The term "hortatory" refers to a particular discourse type characterized by (1) a particular function, (2) a particular notional/ semantic structure, and (3) certain features of *surface structure.* A hortatory discourse is a discourse whose function is to effect behavioral change in another being. The *notional structure* will include three elements: the *situation* believed to be in need of change, the *change* being advocated, and the *motivation* offered to support the change, either as positive benefits or as negative warnings.

Most important, the *surface structure* of a hortatory discourse will be marked by the inclusion of directives that encode the advocated change. The directives will be whatever verb forms and clause types are normally used by the language to express injunction or exhortation. This third characteristic of hortatory discourse is very important because it is the primary means by which hortatory is identified. Because of the function of hortatory discourse to effect change, the change element of the notional structure is the most salient. Therefore, the morphosyntax that a language uses to express this element must be the mark of a hortatory discourse. While the other elements (situation and motivation) sometimes can be left for the interpreter to infer from the textual context or communication situation (as with a stop sign), the change element is not optional. A language may have a large inventory of directives encoding a great variety of semantic and pragmatic messages, but one of them must occur for the text to be identified as hortatory.

We should note before proceeding, however, that a discourse whose function is to change behavior will not necessarily be hortatory. A speaker/writer wishing to affect behavior may choose another discourse type such as narrative. But such a choice would result from a discourse strategy to violate the norm and to choose an option other than the "default case." We will not argue, therefore, that prophecy is always formally hortatory. The Book of Jonah is narrative, although like all prophecy it has a hortatory function.[15] Nathan's message to David in 2 Samuel 12:1-14 is a narrative whose discourse function is to get David to repent.

Confirmation of the normal relationship between prophecy and hortatory is found in introductory texts on prophecy. It is common for such books to list the types of oracles found in the prophets. A typical list includes *indictment* (sometimes called reproach, accusation, or complaint), *judgment* (or threat), *instruction* (or exhortation), and *hope* (or promise).[16] *Indictment* oracles describe the offense of the audience, behavior which the prophet wishes to be changed—for example, idolatry, ritualism, social injustice, or failure to honor Yahweh. *Judgment* oracles describe the punishment to be carried out (or already being experienced) because of the offensive behavior. *Instruction* oracles call for response that will result in changed behavior—for example, a call to return to Yahweh or to put an end to wickedness. *Hope* oracles assure the audience of Yahweh's determination to bless them. These may or may not be expressed conditionally, but their function is to motivate the response the prophet is calling for.

It is interesting that this list matches what we expect to be the notional structure of a hortatory text. Indictment oracles describe the situation that needed to be changed; instruction oracles explain the change being advocated; and both judgment oracles and hope oracles present the motivation offered for the change—judgment presents negative motivation (what will happen if the change is not effected), and hope presents positive motivation (either the blessings that will occur if the change is effected or past/present blessings that render the change reasonable and appropriate).

Discourse Type and Organization

The exegetical procedure being advocated here assumes that language is dynamic. Its purpose is more than to convey meaning; it is to affect the listener or reader in some way—to entertain, inspire, rebuke, persuade, warn, anger, or console. Just as speakers must choose the most effective form of a sentence for their purposes—a statement, question, promise, or command—they must choose the genre of the envisioned text and how to employ the available aspects of that genre. As Thomas G. Long argues, "Texts are not packages containing ideas; they are means of communication. When we ask ourselves what a text means, we are not searching for the *idea* of the text. We are trying to discover its total impact upon a reader—and everything about a text works together to create that impact."[17] The reason discourse typology is so important is that it is used by readers/listeners to interpret texts. One of the requirements for the interpretation of a text is linguistic competence, which John Barton

FOCUS	FRAMEWORK	
	CHRONOLOGICAL	LOGICAL
Agent	Past: **NARRATIVE** Future **PREDICTIVE**	**HORTATORY**
Theme	**PROCEDURAL**	**EXPOSITORY**

Discourse Typology
Table 1

defines as *"the ability to recognize genre."*[18] The primary discourse types, identified on the basis of grammatical features, are narrative, predictive, procedural, expository, and hortatory (see table 1).

Identifying the utterance type sets up certain expectations, among which are the elements or parts to be encountered.

Thus, identifying a discourse as hortatory on the basis of directives in the text[19] leads an interpreter to expect the notional structure to employ the elements *situation, change,* and *motivation.* The primary cohesive device of a hortatory discourse is the *change* slot, which is the focus, nucleus, or naturally most prominent element in the discourse, performing a function similar in this regard to that of the verb of a clause or the root of a word.[20] It is also similar to the climax of a narrative toward which the story rises and from which it usually falls.

Where and how frequently directives occur is determined by the conventions of the language code and the strategies of the writer/ speaker. If there is more than one directive in a discourse, yet related to the same *situation* and *motivation* elements, the sequence of directives will form what Longacre has called a "line of exhortation," related to a narrative story line.[21] The message or macrostructure of such a discourse would be a summary of all the *situation, change,* and *motivation* elements.

If, on the other hand, one of several change slots in a discourse is governing its own separate situation and motivation slots, then it is useful to describe it separately as an embedded discourse. The Book of Malachi furnishes examples of this (see table 2). There are three embedded discourses or addresses, each with an internal chiastic structure. In the first and second addresses, the naturally most salient element in hortatory, the exhortation, is the focus of the chiasm. In the final address the pattern is altered, causing this address to stand out as the most prominent and to end the book with a final exhortation. Thus, an interaction between the surface structure and the notional structure of Malachi gives the book cohesion. While the author may not have had labels (certainly not our labels) for the semantic slots of hortatory discourse, the structure of the book demonstrates a skillful familiarity with them.[22]

FIRST ADDRESS			
Priests Exhorted	1A Motivation	Yahweh's Love	1:2-5
to Honor	1B Situation	Failure to Honor Yahweh	1:6-9
Yahweh	**1C Change**	**Stop Vain Offerings**	**1:10**
1:2–2:9	1B′ Situation	Profaning Yahweh's Name	1:11-14
	1A′ Motivation	Results of Disobedience	2:1-9
SECOND ADDRESS			
	2A Motivation	Spiritual Unity	2:10a, b
Judah Exhorted	2B Situation	Faithlessness	2:10c-15b
to Faithfulness	**2C Change**	**Stop Acting Faithlessly**	**2:15C-16**
2:10–3:6	2B′ Situation	Complaints of Yahweh's Injustice	2:17
	2A′ Motivation	Coming Messenger of Judgment	3:1-6
THIRD ADDRESS			
	3A Change	**Return to Yahweh with Tithes**	**3:7-10b**
Judah Exhorted	3B Motivation	Future Blessing	3:10c-12
to Return to	3C Situation	Complacency toward Serving Yahweh	3:13-14
Yahweh	3B′ Motivation	The Coming Day	3:15-21
3:7-24	**3A′ Change**	**Remember the Law**	**3:22-24**

Structure of Malachi
Table 2

The constituents of a hortatory discourse may also belong to various discourse types. While the *change* slot must be hortatory, the *situation* slot will frequently be realized by an expository discourse. The *motivation* slot will often be a predictive discourse, although motivation by past events would normally be narrative. The discourse type of the paragraph or embedded paragraph will determine which system of verb-clause types will be employed.[23]

Paragraph Analysis in Malachi

The Book of Malachi is in the form of a speech by Yahweh the God of Israel to His people, often referred to as an oracle or a messenger speech. Nevertheless, it contains rhetorical responses from that audience that portray their attitudes. Since the interaction is rhetorical, it can be called pseudo-dialogue.[24] Malachi can be analyzed, then, as a monologue interspersed with exchanges between Yahweh and His audience. Twenty-five times we are given a quote formula announcing that Yahweh is speaking. It varies between "says Yahweh of Hosts," "says Yahweh" (four times), "says Yahweh the God of Israel" (once), and "the declaration of Yahweh" (once).[25] Although some of these could be understood to mark a change of speaker, at least most of them are unnecessary for that purpose and are better understood as markers of prominence or the boundary of a paragraph or sub-paragraph.

The first constituent of Malachi (designated 1A) will be used as a sample of the type of paragraph analysis employed.[26] It is marked as a unit by the theme of Yahweh's demonstrated love for Israel in contrast to His rejection of Esau/Edom. It functions as motivation not only for the first embedded discourse but also for the whole of Malachi, since the audience of the first movement (the priests) is not clarified until 1B and themes are introduced in 1A that are developed in the third (climactic) embedded discourse.[27]

Paragraph analysis relies upon an inventory of semantic relations between sentences. One way of describing these semantic relations is by speaking of paragraph types (see table 3). A paragraph type is a cluster of sentences which have a particular type of semantic relation. For example, a sequence paragraph has sentences that describe events sequentially; an antithetical paragraph has sentences related as thesis and antitheses; a result paragraph has a thesis and a result, and so on.

The constituents of a paragraph may also be sentence clusters or "embedded paragraphs," so that an entire paragraph may be analyzed in terms of a series of embedded paragraphs (e.g., see table 4 on p. 141).

TYPE	CONSTITUENTS
Simple Paragraph	One sentence
Sequence Paragraph	Sequential event sentences
Simultaneous Paragraph	Simultaneous event sentences
Coordinate Paragraph	Coordinate sentences
Alternative Paragraph	Thesis + Alternative (Alter)
Antithetical Paragraph	Thesis + Antithesis (Anti)
Condition Paragraph	Condition (Cond) + Consequence (Cons)
Result Paragraph	Thesis + Result
Reason Paragraph	Thesis + Reason
Attestation Paragraph	Thesis + Evidence (Evid)
Amplification Paragraph	Thesis + Amplification (Ampl)
Paraphrase Paragraph	Thesis + Paraphrase (Para)
Comment Paragraph	Thesis + Comment (Com)
Illustration Paragraph	Thesis + Illustration (Illust)
Dialogue Paragraph	Thesis + Initiating utterance (IU)
	± Continuing utterance (CU)
	+ Resolving utterance (RU)
Quote Paragraph	Quote formula + Quote

Basic Paragraph Types
Table 3

Paragraph analysis is a bottom-up process. That is, the immediate relationship, if any, between adjacent sentences is determined first, then the relationship between sentence clusters, until the entire paragraph is accounted for. Paragraph 1A in Malachi is called a dialogue paragraph because at the highest level of structure its constituents are related as an interchange between Yahweh and the people of Judah. It is called a narrative paragraph because at the highest levels it is a narrative, identified by the narrative perfects (PF) and *waw*-consecutive preterites (wcPRET) in verses 2-3. Traditional exegetical method has attempted to categorize grammatical forms such as the perfect and imperfect as if the Hebrew Bible were grammatically uniform. Rather than concentrating on the aspectual differences between the perfect and imperfect, however, textlinguistic analysis investigates how the various verb forms and clause types function in each discourse type. That is, what kind of information do they carry, or what effect do they have on the reader?

Table 4. 1A—Malachi 1:2-5: Narrative Dialogue

IU:Rem: "I have loved (PF) you,"
  says Yahweh.
CU:Q: And you say (PF),
  "How have you loved (PF) us?"
RU:Ans: Narrative Antithetical
  Anti: "Was Esau not Jacob's brother?" (NOM)
  declares Yahweh.
  Thesis: Result
  Thesis: Antithetical
    Thesis: "Yet I loved (wcPRET) Jacob (v. 2),
    Anti: "And Esau I hated (PF).
  Result: Amplification
  Thesis: "And I made (wcPRET) his mountains
    a desolation and his inheritance
    for the jackals of the wilderness" (v. 3).
    Ampl: Predictive Result
      Thesis: Quote
      QF: If Edom says,
      "We have been battered, but we
      shall rebuild the ruins,"
  Thus Yahweh of hosts says.
  Quote: Antithetical
    Anti: "They will build (IMF).
    Thesis: "But I shall demolish (IMF)."
  Result: Result
    Thesis: "And they will be called (wcPF)
      the territory of wickedness and
      the people which Yahweh cursed
      forever (v. 4).
    Result: Result
      Thesis: And your eyes will see
      (IMF).
      Result: And you will say (IMF),
      "Great is (IMF) Yahweh over the territory of Israel" (v. 5).

Malachi 1:2-5 begins with an initiating utterance which is a remark by Yahweh. It uses a perfect which portrays backgrounded
actions in narrative. Its prominence is also marked by the "says
Yahweh" quote formula. Judah's evaluation of Yahweh's remark is in

the form of a question which serves to continue the dialogue and is therefore called a continuing utterance.

The remainder of the paragraph comprises Yahweh's answer, which concludes this initial dialogue and is therefore called a resolving utterance. It is structured as an antithetical paragraph with an initial antithesis followed by an embedded paragraph functioning as the thesis. The antithesis uses a nominal sentence (NOM), which narrative discourse uses for setting. Although setting is normally low in prominence, its important function in the argument here is marked by its interrogative form[28] and by the quote formula, "declares Yahweh." The thesis slot of the antithetical paragraph is filled by an embedded result paragraph whose thesis is an antithetical paragraph. In spite of Jacob and Esau being brothers, Yahweh formed a unique permanent relationship only with Jacob and rejected Esau ("loved Jacob"/"hated Esau"). The use of the perfect tense rather than a preterite in "And Esau I hated" is due to two factors: (1) contrast is marked by the object-first word order, which does not allow a preterite, as well as the lexical opposition of Jacob/ Esau and loved/hated; and (2) God's rejection of Esau is treated as less prominent than His choosing Jacob; hence the verb form is used whose function in narrative is to mark backgrounded events.

One result of Yahweh's contrasting relationships with Jacob and Esau is that Edom's sin (which is assumed) led to Edom's permanent destruction: "I made his mountains a desolation." Their permanent destruction may also be understood as evidence for the difference in relationships. The permanence of Edom's destruction is amplified in verses 4-5 in three hypotactically embedded result paragraphs, which employ verbs from the predictive discourse system. They begin with a conditional clause, which is used to introduce a divine quote. The quote is an embedded antithetical paragraph using imperfect verbs. Although we would expect clause initial *waw*-consecutive perfects predictive discourse, both clauses front the pronominal subjects, a common feature of clauses in contrast.[29] Fronting also explains the use of imperfects in verses 5a and 5b ("Your eyes will see. And you will say"), although the fronting there does not accompany contrast. It rather reintroduces the "you" topic from verse 1, thereby contrasting the wicked speech of Israel in the present, doubting Yahweh's love ("you say"), with the believing speech of Israel in the future, recognizing the greatness of His love ("you will say").

The imperfect in the final sentence of the paragraph occurs in a quote of what Israel will say in the future. Since the quote itself, then, will be describing a present reality, it is a simple embedded expository paragraph consisting of a single sentence. As Longacre explains, the highest ranking verb and clause types in expository discourse are those which normally encode static concepts, such as the stative verb used here.[30] This constituent, then, is a good example of the interaction of discourse types and verb-clause systems in a single paragraph. It switches from narrative to predictive, then to expository discourse. Longacre's model of paragraph analysis via discourse type and verb-clause ranking provides a very satisfying description of constituent 1A.[31]

The purpose of the paragraph is to declare and demonstrate by contrast that Yahweh's covenant love for Israel would continue. The historical context of postexilic Judah confirms that this was an important word of reassurance during difficult times. The broader context of Malachi's prophecy shows that Judah had allowed their difficulties to hinder their faithfulness to God. But even their faithlessness had not annulled God's pledge to be faithful and restore righteousness and blessing in Israel on the other side of judgment. Meanwhile He would lovingly watch over and care for those who feared Him.[32]

Conclusion

There is much in postmodernism which the evangelical community can applaud because there is much in modernity that was harmful to biblical faith—especially (1) the idolatrous exaltation of the human intellect and the pretentious usurpation of God's position of objectivity and (2) the swallowing of the spiritual by the material resulting in the perception of a mechanistic universe and the analytical fragmentation that followed from that perception. These concepts broadened the gap between the ancient sacred text of biblical studies and the modern world badly in need of a relevant message. The resulting sterility of historical criticism eventually produced "the current methodological ferment in biblical studies,"[33] often called a crisis.

> Interpretation is in crisis. So many questions which once seemed settled, so many foundations which once seemed secure, so many agreements which once seemed firm, have come apart. Issues which go to the bedrock of interpretation have opened deep fissures.[34]

Nevertheless, without a commitment to a divine reality made known historically and eschatologically in Christ and an epistemology founded on the biblical doctrines of God and humanity, postmodernism tends to throw out the concept of truth along with that of objectivity and tries to find meaning and relevance in the amorphous reading community rather than in the revelatory text.[35]

Therefore, although there are many important concepts within postmodernism that must be included in a contemporary hermeneutical paradigm, taken as a whole postmodernism is an inadequate foundation for exegesis. The purpose of exegesis is to bridge the gap between the ancient text and the contemporary world in such a way that we are confronted anew with God's word to us. An exegetical method is necessary that can mediate the transaction between the biblical author in his historical context and the modern readers through an investigation of the biblical text. Our thesis is that in hermeneutics and exegesis we can (and should) consider the dynamics of the reader while not losing sight of the intentions of the author or the message of the text. Communicators do things with texts. Language works. A skillful reader will experience what a skillful communicator intended to accomplish through the agency of a text as an interface takes place between the worlds of the author, text, and reader. An interpreter (or "critical reader") is a reader who is more skillful than certain other readers (because of greater familiarity with the author or his world, and/or with the semantic systems the text relies on to accomplish the author's purpose) and thus can facilitate their experience.

Exegesis must focus on investigation of the text itself, but must integrate it with investigation of the historical context and also the canonical context. This kind of integration is generally lacking in postmodernism.

> The more we move towards a climate in which "my reading of the text" is what matters, the less pressure there will be either to anchor the text in its own historical context or to integrate a wider "message" of the text with other messages, producing an overall theological statement or synthesis.[36]

Textlinguistics is a discipline that treats texts within a theory of communication, an understanding of how language works. This theory is based upon worldwide investigations in hundreds of languages with the assumption that there is a universal infrastructure underlying human language that is an aspect of the *imago dei*.[37] It is thereby well-suited to serve as the interpreter's road map or guide as we attempt to "claim the new postmodern context for Christ."[38]

NOTES

1. Stanley Fish, *Is There a Text in This Class? The Authority of Interpretive Communities* (Cambridge: Harvard Univ. Press, 1980).

2. On authorial intent see N.T. Wright, *The New Testament and the People of God* (Minneapolis: Fortress, 1992), 58–64.

3. See G. Aichele, Jr., "On Postmodern Biblical Criticism and Exegesis: A Response to Robert Fowler," *Forum* 5/3 (1989): 32.

4. Numerous instances could be cited from the Bible and elsewhere of the world being moved and turned by the power of language: e.g., the Book of the Law and King Josiah, the Prophets Haggai and Zechariah and the remnant of Judah, the Apostle Peter at Pentecost, Peter the Hermit and Pope Urban II on the Crusades, Harriet Beecher Stowe and abolition, Martin Luther King, Jr. and civil rights.

5. The concept of the sufficiency of Scripture, however necessary to the Christian faith, is foreign to postmodernism. According to Fowler, "I'm not sure that the notion of canon can survive postmodernity. Whatever canon may have meant in antiquity, has it not become in modernity one of those figures of totality and completeness that is so distrusted by the postmodern?" (R.M. Fowler, "Postmodern Biblical Criticism," *Forum* 5/3 [1989]: 25)

6. Anthony C. Thiselton, *New forizons in Hermeneutics: The Theory and Practice of Transforming Biblical Reading* (Grand Rapids: Zondervan, 1992), 1; Wright, *New Testament and the People of God*, 81.

7. Thiselton, *New Horizons*, 5.

8. See Williston Walker, *A History of the Christian Church*, 3rd ed. (New York: Scribners, 1970), 186.

9. Thiselton, *New Horizons*, 124.

10. See, e.g., E. Ray Clendenen, "Discourse Strategies in Jeremiah 10:1-16," *Journal of Biblical Literature* 106 (1987): 401–8.

11. See, e.g., W. Houston, "What Did the Prophets Think They Were Doing? Speech Acts and Prophetic Discourse in the Old Testament," *Biblical Interpretation* 1 (1993): 167–88.

12. Thiselton, *New Horizons*, 16.

13. The particular model I have found most useful is the tagmemic model of Longacre. See Robert E. Longacre, "The Discourse Structure of the Flood Narrative," *Journal of the American Academy of Religion* 47 (1979): 89–133; idem, "A Spectrum and Profile Approach to Discourse Analysis," *Text* 1 (1981): 337–59; idem, *The Grammar of Discourse* (New York: Plenum, 1983); idem, "Interpreting Biblical Stories," *Discourse and Literature*, 3 vols., ed. T.A. van Dijk (Philadelphia: John Benjamins, 1985), 3.83–98; idem, *Joseph: A Story of Divine Providence — a Text Theoretical and Textlinguistic Analysis of Genesis 37 and 39–48* (Winona Lake, Ind.: Eisenbrauns, 1989).

14. This paper is a major revision of my article "Old Testament Prophecy as Hortatory Text: Examples from Malachi," *Journal of Translation and Textlinguistics* 6 (1993): 336–53. This section in particular is taken from that article.

15. Jonah clearly functions as a prophet in the book and is called a prophet in 2 Kings 14:25.

16. See Andrew E. Hill and John H. Walton, *Introduction to the Old Testament* (Grand Rapids: Zondervan, 1991), 313–14; Claus Westermann, *Basic Forms of Prophetic Speech*, trans. H.C. White (Philadelphia: Westminster, 1967), 45–47; G.M.

Tucker, "Prophecy and the Prophetic Literature," in *The Hebrew Bible and Its Modern Interpreters,* ed. Douglas A. Knight and Gene M. Tucker (Philadelphia/Chico, Calif.: Fortress/Scholars, 1985), 335–42.

17. Thomas G. Long, *Preaching and the Literary Forms of the Bible* (Philadelphia: Fortress, 1989), 12.

18. John Barton, *Reading the Old Testament: Method in Biblical Study* (Philadelphia: Westminster, 1984), 16. Although the terms are sometimes used synonymously, *discourse type* speaks of a universal system of parameters by which discourses from various cultures can be usefully categorized; *genre* describes particular types of literature occurring in a certain culture. Genre may be identified by the use of certain discourse strategies, patterns of organization, and grammatical features. See E.R. Wendland, *Language, Society, and Bible Translation* (Roggebaai, Cape Town: Bible Society of South Africa, 1985), 82–83. They may also be characterized by the use of a certain combination of discourse types.

19. Malachi, for example, is marked as hortatory by seven directives, at 1:10; 2:15, 16; 3:7, 10 (twice), 22.

20. Cf. C. Matthiessen and S.A. Thompson, "The Structure of Discourse and 'Subordination,' " in *Clause Combining in Grammar and Discourse,* ed. J. Haiman and S.A. Thompson (Philadelphia: Benjamins, 1988), 321, n. 27.

21. Longacre, *Joseph,* 120 offers an example of such a line of exhortation in Genesis 41:33-36 (p. 133), in which Joseph the Hebrew offers advice to the Egyptian Pharaoh in view of the coming famine:

And now, *let* Pharaoh *find* a wise man and *let* him *set* him over the land of Egypt. *Let* Pharaoh *act* and *let* him *appoint* overseers over the land and he will take a fifth of the produce during the plenty and *let* them *gather* food during the good years, and let them heap up grain under the hand of Pharaoh and they will guard it. And [motivation] it will be a food reserve for the land. Then the land won't be destroyed by the famine [situation].

22. Baldwin has made the unfortunate claim, "Unlike Zechariah, Malachi does not employ any particular literary structure in order to convey his meaning. The subjects with which he deals follow one another apparently haphazardly" (Joyce G. Baldwin, *Haggai, Zechariah, Malachi,* Tyndale Old Testament Commentary [Downers Grove, Ill.: InterVarsity, 1972], 214). This is clearly not the case. An improvement on the standard view that Malachi is a collection of six "disputations" (e.g., E. Pfeiffer, "Die Disputationsworte im Buche Maleachi," *Evangelische Theologie* 19 [1959]: 546–68) is E. Wendlands argument for a concentric structure ("Linear and Concentric Patterns in Malachi," *The Bible Translator* 36 [1985]: 108–21), refined in G.P. Hugenberger, *Marriage as a Covenant: A Study of Biblical Law and Ethics Governing Marriage Developed from the Perspective of Malachi* (Leiden, Netherlands: E.J. Brill, 1994), 24–25. Concentrating on form, however, these still fail to consider the notional structure of the book.

23. Longacre, *Joseph,* 64–118.

24. See M.L. Larson, *The Functions of Reported Speech in Discourse* (Dallas: Summer Institute of Linguistics, 1978), 77–85; Longacre, *Grammar of Discourse,* 30.

25. The quote formulas used with speeches of Judah function to mark speaker change and occur before the speech, whereas quote formulas in Yahweh speeches

occur after what they specify or in the middle of a quoted sentence (2:2). The only exception is in 1:4 where the formula uniquely begins with *Koh* ("Thus").

26. The method of paragraph analysis and the terminology employed here will be that of Robert E. Longacre ("An Apparatus for the Identification of Paragraph Types," *Notes on Translation* 15 [1980]: 5–22; idem, *Joseph*, 83–118). The primary constituents of paragraphs are taken to be sentences. The biblical Hebrew sentence is defined as having three slots — an obligatory independent clause preceded and followed by optional dependent clauses (i.e., by none, one, or several). According to this analytic model there are no Hebrew "compound sentences" as occur in that of F.I. Andersen, *The Sentence in Biblical Hebrew* (The Hague: Mouton, 1974).

27. Note, for example, the uses of the verbs *sub* ("return") and *gara* ("call") in the first constituent and again in the last movement of the book.

28. Waltke and O'Connor explain, "Rhetorical questions aim not to gain information but to give information with passion" (Bruce K. Waltke and Michael O'Connor, *An Introduction to Biblical Hebrew Syntax* [Winona Lake, Ind.: Eisenbrauns, 1990], 18.2g).

29. The imperfect in the first sentence "They will build" may be understood as modal expressing possibility (Waltke and O'Connor, *Introduction to Biblical Hebrew*, 31.4e) making this couplet an example of a conditional rather than an antithetical paragraph. This is less likely, however, since it would be unmarked.

30. Longacre, *Joseph*, 111–12.

31. For an analysis of the entire Book of Malachi see E. Ray Clendenen, "The Structure of Malachi: A Textlinguistic Study," *Criswell Theological Review* 2 (1987): 3–17; idem, "The Interpretation of Biblical Hebrew Hortatory Texts: A Text-linguistic Approach to the Book of Malachi" (Ph.D. diss., University of Texas at Arlington, 1989).

32. See the critique of this second point by J.P. Martin, "Toward a Post-Critical Paradigm," *New Testament Studies* 33 (1987): 370–85.

33. Ibid., 370.

34. W.D. Edgerton, *The Passion of Interpretation* (Louisville: Westminster/John Knox, 1992). See also Richard J. Neuhaus, *Biblical Interpretation in Crisis: The Ratzinger Conference on Bible and Church* (Grand Rapids: Eerdmans, 1989).

35. See the productive critique in Stanley J. Grenz, "Star Trek and the Next Generation: Postmodernism and the Future of Evangelical Theology," chapter 6 in this volume.

36. Wright, *New Testament and the People of God*, 13.

37. Note the similar commendation of W. Richter's method by J.W. Rogerson, "*Exegese als Literaturwissenschaft:* Revisited," in *Text, Methode und Grammatik* (St. Ottilien: EOS-Verlag, 1991), 386.

38. Grenz, "Star Trek and the Next Generation," 101.

9

The Bible in Stereo:
New Opportunities for Biblical
Interpretation in an A-Rational Age

Michael J. Glodo

As an evangelical writing to evangelicals, we approach the subject of postmodern biblical interpretation concerned to thread a course between the Scylla of not saying anything and the Charybdis of saying too much. This difficulty is compounded severely when one wants to say something positive.

William Larkin has stated that there is a succession of "questions which must be answered if evangelicals are to successfully cope with this new intellectual climate." By success Larkin means

> that the resulting hermeneutic will be able to avoid the twin dangers of obscurantism, no communication, and syncretism, the distortion of Scripture's message by a wrong appropriation of the cultural worldview, in this case the postmodern paradigm. Stated positively, a successful interpretation will articulate a message that is intelligible and relevant to postmodern culture and, at the same time, faithful to Scripture's content.[1]

Following the positive side of this formulation, our purpose will be to describe some windows of opportunity ahead and to stimulate some helpful conversation on these perceived opportunities. This

Michael J. Glodo is Assistant Professor of Old Testament at Reformed Theological Seminary in Orlando, Florida.

is not to ignore the radical skepticism and will to power among many postmodern thinkers, nor is it to mitigate the anti-God cult of the self which lies at its center. In spite of these concerns, this chapter will focus on some potentially positive developments. We must remain clear that, like all autonomous human thought, postmodernist thought is corrupt. This is absolutely essential to attempt any positive evaluations. But biblical interpreters can approach the new cultural paradigm with more than a "making-the-best-of-a-bad-situation" mentality.

Purpose

After briefly articulating the fundamental commitments behind my proposal, we will focus on two tendencies of postmodernism — the preference for image and the social construction of reality — and how those tendencies can play well into the hands of evangelical biblical interpretation.[2] In this process we will attempt to apply insights from Pierre Babin's *The New Era in Religious Communication*[3] in an effort to show how new doors are opened for the use of Scripture in the church.

Commitments

Several fundamental commitments simultaneously compel and restrain this attempt.

Scripture. The primary commitment behind this attempt is an orthodox view of Scripture. In fact, it is just such a view that compels this kind of effort. For Scripture is as much directed to this coming age as the receding one (Rom. 15:4).

History of Interpretation. The history of the interpretation of the Bible has been regarded by some as a comedy of errors.[4] Recent works have attempted to show that, in spite of the errors of the past, the ancients struggled with the fundamental questions with which we still wrestle.[5] A sensitivity to the latter persuades us that, to a limited extent, the history of interpretation is a study in paradigm shifts. These paradigm shifts are brought about partly by the inadequacy of the previous paradigms and partly by cultural shifts.[6] This means that we can look to postmodern developments, in spite of their overwhelmingly negative character, for what inadequacies they might reveal in the way things have been done.

It also means that just as God accommodated Scripture to the languages and cultures of the milieus in which it was inspired, so also interpretive paradigms develop out of the church's drive to make the

Bible perpetually intelligible and relevant in obedience to the Great Commission. This is not to say that Scripture and its interpretation are the same (especially with respect to inerrancy), but that interpretation should be modeled after Scripture. Therefore, with the proper limits against syncretism, we should welcome how new paradigms (even if they are largely wrong) may shed light upon how our interpretive strategy has imbibed of secular and anti-Christian influences.[7] This in no way implies that we should let go of what is valuable in the waning paradigm (in this case, modernity), but that we should welcome the light shined in dark corners by the new one.

Scripture, History, and Interpretation. This view of Scripture and the history of interpretation must be brought together under a Christian view of history in order to properly engage our world. God is the author of history, moving it toward His appointed end in obedience to His word. Insofar as the history of interpretation has been comprised of the engagement of the world by the church with the "living and active" Word of God, there is a proper attitude of expectation toward the new thought of postmodernism. What new opportunities is God presenting His church for the preached word (Rom. 10:14, 17) in this new day dawning?

Postmodernism and the Social Construct of Reality

It might be expected that the definition of postmodernism would be the most frequently discussed question in a volume such as this. Without my attempting an exclusive definition, or a definition at all, a few observations are in order.

Modernism, Postmodernism, and the Self

First, modernism can be characterized by the vesting of authority in the self. Whether following the external canons of empiricism or the internal canons of rationalism and romanticism, the modernist mind accomplished the enthronement of the individual as the final arbiter of truth. This individual authority asserts itself both against corporate authority and divine revelation either in denying them altogether or in subjecting them to the individual for validation.[8] While human autonomy is at the heart of every non-Christian thought system, modernism distinguished itself by its self-consciousness in this regard.

Secondly, postmodernism does not differ in its view of the self as authoritative. Therefore, postmodernism's uniqueness is not in its relativism. Relativism was the rule already.[9] It is not in the establishment of the individual as the final arbiter of truth that modernism and postmodernism differ, it is in their respective *concepts of truth.*

Foundationalism and Construct of Reality

For modernism, there is still a universe to be known, truth to be found. The project of the mind is to go about its discovery. For postmodernism, truth is not to be found but, rather, to be created. What is true is what one believes to be true. Reality is not to be perceived so much as to be conceived or constructed.

> The constructivists . . . say we do not have a "God's eye" view of nonhuman reality, never have had, never will have. They say we live in a symbolic world, a social reality that many people construct together and yet experience as the objective "real world." And they also tell us the earth is not a *single* symbolic world, but rather a vast universe of "multiple realities," because different groups of people construct different stories, and because different languages embody different ways of experiencing life.[10]

Thus seen, Lyotard's definition of postmodernism fits: "simplifying to the extreme . . . incredulity toward metanarratives."[11] There is a fundamental resistance to a unifying principle. There is a shift from foundationalism in epistemology to social construction. In the postmodern mind multiple realities exist, with "to each his own" a suitable motto.

Multiple independent and mutually exclusive realities are incompatible with a biblical view of reality. "Yet for us there is but one God, the Father, from whom are all things, and we exist for Him; and one Lord, Jesus Christ, by whom are all things, and we exist through Him" (1 Cor. 8:6, NASB). Christians live with the conviction of a transcendent reality established by the transcendent God. This is not to deny the variety of interpretations of truth among Bible-believing Christians. And though this variety is due partially to errors contained in each, it is due as well to the variety of endowments and experience contained in the various biblical perspectives. Insofar as these differing perspectives are true we can say that they are ultimately reconciled in God, though our limited faculties do not always make it apparent to us.

But put in sociological terms, the proclamation of the Gospel is the task of construing a reality, of telling people the way the world *really* is, of ordering people's perception of the world around the throne of God. The Bible's reality is variegated but exclusive versus the multiple realities of the constructivists. How can this be persuasively communicated in a postmodern age? How is this time in history uniquely addressed by the Scriptures?

The Postmodern Appetite for Image

One of the ripest fields is in the postmodern appetite for image. Admittedly, this appetite has been at the expense of a staple diet of rational thought. In describing the United States in the typographic age, Postman writes, "The resonances of the lineal, analytical structure of print, and in particular, of expository prose, could be felt everywhere."[12] However, loss of modernist rationality in discourse has accompanied the ascendance of image as the preferred form of public discourse. The important point here is that image has become preferred.

God, the Reality-Constructor

The church may respond to this challenge by seeing the creative word of God as a reality-builder. A fundamental dynamic in Scripture is the Bible's articulation of a transcendent, ultimate reality. This is frequently, if not usually, in contrast to perceived reality. Such is the case when the servant of Elisha sees the armies of God surrounding Dothan (2 Kings 6:8-17), or when the sanctuary makes sense out of the prosperity of the wicked in Psalm 73, when Isaiah sees the vision of God on His throne in the face of pending exile in Isaiah 6. It is found in the Deuteronomic historian's effort to provide hope to those in exile and in John's visions of God enthroned and ruling over the earth as written initially for late first-century Christians under intense persecution (Rev. 4–5). Everywhere in the Scriptures we are urged to look beyond the order which our own senses have construed and look "for the city which has foundations, whose architect and builder is God" (Heb. 11:10).

We don't naturally perceive this transcendent reality. Rather, God has established a host of metaphors and images through which we are to view it.

> God's relationship with his people is presented by means of a variety of metaphors that emphasize different aspects of that relationship. No one metaphor is capable of capturing the richness of God's nature or the wonder of his relationship with his creatures.[13]

The task of biblical interpretation may proceed in this post-modern age with a view to deconstructing false views and reconstructing (rather, proclaiming) true reality. And this can be done effectively through the images of Scripture. In fact, if our view of Scripture be right, the Bible should be able to "out-image" any contemporary imaging because of the divine character of Scripture and because of God, the end of Scripture.

Metaphors and the Social Construct of Reality

This suggestion not only concords well with the nature of biblical literature. It fits the general manner in which metaphors impact the way we live. An important work outside of biblical studies has suggested how our realities are significantly shaped by metaphors.[14] To be sure, Lakoff and Johnson reject "the possibility of any objective or absolute truth,"[15] a position untenable for evangelicals. However, we *may* say that all truth is relative to the Triune God. Everything that is derives its meaning and existence in relation to Him (Acts 17:28). And God's speech is determinative and true, even when He uses metaphors. Even with the limited biblical examples cited above and following, we can see the significant role metaphor plays in the Bible's constructing of reality.

Nothing But the Truth

Sensitivity to the significant image-character of Scripture places demands on an evangelical biblical hermeneutic that realizes its reality-building mandate, especially in an era where consensus worldviews among hearers are minimal. The challenge of the multiplied images of postmodernism may be confronted with the Bible's own multiplicity when we call the world not only to believe, but to imagine.

This new sensitivity will emphasize what is real over what is true. Whereas we as evangelicals might regard the terms "real" and "true" as synonyms, they will be understood as significantly different in a postmodern world. We must not abandon emphasis on the truth. Our suggestion of a stereophonic approach will include such emphasis. But the two terms will be understood as distinct by our hearers.

A metaphor-sensitive approach to reality building stands a chance to persuade the image-friendly/word-resistant postmodernist. It will also—and we emphasize this as vital—provide the connection to propositional truth for the word-resistant.[16] Sadly, but not outside providence, a wholesale frontal assault with propositional truth is less and less effective against the word-resistant. But God has provided in

Scripture a key for the back door — the metaphor-conveyed transcendent reality of Him and His kingdom.

The Whole Truth

A further benefit to a metaphor-sensitive hermeneutic will be its effectiveness in completing reality for the proposition dependent. One modernist contaminant in evangelical exegesis is the preference for proposition. Many consider the task of an exegete to be that of reformulating Scripture into propositions.[17] Preaching often consists of the explanation of words and sentences with little regard for biblical book context or literary forms of the text. It seems that our preference for proposition has made us image- and literature-illiterate. We understand words and sentences, but not imagery and literature. The result is a confusion between truth and precision.

The variety of metaphors of God, for instance, requires the preservation of that very variety in order to preserve the entirety of truth presented in them. Because of their richness, we never entirely see the full implications of each one. A single metaphor simultaneously hides and highlights different aspects of the thing it signifies.[18] Propositional approaches attempt to fit the biblical data into a system even when the metaphors are not easily compatible. For example, how can Jesus be both our husband and our brother? Since our summations of the metaphors are not the inspired Word of God and the metaphors themselves are, we should take care to let the metaphorical character stand without replacing it with reductions.

For example, a young man had some biophysical problems which led to severe psychological difficulties. However, he believed that his situation was the result of a theological/spiritual problem. But his desire for precision on some spiritual matters went well beyond the Bible's own statements. Although his subsequent medical treatment and counseling helped him significantly, another source of help has been his following a suggestion to read the Psalms and to write poetry. It was recommended in an attempt to redirect his aim to God as the end of truth.[19] Although most Christians are not in such dire straits, most could be given a more whole view of the truth by a hermeneutic balanced between image and proposition.

Babin's "Stereo Catechesis" and Biblical Interpretation

In a work not explicitly on the subject of biblical interpretation, Pierre Babin writes about the new media culture and religious communication.[20] Therein he sets forth a method for understanding the impact of the new audiovisual paradigm of popular communication upon religious communication. In the process he asks the question: "What affinity does the audiovisual language have with the gospel?"[21] This question is asked in the face of a youth culture which is "no longer attuned to abstract doctrinal formulas."[22] Through a series of encounters with Marshall McLuhan, Babin concludes that the audiovisual way is more than just a new form of communication. It significantly shapes the message of all, including religious, communication.

The "audiovisual way" is, in many respects, the same as what Neil Postman laments as the "ascendancy of the Age of Television."[23] Postman makes some important points, particularly about the arcane nature of most popular communication. Our interest here, as stated above, is to show how biblical interpretation can (biblically) capitalize upon this new way.

Those who labor in using the Bible in the church have felt the immense pressures brought to bear by our image-oriented culture.

> We are entering a time when putting on a show carries more weight than do values and underlying realities. Both the affective and the imaginative, strongly stimulated by audiovisual images, are becoming the central part of human and religious functioning.[24]

This is because, according to Babin, young people "are more interested in the covenant relationship than in dogmatic formulas. They are more interested in the beauty of God than in the proofs of God's existence."[25]

Does the Bible itself allow us any maneuvering room or any high ground, other than to require our hearers to become eighteenth-century people before they can understand and respond to its message?[26] After surveying the development of religious communication from the invention of the printing press to the present day, Babin summarizes:

> Protestantism was born with printing and has been the religion in which printing—the printed Bible, the catechism, newspapers, and journals—has played a vital part. The present crisis in these publications is undoubtedly a sign of a very deep crisis of identity. How is it possible to be a Protestant in a world in which radio and television are the easiest forms of communication?[27]

While Postman's contrast is between the Age of Typography and Age of Television, Babin sees these two ways of thinking not limited to particular media. He differentiates them first in terms of ground and figure and secondly as two schema of communication—alphabet and modulation.

Ground and Figure

Babin's primary preliminary distinction is the one between ground and figure in communication.

> The "figure" refers to what is the direct focus of our attention: the printed matter on the paper, the persons or action portrayed in photos or on the television screen. The "ground" in print media is the paper of a magazine, the white spaces, the layout, the contrast in titles, the grain in the photos, and even the publishing house and distribution outlets, which quietly signal who is publishing the material.[28]

In biblical exposition, figure would be the words (particularly the main points and sub-points of the sermon) while ground would be voice inflection, hand gestures, facial expressions and, to some extent, the entire worship service, and the church body itself.
According to Babin:

> McLuhan suggests that the ground—what frames and contextualizes explicit figures—is the determining component of the mediated message . . . it is often not the explicit message or the rationalistic arguments that are most important in communicating faith, but the deeper tones of feeling and background, aspects that hardly enter into our awareness.[29]

Whether we go as far as McLuhan in saying that ground is *the* determining component, this distinction can emphasize to us the important element of community in biblical interpretation. Jesus invited emphasis on the community as ground for the Gospel. "By this all men will know that you are My disciples, if you have love for one another" (John 13:35). While this statement may have more in mind the validation of followers of Christ, there is also expressed a truth-telling dimension to orthopraxy. Conduct is declarative.

If we appreciate both the influence of metaphor on the way we structure our existence and on the crucial role that ground plays in communication, we will not restrict to a mere figure of speech Paul's words "for even as the body is one and yet has many members, and all the members of the body, though they are many, are one body, so also is Christ" (1 Cor. 12:12, cf. Eph. 4:12). Christ is ὁ λόγος. This word function is maintained in His body the church as well as in His body the sacrament/ordinance (1 Cor. 10:16). This is not to commit the error of identification, but to admit that we need to appropriate the reality there represented and not limit such statements to mere figures of speech.

Schema of Alphabet and Modulation

Babin's second set of distinctions is between two basic schema of language. The first is the "scheme of modulation."[30] The language of modulation is a "language of ground."[31] His metaphor is the womb. The listener is surrounded by multisensory communication. This scheme is more affective and experience-oriented. Sense of belonging and security takes priority over truth. Interaction is more important than passive listening. Babin's hope is that "theologians become increasingly open to the language of modulation and discover its instruments of analysis."[32]

The second scheme of language is the "scheme of alphabet."[33] In this scheme, speaking is more important than listening and words are the dominant form of communication. Systematization of ideas and response through words predominate. And Babin reflects great esteem for this scheme when he states "the people of the West, including, above all, the French Cartesians, were to become, through the medium of this alphabet, the most gifted in the task of communicating clear ideas and arguments—to such an extent that they made it their principal form of communication."[34]

As Babin describes "modulation church" and the "alphabet church," one can barely resist smiling. Churches in our own experiences can be placed with some facility into either of these categories. The modulation church is less lit, has more stained glass, music resonates with rich repetitive harmonics, gestures are slow, sermons are short, ceremony is rich, and atmosphere replaces explanation. The alphabet church is full of light, pulpits are central, sermons are longer, hymns are complex and modern, and explanation predominates.[35]

The Stereophonic Way

Babin has analyzed faith formation and religious communication in an image-oriented world. His final proposal is that both are important and that the preferred way is a stereophonic way. Just as stereo sound combines melody and background lines to produce a synergistic sound, so also a stereophonic approach to faith formation proposes a balance of ground and figure, modulation and alphabet. Then, reflecting back on McLuhan's priority of ground over figure, Babin proposes

> that priority be given to the symbolic way and, at the same time, to functioning in stereo. Stereo has the specific attribute that two modulations, with different sources, result in a unified effect. . . . Applied to religious teaching, stereo means that we can speak two languages in a simultaneous but really quite different manner: the language of Guttenberg and the symbolic language.[36]

Conversely, he asserts that "the greatest catastrophe that can happen to communication today is for it to be governed by reason alone."[37]

Image and Word in Biblical Interpretation

When applied to the subject of biblical interpretation, this framework can address the evangelical dilemma in speaking the truth of Scripture to the image-driven postmodernist and its deep distrust of logocentrism — the dilemma between resistance and accommodation. Seeing the mixed word/image character of Scripture as analogous to the alphabet/modulation distinction of Babin can open up new opportunities for a postmodern use of the Bible.

Word and Image

Neil Postman, who laments the shift from type/word to image, thinks he finds a basis for his concern in the Bible.

> In studying the Bible as a young man, I found intimations of the idea that forms of media favor particular kinds of content and therefore are capable of taking command of a culture. I refer specifically to the Decalogue, the Second Commandment of which prohibits the Israelites from making concrete images of anything. "Thou shalt not make unto thee any graven image, any likeness of any thing that is in heaven above, or that is in the earth beneath, or that is in the water beneath the earth." I wondered then, as so many others

have, as to why the God of these people would have included instructions on how they were to symbolize, or not symbolize, their experience. It is a strange injunction to include as part of an ethical system *unless its author assumed a connection between forms of human communication and the quality of a culture.* We may hazard a guess that a people who are being asked to embrace an abstract, universal deity would be rendered unfit to do so by the habit of drawing pictures or making statues or depicting their ideas in any concrete, iconographic forms. The God of the Jews was to exist in the Word and through the Word, an unprecedented conception requiring the highest order of abstract thinking. Iconography thus became blasphemy so that a new kind of God could enter a culture. People like ourselves who are in the process of converting their culture from word-centered to image-centered might profit by reflecting on this Mosaic injunction.[38]

Postman admits the possibility that he may be wrong about this interpretation of the Bible. Though Postman is not a biblical scholar, there seems to be an evangelical impulse to "amen" his characterization. If so, that impulse reveals a significant lack of awareness that informs the exclusively negative assessment of an image-driven culture. We must be aware of several things. The concern Postman shares might be directed properly toward television, but not toward image in general.[39]

First of all, Moses recorded this law against images from the midst of a striking tactile-audiovisual display. The fire, smoke, and thunder surrounding Sinai were so awesome "that all the people who were in the camp trembled" (Ex. 19:16b). Once written, these laws were to be placed in an ornate box (the ark). This box was to be harbored in a structure that did not bear inscriptions, but in all of its elaborate construction was a pattern of God's habitation in heaven[40] (Ex. 25:40). Further, this visible box (though draped with a covering, Num. 4:5) was to lead Israel in their journey to the Promised Land, particularly as they entered into battle against their enemies (Num. 10:33, 35). Most importantly, it was from above the ark where God would speak to Moses concerning His will for Israel (Ex. 25:22; 30:6; Num. 7:89).

This law of Moses contained within it stipulations for celebrations, feasts, sacrifices, offerings, and other ceremonies. This law taught Israel about God's holiness through food and diseases. Although formulating objective criteria would be difficult, one could argue the larger portion of the Pentateuch has to do with symbols and images. Added to these explicit instances of image should be the image-like concreteness of Pentateuchal narratives. This recognition of image in the Bible also must be extended to the extensive poetry of the Old Testament, not to mention the shocking images of both New Testament and Old Testament apocalyptic literature and displays of the prophets with metaphorical intent (Isa. 20:2ff; Hosea 1:2ff).

Furthermore, the doctrine of general revelation is founded upon the image nature of revelation. God established in His design and calling the world into being metaphors through which He in turn revealed Himself. He didn't simply, as we do, look around for convenient analogies, but built the analogies into creation. There is a profound image-orientation to both general and special revelation.

With the proper sensitivities, one can see the Bible tailored to an image-driven culture. Biblical interpretation for a postmodernist, a-rational, age should neither be a choice of word over symbol nor of symbol over word, but rather the proper relation of the two. The image/word distinction should not be viewed as a continuum requiring placement on some point, but rather two ideas between which tension should be maintained. Psalm 19 may provide a model for such a "stereophonic" approach to biblical interpretation.

> The heavens are telling of the glory of God;
> And their expanse is declaring the work of His hands.
> Day to day pours forth speech,
> And night to night reveals knowledge.
> There is no speech, nor are there words;
> Their voice is not heard. . . .
> The law of the LORD is perfect, restoring the soul;
> The testimony of the LORD is sure, making wise the
> simple (Ps. 19:1-3, 7).

Justification: Christ, the Image/Word

Ultimate justification for such an interpretive approach comes from the person of Christ Himself. Jesus is ὁ Λογος (John 1:1) of God. He is the consummate statement of God to us (Heb. 1:1-2). But Jesus is also εἰκὼν τοῦ θεοῦ τοῦ ἀοράτου "the image of the invisible God" (Col. 1:15). Truth comes not only in word, but in image, embodiment.

For example, one might be perplexed in reading John 14:6.

"Jesus said to him, 'I am the way, and the truth, and the life; no one comes to the Father, but through Me.' " We can understand how a person could speak the truth, but how is it a person could *be* truth? The key is in understanding truth not simply in terms of propositions (1 Cor. 5:8; 1 John 1:6).

In describing a climactic encounter with McLuhan, Babin relates, "When I asked him whether the formula 'the medium is the message' could be applied to Christ, he replied at once, 'Of course. *That is the only case in which the medium and the message are perfectly identical.' "*[41] Such a statement surely has far-reaching implications, but in a profound, biblical sense it is true. In Christ are reconciled image and word (see figure 1).

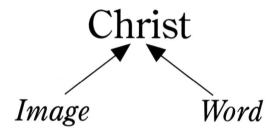

Christ

Image   *Word*

Image/Word Reconciled in Christ

Figure 1

The commandment against fashioning idols is not a commandment against image per se, but a prohibition against fashioning an exclusive image and therefore committing the idolatry of identification. For there was only one image that was exclusively representative of God—Christ Himself. "For in Him all the fulness of Deity dwells in bodily form" (Col. 2:9). And as the authoritative and final word of God to us (Heb. 1:2), Jesus in His person provides a model of biblical interpretation and Gospel communication.

The Bible in Stereo
What does the realization of the image/word nature of Scripture mean for biblical interpretation? Several bear mentioning.

Proposition Plus . . .
First, we should see that, to the extent we have preferred proposition over image in biblical exposition, we have been engaged in an

unbalanced approach. It would seem that, if such a preference exists (and it seems to me rampant in certain varieties of evangelicalism), it is a symptom of modernism.

> According to Spinoza and others who followed him in the Enlightenment, the Bible uses poetry and stories only to beguile the naive minds and pliant wills of the unenlightened masses. The truly enlightened thinker has no need of such devices. For such a person, rational and mathematical rigor will suffice in the search for truth.[42]

Just as Plato "disqualified all image-making activity . . . as intrinsically deceptive,"[43] also many evangelicals view imagination with suspicion. But the inspired writers of Scripture were extremely imaginative when they saw God as a rock, tower, fortress, shepherd, warrior, eagle. Image-ladenness is not found exclusively in figures of speech, but may also be counted in biblical narratives and their pervasive intertextuality. In some ways this is related to what has been called typology, but is also revealed in the creative purposes of narrative as rediscovered in recent years among many in the critical school and a growing number of evangelicals.[44] Such approaches reveal to us how much is going on in biblical narratives besides types and exemplars.[45]

A proper interpretive approach, especially in an image-oriented culture, must receive gladly the rich imagery God has provided in Scripture as an indication that He anticipated this day in His sufficient Word. There is currently a growing appreciation of biblical imagery among evangelical scholars. A major dictionary of biblical imagery is in the beginning stages of production.[46] At least one major work on a particular biblical image is now available.[47] Other works have shown a serious reengagement of the symbolic nature of much of the Pentateuch while avoiding the allegorical excesses of the past.[48]

Image/Word Dialogue

Second, this image/word sensitivity should produce an integrative approach to the Bible where word informs image and *vice versa*. This dialogue can be expressed as in figure 2 below.

The "word" (i.e., propositional, didactic) forms of Scripture must be enriched and vivified by the "image" forms as well as the latter being controlled and organized by the former. What makes an image-

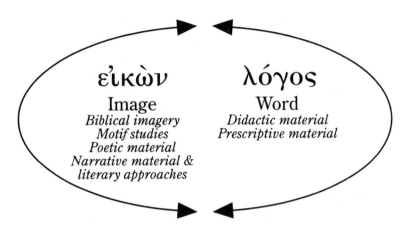

Image/Word Dialogue within the Bible

Figure 2

driven culture arcane or cabalistic (a la Postman) is not its image-drivenness, but the disconnection of image from word. Images become contentless or, worse, connected to propositions to which they bear no relation. An unrestrained dive into the image-character of the Bible without the proper dialogue with word could result in the same arcaneness. *But word uninformed by image will bear the marks of the modernist who proclaims it.*

Imaging God as Image-Maker

Third, biblical interpreters need to be imaginative. The inspired writers give us examples to follow. Our interpretation is not infallible and must always be conducted under the authority and authorial intention of the original authors, but we should interpret Scripture in light of our own concrete realities. This impacts the expository task. Exposition in a postmodern setting should be done in self-conscious reflection upon the connections between Scripture and the concrete experiences of listeners.

Just as God's creative word established a world that mirrored His presence, so also as images of God we should creatively order God's world through His Word. Evangelicals have reacted negatively, and quite appropriately so, to the demythologizers of Scripture. But we may have lost something in the process—something we would do well to recover.

Our rejection of myth may well have caused us not only to cast out the derailed myth but in doing so have moved us to do injustice to the God-given human faculty of imagination and the stories that proceed from it. If we impose on the revelation a literary form that is not there, in effect deciding that God would not have used such literary forms, we may be trying to be wiser than God. If God did not abandon human fantasy after the fall, neither should we. If God honored this human gift in disclosing his will, we should accept it as included in our obedience of faith.[49]

We may find ourselves newly aware of certain literary forms in the Bible if we can reawaken imagination. This must be done with extreme care, with the burden of proof upon establishing authorial intention of those forms. However,

human fantasy should therefore not be suppressed but should be brought into line with God's will. This happens when gifted people exercise their full liberty as children of God. God bless our storytellers.[50]

Only the Christian with an orthodox view of Scripture can attempt this without syncretism. But it does provide hope in the face of the new paradigm of postmodernism.

The Christian alternative to rationalism is not a re-mythologizing of our worldview and of our thinking. Irrationalism, mysticism, the culture of feeling, etc., in whatever form they appear, are no remedy against the evils of rationalism. ... The Christian alternative to mystical and mythologizing thinking is also not a moderate theological or neo-rationalism.[51]

We should seek (legitimate) connections between the Bible and our contemporary world. The task of illustrating biblical truths is not simply attempting to make things more interesting and clear, but it is to model the Bible itself. And in doing so, we will address another negative symptom of modernism—the nature/grace dichotomy. And with a proper dialogue between image and word, we stand a chance to correct a prevalent postmodern heresy—the nature/grace synonymy.

Word/Image in Worship

This image-sensitive approach to the Bible also can have positive benefits for the worship life of the church. A dialogical relationship similar to that above can be proposed as in figure 3 below.

Out of the Protestant reformational concern not to vest the sacraments with autosoterism, evangelicals have neglected the particular

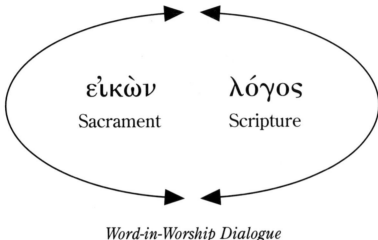

εἰκὼν   λόγος

Sacrament   Scripture

Word-in-Worship Dialogue

Figure 3

powers of image to grip and inform them. There seems to be some stirrings of sacramental renewal among evangelicals, but this may be due more to the migration of many of its children to sacerdotal traditions than to a renewed appreciation for the power of image. In the Reformed tradition, for example, there has always been the insistence upon the preaching of the Word to accompany the sacraments and upon the primacy of that preached Word. Other images could be discussed under this head as well (the role and nature of singing, the use of liturgy, church architecture etc.).

Participation is a key element in this dialogical. The word emphasis eliminates or significantly delays participation. The sacraments weave word and image together in participation.

Divine Construct of Reality

Finally, a proper image/word should be directed at the heart of the postmodern distinctive—the social construction of reality. Postmodernists choose a constructed reality, at least partly, because of the overwhelming task of making sense of their world.[52] The Christian community must be involved in the task of "re-pristining" image inside the community (insofar as it has imbibed of postmodernism) and for those to whom it wishes to speak outside. This is not to be done like popular media images, separated from truth, but as truth. This dialogue may be expressed as figure 4.

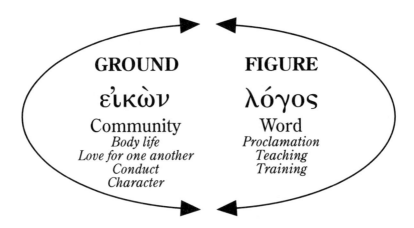

Word and Community: Reality Dialogue

Figure 4

This means that the community of faith needs to embrace its responsibility to "create a reality" — to be heaven on earth, to be the visible manifestation of the kingdom of God.

As Babin puts it:

The incarnation of the Christian message in different cultural epochs, each characterized by different media, has introduced not just a new way of transmitting a message (print or electronic, for example), but a new form of Christian existence and a new form of the church. Unless there is this continual total transformation, the Christian message and Christ himself are not communicated.[53]

For example, in attempting to explain the location of a stereophonic word/image approach to the Bible in the *logos/icon* of Christ, we may be challenged with the fact that we no longer have the body of Christ with us. However, we must remember that the church *is* the body of Christ, and we often come to view this as a mere figure of speech and not a metaphor by which to live.

In summary, the approach we are suggesting would have an overall character something like that illustrated in figure 5 below.

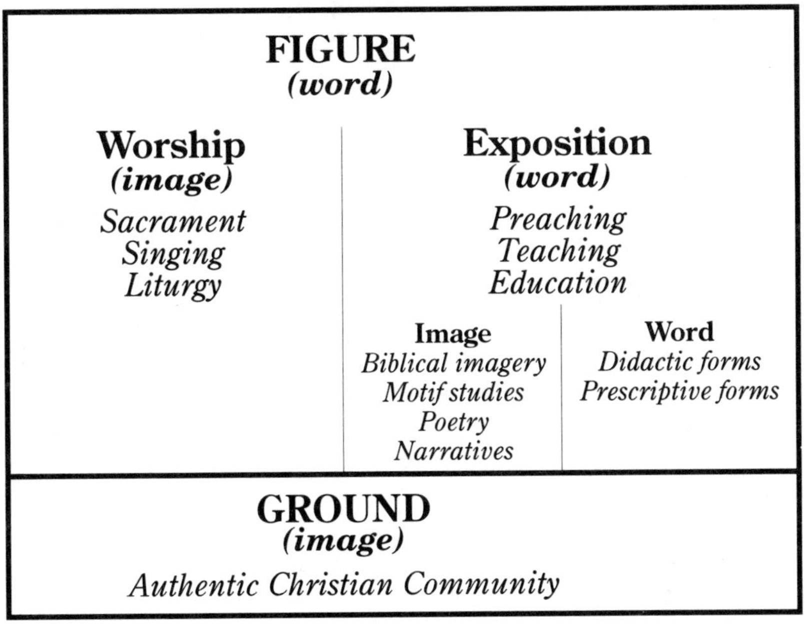

FIGURE
(word)

Worship *(image)*	**Exposition** *(word)*
Sacrament	*Preaching*
Singing	*Teaching*
Liturgy	*Education*

Image	**Word**
Biblical imagery	*Didactic forms*
Motif studies	*Prescriptive forms*
Poetry	
Narratives	

GROUND
(image)

Authentic Christian Community

Comprehensive Diagram

Figure 5

This visual way of portraying things demonstrates how differently all of the scenarios depicted above could function in the context of the whole.

Conclusion: A Hermeneutic of Imagination

Because this essay is intended to be more suggestive than conclusive, the proposals and problems described above will finalize nothing and create many questions and needs for qualification. But evangelical hermeneutics must appropriate the great possibilities presented by the image character of Scripture. We may call this movement a "hermeneutic of imagery," but it is perhaps better termed a "hermeneutic of imagination" because it makes demands upon the imaginations of Bible interpreters. Such imagining must be done within the constraints of the grammatico-historical method and within the bounds of orthodox theology. Those not feeling those constraints have already begun this process in earnest.[54] As evangelicals we should not shy away from exercising our creative capacities because others exercise them autonomously.

"Taking every thought captive to Christ" (2 Cor. 10:5) should restrain our autonomous imaginations. But approaching the Bible under the freedom of the truth (John 8:32) should also be a fantastically liberating experience, imaginative faculties included.

> A biblically Christian conception of imagination will distinguish imagining from perceptual error, from imaging and from being an oracle of truth. Imaginative human activity is quite distinct from sensing or thinking but is also a bona fide activity interrelated with all human functioning. Imagining is a gift of God with which humans make-believe things. . . . Imagination is meant to be an elementary, important, residual moment in everything God's adopted children do. Imagination becomes a curse only if it becomes an exercise in vanity.[55]

Larkin asks, "Can evangelicals find a biblical metaphor or series of metaphors to commend to the postmodern age a fully and finally authoritative Word of God?"[56] It seems uncertain whether we will find an acceptable metaphor for Scripture. But we can find metaphors for God Himself, in keeping with His richness and the beauty and the richness of His Word. Further, general revelation not only functions to condemn those who do not honor God (Rom. 1:18-21), but it invites us to imagine (image) God—to see pictures of God in our world (Ps. 19:1-6). This is not idol-making. This is finding God where He has manifested his reflection in our world. This is mirror gazing until "we shall see face to face."

We can learn much from postmodernism. As Veith has said:

> Confessional Christians can also appropriate the insights of postmodern scholarship by taking sin seriously and emphasizing the epistemological implications of the Fall. Human reason *is* inadequate, as the postmodernists say; but Christians base their beliefs not on reason but revelation. We *are* wholly dependent upon language, as the postmodernists say; but Christians base their faith on God's language, that is, the Bible as the Word of God. Postmodernists say that meaning can only be determined from within an "interpretive community." For Christians, the church is their interpretive community.[57]

What is the proper role for imagination in the interpretation of Scripture within orthodoxy? And, is an evangelical "metaphorical theology" possible? If so, its form and method would require serious thought. That task will be left for the creative community of God's people living in the transcendent reality brought to us by the living and active word of God.

NOTES

1. William J. Larkin, Jr., "Culture, Scripture's Meaning, and Biblical Authority: Critical Hermeneutics for the 90's," *Bulletin for Biblical Research* 2 (1992): 174.

2. For purposes of this paper, several brief definitions are in order. "Modern" is used here to refer to the period of history now drawing to a close. "Modernism" is the ideology which characterized that period and which consisted in, among other things, a belief in the inevitability of progress through technology, and a view of the universe as a closed system. "Postmodern" refers to the period of time which is upon us. "Postmodernism" is the ideology that characterizes this age, the essence of which will be discussed below. "Postmodernist" refers to someone adhering to postmodernism.

3. Pierre Babin with Mercedes Iannone, *The New Era in Religious Communication* (Philadelphia: Fortress, 1991).

4. E.g., "And though we shall be compelled to notice the many aberrations of exegetical theology, we shall also see that scarcely in any age has it been absolutely fruitless. . . . Devious as has been the path of exegesis, it has gathered multitudes of treasures in the course of its wanderings" (Frederic W. Farrar, *History of Interpretation* [New York: Dutton, 1886], 14–15).

5. E.g., David S. Dockery, *Biblical Interpretation Then and Now: Contemporary Hermeneutics in the Light of the Early Church* (Grand Rapids: Baker, 1992), and Moises Silva, *Has the Church Misread the Bible? The History of Interpretation in the Light of Current Issues,* Foundations of Contemporary Interpretation, vol. 1 (Grand Rapids: Zondervan, 1987).

6. For an excellent overview of the connection between Thomas Kuhn, *The Structure of Scientific Revolutions,* 2nd ed. (Chicago: Univ. of Chicago Press, 1962/70) and its applicability to biblical interpretation, see Vern S. Poythress, *Science and Hermeneutic: Implications of Scientific Method for Biblical Interpretation,* Foundations of Contemporary Interpretation, vol. 6 (Grand Rapids: Zondervan, 1988).

7. E.g., how imperialist influences led early Biblical Theology proponents to assert the absolute uniqueness of biblical religion to the detriment of comparative studies. Or how empiricist views of word meaning have led to word study fallacies. See Thomas C. Oden's similar sentiments concerning American fundamentalism in *After Modernity . . . What? Agenda for Theology* (Grand Rapids: Zondervan, 1990), 68.

8. For an excellent discussion of the affinities of empiricism, rationalism, and romanticism, see Roger Lundin, *The Culture of Interpretation: A Christian Encounter with Postmodern Critical Theory* (Grand Rapids: Eerdmans, 1993), 31–52.

9. This statement will not be agreed with by all. The works by Anderson, Lundin, and Veith referenced herein provide the basis on which the statement is made.

10. Walter Truett Anderson, *Reality Isn't What It Used to Be: Theatrical Politics, Ready-to-Wear Religion, Global Myths, Primitive Chic, and Other Wonders of the Postmodern World* (San Francisco: HarperCollins, 1990), x–xi. Anderson asserts the social construction of reality is the distinguishing feature between modern and postmodern thought. The standard work on the social construct of reality per se is Peter Berger and Thomas Luckmann, *The Social Construction of Reality: A Treatise in the Sociology of Knowledge* (New York: Doubleday, 1966).

11. Jean Francois Lyotard, *The Postmodern Condition: A Report on Knowledge,* trans. Geoff Bennington and Brian Massumi (Minneapolis: Univ. of Minnesota Press, 1984), xxiii–xxiv as cited in Lundin, *The Culture of Interpretation,* 4.

12. Neil Postman, *Amusing Ourselves to Death: Public Discourse in the Age of Show Business* (New York: Penguin, 1985), 41. He does not realize there *is* linearity (albeit frequently irrational) in a string of images presented together. For instance, there is no necessary logical or causal relationship between stories placed on the front page of a newspaper, but the effect upon the reader is the establishment of some connection. For instance, a recent newspaper contained a story about the murder of an abortion doctor by an anti-abortion protester on the same page as the story of another abortion doctor's murder for which no suspect or motive had been found. The implication was that the second case involved an anti-abortion protester, in spite of the fact that it was later revealed to be robbery-related.

13. Tremper Longman III, "Current Issues in Biblical Theology: An Old Testament Perspective," paper presented at the annual meeting of the Institute for Biblical Research, Washington, D.C., November 1994.

14. George Lakoff and Mark Johnson, *Metaphors We Live By* (Chicago: Univ. of Chicago Press, 1980).

15. Ibid., x.

16. Others in the evangelical community are emphasizing the critical need for this task. E.g., David F. Wells, *No Place for Truth: Or, Whatever Happened to Evangelical Theology?* (Grand Rapids: Eerdmans, 1993).

17. Even one so dear to me and my own tradition described the task of systematic theology as "the exhibition of the facts of scripture in their *proper* order and relation" (Charles Hodge, *Systematic Theology*, 3 vols. [1871-73; reprint, Grand Rapids: Eerdmans, 1982], 1:19, emphasis mine).

18. Lakoff and Johnson, *Metaphors We Live By,* 10–13.

19. We may look toward the Puritans for a way out of this modernist propensity. The grand height of theological expression in their writing in no way surpasses their hymns and, in the case of Bunyan, similes. As was once said of America's lack of literary greatness, it may well be said of evangelicalism — we don't have enough dead poets.

20. Babin with Iannone, *New Era in Religious Communication.*

21. Ibid., 3.

22. Ibid.

23. Postman, *Amusing Ourselves to Death,* 8.

24. Babin with Iannone, *New Era in Religious Communication,* 13.

25. Ibid., 14.

26. Of course, such a statement in itself reveals a modern notion. If we are to require a complete reorientation of hearers of the Word, to what epoch would we reorient them — preexilic Israel, New Testament church, etc.? If our preference is for

the mid-eighteenth century, this might reflect a thoroughly modern assumption about the superiority of the modern age to all others.

27. Richard Molard, *Horizons Protestants* (June 1975), 3, cited in Babin, *New Era in Religious Communication,* 25.

28. Babin, *New Era in Religious Communication,* 8.

29. Ibid., 8–9.

30. Ibid., 77ff.

31. Ibid., 81.

32. Ibid., 88.

33. Ibid., 84ff.

34. Ibid., 85.

35. Ibid., 89–90.

36. Ibid., 182.

37. Ibid., 104.

38. Postman, *Amusing Ourselves to Death,* 9. Emphasis his.

39. In fact, the problem with television and other "immediate" visual media is that they are too literal. The literalness neutralizes the imagination, which is much more active in less literally-presented images. See chapter 18, "Theology in a Postmodern Culture: Implications of a Video-Dependent Society," by William E. Brown in this volume.

40. For the correlation between the tabernacle and its furnishings and the heavenly courts of God, see Meredith G. Kline, *Images of the Spirit* (South Hamilton, Mass.: M.G. Kline, 1988), 13–56; and Vern S. Poythress, *The Shadow of Christ and the Law of Moses* (Brentwood, Tenn.: Wolgemuth and Hyatt, 1991), 9–68.

41. Babin, *New Era in Religious Communication,* 6, emphasis mine.

42. Lundin, *Culture of Interpretation,* 44–45.

43. Calvin Seerveld, "Imagination" in *New Dictionary of Theology,* ed. Sinclair B. Ferguson and David F. Wright (Downers Grove, Ill.: InterVarsity, 1988), 329.

44. Worthy examples of the latter are Tremper Longman III, *Literary Approaches to Biblical Interpretation,* Foundations of Contemporary Hermeneutics, vol. 3 (Grand Rapids: Zondervan, 1987); and Richard L. Pratt, Jr., *He Gave Us Stories: The Bible Student's Guide to Interpreting Old Testament Narratives* (Nashville: Wolgemuth and Hyatt, 1990).

45. In a not so unusual attempt at exemplarism, a well-known evangelical figure was recently heard pointing out how the Gadarene demoniac was naked while possessed and clothed himself when he was in his right mind.

46. Leland Ryken, Tremper Longman III, and James C. Wilhoit, eds., *Dictionary of Biblical Imagery* (Downers Grove, Ill.: InterVarsity, forthcoming).

47. Tremper Longman III and Daniel Reid, *God Is a Warrior: Studies in Old Testament Biblical Theology* (Grand Rapids: Zondervan, 1995).

48. For example, Poythress, *Shadow of Christ in the Law of Moses;* and James B. Jordan, *Through New Eyes: Developing a Biblical View of the World* (Nashville: Wolgemuth and Hyatt, 1988).

49. Paul G. Schrotenboer, "The Bible and Myth," *REC Theological Forum* 21/2 (May 1993): 10.

50. Ibid., 12.

51. Andries Troost, "Myth and Reason," *REC Theological Forum* 21/2 (May 1993): 12–18.

52. According to Anderson, *Reality Isn't What It Used to Be,* one of the chief factors in the development of the constructivist view is exposure to people and groups which defy one's native organizing system. "Globalizing processes require us to renegotiate our relationships with familiar cultural forms" (p. 25).

53. Babin with Iannone, *New Era in Religious Communication,* 8.

54. E.g., Sallie McFague, *Metaphorical Theology: Models of God in Religious Language* (Philadelphia: Fortress, 1982) and several works by Walter Brueggemann including *Texts Under Negotiation: The Bible and Postmodern Imagination* (Philadelphia: Fortress, 1993).

55. Seerveld, "Imagination," 331.

56. Larkin, "Culture, Scripture's Meaning, and Biblical Authority," 177.

57. Gene Edward Veith, Jr., *Postmodern Times: A Christian Guide to Contemporary Thought and Culture* (Wheaton, Ill.: Crossway, 1994), 221.

10

The Mystery of Paul's Theologizing: A Postmodern Experiment[1]

Carey C. Newman

What do Sherlock Holmes and the Apostle Paul have in common? This chapter provides the "obvious" answer as it utilizes the genre of fictional detective stories to develop a reading strategy for the Pauline corpus.[2] At first blush, juxtaposing Sherlock Holmes with the great apostle appears comical, singular and, possibly, even criminal. Despite fears about exegetical frivolity, this attempt is made in good faith. The appropriateness of employing mystery story as a reading strategy resides in its ability (1) to illumine the plotting of Paul's pretextual story world, (2) to follow Paul as he thinks through the implications inherent in his story world to draft letters, and (3) to model our act of reading. Two suggestive clues drive my abduction of Paul.

Paul's invocation of "mystery" may well be more than just a passing trifle. He characterizes his Gospel as wisdom wrapped in "mystery" (1 Cor. 2:7; Col. 4:3). The Gospel centers in the surprising and unexpected way in which the death and resurrection of Jesus worked out the hidden, secret, mysterious purposes of God for the world (Rom. 16:25; Eph. 1:9; 6:19; Col. 1:26). The firsthand encounter with the risen Jesus wove Paul's life into the unfolding mystery of God and, further, uniquely endowed him to explain to the nations the paradoxical way in which God had chosen to redeem the world (Eph.

Carey C. Newman is Assistant Professor of New Testament Interpretation at The Southern Baptist Theological Seminary in Louisville, Kentucky.

3:3-4, 9). The continuing mystical presence of the risen Jesus in the church and the individual believer entangles both in the intriguing adventure of Gospel expansion (Eph. 5:32; Col. 1:27; 2:2; 1 Tim. 3:9, 16). The events of the end of the world also properly belong to this mysterious drama: God's uncanny future dealings with Israel, the appearance of that enigmatic eschatological criminal (the man of law-lessness), and the Parousia all unite to form the final explanation (Rom. 11:25; 2 Thes. 2:7; 1 Cor. 15:51). From Paul's vantage, the misty, mysterious purposes of God, which for so long have been a complete and utter riddle, have, in the cross and resurrection of Jesus, found substantive explanation. Paul's lexical juxtaposition of "mystery" with revelation, Gospel, apostleship, mission, and Parousia creates, at the very least, an intriguing semantic state of affairs that merits further investigation.

We find further precedent for the present escapade in the others who have purloined the detective story for hermeneutical ends. While G.K. Chesterton, Ronald Knox, Dorothy Sayers, and P.D. James actively blurred the lines between theology and mystery story, it has been the literary critics who have exploited the power of the mystery story for hermeneutics. Tzvetan Todorov's structural analysis of whodunits maps the generic terrain of novels, suspense, and thrillers, while Peter Brooks, building on Todorov, discovers in detective fiction the narrative of all narratives because of the way it so clearly betrays plotting, reading, and, by extension, living.[3] Jacques Lacan, Jacques Derrida, and Barbara Johnson all found themselves intertwined in a web of discourse with the mystery story behaving intersubjectively.[4] Lacan uses the mystery story as a semiotic parable on the way in which the signifier controls the signified. Derrida puts the mystery story to deconstructive ends, celebrating the ellipses, diversions, and contradictions inherent within it. Barbara Johnson completes the trilogy; she frolics in the infinite regresses created by successive readings. In another direction, Thomas Sebeok and Umberto Eco have shown the mystery story to be correlated positively with the logical and scientific methods of C.S. Pierce and Karl Popper.[5] Paul's suggestive use of "mystery," when combined with the hermeneutical value of detective fiction, seems to be sufficient grounds to open an initial investigation.

Holmes as Hermeneutician

Sherlock Holmes is certainly the most beloved fictional detective. The Holmes canon consists of some fifty-six short stories and four novels. Although Holmes is the creation of Arthur Conan Doyle, the author is clearly dependent on Edgar Allan Poe and the latter's trilogy of stories involving the first "real" detective, Chevalier Auguste Dupin. Of the many stories, or even combination of stories, which could joyfully occupy our time, we have only space enough in this investigation to make some cursory observations about the nature of the mystery story as conceived by Doyle and of the activity of his celebrated sleuth.

The Structure of a Holmesian Mystery Story[6]

The Holmes cycle is episodic in character.[7] The discourse of each episode commences in the middle of the story. Holmes learns of some singular events *which have already occurred*. These events form the initial sequence of the story. It matters not what the events were, or even if there was some violation of law; what counts is that the events are bizarre, odd, strange, peculiar, unusual, remarkable, or queer. As related to Holmes, an unidentified malevolent force has disturbed an equilibrium or has created a deprivation which needs redress and restoration. The activity of the unknown agent (or agents) has left the scene in a state of disarray. What *is* known stands disconnected and garbled, so much so, that the events are deemed a "mystery." The who, why, how of the equilibrium's disturbance is unknown to the victim, the interested parties, Watson and, initially, Holmes.

After learning of the events and deciding that their singular character merits his powers of detection, Holmes, with his faithful companion and chronicler Watson, sets out to explain the unexplained. Holmes' hermeneutical quest constitutes the middle sequence of the story and forms the majority of the discourse. Holmes, almost always, successfully becomes the agent through whom the who, why, and how of the curious events become properly ordered.

Holmes is helped by his common sense, his knowledge of certain disciplines of learning, and even at times by Watson. The greatest and, in reality, only true helper to Holmes is, however, his own "logical" prowess. Bordering on the unnatural, Holmes' uncanny abilities routinely amaze all involved. Holmes meets up with opposition in two forms — deceit and ignorance. He sometimes encounters, either directly or indirectly, the principals who are, either actively or passively, still involved in the web of deceit. Holmes also faces the "official" detectives of the police, who, although they sometimes join with Holmes to oppose the malevolent force(s), never fully enter in as Holmes' helpers. They ultimately are merely foils for his interpretive faculties. Despite the impediments of deceit and ignorance, Holmes (re)solves the case through his powers of detection.

Having thoroughly triumphed over confusion, Holmes seeks to restore the equilibrium—but in a fashion unique to his own sense of justice and his status as an "unofficial" adviser. The discovery, entrapment, capture, confession, and final disposition of the forces/powers who initially caused the disequilibrium constitute the story's final sequence. This part of the story typically occupies only a small part of the discourse and sometimes is only partially narrated. The transformation from an unexplained and/or misunderstood disequilibrium to a renewed tranquility by the interpretive charismas of Holmes conquers the disarray created during the transformation from peace to disequilibrium enacted by the sinister forces. This pattern constitutes the episodic structure of a Holmes mystery story.

The pattern can be easily detected in *Silver Blaze.* Only a short time before the running of the Wessex Cup, Holmes learns of the disappearance of the prohibitive favorite, a horse named Silver Blaze, and the accompanying death of the trainer. The case is a complete mystery because no one knows who stole the horse, who, how, or why the trainer was killed, and why the horse has not been found, either dead or alive. Holmes travels to the scene where he faces three additional opponents: (1) the skepticism of the owner of Silver Blaze; (2) the alternative and premature explanation of detective Lestrade, who is convinced he has the guilty party in custody, though he freely admits the evidence is circumstantial and his explanation cannot account for the evidence as it stands; and (3) the trainer of the neighboring stable, who, though taking no part in either the theft of the horse nor in the death of its trainer, has hidden the horse. Holmes is helped by Watson at one key juncture, but only in a way that "saves time." The major portion of the discourse is devoted to Holmes (re)solving the case. His solution explains the who, why, and how of the horse's abduction and the trainer's death. Based upon his (re)solution, Holmes enacts a series of events which will transform the skepticism of the owner into genuine admiration, demonstrate the stillborn nature of Lestrade's detective "imagination," and force the trainer at the competitive stable to relinquish the horse in time to run in the Wessex Cup.

Steps in Holmesian Epistemology[8]

(1) The first step Holmes takes is to acquire data. This occurs through newspaper accounts, personal communication to him via

telegram/letter, or, most often, through a personal visit. Holmes usually enlarges the pool of information through his own interrogations, observations, and inspections. The important fact is that there is a *narrative* disclosure of some kind; a *story* is told in which there are gaps and erasures, and in which there is disparate, disconnected and, oftentimes overlooked, commonplace pieces of information. Although the apparent disconnectedness of the data mystifies those who seek some solution, or points in the direction of some "easy" solution which cannot account for all the data, Holmes is undaunted in the face of such profusion and disarray. The data he collects, the testimony he receives, and the inspections he makes only serve at the surface level of the discourse to complicate the possibility for solution, although this imposed delay actually is the *only* path to the *only* proper conclusion.

(2) Holmes retraces the steps of the mysterious events. Though most of the time when he travels to the scene he also collects more data, the real importance of going to the scene is so that he can retrace the contours of the events themselves. At this stage he is scoffed at by the police or by some involved party, and Holmes' fixation on following the exact tracings of the events is pawned off as nothing other than an expression of his eccentricity. Holmes' apparent madness masks his method. Repetition and reenactment uncover clues missed by the police or lead to the crucial fulcrum upon which the previously unexplained turns. The net effect of Holmes' relentless reenactment of the eventful steps inexorably leads him to recognition; repetition is a hermeneutically full act.

(3) Holmes reconstructs a *prior coherent narrative* which explains the *second seemingly conflicted discourse*. When we, with Holmes, first learn of the mysterious events, we are convinced that the surface discourse cannot stand as told, for something must be untrue or inconsistent. But it is because Holmes treats what he is told or gleans with all seriousness, however inconsistent or however improbable it may seem to be at the surface, that he is enabled to discern further clues and to formulate that explanation which reconciles all that at first appeared inconsistent. It is important at this stage to examine carefully the "logic" of Holmes' reconstructive act.

Deduction	*Induction*	*Abduction*
All p are q (rule)	p (case)	All p are q (rule)
p (case)	q (result)	q (result)
— —	— —	— —
therefore q (result)	All p are q (rule)	p (case)

Most think Holmes to be the purveyor of deductive logic. He gets all the facts and from them deduces the solution. Holmes himself even indicates as much. Surprisingly, though, only in a few places can Holmes' logic in any way be deemed deductive. Careful analysis reveals Holmes' reasoning to follow what C.S. Pierce calls abduction, or retroduction, the process of reasoning backwards. Abduction should be contrasted with its two siblings, deduction and induction.

Deduction syllogistically moves from rule and case to result; induction moves from case and result to rule; abduction works from rule and result to case. Of the three moves, only abduction seeks the prior, *singular* antecedent cause.

That Holmes works from result to cause invites risk and potential error. Abduction commits the fallacy of affirming the consequent:[9] the presence of q does not *necessarily* dictate the presence of p, for there could be other possible explanations for q than the one suggested. And yet this is exactly how science proceeds. As the certainty of any potential reconstruction plummets, its heuristic merit soars. It indeed is ironic that hermeneutical fruitfulness increases at the very moment certainty diminishes.[10]

Holmes' abductive formulation of an hypothesis should not be confused with guesswork. Holmes abhors guessing. The data itself, however conflicted and inconsistent it may appear, *suggests its own explanation.* Holmes was able to decode the suggestive data because he, like Pierce, functionally construed human beings as symbols, the world as full of signs, and the universe as some grand argument. Holmes' uncanny powers to tell others of their own profoundly private thoughts, to recount what had happened without having been there, and to predict with ghostly accuracy what was yet to unfold resides in his decoding of the connectedness of signs. He followed the signs where they led him. Therefore, based upon the suggestive peculiar data, Holmes formulates a prior coherent narrative (p) which explains the subsequent apparently inconsistent discourse (q).

(4) Holmes next tests his hypothetical reconstruction. Can his reconstructed narrative explain other seemingly odd items? In *Silver Blaze* he tests his explanation of the previously unexplained in three ways. He digs in the mud for a candle—and "finds" it, much to the amazement of the police and Watson, precisely because he *suspected* it to be there. He further supposes that the tracks of the missing horse should be found some distance from the scene of the death of the trainer—and he finds them, much to the amazement of Watson.

And, most outrageously, Holmes suspects that the trainer had practiced on other animals a procedure to injure Silver Blaze; sure enough, Holmes "discovered" that several of the sheep had "inexplicably" turned up lame. As suggested by the data (q), Holmes generates a coherent prior story (p), and then tests the *consistency* of the hypothesis "if and only if p, then q" against the data.

(5) Finally, Holmes sets in motion stratagems to bring the events to a conclusion. It is not enough, in most cases, for Holmes to "solve" the case; full (re)solution necessitates a return to some state of equilibrium, and Holmes unpredictably, in many cases, orchestrates some "proper" end for the events. Holmes is therefore not only an agent in the discovery of what happened, but he serves as a catalyst to transform the course of future events.

To sum up: it is our contention that the structure of a Holmes episode and his activity in detection can serve as a heuristically productive analog for our reading of Paul.

Paul as Detective

The past decade has seen several major bends in the road to understanding Paul. The works of Sanders, Beker, Patte, Meeks, Räisanen, Luedemann, Hays, Segal, and Wright (just to name a few) act as pedagogical signposts for those seeking to chart their way. The recent course of Pauline studies is not invoked here with the intention of mapping or rehearsal, but in the context of this chapter we cite recent history to focus our attention briefly on just one aspect of how to read Paul aright.

In this regard the work of Jouette Bassler proves most useful. Professor Bassler organizes her analysis of recent attempts to chart the theology of Paul under the adverbs "whence" and "whither." "Whence" is appropriate because some have suggested Paul's theology should be identified with the surface argument of a letter or with the effects a letter produced upon its first readers/hearers, while "whither" points to that which is behind the surface text. By neither unduly accenting either the posttextual "whence" or pretextual "whither," Bassler drafts a proposal which, she believes, more accurately tracks the "pathing" of Paul's theological activity. She writes:

> The *raw material of Paul's theology* (the kerygmatic story, scripture, traditions, etc.) passes through *the lens of Paul's experience* (his common Christian experience as well as his unique experience as one "set apart by God for the gospel")

and generates a *coherent (and characteristic) set of convictions.* These convictions, then, are refracted through a prism, Paul's *perception of the situations that obtain in various communities,* where they are resolved into specific *words on target for those communities.*[11]

Bassler's proposal incorporates various "elements" or "aspects"—Gospel, Scripture, preformed traditions, experience (both unique and common), surface argument, and the historical situations—into a single descriptive statement without unfairly centering one "aspect" to the neglect of the others. This, in turn, allows her to employ a dynamic, *optical* metaphor to describe the task of reading Paul; his theology is the *movement* from "raw material" to "specific words on target" through a "lens."

Bassler's description marks a real advance: what everyone is (or should be!) looking for is an *activity* rather than a *static entity,* a verb and not a noun. We should be ready to jettison the phrase "Pauline theology" and, much to the dismay of English professors, verb the noun, yielding the semantically abysmal "Paul's theologizing." Theology is not something Paul *has;* it is something Paul *does.*

And yet, Paul did reflect upon *something before* or *as* he wrote a letter. Arguably behind the clutter of a letter's surface text (q) stands a *something* (p). This *something,* though variously appraised, is best characterized as story. Therefore, despite her considerable adverbial wisdom, Bassler's *optical* reading strategy ought to be replaced with a *narrative* one—the fictional detective story.

The Shape of Paul's Story World

Richard Hays has popularized narrative approaches to reading Paul, though his is by no means the only one. Hays argues that standing behind Paul's letters is an epic, foundational story.[12]

The initial scene of this macro story recounts how the malevolent powers of sin and death violently interrupted the peace established by God. Though God seeks to answer the disruption in Eden's shalom by selecting various agents (e.g., Abraham, Moses, David, Israel, and the Prophets) and by providing various helpers (e.g., the Law, Spirit), the powers continue to frustrate and subvert God's intention to bless the world. God remedies the disability of His human agents in the middle sequence. He does this by sending Jesus to transform and empower humanity. Sin and death still seek to work their evil and, in fact, apparently do in their killing of Jesus. God, however, redeems the death of Jesus through resurrection, and this becomes, ironically, the very means of humanity's enablement. In the final sequence, God resumes His grand enterprise to bless the world. The agents are the renewed and empowered humans. The familiar foes of sin and death still seek to subvert, but the believing agents are helped by the Gospel (the re-presentation of the death and resurrection of Jesus) and the Spirit (the resurrection presence of Jesus). At the time of writing, Paul and his contemporaries were living in the final sequence of the unfolding drama.

Some initial observations are in order. (1) The letters presuppose this story, and *presupposing* the story confers meaning upon the surface text of those letters. (2) The clues for recovering the story are present within the surface text of the letters themselves. (3) Theologizing is the process of thinking through the implications inherent within the story (what Hays calls the *dianoia* of the story; cf. Beker's "truth of the Gospel") to address a set of specific and contingent situations. (4) Nested within this macro story are other stories.[13] Though we will have occasion to return to each of these tantalizing observations in time, I want to press the last one a bit further.

Lodged within the middle sequence of the macro story is a Jesus story (Phil. 2:5-11; Col. 1:15-20). This story focuses upon the events of Jesus' life, stretching from preexistence to apocalypse. The initial sequence envisions a pretemporal, heavenly scene with Jesus enjoying equality with God. The potential "evil" here is for Jesus to use this equality selfishly. Instead, Jesus sacrificially empties Himself and takes on the form of a human. The earthly life of Jesus forms the middle sequence of the story. Here Jesus, in repetition of the primal scene, continues to submit to God, even to the point of death. God answers death with resurrection and exaltation. The final sequence chronicles the current reign of Jesus as Lord and the world's final apocalyptic "confession" of what was always and already true. As in the macro story, the events of death and resurrection constitute the key events of the middle sequence in the Jesus story.

The macro story also encloses Paul's own life story (1 Cor. 15; Gal. 1; Phil. 3; Eph. 3). Paul's former, successful life in Judaism governed the plot of the initial sequence in his life story. The apocalypse of the risen Jesus as Lord forms the middle sequence of Paul's life story. The final sequence follows him in living out a new plot — one similar to the scripting provided by the servant in Isaiah 49 — as the unique agent charged with extending God's blessing to the nations. Paul's life is bound up with the Jesus story (and thus with the macro story of the world) because the life he now lives is a replication and repetition of the death and resurrection of Jesus (cf. Gal. 2:20). The cross and resurrection again form the dynamic means of transformation and the critical fulcrum upon which the whole of his life story turns.

The letters also reveal the story of every Christian's life. It too betrays a tripartite structure. The primal scene depicts all humans as enslaved by the destructive powers of sin. These sinful powers enact a series of de-formations which ultimately end in death. Conversion forms the middle part of the story. Hearing and believing the Gospel, the way in which the story of Jesus works the will of God in the macro story of the world, enacts a transfer (movement from the domain of sin and death to the domain of life and spirit in Christ) and a transformation (the believer becomes a new creation). The final sequence is depicted as a series of transformations which culminates in one, final great apocalyptic act of transformation into the image of God in Christ. Again, the cross and resurrection form the indispensable middle of the story.

Although possessing a unique configuration, each story shares the signs of cross and resurrection as the dynamic, plot-making transformation. It is the semiotic, plot-making relationship between cross and resurrection — taken together as a sign — and the other signs within each of Paul's narratives which makes the mystery story a compelling analogical reading strategy.

As opposed to an encoded plot of actions (what Roland Barthes calls the proairetic), a detective story's plot is a code of enigmas and answers (Barthes' hermeneutic code). As Peter Brooks comments:

> The proairetic concerns the logic of actions, how their completion can be derived from their initiation, how they form sequences. The limit-case of a purely proairetic narrative would be approached by the picaresque tale, or the novel of pure adventure: narratives that give precedence to the happening. The hermeneutic code concerns rather the questions and answers that structure a story, their suspense, partial unveiling, temporary blockage, eventual resolution, with the resulting creation of a "dilatory space" — the space of suspense — which we work through toward what is felt to be, in classical narrative, the revelation of meaning that occurs when the narrative sentence reaches full predication. The clearest and purest example of the hermeneutic would no

THE MYSTERY OF PAUL'S THEOLOGIZING

doubt be the detective story, in that everything in the story's structure, and its temporality, depends on the resolution of enigma.[14]

The hermeneutical power wielded by a detective story's structure can be seen in *The Musgrave Ritual*. The mysterious disappearance of Musgrave's butler is resolved by Holmes when he unpacks the hidden significance of, what is to Musgrave, an absurd, family ritual. The decoding of the ritual leads to the discovery of the dead butler. Finding the dead butler, in turn, leads to the recovery of, what seems at first glance, just some old relics. However, when the old relics themselves are decoded, they lead, like a link in a great semiotic chain, to the restoration of Musgrave to his proper place in the larger story of England's monarchical history. The resolution of the central enigma — the ritual — spirals outward in a hermeneutical march, opening up new avenues of understanding all along the way. The deciphering of the central enigmatic metaphor fuels the plotting and determines the shape of narration. To quote Peter Brooks again:

> What lies between the two related poles [beginning and end] is the enactment of the first metaphor as metonymy — and then, a hypothetical and mental enactment of the results thus obtained — in order to establish the second, more fully semiotic metaphor. We start with an inactive, "collapsed" metaphor and work through to a reactivated, transactive one, a metaphor with its difference restored through metonymic process.[15]

The semiotic function of the cross and resurrection within Paul's story world compares favorably. The cross, standing alone, is a collapsed metaphor; it is meaningless, utter foolishness. The collocation of cross with resurrection opens the metaphor. In fact, the collocation creates a plot by the transforming of a metaphor (cross) into narrative through metonymy (cross . . . resurrection).[16] The semiotic activity of the resurrection upon the cross redeems it from meaninglessness and invests it with eschatological plenitude.

The unfolding of the collapsed metaphor of the cross by the resurrection triggers a profound series of semiotic discoveries. (1) The cross and resurrection, when taken together, invest Paul's life story with significance: it enlightens the blinded character of his pre-conversion life pattern, metamorphosing him into a new life plot.

(2) What is true of Paul's life story is also true of every believer's. Without the dynamic unleashed by the operation of resurrection upon crucifixion everyone would remain perpetually veiled (2 Cor. 3–4). (3) Collocating cross and resurrection also opens the blinded metaphor of the Jesus story. Without the vindicating act of resurrection and exaltation, the series of sacrifices, stretching from preexistence and culminating in the cross, would be nothing more than an enigmatic black hole of nonsense. Resurrection rescues the life of Jesus from unnarratibility. (4) The Jesus story, configured as it is by the cross-resurrection, opens the blinded metaphor of the macro story of the world. Up until the appearance of Jesus, up until His death, and, most particularly, up until His resurrection, the purposes of God remained a riddle—and this is exactly Paul's use of mystery—but with the resurrection, what was previously conflicted has now been resolved.

Therefore, the coincidence, order, and priority of cross and resurrection in each of Paul's stories, by rendering a definitive answer to life's only true enigmatic question, structures Paul's paradoxical convictional coherence. The alibi for purloining the detective story as a hermeneutical key hangs upon the way in which the end (resurrection) confers meaning upon the beginning and middle of narration even before the end is reached. Employing the detective story as reading strategy willfully plunders the resolution-without-final-closure structure of Paul's foundational story world.

Pauline Repetition

If our hermeneutical pillaging of the fictional detective story finds a substantive pre-text in the illumination of Paul's story world(s), then a further analogical plea can be found in the *way* in which Paul "thinks through" the implications inherent within his narrative world to draft letters. How is it that Paul *moves* from a fluid, interlocking network of stories—structured by the plot-making dynamic of cross . . . resurrection—to very specific words-on-target? It is my contention that Paul retraced the steps of his narrative world, and it is this repetition and retracing of the story(-ies) to address a specific set of circumstances which yields a letter. In this operation Paul is again Holmesian.

Paul wrote letters precisely because his congregations had taken a detour in the story. Ominous and eschatological subplots abound. When faced with a question about the role of grace and sin in the Christian life (Rom. 6), Paul retells the story of conversion (Rom. 6:1-4), which is itself encoded into the ritual of the baptism. Paul's solution for Corinthian misbehavior, based as it was on their misunderstanding of the resurrection, was to re-narrate the "traditional" Gospel story (1 Cor. 15:1ff). Paul answered the challenge brought by the Galatian troublemakers by retelling the story of how he came be an apostle (Gal. 1). Paul's recapitulation of the Jesus story (Phil. 2:5-11) and its subsequent structuring force upon the plot line of his own life (2:14-18), that of Timothy (2:19-24), and Epaphroditus (2:25-30), serves as the basis for his redirecting the path of the Philippians.

Though examples could be multiplied, in reality Paul faced only two problems—ignorance and deceit. For those disabled by ignorance, repetition (re)opens the closed metaphors by reading them in their proper order. For those bewitched by deceit, Paul again retraced his steps. A metaphor, taken singularly, may be co-opted into another narrative context, thus yielding another and *drama*tically different plot. Repetition subverts such wanton semiotic looting. The reconnection of the metaphor within its story retrieves it from its exile. When the Gospel story is wrongly or absently read, Paul seeks, through repetition, to replace the detours with the only true solution. Like Holmes going over the ground again, Paul's retracing leads to detection and apprehension of the original plotmaker, Jesus, and His plot-making deeds, cross . . . resurrection.

Repeating the initial metonymic chain also invests the metaphoric syntax with ethical importance. The rituals, when correctly plotted, point to solutions. Paul's compulsion to write a letter is, therefore, grounded in his thinking through the story, his retracing of its armature to resolve the problems of his churches.

Though formally identified as Greco-Roman epistolary literature,[17] akin to many other ancient examples, recent interpreters have pointed to the narrative context evoked by Paul's letters. Each letter participates in a story being acted out among Paul, his detractors, and the churches he sought to pastor.[18] Whereas in a Holmes episode only a small portion of the discourse is devoted to the stratagems set in motion to effect a return to equilibrium—the bulk of the narrative recounts the resolution of the central enigma—the opposite is the case with Paul. In a Pauline letter the resolution of the central enigma—the centrifugal semiotic answer of resurrection to crucifixion—occurs *before* the writing of the letter. In the narrative world evoked by the letter, the *letter becomes* the topical sequence which sets in motion the transformation to the final sequence. Through the letter Paul enacts a series of revaluations which will resolve the disequilibrium and move to a new equilibrium.

As the presence of apostolic absence the letter therefore embodies the dynamic plot-making power of cross . . . resurrection. The letter obtains a plot-making power because it formalizes and binds the energy inherent in the story world of Paul. In writing, Paul is attempting to bind the open, dynamic energy of resurrection, which breathes the breath of life into his narrative world, by applying his convictions to a specific situation. Letters, in a sense, are simply the formalization of resurrection. The letter becomes the way in which the displaced or misplaced become reconnected with daily life. The letter not only depends upon and invokes a story world but actively participates in it by structuring future narration.

Conclusion: Licking the Post-Age Stamp

We have sought here to justify my use of the fictional detective story as a reading strategy for Paul. The appropriateness of employing mystery story resides in its ability to illumine the plotting of Paul's pretextual story world, to follow Paul as he thinks through the implications inherent in his story world to draft letters, and to model our act of reading. This strategy is offered in the name of postmodernism[19] and done so with fear and trembling. Whether or not this exercise in criticism earns the postmodernism label must be a judgment rendered by more competent critics.[20] While the final verdict may well be in the hands of others, let us be bold enough to suggest three reasons why the label sticks.

First, what one discovers through this reading strategy comports with postmodernism. The convictional world of Paul, because it is an interlocking network of stories, is open and dynamic. Since there was potential for Paul to produce *new meaning* when his convictional world came in contact with *new* issues about which he cared, Paul's interlocking network of stories remained lexically and syntactically under-formalized. The corollary is also true: the very act of bringing the inherent openness of his paradoxically coherent convictional world to a historical and contingent sense of closure creates a letter which is paradigmatically underdeveloped. There is a semiotic polyvalency and a narrative plenitude to Paul's story world which cannot be exhausted by formalization — either ancient or modern.

Second, we consciously adopt a reading strategy which moves beyond modernism (with science as the final arbiter) and embrace textuality — historically, theologically, and literarily.[21] In this strategy, the reader becomes actively involved in construction/production of meaning. This can be seen in two ways. (1) The character of the letter mandates the abductive creativity of the reader/detective. While sharing interrogations, observations, and inspections with other approaches, this strategy forces readers to exercise a clever, inventive, image-making capacity. Readers must reconstruct a/the *prior coherent story* which explains the *second seemingly conflicted discourse.* Working from effect to cause invites risk and lacks that positivistic certainty we have been taught to crave. However, as certainty plummets, the heuristic value of any reconstruction soars. (2) Adopting this strategy obligates the reader to reenactment and repetition. Such reader involvement uncovers clues and leads to the discovery of the crucial fulcrum upon which the whole of explanation turns. The successful Pauline sleuth must ultimately (re)trace the apostle's steps in writing in order to understand his theologizing.

Readers should not be disturbed by the apparent conflicts and inconsistencies within the discourse. Despite the letter's gaps and erasures, readers should persist with abduction and repetition. The imposed mystification caused by the disconnectedness of the surface text is actually a/the hermeneutical clue. Locked within the letters themselves, however conflicted and inconsistent the surface text may appear, are the encoded clues which *suggest their own explanation.* The letters must be abductively decoded and mimetically repeated by an aggressive reader because the narrative world of Paul's letters is full of signs and its plotting is God's great argument.

Third, the stratagems Paul enacted through letters leaves readers in suspense. The reader is plotted by Paul's letter into the final sequence, and the final sequence has not been brought to closure. The reader, therefore, stands between Paul and final closure. The lack of closure introduces suspense into the act of reading. But reading gives way to living. Paul's convictional world encloses us within it; the letters transform readers into actants who seek through living to bind and formalize and to bring to historical closure the openness that resides in the story. We read and are filled with suspense precisely because we are living the drama.

In short, abducting Paul is postmodern because: (1) what is found is inherently fluid, (2) the way in which one discovers what is found is inherently creative, and (3) the way one appropriates how one finds what one finds is inherently suspenseful.

NOTES

1. This chapter is part of a larger project by the same name which seeks to harness the heuristic power of the mystery power story to track Paul in his theological enterprise and to suggest how Paul's act of "theologizing" might (re)configure contemporary praxis and reflection. The project is divided into three major parts which focus respectively upon (1) the plotting of a mystery story, (2) Paul and his storytelling, and (3) contemporary, theological storytelling.

2. For previous theoretical and exegetical attempts at employing the fictional detective story for reading Paul, see Carey C. Newman, "Christophany as a Sign of 'The End': A Semiotic Approach to Paul's Epistles," *MOSAIC* 25 (1992): 1–13; idem, *Paul's Glory-Christology: Tradition and Rhetoric,* Novum Testamentum Supp 69 (Leiden: Brill, 1992), 196–201.

3. Tzvetan Todorov, "The Typology of Detective Fiction," *The Poetics of Prose* (Ithaca, N.Y.: Cornell Univ. Press, 1975), 42–52; Peter Brooks, *Reading for the Plot: Design and Intention in Narrative* (New York: Vintage: 1984), 22–28.

4. Jacques Lacan, "Seminar on 'The Purloined Letter,' " *Yale French Studies* 48 (1972): 38–72; Jacques Derrida, *The Post Card: From Socrates to Freud and Beyond* (Chicago: Univ. of Chicago Press, 1987); Barbara Johnson, "The Frame of Reference: Poe, Lacon, Derrida," *Yale French Studies* 55/46 (1977), 457–505. See further, John P. Muller and William J. Richardon, *The Purloined Poe: a Lacan, Derrida, and Psychoanalytic Reading* (Baltimore: Johns Hopkins Univ. Press, 1988).

5. Thomas Sebeok and Umberto Eco, eds., *The Sign of Three: Dupin, Holmes, Pierce* (Bloomington, Ind.: Indiana Univ. Press, 1983).

6. The analysis of both Holmes and Paul follows the narrative theory outlined by Algirdas J. Griemas, *Du Sens* (Paris: Sueil, 1970); idem, "Element of a Narrative Grammar," *Diacritics* 7 (1977): 23–40; J. Calloud, *Structural Analysis of Narrative,* Semia Supplements 4 (Philadelphia: Fortress, 1976). Central to Griemas' understanding of narrative are narrative sequences. Every narrative, as Aristotle argued, has a beginning, middle, and end. Griemas labels these three elements "sequences" — initial, topical, and final. The function of an initial sequence is to show/create a lack or deficiency. The function of the topical sequence is to enable or empower a "subject," who, in the final sequence seeks to alleviate the "lack." Each sequence is constituted by three narrative elements, units, or syntagms. In the *contract syntagm* the protagonist is charged with a task to perform. In the *disjuntive/conjunction syntagm* the protagonist sets out on the quest to carry out the contract. In the *performance syntagm* the protagonist carries out or fails to carry out the task. Each of the sequences — the initial, topical, and final — will have these three syntagms. Each sequence can be diagramed according to the roles and network of relations among the various players in the narrative. The *sender* is the figure who establishes the mandate in the contract syntagm. The *subject* is the figure who receives the mandate. The *object* is the thing or quality which the sender wants to communicate to someone. The *receiver* is the figure to whom the sender wants to communicate the object. The *opponent* is the figure or force that seeks to prevent the subject from carrying out the mandate. The *helper* is the figure or force that aids the subject in carrying out the mandate.

7. Though one may argue that the figure of Moriarty in the series links the episodes into a larger narrative.

8. Cf. Irving M. Copi, *Introduction to Logic*, 5th ed. (New York: Macmillan, 1978), 472–81.

9. The only way to rectify this argument is to say:

if and only if p then q

q

———

therefore p

10. Thomas A. Sebeok, "One, Two, Three Spells U B E R T Y," *Sign of Three*, 2.

11. Jouette Bassler, "Paul's Theology: Whence and Whither? A Synthesis (of sorts) of the Theology of Philemon, 1 Thessalonians, Philippians, Galatians, and 1 Corinthians," SPLSP (1989): 418.

12. Richard B. Hays, *The Faith of Jesus Christ*, SBLDS 56 (Chico, Calif.: Scholars, 1983), 85–138.

13. Cf. Ben Witherington III, "Christology," in *Dictionary of Paul and His Letters*, ed. Gerald W. Hawthorne, Ralph P. Martin, and Dan G. Reid (Downers Grove, Ill.: InterVarsity, 1993), 104–5.

14. Brooks, *Reading for the Plot*, 18.

15. Ibid., 27.

16. Cf. "The King died . . . The Queen died."

17. David E. Aune, *The New Testament in Its Literary Environment* (Philadelphia: Fortress, 1987), 183–225; and William G. Doty, *Letters in Primitive Christianity* (Philadelphia: Fortress, 1973), 21–48.

18. Daniel Patte, *Paul's Faith and the Power of the Gospel* (Philadelphia: Fortress, 1983; and N.R. Petersen, *Rediscovering Paul* (Philadelphia: Fortress, 1985).

19. Ralph V. Norman, "M. Dupin's Revenge," *Soundings* 73 (1990): 493–505.

20. Wesley A. Kort, " 'Religion and Literature' in Postmodernist Context," *Journal of the American Academy of Religion* 58 (1989): 575–88; W.H. Smith, "Postmodernist's Impact on the Study of Religion," *Journal of the American Academy of Religion* 58 (1989): 653–70; Stephen D. Moore, "The 'Post'-Age Stamp: Does It Stick? Biblical Studies and the Postmodern Debate," *Journal of the American Academy of Religion* 57 (1989): 543–59.

21. Cf. N.T. Wright, *The New Testament and the People of God* (Minneapolis: Fortress, 1992).

11

The Pauline Gospel in a Postmodern Age

Mark A. Seifrid

A change in perspective on Pauline theology has taken hold over the last twenty years or so, a change that roughly parallels the shift that has occurred in the intellectual consciousness of Western society in the same period. While it is still too early to assess fully the way in which larger currents of thought have caught up biblical scholarship in their drift, a few observations are in order. At a superficial level, the increasing influence of literary and sociological approaches to Paul display in moderated fashion the interest of "academic postmoderns" in the question of the nature of a "text" and its relation to a "community." Yet these outward and evident appropriations of new critical perspectives are in themselves relatively uninteresting and unimportant. Far more significant, and far more difficult to evaluate, is the manner in which presentations of Paul's theology itself are being shaped by the current mood. Here again, the prevailing preference for describing Paul's thought by means of a narrative is an obvious adaptation of socio-linguistic insights, and yet in and of itself it is not of great moment. The crux lies in the actual substance of current proposals regarding Pauline theology.

Contemporary Pauline Scholarship: An Overview

Most contemporary Pauline scholarship is in reaction against Rudolf Bultmann's quintessentially modern reading of Paul, which was

Mark Seifrid is Assistant Professor of New Testament Interpretation at The Southern Baptist Theological Seminary in Louisville, Kentucky.

based upon an existential appropriation of Paul's theology of justification.[1] His sweeping reconstruction of Paul's thought, which was formed already in the 1920s at the height of the modernist impulse, enjoyed considerable influence in the 1950s and 1960s and since then has been in decline. Bultmann freely accepted the notion of a closed, material universe in which no divine interventions take place. All the ground that any "scientific" worldview claimed, Bultmann not only conceded, but readily gave away as a threat to genuine faith. Only in the self-understanding of the human being, alienated and threatened by death, did the question of God arise. Here a theology of justification by faith alone found its relevance. Yet this theology was very far removed from both Paul and Luther. It was in large measure a reaction against the Ritschlean moralism of the late nineteenth century. And it appropriated the article on justification through the filter of Marburg neo-Kantianism which applied especially to the sphere of human scientific accomplishments. An existentialist interpretation of justification by faith became for Bultmann the fundamental criterion for appropriating the message of Paul, and, in fact, of the entire New Testament. For him, Paul's Gospel could be summarized in the lapidary statement: "Life arises out of surrendering one's self to God, thereby gaining one's self."[2] This surrender extended to the sphere of knowledge, thus securing the significance of Paul both within and in opposition to the modernist paradigm.

Of course this truncated analysis of Paul, which furthered the problem Adolf Schlatter called "the pious heart and the pagan head" was not well-received in all quarters, especially not among evangelicals. Yet the measure of Bultmann's influence is seen in the broadly felt need to respond to his reading of Paul. That situation has changed. The Bultmann era is gone. Within the field of New Testament studies it is possible to place one's finger on several responses to Bultmann which have figured largely in effecting this shift. One of the first among them was proposed by Bultmann's own pupil, Ernst Käsemann, who in a 1964 Oxford lecture claimed that with the expression the "righteousness of God" Paul was borrowing from apocalyptic Judaism the concept of the saving triumph of God over the rebellious world. Käsemann was thus able to bring "justification" and "sanctification" together and to find a place for social action within the central element of the Pauline Gospel. Another frequently cited response to Bultmann, which appeared just prior to that of Käsemann, was that of Krister Stendahl. Stendahl, arguing with Lutheran tradition in which he stood, claimed that Paul's concern was not that of Luther: while Luther suffered from an anguished conscience, Paul was a missionary who sought to secure the rights of believing Gentiles alongside the Jewish people within the purposes of God. Some fifteen years later, a pivotal work in the shift in scholarly understanding of Paul appeared: E.P. Sanders' *Paul and Palestinian Judaism.* This lengthy monograph analyzes Paul's soteriology against the backdrop of a thorough survey of early Jewish writings and dismisses the faulty understanding of Judaism that prevailed especially in German Protestant scholarship around the turn of the century. Early Judaism was not a religion of anxiety which focused upon the weighing of good deeds and bad, but one in which mercy and forgiveness are assumed to be available for the people of God. Paul's coming to faith must be understood in terms other than finding the mercy of God. His understanding of salvation centered instead upon "participation in Christ" as Savior of all.

The New Perspective on Paul

While each of these studies undercuts Bultmann's approach in important ways, it is not our purpose here to evaluate the validity of their claims. Whatever their value, these studies have brought with them what James D.G. Dunn has called "the new perspective on Paul."[3] Of primary interest to us is that in each response, the basic lines of thought had been laid in earlier works. Käsemann draws on Adolf Schlatter's interpretation of the "righteousness of God." Stendahl takes up Johannes Munck's insistence that salvation-historical thought and missionary aims are crucial to understanding Paul. And Sanders had his precedents in George F. Moore, Claude Montefiore, and others. Without denying the originality of these pivotal studies, one is struck by the considerable role that current interest within the community of biblical scholars has played in fixing attention on the ideas they have presented.

We are therefore drawn to this question: to what extent and in what manner are our present cultural concerns manifest in the current interpretation of Paul and his understanding of justification? We are not thereby limited to chronicling a defection and decline. Obviously the waning of Bultmann's influence has led to a greater appreciation for the full dimensions of what J. Christiaan Beker calls the "triumph of God" in Paul's thought, that is, the triumph of Christ's lordship over creation in the destruction of sin, death, and corruption. All the same, it is proper to focus on the present dangers to get a proper understanding of Paul. No less than the second generation of believers at the beginning of the second century, we are tempted to "flatten out" Paul, to reduce the inner and vital tensions of his thought in favor of a reading that seems to make Paul relevant to our contemporaries.

Perhaps the most striking feature of recent study of Paul is the frequent insistence that Paul was not concerned with "isolated individuals" (or their consciences) but with believing communities of Jews and Gentiles. This assertion provides a healthy corrective to Bultmann, but carries its own rather weighty set of difficulties. There is a risk in it of enlisting Paul simply for the practical purpose of affirming pluralism. Some recent assessments of Paul's arguments on justification seem nearly parabolic. Conservative Jewish Christians, who force their traditions upon uncircumcised Gentiles, symbolize the defenders of Western culture. By means of his arguments on justification by faith alone, Paul rises to the defense of the oppressed minority, with the aim of securing their rights and equality within the larger body politic.

Obviously some truth inheres in this proposal. A central concern in Paul's letter to Rome is to secure harmonious relations between Jews and Gentiles within the circle of Roman house churches. And Galatians was written to defend the liberty of believing Gentiles. Yet there are dissimilarities between Paul's context and ours which ought to give us pause. All the letters in which the theme of justification figures prominently were sent to communities in which Gentiles were in the majority. In no instance do we find Jewish believers forcing their culture on Gentiles. Quite the contrary: the Gentile believers in Galatia were themselves eager to observe the Law, including the requirement of circumcision. And in the letter to Rome, Paul firmly locates his Gospel within Jewish particularism, even while asserting its universal scope ("to the Jew first, and also to the Greek"). He emphasizes to the Gentile majority at Rome that Israel could yet expect the appearance of the deliverer from Zion,[4] reinforcing their limited place in the working out of salvation in history: "You stand by faith; do not be conceited, but fear" (Rom. 11:20; cf. 11:25, author's trans.). The stumbling block of religious particularism cannot be removed from Paul's Gospel without damage to its integrity.

Individualism vs. Community

At a deeper level, the present tendency to minimize the address to the individual within Paul's Gospel displays a number of serious and unhealthy misunderstandings. In the first place, one may fairly question whether Paul was at all opposed to the cultural and national emblems of Jewish Christianity. His defense of the practices of the "weak" at Rome, his treatment of circumcision as an *adiaphoron* in 1 Corinthians, and even his silence regarding the men from James at Antioch together implicitly point to his full acceptance of Jewish cultural distinctives. We shall argue below that Paul regards the Gospel to be compromised only when Jewish emblems are used to make a claim to religious superiority. The arguments on justification by faith do not concern the encroachment of one culture upon another, they rather are directed against any compromise of the Gospel. This Gospel, precisely because it justifies the ungodly, transcends the distinctions of this age, whether race, class, or gender. In other words, the Pauline Gospel has a heavenly horizon in view and is not properly perceived without this scope.

To restate our point: the deficiencies of the present mood are most clearly manifest in its rejection of individualism in favor of community. This sentiment is both understandable and justified in response to the particular form of isolated individualism present in our culture. Yet the very formulation "individualism versus community" is deeply flawed and fails to address the root of the human problem according to Paul's Gospel. Jonathan Edwards perceived clearly that love for a specific and limited group is nothing other than self-love. It is a mutant individualism, not true beneficence, as we should know from the loud voices of numerous advocacy groups within our society. And as Kierkegaard knew, our common temptation is to hide our selfishness from the searching demands of God by means of community values and standards which provide us with a false righteousness of our own. Carl Braaten has rightly warned that the current shift in interest from individualistic soteriology to ecclesiology may simply represent the exchange of one kind of narcissism for another.[5]

The passage from modernity to "post-" or "ultra-" modernity has not brought to an end the "eclipse of heaven" in our culture.[6] The move from the Paul of Bultmann to the Paul of E.P. Sanders has suffered from the same deficit. Paul's apocalypticism is largely taken for granted, but it is the vision of an earthly transformation, not the judgment seat of Christ, which has captured the imagination of this generation of Paul's interpreters. All too quickly it is assumed that Luther's search for a gracious God was altogether alien to Paul. And worse yet, Luther is often charged with Bultmann's transgressions. Yet Luther, unlike Bultmann, still lived under "the bright shadow of heaven," with a robust consciousness of the transcendent that distanced him not only from Bultmann's existentialism, but also from a distorted sense of community that shelters a *cor incurvatus se.*

"Works of the Law" as Claims to Morality[7]

Virtually all aspects of the "new perspective on Paul," in both its spheres of inquiry — early Judaism and Pauline theology — have been offered before.[8] If it is new, it is so by virtue of its linking a Pharisee who knew divine grace and mercy with the apostle who was sent by Christ to the Gentiles. Everything depends on how one sorts out the relation between this "covenantal nomism" of Paul's past and his transforming faith and work in Christ. Sanders' *Paul and Palestinian Judaism* originally provided only the framework: Paul the Jew rejected God's covenantal mercies because they were not "Christianity."[9] Dunn has been in the forefront of building an explanatory bridge for the gap in the new perspective.[10] In his reading, Paul's arguments on justification chiefly concern his opposition to Jewish exclusivity. The discontinuity between Paul and his past should be understood primarily as his becoming an advocate for the inclusion of Gentiles in the people of God, not as a release from a guilty conscience or a new understanding of divine mercy.

Some central elements of Sanders' work on early Judaism serve his purpose of comparison with Paul rather poorly. The category of "covenantal nomism" becomes relatively meaningless for describing the soteriology of early Jewish groups when the terms of the covenant are in dispute.[11] I have attempted elsewhere to show that Paul broke with a belief which this vague expression fails to articulate sufficiently: that the promise of mercy is given to those who are faithful to the covenant.[12] While remaining covenantal in structure, two representative early Jewish writings, the Community Rule from Qumran (1QS) and the Psalms of Solomon (PssSol), restrict the saving benefits of the covenant to a limited group within the nation. A measure of individualism enters here, especially in the PssSol, since salvation is now contingent upon personal righteousness, adherence to the Law as it was interpreted within the community.[13] Neither writing displays any lack of assurance on the part of the pious, or any indication that salvation was viewed as earned or deserved. The PssSol attribute deliverance to divine mercy. The *sola gratia* stance of the Qumran materials is particularly evident.[14] Paul's brief autobiographical statements about his life prior to his encounter with Christ conform to this pattern, especially as it appears in the PssSol. He does not seem to have suffered from an "introspective conscience" and most likely viewed the righteousness which was his through the Law as a gift from God. Nevertheless, the encounter with Christ worked a conversion in Paul. Faith in the crucified and risen Messiah led him to reject this very understanding of divine favor as a gift to the obedient. Through appropriation of early Christian traditions in which Jesus' death was interpreted as an atonement for sin, he came to believe that salvation was mediated by the Cross to the ungodly.

Jewish Boundary Markers

Despite the inadequacy of Sanders' foundation, others have built upon it. Dunn, in particular, has attempted to fill the lacuna which Sanders originally left between Paul and his background. Discussion of his proposal that circumcision and food laws served as ethnic boundary markers has tended to focus, too narrowly in my view, on the meaning of the expression "works of the Law." We will briefly revisit that exegetical debate below. Here we will examine in broader strokes the claim that Paul rejected a Jewish "national righteousness." There is little doubt that circumcision, along with obedience to food and Sabbath laws, served Jews as "boundary markers." It is highly questionable, however, that these "boundary markers" symbolized *mere* national identity. Ethnic traditions bear values which provide cohesion and continuity in community life. And while early Judaism was a "national" religion, it was nevertheless a *religion.*

That reality presses itself upon us from every angle in the early Jewish sources. It is not hard to find attestation that Jewish "boundary markers" could transcend racial lines. One immediately thinks of Josephus' account of the circumcision of King Izates. Under the urging of a certain Eleazar, he was circumcised in order to become a Jew and, significantly, to ensure that he had truly conformed to the Law.[15] The report, which is reflective of Josephus' views, indicates that the way was open for outsiders to *become* Jews. He states elsewhere, admittedly in an apologetic vein, that Moses the lawgiver took great care

> that we should not begrudge the things of the household (οἰκεία) to those who choose to share them. For as many as come to live under the same laws as us, when they come he gladly welcomes them, supposing that the household relation (οἰκειότης) is not for race alone, but for choice of lifestyle (βίος).[16]

This sentiment, although it does not remove the requirement of circumcision, is epitomized in the saying attributed to Hillel:

Be one of the disciples of Aaron, who loves peace and pursues peace, who loves (all) human beings (הַבְּרִיּוֹת, creatures) and who brings them near to *Torah*.[17]

While it is true that Jews protected their traditions in distinctive practices, especially the "boundary markers" of circumcision and Sabbath observance, and while there does not appear to have been widespread Jewish missionary activity in this period, there is good evidence that in many places Jews were receptive to those outsiders who in varying degrees associated themselves with the Jewish community.[18] The ethical dimension of the language used to describe Gentile adherents to Judaism is unmistakable: "God-fearer" is a designation for a pious Jew in the Scriptures, and the more Hellenistic term "devout" (θεοσεβής) represents a general expression for religious devotion, applied to Jews and pagans as well.[19]

The recognition of "righteous Gentiles" by some Jews led to a certain tension within Judaism regarding the importance of circumcision for salvation. Yet whatever their soteriology, those Jews who concerned themselves at all with Gentile participation in Judaism understood circumcision in ethical terms. Josephus' narrative of Izates' circumcision illustrates the situation well. Ananias and Eleazar disagree in their estimation of the importance of circumcision for Gentiles. The former judges that commitment to Jewish tradition is more important than the act of circumcision. Yet he does not regard Izates as having become a Jew without circumcision, or as having fully obeyed the Law: God will *pardon* Izates, because of the constraints of his situation. Eleazar, on the other hand, regards the failure to be circumcised as an act of impiety. Despite their disagreement, they both look upon circumcision as a completion of the decision to worship God, a position which is reflected in Josephus' own estimation of the divine protection afforded Izates after his circumcision: "The fruit which comes from godliness (εὐσέβεια) is not lost for those who look to him, and trust in him alone."[20]

Circumcision here serves as a mark of faith and piety, not mere national identity.[21] Outsiders might have seen conversion to Judaism only as the transfer to another *ethnos*. For Jews like Josephus it signified the embracing of monotheism: the coming to faith in the one true God and the rejection of idolatry.[22] "Fearing God" did not in itself automatically secure a monotheistic commitment, circumcision effectively did.[23] The other classic conversion story is that of Aseneth, in which precisely the matter of monotheism is central.[24] Israel's distinctiveness is regularly described in such terms elsewhere.[25] Paul and his Judaizing adversaries in Galatia differed in soteriology, but like Ananias and Eleazar they represented an "open" Judaism, ready to find a way to secure Gentile morality and the worship of the one God of Israel. As we have seen with Josephus, such groups and persons draw conceptual distinctions between purity rituals and moral concerns, even where they are joined in practice.[26] Circumcision symbolized not merely separation from other nations, but an ethically superior monotheism.

The religious character of Jewish "boundary markers" becomes even clearer when we turn to writings which reflect tensions between various early Jewish factions. The judgment which we rendered on the expression "covenantal nomism" applies as well to the category of "national righteousness." When one group of Jews regards another as "outside the boundaries," the concept of "nation" is subordinated to a larger idea of true religion and piety. This stance is a prominent feature of a number of the Qumran writings where the covenant is restricted to the community alone and requires no elaboration here.[27] It appears in other materials, although not in precisely the same manner. Where the sectarian stance recedes and intercourse with the larger society increases, the exclusivistic use of terms like "covenant" and "Israel" disappears. A hope for "national" salvation is retained by envisioning the nation as converted to righteousness. An alternative soteriological paradigm conditions the ethnic ideal. In the PssSol this reshaping of covenantal theology takes the form of a distinction between "the pious" (ὅσιοι) and "the sinners" (ἁμαρτωλοί). The former expression, along with similar terms, depicts the circle of the godly to whom the promises of Israel's salvation are assured. The latter term more often than not refers to wayward Jews, whom the coming Messiah will cast out from the covenantal inheritance.[28] The pattern is repeated elsewhere in varying forms. For all its severity, 4 Ezra retains its hope in covenantal mercies for the righteous (*iusti*). True, Uriel rejects any offer of mercy apart from the Law, but he tacitly affirms divine patience and grace toward those who turn toward it. A later vision in 4 Ezra affirms the hope that the Messiah will mercifully deliver the remnant at His judgment seat.[29] The shift to ethical and individualistic categories in these materials subverts and restricts the "national" ideal.

Placed side-by-side, the two features of early Judaism we have briefly examined make it impossible to sustain the claim that Jewish "boundary markers" signaled exclusivism or national identity alone. We must confess considerable puzzlement that Dunn, who recognizes that some Jews could regard other Jews as outside the community of the elect on the basis of *halakhah,* regard distinctive practices as simply "exclusivistic," borders without interior meaning. Insiders saw them as emblems of community values, especially fidelity to *Torah* and covenant. The מעשי תורה which those of the Qumran community are to offer to God as sacrifices are described elsewhere as מעשי טוב and joined with doing "truth, righteousness, and justice."[30] Although we yet await the publication of 4QMMT, the sectarian dispute it reflects is clearly of this nature. The מעשי התורה which divide the Qumran group from their adversaries represent what is right and good and result in righteousness and blessing.[31]

If the reading which we have adopted is correct, the manner in which the Qumran community regarded its practices to function appears in an explicit manner in 1QS 11:2, 3:

> For I belong to the God of my vindication and the perfection of my way is in his hand with the virtue of my heart. And *with my righteous deeds* he will wipe away my transgressions.[32]

Even aside from this passage, it is clear that the Qumran community attributed a sanitizing, atoning efficacy to its deeds.[33] Yet it did so without in any way sacrificing its *sola gratia* stance: God was the source of these works and the salvation which accompanied them. The PssSol do not attain to the same heights of grace as the *Hodayoth,* but they too know of an atonement through deeds of repentance (PsSol 3:3-8) and a saving righteousness gained by works (ἔργα, PsSol 9:4, 5). The *thesaurus operum* accredited to Ezra (4 Ezra 7:77) is not an isolated phenomenon. Nor does it eliminate "covenantalism" or notions of mercy, however qualified they might be.

If we understand Paul's rejection of "the works of the Law" in Galatians and Romans against this background, we overcome a number of interpretive difficulties. The debate between Dunn and his critics has centered on the place the problem of transgression holds in Paul's argument in Romans 2-4.[34] While acknowledging that Paul addresses the issue of disobedience, Dunn now views a "nationalistic righteousness" represented by ἔργα νόμου and epitomized in circumcision as the primary element of disobedience which Paul attacks. Yet Jewish "boasting" is never treated as transgression in the rhetoric of the text. There is no call for repentance, no charge of guilt, simply a dismantling of the Jewish presumption of privilege. The rhetoric involving the term ἔργα νόμου is not forensic but deliberative, as the abundant use of the first-person plural in Romans 3–4 indicates. Once the charge that the Jew is guilty along with the rest of the world is established, Paul moves toward exploring the meaning of the Cross alongside his audience. This shift in the form of argument appears precisely at the point at which Paul begins to set ἔργα νόμου in contrast with Christ's saving work.[35] Now that Dunn has allowed that transgression is a problem in Romans 2–3, he must come to terms with the evidence that Paul treats the "works of the law" here not as transgression, but as a false way to righteousness.[36]

The significance of the expression ἔργα νόμου appears to be different from what either Dunn or his critics have proposed thus far. Dunn is surely correct in claiming that the ἔργα νόμου are visible and outward, in some way markers of Jewish identity.[37] Paul uses this language only in the context of his debate with Judaism and alters his wording where he speaks of obedience to the Law by non-Jews. The uncircumcised person, for example, does not do "the works of the Law," but "keeps the just ordinances of the Law" (Rom. 2:26). The thesis that Paul is opposed to "works in general" as a means of justification, claims just a shade too much.[38] Without question, Paul twice clarifies (or, perhaps, redefines) the relation between "grace" and "works" for his audience at Rome, arguing that recompense for works by its very nature excludes grace (Rom. 4:4; 11:6). Yet his argument remains within the scope of Judaism. The categories of ἔργα and ἐργάζομαι appear in passing as he elaborates his understanding of the experiences of Abraham and Israel, both of which were bound up with the issue of the Law.[39]

At the same time, Dunn's insistence that circumcision stood at the head of the list of (ἔργα νόμου) fails to account for the distinction between the two that Paul presupposes. In Romans 4, having already appealed to Abraham as an example of justification of the ungodly apart from "works," Paul addresses circumcision as a new issue (Rom. 4:9-25). Moreover, his use of ἔργα and ἐργάζομαι in opposition to concepts such as impiety, transgression, and forgiveness indicates that in the first part of Romans 4 he takes up the ethical aspect of ἔργα νόμου, exploring the moral dimension of covenant fidelity, and emphasizing it by the slight shift in language. "Circumcision" was in a sense distinct from "works of the Law," most likely because it was a sign (Rom. 4:11), emblematic of Jewish commitment to the Law (Rom. 4:13; cf. 2:17-29; 3:1, 27-31). The subsequent ἔργα νόμου which the circumcised were to perform marked the difference between the righteous and the ungodly.

Further features of these letters suggest that although the polarity between the universalism of the Gospel and Jewish particularism represents an important element of Paul's argumentative situation, it falls short of doing justice to the whole. Above all else, it fails to account for the strong attraction the message of the agitators had for the Galatian believers. The letter contains no evidence that they had lost the assurance of their salvation. They seem rather to have been attracted to Judaism in and of itself, as a supplement to their faith and a way to order their moral and religious universe, just as other Gentiles elsewhere, like Izates, had been drawn to a full commitment to Jewish monotheism. Moreover, when we turn to Romans, we find a paradoxical relation between universalistic and particularistic themes.[40] Without diminishing the stress of Romans 3–4 and Romans 10 on the universal scope of the Gospel, Paul elsewhere in the letter is intent on gaining Gentile submission to Jewish monotheism. The manner in which he introduces his Gospel is unashamedly Jewish, as is the way in which he closes the massive theological argument, affirming the final salvation of ethnic Israel. His summary appeal in Romans 12:1-2 calls for the submission of his primarily Gentile audience to the one God of Israel. His apostolic task, as he describes it to these readers, is to present the Gentiles as a priestly offering to Israel's God (Rom. 15:16). They, as Gentiles, are indebted to the saints of Jerusalem (Rom. 15:27). And perhaps most significantly, as a response to the Messiah's acceptance of them as Gentiles, they are to welcome those conservative Jewish Christians whose national practices might have been an embarrassment (Rom. 14:1–15:13).

All these observations give us reasons for thinking that in rejecting ἔργα νόμου as a guarantee of salvation, Paul rejects a moral superiority gained by obedience, notwithstanding that Jews who adopted such a stance would have attributed their progress to God's gracious covenant with Israel. There may well have been a distant echo of Luke's Pharisee at prayer in Paul's past which he also heard in his opponents at Galatia: "God, I thank you that I am not like other human beings." Bultmann's picture of the Jew consciously striving to secure righteousness through self-effort is a caricature. But it is equally a caricature to reduce Paul's debates in Galatians and Romans to a matter of Jewish ethnic privilege.

Luther and "the New Perspective on Paul"

Sanders' choice of the term "covenantal" to describe the thought of early Judaism is striking because Luther himself was reacting to a *pactum* theology, in which divine saving action is formally primary — bringing one into a state of grace and subsequently sustaining one there — but materially dependent on human response and "maintenance of covenant status." Sanders' "covenantal nomism" is at root quite similar to the medieval understanding of *facienti quod in se est Deus non denegat gratiam,* particularly in the *via moderna.*[41] God gives His grace to the one who by effort and intent is faithful to the covenant. True, there is a variation in emphasis which should not be overlooked. The theology of the *via moderna* tended to create doubts: one could not know with certainty whether one had done true penance and was in a state of grace. In contrast, everywhere we turn in the early Jewish sources there is an assurance of God's covenantal favor. Not even 4 Ezra is an exception.[42] The psychology of the sinner is entirely peripheral to the issue, however. For Luther, and for Paul whose letters he pondered, the question is where the salvation of the human being ultimately lies. Is it in some practice, disposition, or quality arising within the human being by the assistance of divine grace, or is it fully and radically *ab extra?* Does God find within us some inherent receptivity to grace by which He remolds our corruption, or must He put to death in order to raise to life? Far from furthering "the introspective conscience of the West," as Krister Stendahl has argued, Luther moves in an entirely new direction. His theology of the cross and his affirmation that the righteousness of Christ is given to the believer by faith mark a radical departure from the introspection of the medieval theology of humility.[43]

Likewise, the Pauline article on justification as it was once adopted by the Reformers is absolutely opposed to the privatism rooted in our secularized Western society. Sanders and those who have followed him have trod down the wrong path because they have followed modern categories, exploring grace no further than the superficial level of doubt and assurance. Paul's understanding of grace reaches its profundity by being before all else objective and theocentric. As Conyers reminds us, Paul was overshadowed by heaven. For him, the fallen world, whether it knows it or not, lies beneath the wrath of God, which already is giving over pagans to immorality, and waits with terrible anger for those confident moralists (read: us) who by their (our) self-centered dealings with others reveal that they (we) have loved idols as well. The gift of justification is likewise objective and external: now manifest apart from the Law, in Jesus Christ whom God set forth openly as a ἱλαστήριον, as a public display of His righteousness. To suggest, then, that the forensic understanding of justification in Paul's letters is "individualistic" in a privatistic sense is completely erroneous. On the contrary, it strips us of any hiding place and sets us *in foro Dei,* to be damned for our idolatry and selfishness, and to be graciously forgiven and given Christ as our Lord, as Käsemann forcefully reminded us.[44] Or as Paul says, "Each of us lives or dies to the Lord, for to this end Christ died and lived again, that he might be Lord of the dead and of the living" (Rom. 14:7-9). To attempt to correct the personal nature of forensic justification by "reversing" direction toward social justice is to remove the article on which all true justice hangs: the wrath and love of God manifest in the justifying work of the cross which calls us to account not merely for our outward deeds, but for the secrets of our hearts.[45] Recent interpreters have failed to understand Paul because the focal point of his thought, the necessity of standing before God in judgment, has seemed to them of minor importance.

As is obvious from the thought of the Reformers, the search for a gracious God is inherently joined to the question of what constitutes the true church. Luther's breakthrough was nothing other than the confession of the freedom of God over against the visible church to save "his own little flock" wherever the Gospel is proclaimed.[46] Rather than standing in opposition to the corporate dimension of Christianity, the article on justification provides its necessary precondition. True universalism is impossible without hearing in the Gospel that we stand condemned and graciously redeemed *coram Deo.* Otherwise we see ourselves falsely only as members of a victorious or victimized circle of the pious: self-love and idolatry in either case. Perhaps more than any other time, our generation needs to hear Paul's Gospel with its heavenly dimension preserved intact, and to see its power in the lives of believers. May God in His great mercy and for His own glory grant true renewal in our day.

NOTES

1. See Anthony Thiselton's discussion of the development of Bultmann's hermeneutic in *The Two Horizons: The New Testament and Philosophical Description* (Grand Rapids: Eerdmans, 1980), 205–51.

2. Rudolf Bultmann, *Theology of the New Testament,* 2 vols., trans. Kendrick Grobel (New York: Scribners, 1951–1955), 2:270.

3. I have expressed my own assessment elsewhere. See Mark A. Seifrid, *Justification by Faith: The Origin and Development of a Central Pauline Theme* (Leiden: Brill, 1992), 1–77.

4. I am still persuaded that Romans 11:25-27 reflects the expectation of an eschatological salvation of the nation of Israel. That reading best accounts for the repeated temporal references ("a partial hardening has come about for Israel, until the fulness of the Gentiles has come in," 11:25; "this shall be my covenant whenever I take away their sins [indefinite time, but not iterative, since it is joined to the Redeemer's coming from Zion]," 11:27), Paul's disclosure of this event as a mystery (11:25), and the distinction Paul draws in 11:28 between the Gospel and God's election of Israel.

5. Carl E. Braaten, *Justification: The Article by Which the Church Stands or Falls* (Minneapolis: Fortress, 1990), 10.

6. See the perceptive book by A.J. Conyers, *The Eclipse of Heaven: Rediscovering the Hope of a World Beyond* (Downers Grove, Ill.: InterVarsity, 1992), who borrows the language of Martin Buber.

7. The following material appears as a portion of an article in, Mark A. Seifrid, "Blind Alleys in the Controversy over the Paul of History," the *Tyndale Bulletin,* forthcoming.

8. Douglas Moo, "Paul and the Law in the Last Ten Years," *Southern Journal of Theology* 40 (1987): 287–307; Stephen Westerholm, *Israel's Law and the Church's Faith: Paul and His Recent Interpreters* (Grand Rapids: Eerdmans, 1988), 1–100; Frank Thielman, *From Plight to Solution,* Novum Testamentum Supp 61 (Leiden: Brill, 1989), 1–27; Moises Silva, "The Law and Christianity: Dunn's New Synthesis," *Westminster Theological Journal* 53 (1991): 339–53; P.T. O'Brien, "Justification in Paul and Some Crucial Issues of the Last Two Decades," in *Right with God: Justification in the Bible and the World,* ed. D.A. Carson (London: Paternoster, 1992), 69–95; Donald A. Hagner, "Paul and Judaism: The Jewish Matrix of Early Christianity: Issues in the Current Debate," *Bulletin for Biblical Research* 3 (1993): 111–30.

9. E.P. Sanders, *Paul and Palestinian Judaism: A Comparison of Patterns of Religion* (Philadelphia: Fortress, 1977), 474–511.

10. See especially the collection of essays: James D.G. Dunn, *Jesus, Paul, and the Law: Studies in Mark and Galatians* (London: SPCK, 1990). E.P. Sanders has moved to close the gap in a similar way in his *Paul, the Law, and the Jewish People* (Philadelphia: Fortress, 1983), 154–60.

11. "Covenantal nomism" as Sanders uses the expression represents the idea that God saves those who by effort and intent remain in the covenantal relation that He established with Israel, where forgiveness and cleansing are provided; see his *Paul and Palestinian Judaism,* 422–23.

12. See Seifrid, *Justification by Faith,* previously cited. Timo Laato, working on the basis of Pauline anthropology and the structure of Paul's soteriology in comparison with rabbinic materials, arrives at basically the same conclusion. See his *Paulus und das Judentum* (Abo: Abo Academy, 1991). The same point has been made in an unpublished dissertation, see Mark A. Elliott, "The Survivors of Israel" (Ph.D. diss., University of Aberdeen, 1993).

13. See especially PsSol, 9:4-5.

14. The Qumran writings, by virtue of their predestinarian stance are firmly *sola gratia*, but not *sola fide*. They differ from both the synergism of the medieval *via moderna* and the Pauline theology of the Reformers.

15. Josephus, *Antiquities*, 20.34–48.

16. Josephus, *Contra Apionem*, 2.210. Here we fail to see how Josephus' description of the welcome to Gentiles, "goes so far and no further" (see N.T. Wright, *The New Testament and the People of God* [Minneapolis: Fortress, 1992], 232). True, there is a limited participation for passing visitors, as there is for any "family," but according to Josephus the door is open and the welcome mat out for those who want to stay: in contrast to the Lacedemonians, he claims, the Jews do not expel foreigners; rather, "we gladly welcome those desiring to share our (customs)," *Contra Apionem*, 2.261.

17. m.Aboth 1.12.

18. See Scot McKnight, *A Light Among the Gentiles: Jewish Missionary Activity in the Second Temple Period* (Minneapolis: Fortress, 1991), esp. 11–48.

19. See Folker Siegert, "Gottesfürchtige und Sympathisanten," *Journal for the Study of Judaism* 4 (1973): 109–64.

20. Josephus, *Antiquities*, 20.48.

21. A similar sentiment appears in *Contra Apionem*, 2.226, "Let it be acknowledged: obedience to laws is a proof of virtue."

22. For Philo too circumcision represents self-control and the acknowledgment of one God as creator, *Spec.Leg.*, 1.8–10.

23. See Siegert, "Gottesfürchtige und Sympathisanten," 140–47.

24. JosAsen 11–13. The intramural apologetic interest is apparent. How could Joseph marry a non-Jew? He didn't: she converted. The walls are being preserved, but so are the gateways.

25. E.g., LetAris 134–43, WisSol 13–16; m.Abodah Zarah.

26. See Mary Douglas, "Critique and Commentary" in Jacob Neusner, *The Idea of Purity in Ancient Judaism*, SJLA1 (Leiden: Brill, 1973), 141.

27. See e.g., 1QS1:7-8, 1:16-17; 10:10; CD2:2; 3:13.

28. PssSol 12:6; 17:3.

29. 4 Ezra 7:133; 12:34. Here I am in disagreement with Bruce W. Longenecker, *Eschatology and the Covenant: A Comparison of 4 Ezra and Romans 1-11*, JSNT Supp 57 (Sheffield: JSOT, 1991). See my discussion of his treatment of 4 Ezra in Seifrid, *Justification by Faith*, 133–35.

30. 4QFlor 1:7; 1QS 1:5.

31. A preliminary survey of the contents of the scroll appears in an article by Lawrence Schiffmann, "The Temple Scroll and the Systems of Jewish Law of the Second Temple Period," in *Temple Scroll Studies*, JSPseud Supp 7, ed. George J. Brooke (Sheffield: JSOT, 1989), 239–55. The terms of the dispute crucial for our interest may be found in the fragment 4Q3998. The one who composed this letter regarded certain "works of the Law" as bringing blessing (מעשי התורה שחשבנו לטוב לך מקצת, "the sum of the works of the Law which we esteem as good for you," line 3). Disobedience in these matters involved the doing of evil (הרחיק ממך מחשבת רעה, "put away from you an evil plan," line 5), while obedience held the promise of eschatological blessing (בשל שתשמח באחרית העת, "in order that you might rejoice in the last time," line 6). The "works of the Law," are characterized as "doing what is right and good before God" and result in a divinely given righteousness and blessing (לך

ונהשבה‎, לצדקה בעשותך הישר וטוב לפנו לטוב לך ולישראל‎, "and it will be reckoned to you as righteousness when you do what is right and good before him, for your good and for that of Israel," line 7).

32. Although the reading ובצדקותו‎ ("in his righteousness") has been adopted universally as far as I can tell, reasons for reading ובצדקותי‎ ("with my righteous deeds") are very strong (i.e., taking the final letter as a *yodh;* vav and yodh are indistinguishable in 1QS): (1) According to Qimron, *The Hebrew of the Dead Sea Scrolls,* HSS29 (Atlanta, Scholars, 1986), 33–35, Qumran scribes generally preserve the orthographic distinction between ו‎ and יו‎. (2) In the closing hymn of 1QS10:8–11:22 only the יו‎ ending (which refers to God) appears with feminine plural nouns. (3) In the immediate context the word in question is surrounded by first-person singular endings requiring the use of יו‎ if the reading "his righteous deeds" is to be made evident. (4) In all other instances of pronominal suffixes attached to the plural צדקות‎ which may be found in currently published Qumran materials, the *plene* form, with the י‎ reminiscent of the masculine construct state is retained. For further arguments see Seifrid, *Justification by Faith,* 100–103.

33. E.g., 1QS 3:6-8; 8:6-10; 9:4.

34. See Thomas R. Schreiner, " 'Works of Law' in Paul," *Novum Testamentum* 33 (1991): 217–44; James D.G. Dunn, "Yet Once More – 'The Works of the Law': A Response," *Journal for the Study of the New Testament* 46 (1992): 99–117.

35. Romans 3:20 and Galatians 2:15-21, which introduce the cluster of occurrences of ἔργα νόμου in that letter, take precisely the same form, and the subsequent use of this terminology in Galatians 3 is didactic. Paul wants to teach his audiences about the "works of the Law."

36. Of course Paul regarded reliance on them rather than the Gospel as disobedience, cf. Romans 9:30–10:4.

37. This observation may help in assessing the significance of the ἐὰν μή clause in Galatians 2:16. One wonders if the solution to the debate (viz., whether we have here an exceptive clause such as generally appears with εἰ μή, or an adversative) lies in allowing that ἐὰν μή introduces an (elliptical) exceptive clause, while the phrase ἐξ ἔργων νόμου is adjectival modifying ἄνθρωπος and paralleling the ὅσοι ἐξ ἔργων νόμου in Galatians 3:10. Paul does not confront Peter with a new insight here, but builds on Peter's acknowledgment that even "a person of the works of the Law" is not justified except through faith. If that is so, Paul continues, we are justified by faith, and not through "works of the Law." See James D.G. Dunn, "Yet Once More – 'The Works of the Law'; A Response" *Journal for the Study of the New Testament* 46 (1992): 114.

38. Compare Westerholm, *Israel's Law and the Church's Faith,* 119; Schreiner, *Works of the Law,* 228–29. When in Romans Paul broadens the sphere of application of the topic of justification, he does it under the category of "faith," not "works" (Rom. 11:20). See Seifrid, *Justification by Faith,* 244–49.

39. See especially Romans 4:5-8, where Paul moves directly from Abraham to David's transgression of the Law.

40. See Nils Dahl, "The One God of Jews and Gentiles" in *Studies in Paul* (Minneapolis: Augsburg, 1977), 178–91.

41. See Alister E. McGrath, *Iustitia Dei: A History of the Christian Doctrine of Justification* (Cambridge: Cambridge Univ. Press, 1986), 1:70-91. For the sharpest, and yet entirely fair statement of this matter which so far has been ignored by

proponents of the new perspective, see Silva, "Law and Christianity," 347–49.

42. There too we find a circle of those who have kept the ways of the Most High. See 4 Ezra 7:1-140; 12:1-51.

43. See Martin Brecht, *Martin Luther: His Road to Reformation 1483–1521*, trans. James L. Schaaf (Minneapolis: Fortress, 1985), 221–37; Walther von Loewenich, *Luther's Theologia Crucis 5* (Witten: Luther, 1967); Joseph Vercruysse, S.J., "Luther's Theology of the Cross at the Time of the Heidelberg Disputation," *Gregorianum* 57 (1976): 523–48; James Nestingen, "Luther's Heidelberg Disputation: An Analysis of the Argument" in *All Things New: Essays in Honor of Roy A. Harrisville*, Word and World Supplements Series, ed. A.J. Hultgren, Donald Juel, and Jack D. Kingsbury (Minneapolis: Fortress, 1992), 147–51. I must thank my colleague Marvin Anderson for his bibliographical assistance, and his guidance in this question.

44. Ernst Käsemann, "Gottesgerechtigkeit bei Paulus," in *Exegetische Versuche und Besinnungen 2* (Göttingen: Vandenhoeck & Ruprecht, 1965), 2:181–93. While Käsemann's collapsing of the conceptual categories of "declare righteous" and "make righteous" is flawed, he rightly sees that for Paul an unbreakable link exists between them. To distinguish between the two is essential, to separate the two is fatal.

45. Contra, James D.G. Dunn, "The Justice of God: A Renewed Perspective on Justification by Faith," *Journal of Theological Studies* 43 (1992): 21–22.

46. See Brecht, *Martin Luther*, 236–37.

12

Reader-Response Theories in Postmodern Hermeneutics:[1] A Challenge to Evangelical Theology

Norman R. Gulley

Modern scholars have approached Scripture in various ways. These ways involve three major paradigm shifts: historical, literary, and cultural. The purpose of this chapter is to concentrate on the latest cultural paradigm (reader-response theories) within the context of their growth out of the historical (source, form, and redaction criticism) and literary paradigms (canonical criticism and structuralism). These paradigms concern the way one approaches Scripture. Within this development we will note the challenge that postmodernism presents to evangelical theology.

Three Horizons

One's approach to Scripture is discussed under the term "horizon" which is used by a number of scholars, including Husserl, Heidegger, Gadamer, Jauss, and Thiselton.[2] Thiselton speaks of the two horizons in which the author and text constitute the past horizon and the text and reader constitute the present horizon.[3] James C. McHann, Jr., goes one step further to include the future. This makes three horizons, past, present, and future. McHann's doctoral dissertation evaluates Pannenberg's focus on eschatology as the future horizon.[4] Pannenberg argues that only in the light of the finished product can there be real meaning. As Thiselton put it:

Norman R. Gulley is Professor of Systematic Theology at Southern College in Collegedale, Tennessee.

A work of art, for example, cannot be judged prior to its completion. For Christian theology, the eschatological horizon of divine promise sheds light on the meaning of the present. The future horizon is the time when we will know the meaning of the text after Christ's return. He will explain that which has remained unclear during the past and present. The event of Jesus Christ and his resurrection offers provisional anticipation of this eschatological goal of promise. This projects meaning within a frame which transcends the unfinished history of any particular community.[5]

Thus the eschatological horizon reaches from the Christ event of the past to the Christ event of the future. It embraces the end time which dawned with the coming of Christ into history. The once-for-all (*en hapax*) of crucifixion-resurrection anchors the future. Because of His death and resurrection it is just a matter of time till He returns again. He has already cried out "it is finished" (John 19:30). It only remains to be revealed as such in His return.

Lessing's "Ugly Ditch"

Gotthold Ephraim Lessing (1729–1781) helped launch critical study of Scripture that still influences modern thinking.[6] He spoke of the "ugly, broad ditch" between the biblical past and the present. His famous saying "Accidental historical truths can never become proofs for necessary truths of reason" was his way of presenting the supremacy of human reason over inscripturated truths. Lessing ended up putting more emphasis on the teaching than on the teacher (Christ). The teachings, not history, were paramount to him. He did not care whether a tale was true or not, as long as the fruit was beneficial. He even went so far as to say that the writings of biblical authors could all be lost and yet the religion they taught could still remain. His view did not really attempt to cross the "ugly ditch" to the horizon of the text and author. He chose to remain on this far side and replace the authority of Scripture by the authority of human reason.

By contrast, through a study of the two horizons, or through the spiral metaphor,[7] scholars attempt to cross the "ugly ditch." Some manage to cross over and discover the true meaning of Scripture, and with that in hand recross to the present time to faithfully tell of the significance of Scripture to contemporary church and society. Other scholars do not bother to cross over the "ugly ditch," choosing to remain on this side, just as Lessing did. They confine themselves within their culture and read out of the present happenings in it some ideas that they then take with them across the "ugly ditch" to super-impose upon Scripture. If we liken the "ugly ditch" to a broad ocean joining two continents, then scholars are taking ships in both direc-tions. They travel from this side to the far side and back again. All do the same journey. The difference between them is seen in the cargo they take with them. Some cross from this side to the far side somewhat empty-handed to learn from Scripture in its own faraway setting, what it means in its own right without any subsequent super-imposition by those living since that time up to the present. Others travel with baggage from this side, and cross not to learn but to teach, not to listen to Scripture but to inform it what it means for contemporary culture. The scholars who cross over to learn from Scripture return with new ideas. The others return with the same baggage they took. The first gained from the journey. For the others it was a waste of time.

Diachronic and Synchronic Methods

Two radically opposed methods of interpretation have been used in biblical studies, known as the diachronic and synchronic methods. The diachronic traces the development through history, whereas the synchronic interprets the text for what it is in itself. Diachronic method is employed by various historical critical methods such as source criticism, form criticism, and redaction criticism. Synchronic method is employed by canonical criticism, structuralism, reader-response criticism, and narrative criticism. Diachronic method is oc-cupied with the assumed development behind the writing of the text, encompassing an oral to written transmission. Synchronic method is occupied with the reading community and the effect of the text with-in it. Diachronic method has to do with a focus on what lies behind the text. Synchronic method has to do with a focus on what lies in front of the text. Terence J. Keegan speaks of these two horizons (behind and in front of text) as two poles, the artistic (behind) and the aesthetic (in front of) the text.[8]

It is clear that numerous methods claim to accomplish the her-meneutical task of interpreting Scripture. They are not only many, but are opposed in their way of arriving at biblical understanding. Even within each method there is a diversity, as Gerald T. Shephard reminds us concerning canonical criticism.[9] To better understand the cultural paradigm, we will offer a brief overview of the synchronic paradigm as a movement beyond historical-critical diachronic methods.

Literary Paradigm

Canonical criticism is an umbrella term that covers "a variety of approaches that inquire into the form and function of the Bible as scripture."[10] James Sanders coined the term "canon criticism" in his 1972 *Torah and Canon,* but Brevard Childs chose the term "canonical approach." As Shephard points out:

> Though the various canonical approaches explore the same neglected perspective on the nature of the biblical text, their chief interpreters do not always agree on terminology, on methods of analysis, or on the practical implications for the future of biblical interpretation and commentary.[11]

Scholars like Childs, Rendtorff, and Shephard begin with the canonical text as the locus where the meaning of Scripture is found. Whereas historical critics attempt to focus on the text at pre-canonical levels, canonical critics approach the text in its final form. As Keegan points out, canonical critics derive the meaning of the text from the community that accepts and canonizes it, whereas historical critics see the meaning of the text apart from the community.[12] Whereas the historical critics attempt to probe behind the text, to the assumed historical development leading up to its final form, canonical critics are not interested so much in that assumed historical development, and begin with the text as it is found today.

Brevard Childs considers canonical criticism to be more interested in looking at the larger picture (canon), rather than merely at books or segments as in source and form criticism. Canonical criticism belongs to what is called literary criticism in that it takes the text as it reads in its final form rather than being preoccupied with what may lie behind it. It, therefore, focuses on what the text means rather than on what the text meant. It focuses on the present horizon rather than on the past horizon. There is no interest in authorial intention, or in getting back into the mind of the authors in a type of psychological study. Therefore canonical criticism bypasses the gulf between the two horizons that has been the major concern of modern biblical scholarship. John Barton notes that

> the canonical approach is conceived as a *theological* mode of study. It is an attempt to heal the breach between biblical criticism and theology, and it assumes (at least for the purpose of method) that the interpreter is not a detached, neutral critic

free from religious commitment, but a believer, trying to apply the biblical text to the contemporary life of the Church.[13]

As a study of the anti-Nicene, Nicene, and post-Nicene exegesis of the church fathers documents, they studied texts in the context of the whole Bible. This is also true of Luther and Calvin, although Luther's was confined. For all practical purposes, canonical context was important to biblical exegetes of the pre-critical era. As Barton points out, there is a paradox about the way Childs presents his case. On the one hand he looks to the early church's decision on the canon, and yet does not look to their interpretation of Scripture. But can he have it both ways? Can he depend upon them for one decision and not for others? Does this not suggest a biased selectivity?[14] So canonical criticism is considered "post-critical" rather than a return to the pre-critical era. It has been called "text immanent" exegesis, in which the text has a life of its own apart from the author. Authorial intention is no longer important to gaining an understanding of the text. The meaning of the text is cut loose from the intention of the author and found rather in its relationship to the rest of the canon.[15]

Structuralism "was the first synchronic exegetical method to have an impact on modern biblical scholarship."[16] This happened in France in September 1969. Structuralism attempts to penetrate beyond the literal meaning on the surface to assumed deeper levels. Traditional linguistic study focused on etymology, or history behind the terms under study. By contrast, Ferdinand de Saussure (1857–1913) said words should be studied within the context of their use rather than in the context of their historical development. The issue was how they were used in contrast with the language of the time. This was a change of focus from diachronic study of changing meanings through history to synchronic study of the meaning of the terms in the context of language-use. Primary focus shifted from etymology to linguistic system. Saussure called this new focus *langue* (linguistic system) compared to *parole* (single utterance).

Although many scholars using structuralist methods do not defend biblical inspiration, John Barton rightly notes that "a major theme of structuralist approaches to biblical study has been a desire to undermine the results of conventional 'historical' criticism,"[17] because of "disappointment and disillusionment with the traditional historical-critical methods."[18] As in canonical criticism the focus has moved away from what lies behind (history/development) the text to what is in the text itself. Structuralism denies the importance of authorial intention, and that the biblical critic needs to use the text to get back to the author to discover his/her intention or to enter into the psychology of the author. This historical approach had been the domain of the various methods of historical criticism which structuralism repudiates. By contrast, structuralism claims to be logical rather than historical. With structuralism there is a major paradigm shift in critical biblical studies from the author-text diachronic focus to text-reader synchronic emphasis.

This paradigm shift rejected the historical concerns of post-Enlightenment critical biblical studies. We noted this change already in canonical criticism. The paradigm shift means that source, form, and redaction criticism are removed from the place of primary concern in biblical interpretation. The shift moved away from the meaning of the author behind the text to the meaning of the text in itself. The paradigm shift was away from the author to the reader, from what the author wrote to the effects of what the author wrote. The later Ludwig Wittgenstein and John Barton both use the chess game to describe structuralism. Barton put it this way:

> To discover what a given move "meant," or what significance it had, in a particular game, we need to be in command of (be "competent" in) the game of chess; we do not need a knowledge of the psychology of the players. The possible meanings of moves at chess are determined completely by the structures of the game; and though players can make "original" moves in the sense of moves that *exploit* to the full the possibilities the rules make available, they cannot make moves that contravene the rules (for example, moving a knight as if it were a rook) without ceasing to play the game altogether. Such a move has literally "no meaning" within chess: it is not a real move at all. The meaning that a genuine move has is determined by its contrast with other possible moves, just as the value of the pieces on the board is a function of their relation to each other. Thus a queen has a high value only because it is part of an ordered structure within which it can make a wider variety of moves than any other piece. If the rules were changed so that all pieces could move as the queen moves, it would cease to have this special value; and if one removed it from the board, which is its own cultural context of "world," it would have neither meaning nor value, but would become simply an oddly-shaped wooden object.[19]

So the biblical text is like a chess board with many players. The rules of the game are found within the structural layers within the text, and meaning can only be achieved through playing the game of interpretation according to the rules. "Until one is in command of (or, in technical structuralist terminology, is *competent*) the rules of chess as a whole, one cannot understand an individual piece or make any sense of a particular move. Almost all social and cultural situations are similarly susceptible of structuralist analysis, from law courts and public meetings to meals and parties."[20] For example, James Barr's *The Semantics of Biblical Language* (1961) "represents a turning point in the linguistic study of the Bible." Before his epochal book, biblical linguistics were preoccupied with diachronic or etymological interest in Hebrew and Greek biblical words, as documented in Kittel's *Theological Dictionary of the Old Testament* and *Theological Dictionary of the New Testament*.

> Barr argued that the biblical languages should be studied in accordance with current practice in general linguistics: meaning must be determined by the present context of words and sentences in the biblical text, and must not be read off from the (supposed) derivations of "key words." Barr also argued against the idea that a special "Hebrew mentality" could be deduced from features of the language, such as its verb system or its syntax, showing that this was incompatible with a structural approach to language.[21]

Structuralists believe that literary meaning is determined by the conventions of reading. In other words, reading determines the meaning. But if this is true then what about structuralist's own literature? Applying their thesis to their own literature, the reader could change the meaning. This means that the thesis that the reader changes the meaning would also be changed by the reader reading that thesis. If that is true then structuralism would experience its demise based upon its own premise.

In his *Anchor Bible Dictionary* articles, Oxford University professor John Barton concluded these methods are "widely divergent," "fruitless," "arid," and need "to be abandoned."[22] Other scholars have also called the methods in question. For example, there are critiques by those who once used the methods, such as Walter Wink,[23] Gerhard Meier,[24] Eta Linnemann,[25] and Thomas C. Oden.[26] Besides these, there are important critiques by Gerhard F. Hasel,[27]

Royce G. Gruenler,[28] Vern S. Poythress,[29] Joseph Cardinal Ratzinger,[30] and Archbishop Stafford.[31]

Joseph Cardinal Ratzinger, second only to the pope in theological authority for Catholics,[32] calls for a "self-criticism of the historical method which can expand to an analysis of historical reason itself, in continuity with and in development of the famous critique of reason by Immanuel Kant."[33] He also notes there are "immense reservations" about the methods, which have serious moral consequences and that they can "bring about a rejection of the relevance of the Bible for learning about God and his relationships to mankind."[34] When historical critical methods remove propositional truths from Scripture, the Bible is silenced, the Word of God becomes little better than an incoherent sound.

Eta Linnemann gave up her Bultmannian critical training after rising to eminence in critical circles. She said, "As time passes, I become more and more convinced that to a considerable degree New Testament criticism as practiced by those committed to historical-critical theology does not deserve to be called science."[35] Furthermore she affirmed, "My 'No' to historical-critical theology stems from my 'Yes!' to my wonderful Lord and Savior Jesus Christ and to the glorious redemption he accomplished for me on Golgotha."[36] She had come to place the Living Word and the written Word above the critical methods of the academy. She had become a true evangelical.

Historical-critical methods involve a dissection that majors in minutia. There is such a preoccupation with some details, imagined and real, that the big picture is usually lost. The extensive processes involved often end up with very little enlightenment of the text. It is like exploring a quarry for gold and doing little else than working in the material without finding anything. As Osborne reminds us, "the historical-critical method has produced a vacuum in actually understanding Scripture,"[37] for the historical-critical method does not allow the text to speak for itself.[38] It is only interested in how the text came to be in the form it is. It does not give proper emphasis to the meaning of the text as it is.

It is important that we come to the Bible and meet it on its own terms rather than meeting it on our terms. We need to take seriously its claims to be God's Word. A doctor does not come to each patient with the same diagnosis. He allows the problems and condition of the patient to dictate how he or she can best understand their condition. Scholars already practice this attention to differences in the historical-critical methods, such as attention to different genres. What scholars need to do is to take this one step further and recognize the genre called "divine revelation/inspiration." The genre of divine revelation/inspiration, by its uniqueness, necessitates a different approach by the scholar than he/she takes when approaching secular literature. If biblical scholars would approach Scripture as "revelation/inspiration genre" they would not assume that biblical history is wrong, would not read a modern evolutionary worldview back into an alleged preliterary oral development, nor confine their research within an alleged closed continuum in which God is kept distant from His creation.

Archbishop Stafford noted that the historical-critical method's "assumptions and deficiencies have inspired tremendous and destructive tensions in the churches," for "the results of the historical-critical method on moral theology have been very serious."[39] George Lindbeck notes that most scholars receiving doctorates in biblical studies teach in secular institutions and those who teach catechists have a "disastrous" effect upon them.[40] Historical-critical methods will go to any limits to speak about preliterary traditions, different forms and sources. But there is thunderous silence when they face truth. These methods raise all sorts of questions about how we got the text but say nothing about the truths it contains. It is like a hungry man who sits down to a banquet and only dissects the food, probing down to the plate, cogitating on how each item may have arrived on the dish, but who eats nothing and leaves empty.

Harvard University professor Frank M. Cross states that "history in the modern context means a description and interpretation of human events arrived at by a specific scientific method. Among the stipulations of this method is agreement to eschew discussion of ultimate causation or meaning. . . . You don't speak of divine acts or victories in writing history. . . . Attribution of events to miracles is disallowed on methodological grounds."[41] Hershel Shanks, editor of the *Biblical Archaeology Review,* stated that "Most modern (historical-critical) biblical scholars do not accept the Bible as literally true. So what you have to do is to treat it almost like an archaeological tel, and excavate it, as it were, and analyze it to see whether what it says is historically accurate by modern historians' standards, by modern historiography." So God is not only shut away from human history but from Scripture. Humans are simply left to their own historical-critical methods which are confined to their own making. This, we submit, is the height of human folly. If Scripture claims to be God's Word to humanity, and proclaims that God has entered into and has made a difference in human history, particularly as seen in the person and work of Jesus Christ, then Scripture should determine its own rules of interpretation rather than have those of human creation thrust upon it from outside. But the historical-critical method first doubts that God has so acted in human history, then doubts the Bible as true, and then proceeds to confine itself to human historical methods to try to get something within Scripture that it can accept as true.

Is this not the final result of Descartes' famous call to doubt? He launched the modern era of philosophy that centers on the human self. This so-called "Enlightenment" era thrust biblical study into a new dark age. Gone is the light of God's Word and the certainty that attends that light. None of the methods have really helped us understand the text better. As Barton asked, "When we have learned to apply all the methods biblical critics have devised, what have we really achieved?[42] Any rejection of the "historical-critical" method in biblical study must also include those of the literary and cultural paradigms.

Cultural Paradigm

Narrative criticism. Historical-critical methods have been used for less than two centuries. They grew out of the Enlightenment period and its celebration of human reason. These methods were launched to break the guardian knot between academia and the church. For centuries ecclesiastical tradition stifled scholarly freedom. As history documents, reactions often overplay themselves. So it is with the historical-critical methods which bought into philosophical presuppositions that confined biblical truth to naturalism. Jettisoned were the miracles, the divinity of Christ, the Second Advent, to name but a few.

These events depend upon the supernatural breaking into the realm of the natural. Naturalism presents a closed continuum of cause and effect in which events follow laws of predictability. This closed worldview shuts out any in-breaking from beyond by the supernatural. Thus God, who resides throughout the universe, transcending space and time as the Creator of both, is shut out from this part of His creation. Such a philosophical worldview is in direct conflict with the biblical worldview.

Historical-critical methods are preoccupied with segments of texts. Narrative criticism broadened the focus by taking in the whole story. But narrative criticism is not interested in the historical connection and so is more interested in the present horizon between text and reader than in the past horizon between author and text. To this degree narrative criticism does not do full justice to the whole story that requires the past dimension.

Reader-response criticism.[43] Post-structuralism shifts attention to the reader, not only as an individual (Wolfgang Iser), but within the reading community as a socio-cultural phenomenon (Stanley Fish).[44] The focus on individual consciousness of author (Schleiermacher) or reader (Heidegger) is replaced by the inter subjectivity of the community,[45] or the creativity of the individual interpreter. As Thiselton argues, when meaning "is subsumed within the prior horizons of the reading community," we have gone beyond Gadamer's two horizons that respect both horizons, and not just that of the reader.[46] Reader-response theorists run the gamut from the radical Stanley Fish to the moderate Wolfgang Iser.[47]

Within that spectrum of difference, the swing away from the past to the present continues from the same trend already noted in canonical criticism and structuralism. For the more radical reader-response theorists the text no longer has a fixed meaning. The "autonomous text" is repudiated. Rather, the text is open-ended to multiplied meanings, because the text only comes to meaning in the reader's response to it. Here hermeneutics no longer is a search for the meaning of the text behind the text, but rather a search for the meaning of the text in front of the text. It is not the author's intention, nor the meaning of the text in its initial context, that is important. Now the context of the reader is of primary significance. The interpretive context has moved from the author-text horizon to the text-reader horizon.

It was Wolfgang Iser's concept of the "implied reader" that introduced the reader as important to the interpretation of texts. The "implied reader" was a counterpart of the "implied author" in preliterary studies. It was said that the "implied reader" would be equipped with a certain minimum of knowledge to understand what the author or "implied author" meant by what he wrote. Beyond this shared knowledge, reader-response criticism "insists that indeterminacy is a basic characteristic of the literary texts. What is revealed in the text is at the same time accompanied by what remains concealed." These "gaps" between the known and unknown necessitate the reader to contribute to the meaning of the text.[48]

The historical paradigm (source, form, and redaction criticism) moved to the literary paradigm (canonical criticism and structuralism) and then to the cultural paradigm (narrative and reader-response theories). Thomas Kuhn, in *The Structure of Scientific Revolutions,* speaks of various scientific paradigms; he says that each new paradigm grows out of a reaction to a prevalent paradigm.[49] We have seen that this is true in the context of biblical interpretation. In different ways, both the literary and cultural paradigms are a reaction to the historical critical methods of the historical paradigm. It is clear, then, that any rejection of the historical-critical methods may be a rejection of one form of biblical criticism for another, and equally devastating, critical method. Such is true of reader-response theories which place culture above Scripture.

Culture above Scripture

A growing number of scholars around the world are placing culture above Scripture, so that authority resides in culture rather than within the Bible. These scholars do not bring their culture to be critiqued and interpreted by Scripture. They bring Scripture to be critiqued and interpreted by their culture. The October 1993 meeting of the "Jesus Seminar" completed the first phase to redefine the New Testament canon. This group of about seventy scholars has been at work since 1985 in the Gospels and has reduced the authentic sayings of Jesus to a mere handful. Robert Funk, head of the seminar's Westar Institute in Sonoma, California, considers that it is legitimate for scholars to call in question the present canon for he argues that the Bible is a "cultural artifact."[50]

An international conference on biblical interpretation convened at the Divinity School, Vanderbilt University, October 21–24, 1993. The focus of the conference was on social location as an important part of biblical interpretation. Social location refers to the reader's cultural context. It is a reading of Scripture from within the reader's own social setting, so that his or her location becomes more important to the interpretative process than does the social location of the biblical author and text. The program called for papers to be presented by scholars from Argentina, Australia, Brazil, Canada, Costa Rica, Denmark, England, Hong Kong, India, Japan, Korea, Nigeria, Norway, South Africa, and the United States. Most of these came to give their papers. Present were people from fifteen different locations, reading Scripture from their own cultural setting.

Following is a list of twenty major assumptions observed during the conference, either expressed by the participants or obvious from their presentations.

(1) The biblical interpreter does not begin with the biblical text but with the reader. This is in contrast to the historical paradigm which begins with the history behind the text, and the literary paradigm that begins with the text itself.

(2) The reader is unable to transcend his/her social location.

(3) The various liberation theologies, whether racial or feminist, are more interested in their personal agenda for liberation than in what the biblical text says in its own location.

(4) True objectivity is impossible. At best, only a relative objectivity is attainable, for objectivity is itself a human construct.

(5) All exegesis is eisegesis.

(6) Socio-analytical reading of Scripture finds in the text what is relevant to the reader in his or her cultural location, the rest is ignored.

(7) Global or universal interpretation of biblical texts is impossible. There are only local meanings.

(8) The reader gives the biblical text its meaning.

(9) The reader must liberate Scripture before it liberates the reader.

(10) Victims, or the colonized, repudiate biblical texts that are products of oppressors, or the colonizers.

(11) All Scripture is patriarchal or andro-centric, male- dominated and, therefore, is repudiated by feminist liberation.

(12) Scripture was culture originated and can be rejected by readers living in the different social location of modern culture.

(13) Readers need to appropriate Scripture to their social location.

(14) Revelation never ceases. It is present in preaching today.

(15) There are no absolute statements in Scripture.

(16) Certain biblical texts are offensive to readers in cultural locations where their practice is different from that given in Scripture, such as in polytheistic cultures.

(17) Yet, the claim is also made that polytheism is taught in Scripture.

(18) Pluralism is presented as true liberation beyond the narrower confines of Scripture.

(19) Because of Scripture, the history of Christianity has been the most destructive religion in history.

(20) Because of Scripture, missionaries have equated deculturization as christianization. So to become a Christian, an Indian, for example, had to renounce his Indian culture.

In all of these assumptions culture, as expressed in the social location of the reader, is placed above Scripture. Although one participant said the place of the biblical text is on the same level as the cultural context of the reader, with neither one authoritative over the other, it is clear that culture is considered authoritative over Scripture. For Scripture is confined within the cultural context of the reader rather than the cultural context being critiqued by Scripture. We will cite some examples given which document this conclusion. Isaiah 40 is a servant song about Christ. This passage was wrenched from its soteriological context and forced to fit into the cultural context of liberation. Isaiah 44:9-20 is disconcerting to the Indian mind because it is offensive for satire to occur in a religious context. Furthermore, the statement against polytheism is offensive because India is polytheistic. It is argued that in India one sees the divine image rather than hearing the divine word. It is claimed that the sin of idolatry is only in the eye of the beholder. For Indians beholding many gods there is no sin. It is culturally acceptable, and so biblical monotheism is offensive.

Christ's dialogue with the woman taken in adultery is reconstructed (John 8:3-11). The question is raised, "where is the man that was taken in adultery, for it takes two persons to commit the act?" Because only the woman is mentioned the text is considered male-biased. The reader postulates that it was really the man's fault, and that the woman was an innocent victim. As an innocent victim it was reprehensible of Christ to tell the woman, "Go now and leave your life of sin" (John 8:11, NIV). So either Christ did not say these words, or the Christ portrayed in the narrative is a male-prejudiced Christ, or a Christ portrayed by a male recorder of the text, and therefore not a relevant Christ to a female reader.

Christ's dialogue with the Canaanite woman is also read out of a modern cultural context (Matt. 15:21-28). She asks for healing for her demon-possessed daughter. Jesus did not respond. It was claimed Christ marginalizes the woman while focusing on something else. Christ then says He was sent only to the lost sheep of Israel and thereby shows racism. This is compounded by Christ saying, "It is not right to take the children's bread and toss it to their dogs" (v. 26). None of this dialogue is perceived from the standpoint of Christ testing her faith, even though Jesus concluded that she had "great faith" (v. 28). This option is ignored in a quest to picture Christ as irrelevant to female readers, as either a Christ presented in a male-dominated social location or a Christ who was the product of His male-dominated culture.

Here were scholars from various denominations placing their different cultures above the Word of God. Each was reading Scripture from a national, tribal, or local perspective. The result was a hopeless and complex pluralism. There was no one Word from God but a multiplex of cultural words from humans. Protestantism caused the liberation of God's Word which brought liberation from Rome. Now, on the eve of the twenty-first century, we find that the strongest adherence to critical biblical methods comes from Protestants. But these methods are destroying the Bible that once gave birth to Protestantism. This is Protestantism using methods that undermine the biblical foundation of its existence. Paradoxically, it is sometimes Catholic scholars who call attention to the destructive nature of these methods[51] mostly used by Protestants for decades.[52]

Actually some Protestants are more Catholic than the Catholic

Church from which they revolted, for at least tradition has a function in some Catholic interpretation whereas the authority of denominational interpretation is repudiated in the name of liberation by so many contemporary Protestant interpreters. The social location is national and tribal but rarely, if ever, denominational. For all authority is jettisoned, apparently in the rush to place self as supreme authority over Scripture. The social location is not just national or tribal; it is personal. Thus every person in every social location is free to read Scripture from his or her own personal social and cultural perspective. In principle, therefore, there can be as many readings of Scripture as there are readers. One has to ask what is the relevance of Scripture in this process. For has not the individual really displaced the divine and culture overthrown Scripture? We may even ask ourselves why these scholars even bother to use Scripture in their attempt to promote their liberation agendas. Why not make culture their Scripture? Why not become sociologists rather than promote their culture under the cloak of scriptural interpretation?

In one session a scholar from Argentina interpreted Revelation 18. In this passage the riches of Babylon are pictured as received from trade with merchants (vv. 11-16). The Argentinean approached this passage from the perspective of a poverty-stricken victim of colonization triumphing over the rich colonizers. Babylon represents the colonizers and their riches which will be destroyed.

At the end of the day it is Scripture that is colonized by the colonizing interpreters. It is Scripture that is suppressed by the oppressive interpreters. It is Scripture that is bound in the cause of personal liberation. Reader-response criticism has its critics. "Some maintain that the method destabilizes the text, ignores its constraints, and opens up the gates for all forms of subjectivism."[53] Deconstructionists question the validity of reader-response theory. As we noted in structuralism, if the reader brings meaning to the text, then the reader will bring meaning to reader-response theory, and so there cannot be any conclusive reader-response theory.[54]

As noted above, reader-response theories place culture above Scripture. Culture judges Scripture and not Scripture culture. Scripture is used selectively according to what is considered useful to any contemporary cultural context. Culture determines the usefulness of Scripture. Culture is the norm that determines what part of the Bible is Scripture and what part can be rejected. Reader-response theorists of the cultural paradigm are quick to attest to their superior method over literary and historical paradigms. Such attestation is too glib, for who is to say that the cultural paradigm has immortality beyond that of the historical and literary paradigms which it critiques. Maybe another paradigm will appear that will call in question the cultural paradigm to the same extent that the cultural paradigm has called the historical and literary paradigms in question. Pannenberg's work on the eschatological horizon in the text is a possible case in point. History tells us that schools come and go, and this is not to say that the historical and literary paradigms are not alive and well. They are. But the contemporary debate has moved beyond them to the cultural paradigm, and in like manner the future debate could go beyond the cultural paradigm. Before considering this, we pause to note the challenge of postmodernism.

The Challenge of Postmodernism

In recent times the supporting structures of modernity have collapsed. As Thomas Oden has observed, "We have already witnessed in the third quarter of the twentieth century the precipitous deterioration of social processes under the tutelage of autonomous individualism, narcissistic hedonism, and naturalistic reductionism, all of which have been key features of modern consciousness."[55] In his seminal book *Agenda for Theology,* Oden, as early as 1979, wrote about postmodern students.

> These postmodern students have explored the edges and precipices of the ecstasies of modern freedom and have fallen into their share of its abysses. Having painfully experienced the limits of modernity, they are now engaging in a lengthy pilgrimage in which they have at long last stumbled, almost by accident, on the texts and spiritual directions and liturgies of classical Christianity.[56]

As Diogenes Allen put it:

> Our intellectual culture is at a major turning point. A massive intellectual revolution is taking place that is perhaps as great as that which marked off the modern world from the Middle Ages. The foundations of the modern world are collapsing, and we are entering a postmodern world. The principles forged during the Enlightenment (c. 1600–1780), which formed the foundations of the modern mentality, are crumbling.[57]

In 1981 Charles Wood spoke of the Christian understanding of Scripture, just as there are historical and literary understandings.[58] He wrote, "Although the Bible can be understood like any other book, not every understanding of it is a Christian understanding."[59] Christians come to Scripture with a worldview that believes in a God who reveals Himself in space and time, where the biblical accounts are not myths but the record of God in His salvific work for humankind. A true Christian understanding of Scripture places authority in the Bible rather than in the believing community (Brevard Child's canonical criticism),[60] or individual reader (reader-response theories), or individual experience (Schleiermacher).

This collapse of modernity, and return to the pre-critical view of Scripture, opens up the possibility of freeing the Bible from its perception as a domesticated casebook to a universal guidebook.[61] A broader view of Scripture, beyond the domesticating influence of the Enlightenment, opens up the possibility of a true reader-response theory—a faithful listening to the Word of God through Scripture. Postmodernism gives opportunity to return to a pre-critical view of Scripture that is more open to classical interpretations than those of modernity.[62] These can take into account the function of the Holy Spirit in the giving and reading of Scripture.

Spiritual Location of Scripture: The Function of the Holy Spirit

The future debate needs to go beyond social location of the reader to the spiritual location of Scripture. This is not to suggest that Scripture was written in the same cultural context as far as human authors are concerned. It is to suggest, however, that Scripture has the same Holy Spirit author working through all the human authors in different locations so that the divine authorship is in one spiritual location. That one spiritual location has far more of a molding influence on Scripture than do the various cultural contexts in which the story of Scripture and its human authors are located. Reader-response theorists ignore the divine dimension of the Bible and treat it as a mere human book subject for their manipulation. By contrast, the meaning of Scripture is found in the spiritual location of the divine author rather than in the social location of the human readers.

Have reader-response theories made an authentic contribution to readers beyond that received in the historical and literary paradigms? The emptiness from the historical critical methods has given way to literary methods in which (1) the text is autonomous, cut off from its author, and therefore open to multiple meanings; or (2) the reader is autonomous and adds to the text to give it its meaning as coauthor. These two positions represent two further steps away from the historical critical focus and also steps away from the authorship of the Holy Spirit. All of the critical methods discussed above call in question the divine authorship of Scripture. In our discussion we have moved away from the past horizon of the author-text and its diachronic emphasis to the "immanent text" as it is and moved further to the "text as it will be" of the text-to-reader present horizon with its synchronic focus. Have these two steps away from the historical dimension solved the "emptiness" problem of the historical critical methods?

To answer this question we will return to the analogy of the person who sits down to a banquet. The starving man sits down to the banquet once more. This time he does not probe into the different items on the plate, nor does he try to speculate on how these items got onto the plate, nor does he try to figure out the cook's intention in choosing the items and why he arranged them as they are. Rather, he comes to the food to see what he can add, by way of thinking, to make the food come alive, to give it meaning. He realizes that he is a co-cook and must apply his human reason to give the real meaning to this scrumptious feast. He comes to force onto this cooking his cultural ideas of cooking. After much thought he believes that he has added significantly to the meaning of the food. With that he gets up and leaves — empty once more. He may claim to be liberated by the process, but he remains unfed. Why? He ignored the cook who handed him the plate.

Immanuel Kant wrote a book entitled *Religion within the Limits of Reason Alone.* Karl Barth calls Kant's hermeneutics the interpretative method of pure rationalism, for Kant believed that "the God who is within us is the interpreter."[63] The introspection into human reason (Kant) or feeling (Schleiermacher) confined humans to themselves rather than allowing them to be open to revelation that comes from outside of themselves. Little better is Brunner's "truth as encounter" or Barth's revelation in preaching (*kerygma*) or locating revelation within Christ. All these fail to give primacy to Scripture and its own self-revelation. For revelation in Scripture is the result of the Holy Spirit inspiring prophets and guiding in the formation of the canon and giving to the interpreters the same guidance in understanding as He gave to the prophets in writing. One of the weaknesses of contemporary study into the process of revelation/inspiration and hermeneutics is the lack of space given to the function of the Holy Spirit.

Modernity emphasizes the function of human beings in the process of writing Scripture and its interpretation. It is true that the written Word (Scripture), just like the Living Word (Jesus Christ), is a union of the divine and the human. God could not reveal Himself in heavenly language for we would not understand. Neither could He reveal Himself in an encounter or we would perish. Of necessity God comes in accommodation to our level, both in written and living form, clothing divine content with human garb. Just as He took flesh and dwelt among us, so He gives divine thought content through human expression.

Hermeneutics, to accomplish its task, must approach Scripture as Moses approached the burning bush (Ex. 3:1-5). One approaches God's Word as holy ground. The interpreter needs to come to Scripture as a scientist comes to nature. He or she should not try to force ideas upon Scripture, but allow the Bible to present its own ideas about itself. Often interpreters come to Scripture as a technocrat. For just as a woodsman looks at the tree for what he can get out of it, so many interpreters approach Scripture. This often leads to selective use of Scripture and often to a canon within a canon, as is seen in cultural hermeneutics. By contrast, the whole of Scripture is inspired by God and deserves to be listened to carefully.

What does the Bible say about itself? It is clear that the biblical writers thought of the Scriptures as unique when compared to other writings. They spoke of them as "sacred writings" (2 Tim. 3:15, NASB), "oracles of God" (Rom. 3:2; Heb. 5:12, NASB) and therefore as "holy Scriptures" (Rom. 1:2, NASB). Biblical writers never claim to have originated their writings. Rather they speak of seeing in vision (Isa. 1:1; Jer. 38:21; Amos 1:1; Micah 1:1; Hab. 1:1). Nehemiah said to God, "By your spirit you admonished them through your prophets" (Neh. 9:30; cf. Zech. 7:12). David said, "The Spirit of the Lord spoke through me; his word was on my tongue. The God of Israel spoke" (2 Sam. 23:2-3). Prophets spoke of being filled or moved by the Holy Spirit. Thus Ezekiel exclaimed, "the Spirit came into me and raised me to my feet, and I heard him speaking to me" (Ezek. 2:2). He continues, "Then the Spirit of the Lord came upon me, and he told me to say: 'This is what the Lord says' "(Ezek. 11:5). In his work of speaking God's messages, Micah testified, "I am filled with power with the Spirit of the Lord" (Micah 3:8).

The New Testament gives insight into the function of the Holy

Spirit in the writing of the Old Testament. Jesus said that David spoke by the Holy Spirit (Mark 12:36). Paul said in Rome, "The Holy Spirit spoke the truth to your forefathers when he said through Isaiah the prophet" and quotes Isaiah 6:9-10 which speaks of those who listen but never understand for they have closed their eyes (Acts 28:25-27). The Old Testament people of Israel were often that way. They did not perceive that the prophets really had a divine message from God. They only listened to them as human messengers. This is a recurring problem through human history, and is evidenced so remarkably since the Enlightenment in the way people come to Scripture not as a divine message from God but merely as a human message.

Peter said ancient prophets had "the Spirit of Christ in them . . . pointing when he predicted the sufferings of Christ and the glories that would follow" (1 Peter 1:11). "For the prophecy never had its origin in the will of man, but men spoke from God as they were carried along by the Holy Spirit" (2 Peter 1:21). The origin of Scripture is clearly not human, but the Spirit of God. It is appropriate then that biblical writers refer to their writings as written by the Holy Spirit. Thus the author of Hebrews says, "So, as the Holy Spirit says" (Heb. 3:7) and "The Holy Spirit was showing by this" (Heb. 9:8).

The New Testament writers not only testified that the Holy Spirit spoke through the Old Testament prophets but that He was the same divine person speaking through their writings. Thus Christ gave "instructions through the Holy Spirit to the apostles he had chosen" (Acts 1:2), many of whom became writers of New Testament books/letters. John could speak of being "in the Spirit" (Rev. 1:10) when he was given a vision and commissioned to "write on a scroll what you see and send it to the seven churches" (Rev. 1:11).

The Bible provides an example of how inspiration works. When Moses said he could not speak to Pharaoh, God appointed Aaron to be the spokesperson. The relationship between Moses and Aaron illustrates the relation between God and the prophets in giving God's messages. "Then the Lord said to Moses, 'See, I have made you like God to Pharaoh, and your brother Aaron will be your prophet. You are to say everything I command you, and your brother Aaron is to tell Pharaoh to let the Israelites go out of his country' " (Ex. 7:1-2). So the message given by the prophets is the message given to them by God. The ultimate author is not the prophet but God. The prophets function not so much as authors but as spokespersons for God.

Hence the meaning of "prophesy" is "to speak on behalf of."

One does not treat the Bible as any other book. It is not a book with merely human authorship. God's Word is His book. He merely used human writers and words in order to communicate with humans just as He became incarnate in order to reach humankind. Source criticism spends too much time considering the possible oral tradition behind the final writing as we have it in Scripture. Little, if any, time is given to considering the divine process behind the writing of Scripture. Holy men of God spoke as they were moved by the Holy Spirit (2 Peter 1:21); Scripture is God-breathed (Gk., *theopneustos*). God inspired the prophets, not their words. Verbal inspiration claims infallibility or inerrancy for the biblical words. By contrast, thought inspiration claims infallibility or inerrancy for the God-breathed thoughts communicated through human fallible words.

Propositional revelation believes that God-breathed thoughts are inscripturated in the Bible. These propositions are the infallible divine thoughts that are wrapped in fallible human language. It is not the words that are of primary interest, but the thoughts they attempt to convey. The preoccupation with word studies in Kittel's *Theological Dictionary of the Old Testament* and the *Theological Dictionary of the New Testament* can be a focus on the human side of Scripture. Hermeneutics has to take cognizance of the human words as they are the vehicle for conveying the divine thoughts. But word studies must always be a means to the end of arriving at the thought content they convey, or else hermeneutics fails to arrive at the divine content given in Scripture, and therefore fails to complete the work of interpretation. We need to emphasize once more, that *genre* study has played an important role in understanding the types of literature found in Scripture. But to stop there is to stop before completing the hermeneutical task. To be fair to Scripture, hermeneutics must follow a method that is appropriate to the object of its study. Hermeneutics must approach the divine content conveyed by the words, and allow word studies to be only a means to arriving at divine thoughts given through them. For the final *genre* is not just the types of literature used, but the divine *genre* that they convey.

In the *Journal of the Evangelical Theological Society,* Daniel B. Clendenin tells why the classic exegetes are to be preferred over many contemporary exegetes. He asks:

Why are they better? Not just because they are earlier but because the classic exegetes were "more attentive" to the text, which is to say that they came to the text to listen and not to question. Instead of coming to the texts as subjects who lord it over an objective datum they saw themselves as objects and the text as the subject.[64]

Classic exegetes did not engage in various methods of biblical criticism. Biblical criticism is not commensurable with belief in Scripture as God's Word. It is a questioning that may be appropriate for other books, but is inappropriate when used of the Bible. John Calvin, one of the classic exegetes, spoke of Scripture as follows: "Scripture . . . shows us the true God clearly. God therefore bestows a gift of singular value, when, for the instruction of the Church, he employs not dumb teachers merely, but opens his own sacred mouth."[65] Calvin continues in another place, saying, "Scripture exhibits clear evidence of its being spoken by God, and, consequently, of its containing his heavenly doctrine."[66]

Classic exegetes believe in the function of the Holy Spirit in the process of both inspiration and illumination of the Bible. The Holy Spirit conveys truth to the inspired prophets in the past horizon, and illumines the seeking reader in the present horizon. It is the function of the Holy Spirit to actualize the "fusion of horizons." Calvin affirms, "The same Spirit, therefore, who spoke by the mouth of the prophets, must penetrate our hearts, in order to convince us that they faithfully delivered the message with which they were divinely intrusted."[67]

Trans-cultural Context of Scripture

Radical reader-response theories begin with the local sociological/cultural context and read that into the text, such as in liberation (Boff, Gutiérrez), black (Cone, Mosala), and feminist (Radford-Ruether, Fiorenza, Tolbert) hermeneutics. For example, the exodus out of Egypt is used to encourage liberation from the restrictions of contemporary society. The *intifada* of the Palestinians is inspired by the return from Babylonian exile model. But there is a basic weakness in the hermeneutics of liberation because it takes up the tools of the oppressor in its quest to liberate, and in so doing calls in question its agenda against oppressors. Anthony Thiselton summarizes this concern incisively.

Historically hermeneutics emerged as a critical discipline precisely to deliver and to free communities from being browbeaten and placed under socio-political pressure by purely *instrumental* appeals to biblical texts *as supports for some prior interest.* Predominantly pragmatic uses of biblical texts have the statues of exercises in self-justification and potential manipulation, whether we are considering a dominant social tradition or a social minority, women or men, pietists or skeptics. Liberation hermeneutics cannot *liberate anyone* if it uses the oppressor's weapons."[68]

A fact which these extreme liberation hermeneutics apparently overlook is the function of the text over the reader. Fuchs believes that "the texts must translate us before we can translate them."[69] In other words, true liberation is not achieved through wresting the text from its own context and forcing it into a socio-pragmatic *mould,* rather true liberation comes from allowing the text to speak to the reader with all its liberating power. In *The Two Horizons,* Thiselton speaks persuasively of the importance of the transforming quality of the text, so that it is not just what the reader brings to the text, but what the text brings to the reader that is determinative. When a reader is transformed by a text, one will come to the text with changed presuppositions compared to when one first approached it. This is a process of change in understanding in front of the text, between text and reader rather than a diachronic preliterary process behind the text.

Although preunderstandings are unavoidable, one must be careful not to read modern issues or modern meanings of language back into the texts. Dennis Nineham opposes efforts to force biblical texts to solve modern problems such as the ordination of women or ecumenism, although there are biblical principles that can apply to both.[70] The paradigm shift from text to reader resulted from a switch from understanding the text "to inquiry into the structure of understanding itself."[71] Understanding came to be inclusive of the one who understands as well as the author's understanding. Gadamer's fusion of these two horizons (*Horizontverschmelzung*) recognizes the importance of both author and reader to understanding the text. The problem with reader-response theory is its tendency to polyvalence, or multiple meanings. These lead to pluralism and relativism as a result of the subjective influence of the reader. Gadamer's fusion of the two horizons shows respect for authorial intention which calls in question the subjectivism of reader-response theories. As Thiselton rightly says:

The hermeneutical goal is that of a steady progress towards a fusion of horizons. But this is to be achieved in such a way that the particularity of each horizon is fully taken into account and respected. This means *both* respecting the rights of the text *and* allowing it to speak.[72]

This contrasts with Dennis Nineham's rather negative conclusion that we cannot think the same as those from another age. He claims that such an idea is an "illusion" comparable to saying we can "think in a wholly different way."[73] If this were true, how could Scripture communicate with any contemporary person?

Philosophy influenced hermeneutics in much of its history, but in recent times the social sciences (sociology, anthropology, and psychology) have replaced philosophy.[74] There has also been a development through linguistics to literary criticism. As Osborne notes:

Hermeneutics originated as a biblical discipline. Yet many fields of study have provided input. Until recent decades, the primary influence was always philosophy. Then with structuralism linguistics came to the fore, and at the present time literary criticism has seemingly assumed the throne.[75]

Understanding does not come through methods of interpretation, as perceived for much of the history of hermeneutics, but is found in "orienting all understanding to language" (Gadamer, Heidegger).[76] But "language only communicates meaning when it expresses an experience that is shared" (Schillebeeckx).[77] This "hermeneutics of experience"[78] is, as Thiselton rightly points out, "a defence of the category of pre-understanding as a necessary hermeneutical tool and as grounded in human-life."[79] So understanding is enabled by the life-world that the reader brings with him or her to the text, including the function of language as used in that life-world.

More than that, the reader functions as a second author, or as Bernard C. Lategan puts it, the reader is "co-responsible for the creation of the text as a meaningful communication."[80] For it is not the meaning of the text that is brought to the reader that is determinative, but the meaning that the reader brings to the text that is decisive. Here we are squarely in the area of pragmatics, which is popular in North America. "Pragmatics is interested in language in action and the effects that can be achieved by language."[81] Behind reader-response theory in biblical studies is the wider field of pragmatics, the rise of "reception theory" (Jauss), "effective history" (*Wirkungsgeschichte*, Gadamer), and "speech act theory." All focus on the effects that history/ text/speech produces.[82]

By contrast, the Reformers spoke of Scripture as *sola scriptura, tota scriptura*, and *prima scriptura*. These terms represented the way that the Bible should be approached, allowing Scripture to interpret Scripture (*sola scriptura*). This means that Scripture is the primary source for interpreting Scripture (*prima scriptura*), and that all of Scripture can be used in this process (*tota scriptura*). As God is the author of Scripture it is transcultural with its social location primarily in the person and function of the Holy Spirit, and only secondarily within the social location of the human writers who under inspiration presented God's worldview. God in Scripture stands in judgment of human culture as He did in Christ in His social location in Palestine. Reader response theorists stand in judgment of God from their innumerable social locations. David S. Dockery, in his book *Biblical Interpretation, Then and Now,* compares the early church's hermeneutical methodologies with contemporary models. The reader-response theories are compared to the "allegorical" or "reader-oriented" model of the Alexandrians.[83] Dockery's evaluation of the present scene is insightful.

> The idea of illumination as enablement for understanding the text in this manner (see 1 Cor. 2:10-16) has at times disappeared from the contemporary discussion. We need to realize that we search not only for the external meaning of the text but for its inner meaning as well. We are suggesting that discovering Scripture's meaning involves not only examining the author's result in the written text, but also the Holy Spirit's work of illuminating the reader's mind to interpret the text. With the enablement of the Spirit, discerning a text's meaning and significance is not only possible but plausible.[84]

In view of this correct analysis, reader-response theories, like their predecessors, are out of vogue in the postmodern period. They are a product of the Enlightenment, a result of modernity. In the post-Enlightenment, postmodern world there is new opportunity to restore the Holy Spirit's function in understanding to its proper place. In the critical methods of the historical, literary, and cultural paradigms, focus was more on what the reader could do with the text than upon what the text could do with the reader. That is to say, transformation of the text was more likely than transformation of the reader. The function of the Holy Spirit's illumination was absent in these critical methodologies. It is now time to restore the role of the Holy Spirit in the writing and interpretation of Scripture.

Conclusion

How does authentic liberation occur? In the transcontextual horizon of the biblical worldview humanity is confronted with the greatest liberation event at the cross. Self is critiqued by the cross. "Genuine *liberation* de-centers both the individual and corporate self."[85] The problem with liberation or reader-response hermeneutics is that it takes from Scripture only that which seems to contribute to its cause. The rest of Scripture is not given equal time or place. This selective use of Scripture is opposed by the Bible itself in its *sola scriptura, tota scriptura,* and *prima scriptura* hermeneutical principles. Hermeneutics must place itself under the guidance of Scripture, to follow its own principles of interpretation, rather than sitting as judge over Scripture and forcing upon it contemporary sociological and cultural ideas that are foreign to it. Thomas C. Oden speaks in principle to this need.

> When criticism is working speculatively, as if historians could be the judges and arbiters of the documents of testimony rather than the text being the judge and constrainer of the interpreter, then there is danger that pretentious criticism may set itself between the apostolic testimony and contemporary hearers, as if to say, "Sorry, you can meet the real apostles only if we historians introduce you to them." This premise has led to the temporary expanding employment of a knowledge elite, but hardly to improved historical inquiry. Good textual inquiry does not lord it over the texts but is called to listen to them.[86]

As interpreters come to listen and learn from the text then Scripture will fulfill its prophetic function. As Thiselton reminds us, if textual meaning is the product of readers, then "texts cannot reform these readers 'from outside.' "[87] All we are left with are polyvalent words from men rather than the authoritative Word of God.

With the collapse of the Enlightenment we have entered the postmodern world. The historical, literary, and cultural paradigms speak of the changing hermeneutical methods during the reign of modernity. The time has come for a change. Scripture must be freed from modernity that has bound it for too long. The postmodern era gives promise of the greatest liberation movement yet — the liberation of Scripture. This evolution through the multiple methods of interpretation into the new opportunity to really listen and learn from Scripture demonstrates the wisdom of the high view of the Bible espoused by the evangelical community.

NOTES

1. Postmodern hermeneutics is a post-Enlightenment understanding of Scripture. It involves holism that calls in question the post-Kantian theory of analogy. See A.G. van Aarde, "Holisme as 'n postmodernistiese filosofie in teologiese lig," *Hervormde Teologiese Stud* 46 (1990): 293–311. The accomodation to modernity is giving way to postliberalism, with an emphasis on narrative, community, tradition, and particularity. Cf. Joseph A. DiNoia, "American Catholic Theology at Century's End: Postconciliar, Postmodern, Post-Thomistic," *The Thomist* 54 (1990): 499–518. The proper place of faith in knowledge distinguishes postmodernity from modernity, and liberates from the neo-Kantian constrictions on faith. See Alan M. Olson, "Postmodernity and Faith," *Journal of the American Academy of Religion* 58 (1990): 37–53. Eastern Christianity, with its post-critical exegesis and employment of typology, is one example of postmodernity. Cf. R. Slesinski, "Postmodernity and the Resources of the Christian East," *Communio: ICR* 17 (1990): 220–37. John Cobb discusses two types of postmodernism; see, "Two Types of Postmodernism: Deconstruction and Process," *Theology Today* 47 (1990): 149–58. It can be argued that postmodernism includes reader-response theories (see Anthony C. Thiselton, *New Horizons in Hermeneutics* [Grand Rapids: Zondervan, 1992], 15, 50, 60, 112, 314, 414) where the cultural paradigm is apparently linked to postmodernism. For this essay I define postmodernism as post-Enlightenment/ post-critical, and therefore post-historical/literary and cultural paradigms. Hence postmodernism in this paper is a return to the precritical hermeneutics with its high view of Scripture.

2. Thiselton, *New Horizons in Hermeneutics,* 33.

3. Anthony C. Thiselton, *The Two Horizons: New Testament Hermeneutics and Philosophical Description with Special Reference to Heidegger, Bultmann, Gadamer and Wittgenstein* (Grand Rapids: Eerdmans, 1980).

4. James C. McHann, Jr., *The Three Horizons: A Study in Biblical Hermeneutics with Special Reference to Wolfhart Pannenberg* (Ph.D. diss., Aberdeen University, 1987).

5. Thiselton, *New Horizons,* 25–26.

6. Warren F. Groff and Donald E. Miller, *The Shaping of Modern Christian Thought* (New York: World, n.d.), 32.

7. See Grant R. Osborne, *The Hermeneutical Spiral: A Comprehensive Introduction to Biblical Interpretation* (Downers Grove, Ill.: InterVarsity, 1991).

8. Terence J. Keegan, O.P., *Interpreting the Bible: A Popular Introduction to Biblical Hermeneutics* (New York: Paulist, 1985), 82.

9. Gerald T. Shephard, "Canonical Criticism," in *The Anchor Bible Dictionary,*

ed. David N. Freedman (New York: Doubleday, 1992), 1:863.

10. Ibid., 1:865.

11. Ibid., 1:862.

12. Keegan, *Interpreting the Bible*, 133.

13. John Barton, *Reading the Old Testament: Method in Biblical Study* (Philadelphia: Westminster, 1984), 90.

14. Ibid., 96–97.

15. Ibid., 101–3.

16. Keegan, *Interpreting the Bible*, 40.

17. Barton, "Structuralism," *Anchor Bible Dictionary*, 6:216.

18. Barton, *Reading the Old Testament*, 105.

19. Ibid., 112–13.

20. Barton, "Structuralism," *Anchor Bible Dictionary*, 6:215.

21. Ibid.

22. Barton, *Reading the Old Testament*, 190, 199, 207, 211, 184. Same problem caused the demise of logical positivism.

23. Walter Wink, *The Bible in Human Transformation: Toward a New Paradigm for Biblical Study* (Philadelphia: Fortress, 1973).

24. Gerhard Meier, *The End of the Historical-Critical Method* (St. Louis: Concordia, 1974).

25. Eta Linnemann, *Historical Criticism of the Bible: Methodology or Ideology?* (Grand Rapids: Baker, 1990).

26. Thomas C. Oden, *After Modernity . . . What? Agenda for Theology,* (Grand Rapids: Zondervan, 1990).

27. Gerhard F. Hasel, *Biblical Interpretation Today* (Washington, D.C.: Biblical Research Institute, 1985).

28. Royce G. Gruenler, *Meaning and Understanding: The Philosophical Framework of Biblical Interpretation* (Grand Rapids: Zondervan, 1991).

29. Vern S. Poythress, *Science and Hermeneutics* (Grand Rapids: Zondervan, 1988).

30. Joseph Cardinal Ratzinger, "Biblical Interpretation in Crisis: On the Question of the Foundations and Approaches of Exegesis Today," in *Biblical Interpretation in Crisis: The Ratzinger Conference on Bible and Church*, ed. Richard J. Neuhaus (Grand Rapids: Eerdmans, 1989), 6, 103–4.

31. Archbishop Stafford as reported by Paul Stallsworth, "The Story of an Encounter," in Neuhaus, *Biblical Interpretation in Crisis*, 164.

32. Neuhaus, *Biblical Interpretation in Crisis*, x.

33. Ratzinger, "Biblical Interpretation in Crisis," 6.

34. Ibid., 103–4.

35. Linnemann, *Is There a Synoptic Problem? Rethinking the Literary Dependence of the First Three Gospels*, trans. Robert W. Yarbrough (Grand Rapids: Baker, 1992), 9.

36. Linnemann, *Historical Criticism of the Bible*, 17.

37. Osborne, *Hermeneutical Spiral*, 139.

38. Ibid., 368.

39. Stafford as reported by Stallsworth, *Biblical Interpretation in Crisis*, 164.

40. George Lindbeck, as reported by Paul Stallsworth, "The Story of an Encounter," in Neuhaus, *Biblical Interpretation in Crisis*, 120.

41. Frank M. Cross, "The Development of Israelite Religion," *Bible Review* 8 (October 1992): 29, 50.

42. Barton, *Reading the Old Testament,* 9.

43. Some articles on different aspects of reader-response theory include, Clarence P. Walhout, "Literary Criticism in the Christian Community," *Christian Scholars' Review* 8 (1979): 295–306; Jouette Bassler, "The Parables of the Loaves," *The Journal of Religion* 66 (1986): 157–72; Fred B. Craddock, "The Gospels as Literature," *Encounter* 49 (1988): 19–35; John P. Heil, "Reader-Response and the Irony of Jesus Before the Sanhedrin in Luke 22:66-71," *Catholic Biblical Quarterly* 51 (1989): 271–84; Adele Reinhartz, "The New Testament and Anti-Judaism: A Literary-Critical Approach," *Journal of Ecumenical Studies* 25 (1988): 524–37; Carol S. LaHurd, "Reader-Response to Ritual Elements in Mark 5:1-20," *Biblical Theological Bulletin* 20 (1990): 154–60; Richard A. Edwards, "Narrative Implications of *Gar* in Matthew," *Catholic Biblical Quarterly* 52 (1990): 636–55; John P. Heil, "Mark 14:1-52, Narrative, Structure and Reader-Response," *Biblica* 71 (1990): 305–332.

44. Thiselton, *New Horizons,* 496, 523.

45. Ibid., 497.

46. Ibid., 515–16.

47. Ibid., 508.

48. Bernard C. Lategan, "Reader-Response Theory," in *The Anchor Bible Dictionary,* ed. David N. Freedman (New York: Doubleday, 1992), 5:627.

49. Thomas Kuhn, *The Structure of Scientific Revolutions* (Chicago: Univ. of Chicago Press, 1970).

50. Jeffery L. Sheler, "Cutting Loose the Holy Canon: A Controversial Re-examination of the Bible," *U.S. News and World Report,* 8 November 1993, 75.

51. For examples, see notes 47–50.

52. Bishop Lazareth as reported by Paul Stallsworth, "The Story of an Encounter," in Neuhaus, *Biblical Interpretation in Crisis,* 166.

53. Lategan, "Reader-Response Theory," 5:627.

54. Ibid.

55. Thomas C. Oden, *The Living God: Systematic Theology: Volume 1* (San Francisco: Harper and Row, 1987), 323.

56. Thomas C. Oden, *Agenda for Theology* (San Francisco: Harper and Row, 1979), 4–5.

57. Diogenes Allen, *Christian Belief in a Postmodern World: The Full Wealth of Conviction* (Louisville: Westminster/John Knox, 1989), 2.

58. Charles M. Wood, *The Formation of Christian Understanding: An Essay in Theological Hermeneutics* (Philadelphia: Westminster, 1981), 21.

59. Ibid., 26. Wood states that the principle aim of Christian understanding of Scripture is the knowledge of God.

60. For an excellent analysis of canonical criticism, see Dale A. Bruggemann, "Brevard Child's Canon Criticism: An Example of Post-Critical Naivete," *Journal of the Evangelical Theological Society* 32 (September 1989): 311–26.

61. See Charles H. Kraft, *Christianity in Culture: A Study in Dynamic Biblical Theologizing in Cross-Cultural Perspective* (Maryknoll, N.Y.: Orbis, 1981). Chapter 10, "God's Inspired Casebook," pp. 194–215, is particularly helpful.

62. This is what Thomas C. Oden has done in his three-volume *Systematic Theology.*

63. Karl Barth, *From Rousseau to Ritschl*, trans. Brian Cozens (London: SCM, 1959), 171.

64. D.B. Clendenin, "Learning to Listen: Thomas C. Oden on Postcritical Orthodoxy," *Journal of the Evangelical Theological Society* 34 (March 1991): 99.

65. John Calvin, *Institutes of the Christian Religion*, trans. Henry Beveridge (London: Clarke, 1962), 1:64.

66. Ibid., 1.71.

67. Ibid., 1.72.

68. Thiselton, *New Horizons*, 452.

69. Thiselton, *Two Horizons*, 73.

70. Dennis E. Nineham, "The Use of the Bible in Modern Theology," *Bulletin of the John Rylands Library* 52 (1969). See Thiselton, *Two Horizons*, 54.

71. Osborne, *Hermeneutical Spiral*, 368.

72. Thiselton, *Two Horizons*, 445.

73. Dennis E. Nineham, *The Use and Abuse of the Bible* (New York: Macmillan, 1976), 39.

74. Osborne, *Hermeneutical Spiral*, 366.

75. Ibid., 367.

76. Ibid., 370.

77. Edward Schillebeeckx, *The Understanding of Faith: Interpretation and Criticism* (London: Sheed and Ward, 1974), 15.

78. Ibid., 6.

79. Thiselton, *Two Horizons*, 109–10.

80. Lategan, "Reader-Response Theory," 5:627.

81. Ibid., 5:625.

82. Ibid., 5:626.

83. David S. Dockery, *Biblical Interpretation: Then and Now. Contemporary Hermeneutics in the Light of the Early Church* (Grand Rapids: Baker, 1992), 158.

84. Ibid., 181.

85. Thiselton, *New Horizons*, 450.

86. Thomas C. Oden, *Life in the Spirit: Systematic Theology: Volume 3* (San Franciso: HarperCollins, 1992), 360.

87. Thiselton, *New Horizons*, 549. Thiselton gives five important reasons why radical reader-response hermeneutics is detrimental.

13

The Uneasy Alliance between Evangelicalism and Postmodernism: A Reply to Anthony Thiselton

Dan R. Stiver

The postmodern frenzy has recently attracted the attention of evangelicals. Recent conferences on postmodernism at The Southern Baptist Seminary and Wheaton College offer notable testimony. The willingness of evangelicals like Thomas Oden and Clark Pinnock to claim the title is also witness.[1] All of the interest has not been favorable, however. For some conservative thinkers, postmodernism represents not an ally but an enemy; if a paradigm change to postmodernity is occurring, it is not opportunity but threat. In a recent issue of *Christianity Today,* Richard John Neuhaus manifests the reaction of many conservatives by charging postmodernism with relativism, subjectivism, radical individualism, and being the enemy of "clear thinking about moral truth."[2] What is even more interesting is that an evangelical like Anthony Thiselton, whose thought can itself be considered postmodern and who affirms thinkers who are considered postmodern, has vehemently rejected postmodernism.[3] Thiselton is always a generous critic and has led the way in the evangelical world in appropriating contemporary philosophy,[4] yet when it comes to postmodernism, his customary charity is for the most part laid aside. At best, then, there is an uneasy alliance between postmodern and evangelical thought. What is going on? Given the acknowledged diversity among postmodern thinkers, is

Dan R. Stiver is Associate Professor of Christian Philosophy at The Southern Baptist Theological Seminary in Louisville, Kentucky.

there any way, to use Pinnock's language, to "track the maze"? And does it matter anyway?

In order to answer these questions in a focused way, we will take Thiselton as a representative case of a negative evangelical response to postmodernism. He is an interesting choice for the reasons already cited, plus he has extensively discussed some postmodern thinkers. If a case can be made for the positive significance of postmodernism for evangelicals in the face of Thiselton's rebuke, then the way may be opened for others. In order to demonstrate the problems with Thiselton's approach to postmodernism, we will first indicate the narrowness of the range of postmodern thinkers that he treats. Beyond such a simple enumeration of a more diverse group of postmodernists, however, we need to offer a more substantial account of postmodernism that enables us to see the similarities while at the same time doing justice to the diversity, thus overcoming the charge that it is merely a faddish, vacuous label. Such a substantive formulation will hopefully offer a reasoned, noncapricious way of dealing with the vexed question of what does and does not count as postmodern. It will further underscore the inadequacies of Thiselton's understanding of postmodernism and raise the interesting question of whether Thiselton himself should be considered postmodern. Third, we will explore the implications of such a postmodern paradigm change for evangelicals.

Seeking a Broader Definition

Thiselton consistently identifies postmodernism with thinkers he deems to be relativists and then rejects postmodernism on that basis. He considers postmodernism antithetical to faith, which is all the more striking in light of his willingness to appropriate thinkers whom other evangelicals have regarded with suspicion. Despite Thiselton's encyclopedic proclivities, he seems to be unaware of some initial obvious facts that should have given him pause, namely, that those who come under the label of postmodernism are far more extensive than he allows and include some of the thinkers that he himself favors. At this point, the issue is not the appropriateness of such labels or the true nature of postmodernism, it is that his use of the term flies in the face of the actual breadth of usage. It is, therefore, misleading and inaccurate without some sort of accompanying rationale — which he never supplies. This point is important because Thiselton's narrow identification of postmodernism is a common mistake.

Who then is included in the broader range of postmodernism? Thiselton is correct to associate postmodernism with those most popularly associated with it, the French poststructuralists Jacques Derrida, Roland Barthes, Michel Foucault, and Jean-Francois Lyotard. He is also on target in including the American neo-pragmatists Stanley Fish and Richard Rorty. What he does not realize is that thinkers he favors such as Hans-Georg Gadamer and Paul Ricoeur, whom one might call hermeneutical philosophers, are also considered postmodernists.[5] Moreover, neo-pragmatists or post-analytical philosophers such as Jeffrey Stout, Cornel West, and Hilary Putnam also give a more balanced critique of modernism.[6] Similarly, the neo-Reformed epistemology of Alvin Plantinga and Nicholas Wolterstorff, among others, provides one of the most devastating critiques of modernism that is available along with a robust affirmation of truth.[7] Diogenes Allen in his own way advocates postmodernism as a means of being more bold in making truth claims rather than less. The communitarian approaches of ethicists like Alasdair MacIntyre and Michael Walzer, who are very close to the work of Gadamer, can also be included.[8] The work of the later Wittgenstein, which Thiselton endorses probably more than any other philosophical position, is considered to be postmodern. In the area of the philosophy of science, postmodernism includes the contextualist approaches related to Wittgenstein's work such as that of Stephen Toulmin and Thomas Kuhn. In theology, the postliberal narrative theology—also influenced by the later Wittgenstein—identified with people like George Lindbeck, Ron Thiemann, Stanley Hauerwas, and Paul Holmer is deemed postmodern.[9] Similarly, James McClendon and Nancy Murphy regard their narrativist approaches as postmodern.[10] As I have mentioned, evangelical thinkers like Oden and Pinnock regard the postmodern condition as favorable for Christian faith. Jerry Gill and Ted Peters should also be added to this list.[11] Other theologians and biblical scholars identified with postmodernism are Hans Küng, David Tracy, David Griffin, Walter Brueggeman, and Stephen Moore.[12] In this light, the restricted identification of postmodernism with the thought of Derrida, usually accompanied with the most radical reading of him, is a serious distortion. On simply empirical grounds, so to speak, Thiselton's usage of the term is suspect.

Seeking a Substantive Definition

In addition, there are conceptual grounds for questioning Thiselton. In light of the broad range of thinkers listed above, the obvious question is whether they have anything in common. If post-modernism is to mean anything at all, a case must be made for some characteristics that would include most of those claiming the term. If these criteria can be found, they would then provide at least some means by which to evaluate critically who is and who is not a postmodernist. What we will find is that such criteria further under-mine Thiselton's categorization.

Given the diversity of postmodern thought, it is understandable that people uncritically assume that there is no "tie that binds." Realistically, though, one should not expect a movement like postmodernism to evince a tight conformity. We use terms like ana-lytical philosophy, existentialism, phenomenology, structuralism, pro-cess philosophy, and pragmatism with meaning but also with the awareness that it is notoriously difficult to come up with demarcation criteria that will tell us in any and every case who is and who is not in the pertinent group. Postmodernism is that kind of term. What makes it more difficult is that, if a postmodern paradigm shift is occurring, we are in the middle of the process and do not have the benefit of hindsight as we do with many of these other movements. Even in our criticism of Thiselton, we must realize the difficulties involved.

Notwithstanding the difficulties, attempts to survey the landscape in the middle of the journey can be very helpful, just as in all of these other movements people did not wait until years afterward to begin the mapping process. In fact, reflection on the way, so to speak, is a part of determining the shape and contours of a movement. The challenge in this case is whether one can discern enough of a family resemblance to use the word postmodern meaningfully. If we cannot, we should gladly forego the term altogether or find a new and better one.

The problem, however, is often not so much that the meaning of the term is too fluid but that it is too narrow, a problem that Thiselton exemplifies. Over and over, one finds postmodernism equated simply with French poststructuralism or deconstruction. What we want to show, beyond the empirical fact that this is much too restricted a field to make sense out of the use of the term postmodernism, is that there is a way of doing justice both to the similarity and the diversity among the thinkers mentioned above. It is possible to see how postmodernism usefully identifies a significant paradigm change which is occurring in our time, a change that repre-sents a challenge to Christian faith in some ways more promise than peril. Whatever term a person uses, one of the surest ways to miss the promise and to realize the peril is to overlook what is happening altogether. All the sound and fury over a name is perhaps justified if the name opens us to an apologetic potential that we would have forfeited otherwise.

When one surveys the panorama of contemporary thought, it is evident in field after field, in discipline after discipline, that a significant critique of modernity has arisen along with discussion of a paradigm change.[13] The upshot is that the kind of change under discussion is not incremental or piecemeal, but structural and thoroughgoing. Almost invariably, those who go by the name of postmodernist use it to refer to this phenomenon, which more specifically entails three dimensions. One is the severe criticism of major features of modernity—without rejecting every aspect of modernity. Ostensibly the name "postmodern" itself suggests some legacy of modernity in what comes after, not to mention the impossibility of turning back the clock.[14] A second is the notion that modernity's ailments will not be solved by Band-Aid treatment; rather, radical surgery is required. Even more than that, something like a massive reconfiguration, namely, a paradigm switch, is unavoidable. The third dimension is some sketch, usually rather vague, of what such a new paradigm would look like. At this broad level, one finds surprising similarity among thinkers. But one can be even more specific.

The most remarkable congruence occurs at the level of the critique of modernity. From Derrida to Oden, from Fish to Gill, one finds the rejection of certain major features of the modernist paradigm. These have been identified in more detail elsewhere.[15] Among other things, people have seen among the major features of modernity, which can be identified broadly as the period in the West running from Descartes in the seventeenth century to the mid-twentieth century, related demands for certainty, clarity, objectivity, and universality, all based on a dualistic intellectualism. Whether explicitly stated or not, and often what is philosophically most important is what is taken for granted, modern thinkers seemed to be operating with these criteria. One should be as clear and certain as possible.[16] Insofar as one was not certain and not clear, one's knowledge claim was tarnished. Whether rationalist or empiricist, the standards were the same—only what was identified as the secure and certain starting point differed. In this light, skeptics like Hume and Nietzsche can be seen to be operating in the same paradigm as Locke and Hegel.[17] With the standards of reason ratcheted so high, skeptics could only conclude that virtually nothing counts as knowledge. Rather than question the paradigm, they simply drew radically negative conclusions from it.

The demand for certainty and clarity usually entailed appeal to some method or foundation that could guarantee results. Variously called foundationalism or objectivism, this characteristic, as well as its consequences, is aptly described by Richard Bernstein.

> By "objectivism," I mean the basic conviction that there is or must be some permanent, ahistorical matrix or framework to which we can ultimately appeal in determining the nature of rationality, knowledge, truth, reality, goodness, or rightness. An objectivist claims that there is (or must be) such a matrix and that the primary task of the philosopher is to discover what it is and to support his or her claims to have discovered such a matrix with the strongest possible reasons. Objectivism is closely related to foundationalism and the search for an Archimedean point. The objectivist maintains that unless we can ground philosophy, knowledge, or language in a rigorous manner we cannot avoid radical skepticism.[18]

Also allied with the quest for rigorous foundations or methods was the assumption that they would deliver valid knowledge for anyone at any time. The goal of the thinker, utilizing rigorous methods, is to be able to bracket or rise above history and find a truth uncontaminated by prejudice or custom. Putnam calls this the "God's-eye point of view," and Thomas Nagel strikingly characterized it as the "view from nowhere."[19]

Common to modern thinkers is also a sharp split between mind and body, reason and the passions. The dualism that runs from Descartes to Kant is coupled with the classical quest for reason unswayed by the passions. One can see how the interest in indubitable foundations or rigorous methods is a way of achieving both the desired universal point of view and the protection from the distorting influence of the emotions and the body. These hang together in a cohesive framework that allows for endless permutations. One can be rationalist or empiricist, objectivist or relativist, idealist or romantic—all can be plotted on the modernist grid.

The postmodern thinkers mentioned above exhibit virtual unanimity in rejecting all of these characteristics. The similarity one finds, as is often the case, lies in what they reject more than in their constructive alternatives. When they turn to offering something in modernity's place, then one discovers the diversity, a bewildering plethora of views that would delight even Derrida's desire for an infinite play of interpretation. As a bare minimum of agreement on the positive side of things, they would agree in this, that they reject the above characteristics of modernity. Whatever view they espouse, it would not demand certainty and clarity as requirement for legitimate knowledge. Nor would the foundations of one's thought have to be indubitable or based on a rigorous method. The claim of ahistorical universality is given up in favor of the role that tradition, authority, context, and community plays in shaping what counts as knowledge. While there is probably less agreement on the last characteristic, most reject a dualistic intellectualism and allow for the inextricability of our entanglement in the body and in the passions. In other words, an incarnational and holistic approach to the self as well as to epistemology is widely accepted among these thinkers. In terms of what is retained from modernity, most would want to preserve the positive gains of science, the emancipatory impulses, and the passion for truth over ideology.[20] How far this preservation is possible and how far these factors are transformed is itself part of the challenge and the plurality of postmodern approaches.

These criteria allow us to make some critical judgments on who is and who is not a postmodernist. All those pointing toward a middle way between objectivism and relativism that avoids the modernist criteria for knowledge are included.[21] In this light, thinkers who do not use the term of themselves are ruled in, such as Ricoeur, Gadamer, Plantinga, and Placher.[22] Those who still seek some objectivist criteria, like Jurgen Habermas and John Rawls, are ruled out, as Placher's work indicates.[23]

The irony of this heuristic for collating postmodern thinkers is that the thinkers most readily identified in the popular mind with postmodernism, the French poststructuralists, are the most suspect. Why is this so? As Bernstein suggests, modernity oscillates between the false dilemma of objectivism and relativism. When the standards of reason are elevated precipitously, then they are difficult to attain, leaving the only alternative as relativism and skepticism.[24] The most radical and visible of postmodern thinkers tend to be the ones closest to giving up on the claims of reason altogether, thus actually exhibiting the modernist dilemma rather than the postmodern avoidance of it. As MacIntyre says, theirs is only an "inverted mirror image" of modernity.[25] Here one could include Rorty with Derrida, Foucault,

Lyotard, and company. Rather than switching paradigms, this flirtation with relativism as the only alternative to failure to meet the extreme standards of reason is precisely a hangover from modernism, not postmodernism. In radical Derridean terms, if there is no absolute presence, then there is absolute absence!

Conversely, the implication of postmodernism is that the paradigm itself is faulty, not that one should just swing to the other side. The surprising but logical implication of postmodernism then is that truth claims can be made more easily than before—not less. More can count as knowledge, not less. If meeting the strictures of knowledge has seemed to be a Western will-o'-the-wisp, then the conclusion postmodernists have drawn is not to give up on knowledge but to change the definition.

There are good grounds then for the observation of several postmodernists that the poststructuralists in many ways are actually "ultramodern" or in Griffin's terms, "most-modern"![26] In an "advertising age," it is not hard to understand why the most radical claims get the most publicity; we have also learned, however, to be suspicious of such popular identifications. What Thiselton and others also do not recognize is that there are milder readings of even the poststructuralists that make them, in light of my heuristic, less relativistic and thus more postmodern.[27] A dramatic example with regard to Derrida comes from John D. Caputo in the conservative journal *Faith and Philosophy*.

> Unfortunately, the significance of Derrida's work has been obscured by a particularly perverse misunderstanding of deconstruction, one which, to anyone who has taken the considerable trouble required to gain familiarity with his texts, seems quite ironic (if not amusing). For the notion has gained currency that deconstruction traps us inside the "chain of signifiers," in a kind of linguistic-subjective idealism, unable to do anything but play vainly with linguistic strings. That, were it true, would be an odd result for a philosophy of alterity, a very unkind fate to visit upon a philosophy whose every effort is bent upon turning toward the other.[28]

In other words, if one gives Derrida, Lyotard, and others of that stripe the same kind of reading that Thiselton gives Gadamer and Ricoeur—as other philosophers have done—they are less radical and less newsworthy but probably more helpful.[29] The irony is, the more radical the interpretation, the more modern are the thinkers — rather than postmodern.

It should be clear now how problematic Thiselton's — and others' — understanding of postmodernism is. His approach does justice neither to the range of postmodern thinkers nor to an adequate conceptualization of postmodernism. In fact, he ends up identifying postmodernism with an interpretation of certain thinkers that is probably more modern than postmodernism. The surprising result is that with this substantive understanding of postmodernism, solid grounds exist to regard Thiselton himself as a postmodernist and to see his work ironically as itself one of the best examples of the promise that postmodernism holds for evangelical thought!

While audacious perhaps, such a claim is not capricious. His views fit very well the broader range of postmodernists detailed above. His enthusiastic endorsement of the later Wittgenstein plus his strong affirmation of the work of Gadamer and Ricoeur are strong clues at the outset.[30] In fact, his approbation of these thinkers is based on a reading of them that is more consistent with the conception of postmodernism detailed above as a way beyond objectivism and relativism than the relativist and subjectivist reading of them by some.[31] For example, in an endorsement of Gadamer, Thiselton specifically draws on Bernstein: "Gadamer's conclusion about the relation between historical situatedness and tradition is expressed in terminology taken up by Richard Bernstein . . . : it entails moving *beyond objectivism;* but it also entails going *beyond relativism.*"[32] Insofar as their work, however, is susceptible to relativist readings, he rightly rejects them.[33] What he does not recognize, though, is that what makes them postmodernist is precisely seeing them not as relativist (and thus modern) but as pointing toward a different paradigm. Thiselton applauds Gadamer's critique of the Enlightenment prejudice against prejudice and Ricoeur's emphasis on the need for interpretation from within one's context whose truth cannot be objectively and absolutely guaranteed. Thiselton rejects in modernity what the postmodernists reject but, like the most authentic postmodernism, does not see this as issuing in relativism, skepticism, or nihilism. He is concerned that we can still deal with the category of truth, but from out of the context of our history and our context.[34] He recognizes that religious faith cannot measure up to modernist standards of rationality, but he makes the postmodern turn to see that these standards are misguided; faith, therefore, is not more tenuous than other kinds of knowledge. It too has its own kind of rationality.

Seeking Implications for Evangelicalism

What, more particularly, are the implications and promise of a postmodern paradigm for faith? We shall highlight four. First of all, part of the promise lies in what Thiselton well recognizes: there are no overriding philosophical reasons to marginalize faith as somehow less rational than other areas. Modernity, however, placed precisely that demand upon faith. The burden of proof was constantly on faith to measure up to the standards of other sciences. Sometimes it tried to do so, to disastrous effect.[35] The other strategy was to throw in the towel, claim that it was not rational, and insist nevertheless that it was immune to reason. Neither approach has been satisfactory. Faith has been marginalized and put on the defensive. With the removal of the strictures of modernist reason, however, the playing field has been philosophically leveled, so to speak. Or to change the metaphor, a new door has been opened for the Gospel. Faith may not win its way, but it is not because it is de facto lacking in rationality since it appeals to tradition, to passion, to community, or to authority. What kind of "reason" does not? That is the question that postmodernism raises. Diogenes Allen illustrates this renewed possibility of boldness in the opening lines of his book on postmodernism: "Now and again I have met a person who has claimed that religion has nothing to offer. 'Why should I go to church,' someone once said to me, 'when I have no religious needs?' I had the audacity to reply, 'Because Christianity's true.' "[36] Such a reply is on firmer ground in a postmodern context than in a modern.

A second implication lies in the obvious fact that the positive shape of postmodernism has yet to be determined. The raw materials stand ready, but a host of architects are vying for them. The new-found cultural strength of evangelicals, which itself may be in part due to the crumbling of modernity, offers an opportunity to draw the blueprints of a friendlier edifice than modernity. In other words, evangelicals have the chance to fill in important details of the postmodern paradigm.

A third implication comes from the realization that the understanding of reason of modernity is itself not new: it runs back to the beginnings of Western thought.[37] Modernity, of course, wove other unique fibers into these long threads. Oden aptly identifies some of these—autonomous individualism, narcissistic hedonism, reductive naturalism, and absolute moral relativism—but by making these the whole of postmodern consciousness, he misses the larger significance of the postmodern paradigm change and ends up focusing on symptoms more than the cause.[38] The difference between modernity and premodernity in this respect is not so much in the understanding of reason and faith but in the prestige of faith and authority as another way of grasping truth. After the horrors of the religious wars of the sixteenth and seventeenth centuries, many thinkers took the "flight from authority" and eschewed tradition and authority in favor of a faith "within the bounds of reason," if faith was affirmed at all. One can also see how the major conceptions of faith and reason all have this in common—they assume the particular paradigm of reason described above that is then set in relationship to faith, which is considered to be a different kind of phenomenon altogether. Whether it be reason preceding faith, or faith preceding reason, or reason rejecting faith, or faith rejecting reason, all assumed common parameters of reason. These alternatives run through the medieval period as well as the modern. If the paradigm has changed, however, there is the need and the possibility for a reconceptualization of a kind that Christianity has never faced, having lived all of its existence, in the West at least, within this broad understanding of reason. Such a reworking of the meaning of faith and reason and their relationship has momentous implications for missions, evangelism, preaching, and theology.

The previous challenges bear particularly on the church's mission to the world. The fourth implication of postmodernism is more internal. One of the besetting faults of evangelicals has been the strife that has fractured its fellowship and soiled its witness. While some things are worth fighting for, few would defend that all of the *fundamentalist's fights* of the past two centuries have been either necessary or productive. As Pinnock once commented, "There is something terribly wrong when we argue about the Bible more and enjoy it less."[39] At this point, the routines and rituals of conflict have become like deep ruts in which the same bumps and potholes are hit with wearying regularity. Like a dysfunctional family where everything seems to work together to foster the same old animosity, what is often needed is an interruption and reconfiguration of the relationship. The postmodern context not only levels the playing field, it promises new and different ball games. A new gestalt offers new possibilities of unity that transcend and open up new pathways of relationship.

In all of these challenges, Thiselton has himself sketched out promising directions for evangelicals. His misidentification of postmodernism, however, as common as it is, threatens to point in as many false directions as true. The name itself is not crucial. Most likely a more positive term will emerge. Confusion about the name, however, can easily lead to confusion about what it symbolizes. However uneasy the alliance between postmodernism and evangelicalism, confusing or rejecting the alliance undermines the chance to play a role in christening a new, more congenial name. It runs the risk of preparing to fight battles that no one is any longer fighting, of answering questions that no one is any longer asking. It does not realize that, at this point, postmodernism may be more ally than enemy.

NOTES

1. See Thomas C. Oden, *After Modernity . . . What? Agenda for Theology* (Grand Rapids: Zondervan/Academie, 1990), 75–77; idem, *Two Worlds: Notes on the Death of Modernity in America & Russia* (Downers Grove, Ill.: InterVarsity, 1992), 43; and Clark H. Pinnock, *Tracking the Maze: Finding Our Way through Modern Theology from an Evangelical Perspective* (New York: Harper & Row, 1990).

2. Richard John Neuhaus, "A Voice in the Relativistic Wilderness," *Christianity Today,* 7 February 1994, 34.

3. See, e.g., Anthony C. Thiselton, *New Horizons in Hermeneutics* (Grand Rapids: Zondervan, 1992) 21, 92, 113, 125–26, 461.

4. Besides the aforementioned book, see his pathbreaking *The Two Horizons: New Testament Hermeneutics and Philosophical Direction with Special Reference to Heidegger, Bultmann, Gadamer, and Wittgenstein* (Grand Rapids: Eerdmans, 1980).

5. See, e.g., Ted Peters, *God—the World's Future: Systematic Theology for a Postmodern Era* (Minneapolis: Fortress Press, 1992), 27–28, on Ricoeur; and Susan J. Hekman, *Gender and Knowledge: Elements of a Postmodern Feminism* (Boston: Northeastern Univ. Press, 1990), on Gadamer.

6. Jeffrey Stout, *Flight from Authority* (Notre Dame, Ind.: Univ. of Notre Dame Press, 1981); Cornel West, *Prophetic Thought in Postmodern Times* (Monroe, Minn.: Common Courage, 1993); Hilary Putnam, *Reason, Truth, and History* (Cambridge: Cambridge Univ. Press, 1981).

7. For an account of their views, see the groundbreaking collection of essays they edited: Alvin Plantinga and Nicholas Wolterstorff, eds., *Faith and Rationality: Reason and Belief in God* (Notre Dame, Ind.: Univ. of Notre Dame Press, 1983). For a tie-in of their views with postmodernism, see Merold Westphal, "Levinas and the Immediacy of the Face," *Faith and Philosophy* 10 (October 1993): 487.

8. See Alasdair MacIntyre, *Whose Justice? Which Rationality?* (Notre Dame, Ind.: Univ. of Notre Dame Press, 1988). Michael Walzer, *Spheres of Justice: A Defense of Pluralism and Equality* (New York: Basic, 1983). For an account that relates Gadamer's and Walzer's thought, see Georgian Warnke, "Walzer, Rawls, and Gadamer: Hermeneutics and Political Theory," in *Festivals of Interpretation: Essays on Hans-Georg Gadamer's Work,* ed. Kathleen Wright, SUNY Series in Contemporary Continental Philosophy (Albany, N.Y.: State Univ. of New York Press, 1990), 136–60. See also Glen H. Stassen, "Michael Walzer's Situated Justice," *Journal of Religious Ethics* (Fall 1994).

9. See Frederic B. Burnham, ed., *Postmodern Theology: Christian Faith in a Pluralist World* (San Francisco: Harper & Row, 1989).

10. Nancy Murphy and James McClendon, Jr., "Distinguishing Modern and Postmodern Theologies," *Modern Theology* 5 (April 1989): 191–215.

11. Jerry Gill, *Mediated Transcendence: A Postmodern Reflection* (Macon, Ga.: Mercer, 1989); Marie Sorri and Jerry Gill, *A Postmodern Epistemology: Language, Truth, and Body* (Lewiston, N.Y.: Mellen, 1989); Peters, *God—the World's Future;* and Diogenes Allen, *Christian Belief in a Postmodern World: The Full Wealth of Conviction* (Louisville: Westminster/John Knox, 1989).

12. Hans Küng, *Global Responsibility: In Search of a New World Ethic* (New York: Crossroad, 1991); David Griffin, William A. Beardslee, and Joe Holland, eds., *Varieties of Postmodern Theology,* SUNY Series in Constructive Postmodern Thought (Albany, N.Y.: State Univ. of New York Press, 1989), 3; Walter Brueggeman, *Texts under Negotiation: The Bible and Postmodern Imagination* (Philadelphia: Fortress, 1993). With regard to Tracy, see Richard Lints, "The Postpositivist Choice: Tracy or Lindbeck?" *Journal of the American Academy of Religion* 61 (Winter 1993): 655–77.

13. An excellent discussion of paradigm change in the context of theology is in Hans Küng and David Tracy, eds., *Paradigm Change in Theology: A Symposium for the Future,* trans. Margaret Kohl (New York: Crossroad, 1989).

14. Even Oden, who terms himself "paleoorthodox" and who almost implies that the Reformation period is too modern, discounts any return to premodernity. Oden, *Two Worlds,* 86. He says:

> Postmodern orthodoxy is not a simplistic, nostalgic return to premodern methods as if modernity never happened. Rather it is a rebuilding from the ashes of modernity using treasures old and new for the restructuring process.
>
> What makes this consciousness "post" is the fact that it does not have to go once again through the pedagogies of modernity. It has paid its dues to modernity twice over, and now is searching for meanings and truths ruled out by these methods (p. 81).

15. Dan R. Stiver, "Much Ado about Athens and Jerusalem: The Implications of Postmodernism for Faith," *Review and Expositor* 91 (Winter 1994): 87–90.

16. The locus classicus, of course, is René Descartes, *Discourse on Method,* in *Descartes, Spinoza,* Great Books of the Western World, vol. 31 (Chicago: Encyclopaedia Britannica, 1952).

17. Stout, *Flight,* 90, refers to Hume as suffering from "nostalgia" for knowledge. On Nietzsche, see Samuel C. Wheeler III, "True Figures: Metaphor, Social Relations, and the Sorites," in *The Interpretive Turn: Philosophy, Science, Culture,* ed. David R. Hiley, James F. Bohman, and Richard Shusterman (Ithaca, N.Y.: Cornell Univ. Press, 1991), 198.

18. Richard Bernstein, *Beyond Objectivism and Relativism: Science, Hermeneutics, and Praxis* (Philadelphia: Univ. of Pennsylvania Press, 1985), 8. I regard objectivism as a more inclusive term than "foundationalism" since objectivism includes any kind of evaluating matrix like a rigorous method as well as indubitable first principles or empirical data. Further, Alvin Plantinga distinguishes between an objectivist foundationalism and a non-objectivist foundationalist noetic structure, calling the former "classical foundationalism." Alvin Plantinga, "Reason and Belief in God," in *Faith and Rationality: Reason and Belief in God,* ed. Alvin Plantinga and Nicholas Wolterstorff (Notre Dame: University of Notre Dame Press, 1983), 48.

19. Putnam, *Reason*, 49; Thomas Nagel, *The View from Nowhere* (New York: Oxford, 1986).

20. For example, see Oden, *Two Worlds*, 42; and Pinnock, *Tracking the Maze*, x.

21. For explicit discussion of such a middle way, see Bernstein, *Beyond Objectivism and Relativism;* Stout, *Flight from Authority*, chap. 12; Paul Ricoeur, *Oneself as Another*, trans. Kathleen Blamey (Chicago: Univ. of Chicago Press, 1992), 21–23; MacIntyre, *Whose Justice?* chap. 18; William C. Placher, *Unapologetic Theology: A Christian Voice in a Pluralist Conversation* (Louisville: Westminster/John Knox, 1989), chap. 7; and Hekman, *Gender and Knowledge*, 134, 144, 152.

22. In this light, Peter Hodgson, a critic of postmodernists (identified as the French deconstructionists) is himself a postmodernist. Peter C. Hodgson, *Revisioning the Church: Ecclesial Freedom in the New Paradigm* (Philadelphia: Fortress, 1988).

23. See Placher, *Unapologetic Theology*, chap. 5. This objectivistic critique applies more clearly to their early work than their most recent, more pragmatist inclinations.

24. Cf. MacIntyre, *Whose Justice?* 6:

It was a central aspiration of the Enlightenment, an aspiration the formulation of which was itself a great achievement, to provide for debate in the public realm of standards and methods of rational justification by which alternative courses of action in every sphere of life could be adjudged just or unjust, rational or irrational, enlightened or unenlightened. So, it was hoped, reason would displace authority and tradition. . . .

Yet both the thinkers of the Enlightenment and their successors proved unable to agree as to what precisely those principles were which would be found undeniable by all rational persons. . . . Consequently, the legacy of the Enlightenment has been the provision of an ideal of rational justification which it has proved impossible to attain.

Stout underscores the same insight in *Flight from Authority*, 8: "If we identify knowledge with *scientia*, it may well turn out that knowledge is in rather short supply. But this would show only that knowledge, thus identified, presupposes standards of judgment too stringent to matter."

25. MacIntyre, *Whose Justice?* 353.

26. David Ray Griffin, *God & Religion in the Postmodern World* (Albany: State Univ. of New York Press, 1989), 8; Griffin, "Introduction" in *God & Religion*, 3. See also Küng, *Global Responsibility*, 23–24; and Oden, *After Modernity*, 77.

27. See also Stephen D. Moore, *Poststructuralism and the New Testament: Derrida and Foucault at the Foot of the Cross* (Minneapolis: Fortress, 1994).

28. John D. Caputo, "The Good News about Alterity: Derrida and Theology," *Faith and Philosophy* 10 (October 1993): 453–54.

29. See, e.g., the way Fish relates his approach to walking by faith in the spirit of Hebrews 11:1. Stanley Fish, "Fish Tales: A Conversation with 'The Contemporary Sophist,' " in *Philosophy, Rhetoric, Literary Criticism: Interviews*, ed. Gary A. Olson (Carbondale, Ill.: Southern Illinois Univ. Press, 1994), 54. He says of this and another reference, "I think there is *nothing* in my work that couldn't be generated from those two assertions and their interactions" (p. 54). A response article in the same book by Patricia Bizzell indicates that the problem with Fish is not, as

Thiselton indicates, that he is anarchistic but that he implies "total conformity and lack of change," in other words, that he implies too much rigidity! Bizzell is compelled to argue that "Fish's view of rhetoric permits dissensus." Patricia Bizzell, "A Response to Fish Tales: A Conversation with 'The Contemporary Sophist,' " 69.

30. For more details on each of these see Olson, *Philosophy, Rhetoric, Literary Criticism:* on Gadamer, see chap. 9; on Ricoeur, see chap. 10; and on Wittgenstein, for whom his endorsement is ad hoc throughout the text rather than occurring in a sustained section, see ibid. 323–25, 400, 541. For a more systematic treatment of Wittgenstein, see Thiselton, *Two Horizons,* chaps. 13–14. Note Thiselton's endorsement of a post-Gadamerian and post-Wittgensteinian paradigm over against E.D. Hirsch's "pre-Wittgensteinian" paradigm. Thiselton, *New Horizons,* 13. See also the way he follows Gadamer's critique of objectivism (p. 319).

31. Note this approval of Gadamer in Thiselton, *New Horizons,* 329–30: "Gadamer's work convincingly demonstrates that hermeneutical, historical, or contextual understanding radically relativizes the claims of any a-historical version of rationalism, such as the critical rationalism of the Enlightenment."

32. Ibid., 327.

33. Ibid., on Gadamer, see p. 320.

34. Thiselton, *New Horizons,* 612 expresses well the way one can make universal truth claims within a contextualist and historicist framework. His use of the language of "trans-contextual" truth claims is misleading, however (pp. 440, 613). It is clear that he does not mean by that a denial of contextualism but the freedom to make and defend universal claims on non-objectivist grounds. This same lack of clarity causes him to endorse Habermas, who as Placher has shown, does not fit this paradigm very well (p. 329). This is partly due to the fact that he uncritically accepts a reading of Gadamer in which Gadamer purportedly rejects method altogether, which is patently false. Eg., see pp. 348, 357. See where Gadamer explicitly rejects this interpretation in the foreword to the second edition of *Truth and Method,* trans. Garrett Barden and John Cumming (New York: Crossroad, 1975), xvii. He clarifies that he did not intend to "deny the necessity of methodical work within the human sciences," as many thought. Rather he says, "The question I have asked seeks to discover and bring into consciousness something that methodological dispute serves only to conceal and neglect, something that does not so much confine or limit modern science as precede it and make it possible." In fact, one of Habermas' students, Seyla Benhabib, has shown the flaws of Habermas' approach while making one of the most carefully argued presentations of the legitimacy of making universal truth on non-objectivist grounds, which she terms an "interactive" or "situated" universality." See *Situating the Self: Gender, Community, and Postmodernism in Contemporary Ethics* (New York: Routledge, 1992).

35. An excellent essay on this point is George Marsden, "The Collapse of American Evangelical Academia," in Plantinga and Wolterstorff, *Faith and Rationality,* 219–64.

36. Allen, *Christian Belief,* 1.

37. See Stiver, "Beyond Athens and Jerusalem," 90–92, for further elaboration of this argument.

38. Oden, *Two Worlds,* 33–36. Also see his chapters, 2 and 23, in this volume.

39. See Pinnock, *Tracking the Maze,* 224.

PART FOUR
THE CHALLENGE FOR APOLOGETICS/MINISTRY

14

Religious Pluralism in a Postmodern World

Gary Phillips

Defining the idea of postmodernism is a bit like nailing down Jell-O. Its amorphous shape and elasticity allow it to pop out in places one might not expect. Some contend that postmodernism is simply a collection of different forms of *anti-modernism*. Others see it as a rather benign or neutral movement which takes different shapes within different areas of the arts, physical sciences, and the metaphysical disciplines. Still others view it as a self-contradictory attack on the very concept of truth itself, which would jettison all attempts at a singular worldview. Postmodernism has never received a single definition agreed upon by all.[1] Thus, whenever one speaks of postmodernism, one runs the risk of faulty generalization; and this chapter is no exception. We shall first make an attempt at description, if not definition.

Postmodernism

Postmodernism is a notoriously self-conscious movement which stands in a long tradition of skepticisms—from Protagoras, Socrates/Plato until today—regarding both the nature of *reality* and the nature of *truth*. Steward and Blocker observe, "Postmodernism challenges the fundamental epistemological assumption of modern philosophy and science—the possibility of discovering the truth about anything.

Gary Phillips is Professor of Bible and Theology at Bryan College in Dayton, Tennessee.

Postmodernists claim that any attempt to verify the truth of a claim by its correspondence with reality is an impossible illusion."[2] Because truth is individual and subjective, there is no aim for consensus, except the consensus that there is no consensus.

Classical philosophy, and even modern philosophy after it, always tacitly assumed that there was a single target at which everyone was aiming, and various attempts to arrive at truth (the bull's-eye) were close or remote in varying degrees.

The epistemology of modernity had its own skepticisms, but it usually regarded its obstacles as challenges to circumvent.[3] Autonomous human reason can understand and to some extent control reality. Gradually, however, it became clear that modernity had arrived at no absolute truth and was cut from the same cloth as the Emperor's new clothes. Eventually, the quest for truth as absolute and knowable was abandoned. No longer was there belief in a bull's-eye (center of absolute truth and ethical normativity) toward which meaning was aimed. Now modernity asserted that all knowledge is mediated through the subjective perspective of the knower. A knowable reality probably exists, but this reality can never be known objectively.

In our postmodern world, no longer do we assume there is one reality which, although it cannot be known with certainty, is still "out there." Indeed, the very concept of reality, as a legacy of modernity, is seen as a social construction. In postmodernism, there is no bull's-eye because there is no target. "Shots going up, down, north, south, east, and west [are] . . . equally accurate. . . . Everyone's opinion is as good as anyone else's. The main criterion . . . becomes how you, as an individual, feel about it."[4] The very concept of meaning itself becomes unstable.

Social groups in power interpret the world for themselves and for others whom they dominate by means of a worldview, or "meta-narrative." A meta-narrative is an interpretive structure which gives meaning to reality and common experience. Postmoderns often assert that the world has most recently been dominated by the worldview (meta-narrative) of Western progress. This meta-narrative has shaped our social agenda so that "marginalized" groups must either conform (become homogeneous) or else be repressed and possibly face violent extinction. This has happened repeatedly (Marxist-Leninism, the Crusades, Nazism, etc.). Thus postmodernism also has a social agenda: the aim of education is not the search for truth but the transformation of education society. Postmodernism is easily identified with multiculturalism and does not hesitate to "deconstruct" history, so that the marginalized thought of women, minorities, Native Americans, African Americans, Hispanics, and even homeless street people may be "liberated."[5] The Euro-American male wears the black hat.[6] In social life, ideas and reason no longer have power to determine any ideological agenda. Not powerful ideas, but powerful forces and the emotions which undergird them, shape the world. Thus postmodernism delights in its multiperspectivism, its acceptance of multiple realities with no correspondence to language, and its radical application of this rejection of all absolutes to all areas of life. In ethics, anything becomes possible. "There are no external standards nor even internal standards of personal or cultural consistency and coherence to restrict us."[7]

Because there is no single meta-narrative, the epistemological quest has moved off center stage. According to postmodernism, no single meta-narrative is possible because none is large enough to encompass the experiences of all people, marginalized or not. Further, our *knowledge* is always mediated through conceptual and linguistic "constructions." We cannot escape this epistemological circularity. What marks postmodern epistemology as different from modernity is its view that "reality isn't what it used to be!"[8] Therefore philosophers are now reporters, functioning as mere "mirrors, reflecting what is taking place in society."[9]

In historical studies, postmodernism eliminates distinctions between fact and fiction, and takes the position that history has no reality beyond that which the historian creates.[10] Richard Stengel claims that history is not "truth"; rather, "history becomes a minstrel show glimpsed through a musty lens distorted by tradition, popular culture and wishful thinking."[11] Thus the past has no normative interpretation and no normative significance for the present. Because historiography deals inevitably with meta-narratives, it is understandable that professional historians have been slow to welcome postmodernism, primarily because of epistemology and ethics (some "historical" events — such as the Holocaust — are still said to be simply "wrong"). Slow to embrace, perhaps, but apparently quite willing to be courted.[12]

Postmodernism thrives in art, architecture, and photography, where images (perceptions) have greater conceptual reality and vitality than objects (concrete reality). In these disciplines postmodern structure is the structure of fragmentation. In psychology, postmodern psychoanalysis is called schizoanalysis in that it may reflect different realities.[13]

In literature, "pluralism in interpretation is a mark of post-modernism."[14] Postmodernism makes a hermeneutical distinction between the text and any objective meaning. There is no fixed meaning in any proposition or in language itself. The postmodernist is free to "play," as Derrida calls it, with the "reading" (interpretation) of the "text"; one may, with joy, interpret "freely without being restricted by considerations of correctness or truth."[15]

In theology, not only do different "Christian" theologies contain various conflicting meta-narratives (such as evangelical theology, liberation theology, feminist theology, black theology, gay theology), but the meta-narratives of other religions have equal claim to truth — but to a truth which is non-absolute and nonnormative.

Several postmodern assumptions give rise to theological questions, particularly as one considers pluralism — the question of other religions. First, if there is no single meta-narrative, what implications follow regarding the concept of biblical revelation? Second, if meaning in interpretation is located in the knowing subject (not in the text), and if that text is interpreted according to a predetermined social agenda, what does this imply regarding the exegetical task? Third, what does a postmodern view of truth imply regarding the Christian claim of the finality of Jesus Christ, vis-a-vis other truth-claims? Fourth, how does a pluralism steeped in postmodernity deal with interreligious dialogue — what are its purposes? There is one final larger question: Are there any components of traditional biblical Christianity which serve to answer postmodern concerns?

Pluralism

Nicholas Rescher defines pluralism as "the doctrine that any substantial question admits of a variety of plausible but mutually conflicting responses."[16] He suggests four components of pluralism: *Legitimate Diversity, Restrained Dissonance, Acquiescence in Difference,* and *Respect for the Autonomy of Others.* None of these demands that one deny oneself in adopting a stance toward truth which requires a pluralistic perspective toward the nature of truth itself. Rescher argues that we must learn to live not with consensus but with what he call *dissensus* — getting along in spite of the fact that we do not agree. If this be pluralism, then let us be pluralists, and "strive to make the world safe for disagreement."[17]

But when people speak of religious pluralism from a postmodern perspective, they often mean something more than that which Rescher's important work describes. Closer to the mark is D.A. Carson, who describes three usages of the term "pluralism": (1) the growing diversity of race, heritage, religion, and value systems within Western culture; and (2) the value of toleration for this diversity. The combination of these first two meanings is consistent with Christian truth and fits very nicely with an appropriate pluralism described by Rescher.[18] Indeed, the early church had to deal with several competing worldviews, and attempted to hold fast to biblical truth while treating ideological opponents with grace (2 Tim. 2:24-26).[19]

However, Carson's other meaning for the term "pluralism" is (3) the philosophical posture which insists that tolerance must be granted to all views on the ground that none can claim to be *true*.[20] This statement bears striking resemblance both to postmodernism and to the liberal religious pluralism put forth by people like John Hick, William Cantwell Smith, and S. Wesley Ariarajah. For example, the Bible claims that Jesus died on the cross, and the Koran claims that Jesus did not die on the cross.[21] The appropriate pluralisms of Rescher and Carson (his first and second meanings) would not necessarily allow both of these statements to stand as true, but would advocate tolerance for those who put forth such conflicting truth-claims. However, postmodern pluralism has few criteria to exclude any truth-claim. Indeed, the goal is now to place all religions on a level playing field, and few people do it better than Hick, Smith, and Ariarajah.[22]

John Hick argues that once one accepts the idea of divine incarnation, one inexorably ends with soteriological exclusivism. If Jesus is God the Son, then the doctrine of the Trinity follows, and with it Christian uniqueness and soteriological exclusivism. "We have, then, to work back up the chain of inference and eventually to question the original premise."[23] For Hick, this means denying the doctrine of inspiration as an important first step to reconstruction (after deconstruction) of a more pluralistic Christianity, devoid of incarnational Christology.[24]

William Cantwell Smith observes that truth is not objective and does not lie in propositions.[25] Western logic may work for computers but is ill-suited for thinking about spiritual matters.[26] Indeed, the term "God" has no objective content; its meaning is "humane" — that is, personal and individual to each human. The historical questions of the truth or reality of a religion (what it *meant*) are irrelevant to the theological questions of its present truth or reality (what it *means*). Thus divested of historical questions, all religions may be "true."[27]

In similar terms, S. Wesley Ariarajah suggests that claiming

Christianity is superior to other religions is tantamount to spiritual terrorism. Writing under the auspices of the World Council of Churches, Ariarajah examined what the Bible says about other religions, and did not like what he found; therefore he reconstructed a hermeneutic within which to "recontextualize" the exclusive message of certain texts.[28]

For Ariarajah, exegesis is functionally irrelevant; hermeneutics is key. The Bible was written by people whose thoughts were influenced by their faith. While admitting that Christianity has claimed to be at its nature an exclusivistic faith, Ariarajah feels this claim is socially inappropriate in our modern context. When we reinterpret exclusivistic texts, this "free[s] us as faithful people to be in dialogue with other faithful people." The new pluralism asks for a theocentric meta-narrative, not a Christo-centric one. "Today we have indeed a new situation. . . . The past models within which Christians sought to accommodate the other faiths can no longer suffice. There is new wine, and we need new wineskins."[29]

John Hick agrees: he suggests a "paradigm shift from a Christianity-centered or Jesus-centered model to a God-centered model of the universe of faiths. One then sees the great world religions as different human responses to the one divine Reality, embodying different perceptions which have been formed in different historical and cultural circumstances."[30]

Basically, Hick, Smith, and Ariarajah seem to think that (1) in general, a multiplicity of views implies a multiplicity of truths (except the "truths" of Christian or Islamic exclusivism), which in turn invite syncretism and, (2) in particular, some "higher" criterion should be invoked as a hermeneutic to abort scriptural claims of Christ's uniqueness and finality.

Observations

Without question we live in a pluralistic world—we always have. The significant change, however, is that divergent worldviews or meta-narratives are now in competition within cultures which had been relatively monolithic (particularly in North America). For the postmodernist, reality is pluralism, and pluralism is reality.[31] In theology, David Wells observes "there is little agreement as to what it means to be postmodern in theology, precisely because pluralism is at the center of it."[32]

Several observations can be made about the relationship of postmodernism and liberal religious pluralism. First, what are the

implications regarding the concept of biblical revelation and inspiration which may be found in the writings of pluralists such as Hick,
Ariarajah, and Smith? It seems that postmodernism and their approach to religious truth share the same epistemology. We have
already seen that Hick's prior acceptance of pluralism became the
reason for his subsequent denial of biblical revelation and inspiration.
According to Ariarajah, even the idea of revelation "is a part of a
faith-claim, and its validity also has to do with the faith of the community."[33] Of course, he would not deny its "truth," but he would deny
its normativity, as would William Cantwell Smith: "if St. Paul or
anybody else thought or thinks that only Christians can be saved, St.
Paul was wrong. It is Christ, and the God who has given me faith
through Christ, that saves me from believing so blasphemous a doctrine."[34] Thus, postmodern forms of pluralism deny the concept of
revelation as given in the Bible; there is no single revealed meta-
narrative which encompasses all religious experience.

Second, if meaning in interpretation is located in the knowing
subject (not in the text), and if that text is interpreted according to a
predetermined social agenda, what does this imply regarding the
exegetical task? Actually, the goal of exegesis is transformed from
questions about what the text *meant* into how the text can be used to
serve the new social agenda of the postmodernist.

For example, Ariarajah begins with this principle imbedded in his
hermeneutic: "exclusive claims, presented as absolute truths, only
result in alienation."[35] Thus "truth in the absolute sense is beyond
anyone's grasp, and we should not say that the Christian claims about
Jesus are absolute because St. John, St. Paul and the scriptures make
them. There will be others who make similar claims based on au-
thorities they set for themselves."[36] Further, all biblical truth-claims
are functionally relative. "However convinced we are about a faith-
claim, it has to be given as a claim of faith and not as truth in the
absolute sense."[37]

Ariarajah's hermeneutic allows him to deconstruct what he calls
the "virtual Christomonism" of Protestant theology which says that
God's revelation in Jesus was final and decisive.[38] This "marginalizes" (excludes) non-Christians and simply will not fit his social agenda; therefore, he reinterprets the texts to mean what he believes
they ought to mean: not Christianity, but theism.

How does he get to this point? He begins by discounting the
Gospel of John's christocentric focus and turning to what he calls the
theocentric synoptics.[39] Regarding the Christology of John, the Acts,

and all the epistles, they are "statements of faith about Jesus, the Christ. They derive their meaning in the context of faith, *and have no meaning outside the community of faith.*"[40] The recovery of a theocentric theology will enable Christians, without denying their witness to Jesus Christ, "to stand alongside people of other faiths as children of the one God."[41] He maintains that this is a needed "corrective that will enable Christians to live in a religiously plural world" and help set the pattern for dialogue between Christians and Hindus, Buddhists, Muslims, and other religions.[42] Thus Christology and the doctrine of the Trinity[43] are not deeply ingressed components of what it means to be a Christian! Smith takes this approach even beyond Ariarajah: "let the word 'God' mean to each of my readers whatever it does mean personally to him or her, as a theist; or if not one [a theist], then what he or she thinks that it has meant to theists."[44]

A third question posed above was, what does a postmodern view of truth imply regarding the Christian claim of the finality of Jesus Christ, vis-a-vis other truth-claims.

Of course, this has already been partially answered. First, there is no absolute truth. Aristotle's law of noncontradiction, foundational for the concept of absolute truth, has fallen on hard times.[45] In direct parallel, exclusivist religions have not fared well in modern pluralistic society. One may venture to say "*this* is true" as long as one does not add, "therefore *that* is false." Clark reminds us, however, that "the law of [non-]contradiction means that each word, to have a meaning, must also *not* mean something."[46] Yet the coexistence of a multiverse of worldviews promotes a psychological unwillingness to adopt even one's own views as truth. Rather, they are true for *me*. G.K. Chesterton once observed that humility was becoming misplaced; humility was no longer on self-opinion, where it ought to be, but was on truth, where it ought not to be.[47]

Since there is no such thing as absolute, normative religious truth, then Jesus Christ can no longer be considered "the Truth" (John 14:6) for all humankind. Smith maintains, "I do not say that God was revealed in Jesus Christ ... I do say that God has been revealed to *me* in Jesus Christ."[48]

Indeed, postmodern pluralistic interpretation of the doctrines of the finality and centrality of Christ (and perhaps even theism) see these teachings as a part of an agenda of oppression. According to Hick, "the resulting doctrine of a unique divine incarnation has long poisoned the relationships both between Christians and Jews and between Christians and Muslims, as well as affecting the history of

Christian imperialism in the Far East, India, Africa, and elsewhere."[49] And if adherence even to theism causes others (pantheists or atheists) to be marginalized, then theism is also negotiable.

Fourth, what is the purpose of inter-religious dialogue for a pluralism steeped in postmodernity? It is true that in past debates, those who are not universalists began their argument — and effectively so — with the assumption that because the religious systems of the world can't all be true, therefore the task was finding out which one (if any) was *true*. This used to be one of the most important questions in pluralistic debates. Even under modernity, this methodology was a viable procedure. But under postmodernism, the truth-claim of any religion is not the issue. Indeed, it is no longer a significant question.

Therefore the aim of dialogue is no longer a search for any kind of normative truth, but an exercise in social healing for marginalized groups. As was mentioned earlier, "exclusive claims, presented as absolute truths, only result in alienation."[50]

Ironically, postmodern pluralism engages in a type of dogmatism which makes all views relative and cuts off all discourse (thereby denying the value of the exchange of ideas valued in true pluralism). It is no longer that we are tolerant of *people* who hold weird and unsubstantiated ideas, we are now tolerant of and fascinated by the weird *ideas* themselves and intolerant people who disagree with our tolerance![51]

Conclusion

Rather than generating dialogue, a postmodern view of truth ultimately makes genuine dialogue impossible. Religious diversity does not require that one view all competing truth-claims as equally true. As Alan Bloom reminds us, "openness" does not necessarily require relativism in truth.

Walter Truett Anderson tells the story of three umpires relaxing together after a baseball game. The first umpire said, "There's balls and there's strikes, and I call 'em the way they are." The second ump remarked, "There's balls and there's strikes, and I call 'em the way I see them."[52] But the postmodern umpire said, "There's balls and there's strikes, and they ain't nothin' until I call 'em!" For the last umpire, the subject's knowledge is all that there is, or all that matters. We can never get outside our knowledge to check its accuracy against "objective" reality.[53] But the problem is precisely this: The umpire's call becomes normative for all; what validates the interpretation of the umpire who rules the game?

The biblical claim is that there is a meta-narrative which is descriptive of all, and normative for all. God is the sovereign Creator, whose word spoke all into existence, and who continues to work through history bringing the biblical meta-narrative to its fulfillment (Gen. 50:20; Rom. 8:28).

Humans were created as theonomous, derived beings, whose point of reference for accurately interpreting reality was the word of their Creator. In the Fall, they asserted autonomy, and reduced God's interpretation to the status of one alternative among others; the effects of sin upon the human mind (the "noetic" effects) have thus become significant for epistemology. Through divine revelation, God's signifying word (illumined by the Holy Spirit who inspired it) assumes that reality may be understood, though in part, by the human knower, and that reality is larger than that which can be ascertained by empirical methodology (Job 1–2; 2 Kings 6:16-17; 1 Cor. 13:9-12; 2 Cor. 4:17-18).[54]

In redemption, the meta-narrative places the focus of history on the Incarnation and on the person and work of God the Son. At the Cross the work of the first Adam was reversed in the work of the Last Adam. Jesus Christ is the one who showed sacrificial compassion for the marginalized: the outcasts, the lepers, the prostitutes, the tax collectors, and the sinners. His self-sacrifice was not for any single marginalized social or ethnic group, but was in behalf of all humankind (John 3:16). The culmination of all things will include judgment—the casting into outer darkness—of a new group of those who are "marginalized" (or who have marginalized themselves) for eternity.[55] This judgment does not involve ethnicity or geography, is the fulfillment of repeated warnings, and is considered an act of justice, not of oppression.[56]

How can this meta-narrative be told in a postmodern world without giving in to a self-defeating form of pluralism? Since in postmodernism (and in some forms of pluralism) everything can be true, therefore why should one dialogue to search for truth?

Geisler notes that in a search for common ground for dialogue, Christianity and other religions will not accept each other's hermeneutic as authoritative, and thus have no common ground there.[57] But for religions which do hold to truth as absolute, there is epistemological common ground. "Both participants believe it is their system that makes meaningful dialogue possible."[58] Muck rightly observes, "the best dialogue takes place between people committed to the absolute truth of their religious traditions."[59]

NOTES

1. See Marjorie Perloff, "Postmodernism: The Prospects for Openness in a Decade of Closure," *Criticism* 35/2 (Spring 1993): 161–92; and Gabriel Josipovici, "Life Between Inverted Commas," *Times Educational Supplement* 3998 (12 February 1993), S9.

2. David Steward and H. Gene Blocker, *Fundamentals of Philosophy*, 3rd ed. (New York: Macmillan, 1992), 241.

3. Ibid.

4. Ibid., 242.

5. Ibid., 245. Steward and Blocker argue that postmodernism implodes, in that since it affirms any theory which enjoys popular acceptance as almost certainly socially repressive and therefore wrong—yet if postmodernism becomes the prevailing theory, it becomes guilty of violating its own criterion (p. 244).

6. See William V. Dunning, "Postmodernism and the Construct of the Divisible Self," *The British Journal of Aesthetics* 33/2 (April 1993): 132–41. Dunning exalts the divided sense of self which he finds laudable among the ancient Aztecs.

7. Steward and Blocker, *Fundamentals of Philosophy*, 248.

8. Walter Truett Anderson, *Reality Isn't What It Used to Be: Theatrical Politics, Ready-to-Wear Religion, Global Myths, Primitive Chic, and Other Wonders of the Postmodern World* (San Francisco: HarperCollins, 1990).

9. David Wells, *No Place for Truth: Or, Whatever Happened to Evangelical Theology?* (Grand Rapids: Eerdmans, 1993), 61. The reader may observe that I have defined a particular postmodernism which is skeptical, culturally broadbased, and badly in need of redemption. While many see postmodernism as benign or neutral, a survey of the literature in the broader culture shows that the term is used in an almost epistemologically nihilistic way, particularly in the arts.

10. See the discussion in Lawrence Stone, "History and Postmodernism," *Past and Present* 135 (May 1992).

11. Richard Stengel, "American Myth 101," *Time*, 23 December 1991, 78, cited in Dunning, "Postmodernism."

12. See Wulf Kansteiner, "Hayden White's Critique of the Writing of History," *History and Theory* 32/3 (October 1993).

13. See Stephen Frosh, "Psychoanaylsis, Psychosis, and Postmodernism," *Human Relations* 44/1 (January 1991).

14. Manfred Jahn: "Postmodernists at Work on Joyce," *James Joyce Quarterly* (Summer 1992), 29:4.

15. Steward and Blocker, *Fundamentals of Philosophy*, 243.

16. Nicholas Rescher, *Pluralism: Against the Demand for Consensus* (Oxford: Clarendon, 1993), 79.

17. Ibid., 3, 5.

18. D.A. Carson, "Christian Witness in an Age of Pluralism," in *God and Culture: Essays in Honor of Carl F.H. Henry*, ed. D.A. Carson and John Woodbridge (Grand Rapids: Eerdmans, 1993).

19. See Richard Mouw, *Uncommon Decency: Christian Civility in an Uncivil World* (Downers Grove, Ill.: InterVarsity, 1992), chaps. 6–7.

20. Carson, "Christian Witness."

21. *Sura* 4:154–159. Netland argues that other religions which have fundamen-

tal elements of mutually incompatible truth-claims include Hinduism, Buddhism, Islam, and Shinto. See Harold Netland, *Dissonant Voices: Religious Pluralism and the Question of Truth* (Grand Rapids: Eerdmans, 1991), chaps. 2–3.

22. We must not assume that shared characteristics of pluralists makes them postmodernists in ideology or methodology, and vice versa (this would be the fallacy of excluded middle). Yet they do travel in the same direction, which this chapter attempts to demonstrate.

23. John Hick, *God Has Many Names* (Philadelphia: Westminster, 1980), 58.

24. Similarly, Hick's universalism drove him to posit that Christianity could not therefore be the only way. See Hick, *God Has Many Names,* 17, 131.

25. William Cantwell Smith, *Towards a World Theology* (Maryknoll, N.Y.: Orbis, 1981), 190. "In so far as truth is apprehended by persons, it is apprehended within history; yet in so far as it is true, it transcends history [and any particular formulation]" (p. 190).

26. Cited in Netland, *Dissonant Voices,* 144.

27. Ibid., 154, 164–70.

28. S. Wesley Ariarajah, *The Bible and People of Other Faiths* (Maryknoll, N.Y.: Orbis, 1989), xii.

29. Ibid., xiii, 27, 61, 63.

30. Hick, *God Has Many Names,* 18–19.

31. See Ziauddin Sardar, "Do Not Adjust Your Mind: Postmodernism, Reality, and the Other," *Futures* 25/8 (October 1993).

32. Wells, *No Place for Truth,* 66. Wells does observe, however, that to be postmodern is often to be Eastern in one's spirituality.

33. Ariarajah, *Other Faiths,* 28.

34. Smith, *World Theology,* 171.

35. Ariarajah, *Other Faiths,* 28.

36. Ibid., 27. Note that simply the existence of rival truth-claims nullifies the normativity of Scripture.

37. Ibid., 67; see also p. 68.

38. Ibid., 64.

39. Ariarajah, *Other Faiths,* 21, asserts that in the synoptics "there seems to be no claim to divinity or to oneness with God: what we have is the challenge to live lives that are totally turned towards God."

40. Ibid., 23, emphasis mine. In another context — Athens — Paul "adopted a new method and a new idiom" and became theocentric in his presentation, not Christocentric (see also pp. 39–47).

41. Ibid., 65.

42. Ibid., 66, 44.

43. Speaking of Matthew 28:18-20, Ariarajah, *Other Faiths,* opines that the "trinitarian formula would suggest that the particular formulation comes from the early church, and not from Jesus himself" (p. 49).

44. Smith, *World Theology,* 153.

45. This is also called the law of contradiction. See Irving M. Copi, *Introduction to Logic,* 7th ed. (New York: Macmillan, 1986), 306–8. See also Alan Bloom, *The Closing of the American Mind* (New York: Simon and Schuster, 1987), 25.

46. Gordon Clark, *Logic* (Jefferson, Md.: Trinity, 1985), vii, emphasis mine.

47. See Rescher, *Pluralism,* chaps. 9 and 10.

48. Smith, *World Theology,* 174, emphasis mine.

49. Hick, *Many Names,* 8.

50. Ibid., 28.

51. Carson, "Christian Witness," 31–34.

52. The first umpire holds the view of naive realism: epistemological judgments are descriptions of the real world; the second is a perspectivalist: knowledge is mediated through the grid of the subjective knower.

53. Anderson, *Reality Isn't What It Used to Be,* 75. This analysis was provided by Walsh in a paper by Brian Walsh and J. Richard Middleton, "Postmodern Pluralism and a Biblical Worldview," presented at the Wheaton Theology Conference, 7 April 1994.

54. Wells, *No Place for Truth,* 280, observes, "a Christian mind sees truth as objective. It seeks to understand reality as it is in itself, not as it seems to the subject."

55. Postmodernism and pluralism both tend toward universalism, since no meta-narrative has priority and all are valid (or at least some would advocate a form of wideness which far exceeds biblical assertions that there are few who will embrace the Gospel).

56. Some of these thoughts were expressed in a response paper by Stephen Spencer at the 1994 Wheaton Theology Conference, 7 April 1994.

57. The illustration given was that Christians don't accept the absolute authority of the Koran, and Muslims don't accept the absolute authority of the Bible.

58. Norman Geisler, "Some Philosophical Perspectives on Missionary Dialogue," in *Theology and Mission,* ed. David Hesselgrave (Grand Rapids: Baker, 1979), cited in Terry Muck, "Evangelicals and Interreligious Dialogue," *Journal of the Evangelical Theological Society* 36/4 (December 1993): 527.

59. Muck, "Evangelicals and Interreligious Dialogue," 529. See I. Howard Marshall, "Inter-Faith Dialogue in the New Testament," *Evangelical Review of Theology* (July 1989): 196–215 for a study of *dialegomai.* The term occurs ten times in Acts, usually with the meaning of preaching (proclamation) with some time afterward for discussion. Significantly, the "dialogue" neither *formulates* nor *reformulates* truth; rather it is intended to clear up misunderstandings and always aims at conversion.

15

Is That All There Is? Moral Ambiguity in a Postmodern Pluralistic Culture

C. Ben Mitchell

Not long ago at a genetics conference about 100 physicians, ethicists, and pastors listened to a number of speakers describe the ethical dilemmas and conundrums presented by the new genetics. One by one they helped the audience gaze presciently into the future of genetic engineering. The clinicians were, to a person, in a quandary. Ought they do what they were presently able to do with human genes? Ought they do what they believe they soon will be able to do? The technological imperative has run broadside into the moral imperative.

Finally, a theologian stood to address the issues raised by the clinicians. This university divinity school professor began by confessing he was more at home in analytic philosophy than in ethics and that the new genetics had given him pause in his otherwise esoteric pursuits (his characterization, not mine).

For nearly an hour the professor of theology read his densely argued paper, rehearsing the same dilemmas the clinicians had described only minutes before. Then he launched into a discussion of the classical formulation of the problem of evil and argued that the wisdom of the ages was little help. Next, he embarked on a discourse on ethical pragmatism and its proponents. Just when the convener was going to call time on our speaker, he got to his point. His

C. Ben Mitchell is Director of Biomedical and Life Issues for The Christian Life Commission of the Southern Baptist Convention in Nashville, Tennessee.

answer to the dilemmas presented by the explosion of genetic technology: *moral ambiguity*. Should we genetically engineer so-called
"designer children"? Should we screen for genetic diseases and abort
children who would be born with those diseases? Should we mix
animal and human genes? The professor gave a long-argued, unqualified *maybe!* Moral ambiguity.

The clinicians who had made an impassioned plea for help in
discerning whether their pangs of moral conscience were justified
were visibly crushed. They had begun the morning with a truckload
of critical and urgent questions — questions that radically impact their
own lives and the lives of their patients. They submitted those queries, if not for answers, at least for some clarification, to persons who
were supposed to speak with some degree of moral force. What they
received was a large dose of more questions topped off with moral
ambiguity. They were worse off than when they started.

It was upsetting, not because of expecting easy resolutions to
exceedingly difficult problems. Human genetic engineering presents
incredibly tough questions. It was upsetting to witness that theology
once again had been seen to be at best irrelevant, at worst, harmful.
Rather than answering questions or, at least, helping clinicians to
focus on better questions, theological distillation produced moral ambiguity. Is that all there is?

How many times will clinicians and policy-makers dip for answers in the once-teaming waters of theological discourse, only to
draw up the dust of the earth? Will they continue to ask for bread
when they receive stones and for fish when they receive snakes?
Jeffrey Stout observes that

> secular intellectuals have largely stopped paying attention.
> They don't need to be told, by theologians, that Genesis is
> mythical, that nobody knows much about the historical Jesus,
> that it's morally imperative to side with the oppressed, or
> that birth control is morally permissible. The explanation for
> the eclipse of religious ethics in recent secular philosophy
> may therefore be rather more straightforward than I have
> suggested so far. It may be that academic theologians have
> increasingly given the impression of saying nothing atheists
> don't already know.[1]

Now we must be careful not to be too hard on the divinity school
professor. But our fear, and one that is well-founded, is that scien-

tists, businesspersons, educators, and policy-makers will cease to engage theological voices if all they hear are distant echoes reflecting their own bewilderment.

We must take seriously Alasdair MacIntyre's challenge: "Theologians still owe it to the rest of us to explain why we should not treat their discipline as we do astrology or phrenology."[2] Scenarios like the one which opened this chapter do not help to extricate theology or theologians from the realm of necromancers. The burden of theology on the threshold of the third millennium is to demonstrate that it makes a difference. Moral ambiguity does not.

Perhaps we should be encouraged by the fact that at least one theological voice was permitted in a discussion of the ethics of molecular genetics. It is becoming increasingly difficult to find the theologians qua theologians on programs dealing with medical ethical issues. Even though the majority of the early literature in bioethics was written by theologians or persons with theological backgrounds, most recently, academic ethics in general and medical ethics in particular has become part of the naked public square. "The naked public square is the result of political doctrine and practice that would exclude religion and religiously grounded values from the conduct of public business," says theologian Richard John Neuhaus.[3] As American culture has become increasingly pluralistic, attempts have been made, more or less successfully, to sanitize political and moral discourse of its religious dimensions. The ethics of medicine, once rich in religious discourse, has likewise been sanitized in favor of moral discourse grounded in only one tradition, namely secularism.

Unlike some cynics, we should not posit behind every bush a secular humanist conspiracy clandestinely working for the eradication of religion. Hence, we will use "secular" and "secularism" in the same way one of its own proponents uses the terms. H. Tristram Engelhardt, Jr., in his important volume, *Bioethics and Secular Humanism: The Search of a Common Morality,* defines secular humanism as, "the cluster of philosophical, moral, and literary ideas, images, and commitments, which have been associated with the historical phenomena of humanism in dissociation from particular religious or ideological commitments."[4] Because of the failure of religion and reason to produce a common, content-full moral framework shared by a majority of individuals in our culture, we live, says Engelhardt, in a society of "moral strangers." That is, there are growing numbers of persons "who do not share a common concrete religious, moral, or philosophical viewpoint."[5] Engelhardt describes

secular humanism as "the attempt to ground culture and public policy in non-religious terms by appeal to what we share as humans."
This view, he maintains, "underlies most contemporary understandings of bioethics and health care."[6]

In light of the sanitization of the public square and the securiza-
tion of bioethics, is there a place for religious talk or religious discourse in policy related to bioethics? Is the patient's bedside a little
corner of the naked public square in which it is appropriate only to
speak in a form of moral Esperanto? If so, with whom does one
speak? Most patients come in discernible moral shapes and sizes. If
so, who does the speaking? Most physicians and ethicists come to
the bedside with moral commitments. So as not to be guilty of what
we have criticized, we not only want to ask these questions, but to
suggest a few modest answers.

Medical Ethics and Pluralism

Not only has the public square become secularized, so also has academic medical ethics. Religious talk about ethical issues in medicine
is less welcome today than in the past. In policy considerations of
abortion, physician-assisted suicide, and the ethical, legal, and social
implications of the Human Genome Project, religious discourse has
been largely marginalized if not ignored entirely. The same could be
said for most medical ethical issues and, therefore, especially of public policy related to such issues. In a discussion of public policy
related to euthanasia, for instance, Dan Brock, Professor of Philosophy at Brown University, has maintained: "in a pluralistic society like
our own with a strong commitment of freedom of religion, public
policy should not be grounded in religious beliefs which many in that
society reject."[7] So, public policy, because it is policy for a pluralistic
society, must, presumably, be framed by rational, secular, and nonreligious notions. Freedom *of* religion has become freedom *from* religion.

Ethicists Albert Jonsen and Lewis Butler have correctly observed
that "there is an undeniable affinity between ethics and policy-mak-
ing—an affinity that arises from their interest in an identical question: What is good for society?"[8] If this is true of ethics in general,
that which is concerned with the "good for society," it seems true
especially of religious ethics. Yet, religious communities are routinely ignored or marginalized because their moral and ethical discourse
contains "God talk." Have religious communities no stake in the
"good for society"? Must religious ethicists be confined to the semi-

nary and the pulpit even though they themselves have an interest in the good of society? If so, it is not surprising that theologians suffer a failure of nerve and use their "prophetic voice" to proclaim (or should we say, "whisper") moral ambiguity.

Varieties of Pluralism

No one doubts that we live in a pluralistic culture. Variety in religion, ethnicity, and lifestyle is a fact of life. Such has always been the case to a greater or lesser degree. There are, however, as Oxford theologian Alister McGrath observes, two kinds of pluralism — "pluralism as a fact of life" (descriptive pluralism) and "pluralism as an ideology" (ideological pluralism).[9] The existence of rival religious, moral, and philosophical presuppositions and convictions constitute the former pluralism. Socrates and Plato argued their worldviews against the backdrop of Thales, Heraclitus, and Pythagoras. The early Christians found their views in conflict with Epicureanism, Stoicism, and even ancient Judaism.

Likewise, we moderns (or, more appropriately, postmoderns) find ourselves in an extremely pluralistic culture. Protestants, Catholics, and Jews no longer constitute the religious triumvirate in American society. Islam, Buddhism, and a host of sects and cults have found homes on North American soil. Atheists, agnostics, New Agers, and self-avowed pagans are common enough that few of us are surprised when we meet a member of one of these groups. It is palpably obvious that, descriptively speaking, we live in a pluralistic environment. This is nothing new. Throughout the ages, few eras and civilized cultures have been monolithic.

The second type of pluralism — pluralism as an ideology — is far more troublesome. This brand of pluralism advances the view "that normative claims to truth are to be censored as imperialist and divisive. . . . Claims by any one group or individual to have an exclusive hold on 'truth' are thus treated as the intellectual equivalent of facism."[10] For instance, postmodernist Zygmunt Bauman has said, "Truth is, in other words, a *social relation* (like *power, ownership,* or *freedom*): an aspect of a hierarchy built of superiority-inferiority units; more precisely, an aspect of the hegemonic form of domination or a bid for domination-through-hegemony."[11]

Framing ethics and public policy in a pluralistic environment is challenging at best. As both Bauman and Engelhardt warn, religious discourse applied to policy issues may be coercive. Says Engelhardt, "The risk to humanity from war and brutal repression in the name of religious and ideological rectitude far outweighs the harms likely to come from tolerating such evils as self-dermination, abortion, and infanticide."[12] Similarly, in another place he says, "Insofar as individuals do not share in the consensus of a common religious belief, including the divine roots of state authority, appeals to religious consideration will appear to those without faith or with a different faith as an appeal simply to force in order to support private interests."[13]

But there are problems with Engelhardt's claims. First, his view fails to acknowledge that nonreligious appeals may be just as coercive and threatening as religious appeals. For instance, in his refreshing treatment of the trivialization of religious faith, *The Culture of Disbelief,* Yale law professor Stephen Carter tells the story of a Colorado public school teacher who was "ordered by his superiors, on pain of disciplinary action, to remove his personal Bible from his desk where students might see it. He was forbidden to read it silently when his students were involved in other activities."[14] Such a policy seems highly coercive, if not unconstitutional. Or, to cite another example, the major proposal for national health care reform, The Health Security Act, enjoins employers to provide insurance coverage for abortion. Specifically, the proposal makes it illegal for persons to opt out of the plan based upon their religious belief that abortion is morally reprehensible except to save the life of the mother. Again, this seems fairly coercive. We must, therefore, recognize the evangelistic agenda of secularists who invite us to join what Gustafson and Hauerwas have called, "that fictional denomination called autonomous rational moral agents."[15]

Second, it must also be pointed out that Engelhardt seems to be attributing to religious ethical discourse a radical individualism that is unfounded. Especially in the Christian tradition, the good of the community, not "private interests," is paramount. For Christians, of course, this is most clearly demonstrated in the atoning work of Jesus Christ who died for persons of every nation, kindred, tongue, and tribe and tore down the walls that falsely partitioned segments of society (Eph. 2:14-17). Moreover, Jesus' command to love neighbor as self certainly repudiates any radical individualism or support of merely private interests.

The most critical problem for ideological pluralism is, of course, that it turns and devours itself. It is rabidly self-refuting. First, by denying the possibility of truth, it effectively squelches every effort to set forth, recognize, or aspire to truth. Since truth is not available nor discoverable, the search for truth becomes futile.

Second, by the ideological pluralist's own admission, no one can (or at least, should) claim to know truth. Self-avowed pluralists who espouse this pluralist doctrine thus become the worst form of imperialist — denying to others what they themselves claim to have. That is, epistemological agnosticism is, in fact, a covert claim of knowing the truth about truth. "That no one can or should claim to know the truth" is a truth-claim. Furthermore, for most ideological pluralists, this is a universal truth-claim; it holds all of the time, everywhere. The truth or individual truths do not exist — anywhere. Unlike its descriptive cousin, ideological pluralism is pluralism with a vengeance. Thus, postmodernist philosopher Richard Rorty says his role is to "decry the notion of having a view while avoiding having a view about having views."[16]

If ideological pluralism were "true," could the ideological pluralist "know" it, since he or she denies the existence (or, at least, knowability) of universal truth? The ideological pluralist has no way of justifying his or her own claims. Viewlessness (read nihilism) abounds. Thus, ideological pluralism is not, in fact, suitable as a moral orthodoxy. English historian E.R. Norman has observed perceptively that " 'pluralism' is a word society employs during the transition from one orthodoxy to another."[17] Indeed, these are days of transition.

In a genuinely pluralistic society (of descriptive pluralism), individuals recognize that all moral discourse is embedded in a moral tradition or moral traditions. Whether that tradition is identified as religious or not, it remains the case that it is a moral tradition. Notions of a so-called "peaceable neutral framework"[18] and an "unbiased analysis of settled moral viewpoints"[19] are temptingly deceptive. Whether it is a Christian, Buddhist, or secularist moral tradition, all ethical statements are grounded in a tradition.

> None of us starts from scratch in moral reasoning. Nor can we ever start over again, accepting only beliefs that have been deduced from certitudes or demonstrable facts. We begin already immersed in the assumptions and precedents of a tradition, whether religious or secular, and we revise these assumptions and set new precedents as we learn more about ourselves and our world.[20]

It is, therefore, unfair, if not morally myopic, for secularists to assume the posture of "rational moral agents" who are not indebted to a particular universe of moral discourse for their ethical perspectives and policy recommendations. There is no Nagelian "view from nowhere." All ethics and, therefore, all public policy is grounded in some moral tradition or traditions. Instead of being depreciated or ignored, in a genuinely pluralistic culture diverse moral traditions must evangelistically push their own notions of the good society. Public policy is, obviously, not stated in terms of religious dogma or creedal statements, but in a specific conception of the good for society. That is, public or institutional policies are not likely to include textual references from any religious scripture, but may nonetheless reflect a conception of the good that is either consonant with or accommodating to one or more of those traditions.

When religious persons are accused of trying to impose their morality upon the public policy process, it is important to ask what alternative source of morality is to be preferred, and why. If the reply is, "it is a nonreligious morality," one should probe deeper to discover what variety of morality is being proposed. It should then be pointed out that religious commitments have at least as much moral force and right to be heard in the public arena as any other commitment.

"Public" Public Policy?

Critical in discussions of public policy is the reminder that "public" policy is policy of, by, and for the public. In American society, and indeed in most parts of the world, the public is decidedly religious. In a survey of persons in thirteen countries, The International Social Survey Program, a consortium of social science research centers, found that "most of them believe in God and in life after death, rebutting perceptions of social scientists that society isn't as religious as it used to be."[21] The survey included the United States, Britain, Hungary, Ireland, Israel, Italy, New Zealand, the Netherlands, Norway, Poland, Slovenia, East Germany, and West Germany. According to the survey, 94 percent of Americans, 92 percent of Irish, 50 percent of Dutch, and 26 percent of East Germans believe in God. Majorities in nine countries believe in life after death, including 80 percent in Ireland, 78 percent in the United States, 33 percent in Slovenia, 26 percent in Hungary, and 12 percent in Germany. Interestingly, the survey also found that as many as 64 percent of Americans favored prayer in schools.

For the second consecutive year, Gallup polls have shown that the importance Americans attach to religion is on the rise. A 1992 poll found that 58 percent of Americans believe religion is "very important" in their lives and 29 percent believe it is "fairly important."[22] While it is certainly true that this is substantially lower than the 1952 high of 75 percent who considered religion very important, it is noteworthy that this finding is up from the 1987 low of 53 percent. Additionally, according to the poll, 70 percent of adults claim membership in a church or synagogue.

The great majority of the American people are a self-professedly religious people. If public policy is truly policy of, by, and for the "public," it must demonstrate appreciation for the religious nature of the American public for whom it exists. That is not at all to say that "might makes right" or that "majority rules" in policy matters. That is a far too simplistic conception of representative democracy. What it does mean is that policy-makers should shape policy which accommodates the religious nature of the American public and does not ignore the religious sentiments of their constituency. To do otherwise would be to make something less than "public" policy.

Furthermore, with respect to medical ethics and public policy, since medical ethics has to do with the practice of medicine and the practice of medicine has to do with real, and more often than not, religious persons, policy related to medicine must also accommodate the religious nature of physicians, nurses, and patients. The patient's bedside must not be seen as a corner of a so-called "naked public square." It is likely that the patient (and the physician for that matter) is a very religious person and her religious commitments must be respected and accommodated in policy that stops at her bedside. In fact, it could be maintained that it is at the bedside that the most profound religious commitments are exposed and expressed. Often, at the bedside questions of ultimacy—of life and death and disability—are faced squarely.[23] "We ought to pay attention," reminds Elton Trueblood, "to the fact that in spite of the apparently dominant humanism, many people turn, in genuine crisis, to the great affirmations."[24] Truly "public" public policy must respect those affirmations; otherwise, that policy exists for a patient who does not exist. That is, there are no patients who present to the emergency room without a moral tradition—most often a religious moral tradition. There is no procedure of "radical traditionectomy" by which a patient can have his or her own moral tradition surgically removed.

Finally, medical ethicists, even those involved in the development of public policy statements, should not be coerced or intimidated into attempting to speak in a form of moral Esperanto. There is a place for religious discourse in medical ethics and, therefore, in policy related to medicine. Unfortunately, some medical ethicists have been of the opinion that in order to get the ear of our culture, theology must assume a voice not its own and merely repeat what Jeffery Stout calls, "the bromides of secular intellectuals in transparently figurative speech."[25] Other ethicists have been more forthright and courageous. Martin Marty characterizes persons such as James Childress, James Gustafson, Stanley Hauwerwas, William F. May, and Paul Ramsey as persons who "exercised more durable influence [in medical ethics] because they gave most attention to the matrix and context of theology and ethics as a background to the medical ethics world."[26] No one can deny that these scholars have been major shapers of medical ethical theory and practice. More than one of them served on the President's Commission on Bioethics and with other august policy-writing bodies. Their effectiveness in shaping both the discussion of medical ethics and the nuances of public policy has been largely due to their refusal to be "just like everybody else."[27]

Conclusion

Religious medical ethics must be a distinctive contributor to public discourse in our culture. The failure of ideological pluralism, the relevance of religious moral tradition, and the religious nature of the American public argue for forthrightness and candor on the part of medical ethicists of religious faith. Secular ethicists and policy-makers who discriminate against or trivialize moral discourse of a religious sort demonstrate ethical bigotry. It may be said of medical ethics what Carl F.H. Henry has said of secular education.

> The main complaints against American education today, from elementary to graduate learning, are its prejudicial exclusion of the Christian world view, the promulgation of which was the primary reason for which many great universities were founded, and its ready misunderstanding of the doctrine of church and state as an occasion for secular naturalistic reductionism.[28]

Medical ethicists often attend to the religious sentiments of patients when considering a particular case study. But when religious ethics — as a way of conceptualizing medicine, not just patients — are marginalized or altogether ignored by medical ethicists, they reveal that they have forgotten the rock from which medical ethics was first hewn and, without great caution, they may display the ugly bias of reverse discrimination.

Furthermore, secularism ignores a critically important component of human nature, namely, the religious dimension. To call for ethicists and policy-makers to neglect the religious nature of human beings is tantamount to calling for physicians to be merely body plumbers. Ethics, policy, and medicine would be severely disabled were that the case. As Steven Lammers and Allen Verhey have said:

> A genuinely pluralistic society requires the candid expression of different perspectives. Candid attention to the religious dimensions of morality, including medical morality, could prevent the reduction of morality to a set of minimal expectations necessary for pluralism and could remind all participants in the public discourse of broader and more profound questions about what human beings are meant to be and to become.[29]

We would suggest then that academic medical ethicists and public policy-makers acknowledge descriptive pluralism as a fact of life. There are, indeed, a multitude of voices to be heard and values to be weighed in medicine and public policy. No one said it would be easy to develop policy that takes into account the perspectives of those who live under its aegis. Great effort will need to be expended to analyze and translate religious concerns into appropriate and effective public policy.

Furthermore, religious voices should not only be *heard* by those who shape health care policy, they should be *encouraged* and *invited*. Fortunately, groups such as the Park Ridge Center for the Study of Health, Faith, and Ethics in Chicago and The Institute of Religion in Houston provide forums for research and discussion of the religious implications of medicine and policy. Their efforts should be applauded and multiplied.

Especially encouraging for the future was the commencement of the first master's degree program in bioethics at an evangelical seminary. Under the leadership of Nigel M. de S. Cameron and Harold O.J. Brown, Trinity Evangelical Theological School began specialized training in bioethics from a distinctively Christian perspective in the summer of 1993. There are ongoing discussions of the possibility for a Center for Bioethics at Trinity.

Interestingly, and to take us back to where we began, one of the results of a series of conferences sponsored by the Institute of Religion and the Baylor College of Medicine on the religious dimensions of the Human Genome Project, was a summary statement which represents the collaborative efforts of a host of scientists, theologians, and ethicists. The *Summary Reflection Statement* appropriately portrays the profundity of the issues raised by the explosion of genetic information, but by no means for moral ambiguity with respect to the uses of that information. For instance, the statement declares:

> Religious values mandate the defense of personal privacy, integrity of the family, and good social relations. Therefore, they support policies and methods of securing consent to have access to genetic information obtained through screening. Moreover, the use of confidential information must be carefully circumscribed to avoid embarrassment, social stigmatization, disruption of marital and familial relations, and economic discrimination. Care should be taken to avoid or prevent the unjust uses of an individual's genetic data in respect to securing and holding employment, insurance, and health care.[30]

This position statement reveals conclusions which are embedded in a particular conception of human persons, the family, their rights, and the good for society. Some may disagree with these conclusions, but they are hardly ambiguous.

Finally, in a cultural environment of descriptive pluralism, religious ethicists and moral theologians will not fear "hanging out their shingle." That is, medical ethicists who represent specific faith communities will be free to work under the banner of their faith commitments and will be enlisted to bring those commitments to bear on the issues of high-technology medicine without fear of being labeled imperialist or without being ignored as irrelevant.

NOTES

1. Jeffrey Stout, *Ethics After Babel: The Languages of Morals and Their Discontents* (Boston: Beacon, 1988), 164.

2. Alasdair MacIntyre, "The Theology, Ethics and the Ethics of Medicine and Health Care: Comments on Papers by Novak, Mouw, Roach, Cahill, and Hartt," *The Journal of Medicine and Philosophy* 4 (December 1979): 443.

3. Richard John Neuhaus, *The Naked Public Square,* 2nd ed. (Grand Rapids: Eerdmans, 1986).

4. H. Tristam Engelhardt, Jr., *Bioethics and Secular Humanism: The Search for a Common Morality* (Philadelphia: Trinity, 1991), 3.

5. Ibid.

6. Ibid., 4

7. Dan Brock, "Voluntary Active Euthanasia," *Hastings Center Report* 22 (August 1992), 21.

8. Albert R. Jonsen and Lewis H. Butler, "Public Ethics and Policy Making," *Hastings Center Report* 5 (August 1975), 21.

9. Alister E. McGrath, "The Challenge of Pluralism for the Contemporary Christian Church," *Journal of the Evangelical Theological Society* 35 (September 1992): 361.

10. Ibid., 361–62.

11. Zygmunt Bauman, "Postmodernity, or Living with Ambivalence," in *A Postmodern Reader,* ed. Joseph Natoli and Linda Hutcheon (Albany, N.Y.: State Univ. of New York Press, 1993), 11. Other examples of what I am calling ideological pluralism are treated in Richard J. Mouw and Sander Griffioen, *Pluralisms and Horizons: An Essay in Christian Public Policy* (Grand Rapids: Eerdmans, 1993).

12. H. Tristam Engelhardt, Jr., *The Foundations of Bioethics* (New York: Oxford Univ. Press, 1986), 13.

13. H. Tristam Engelhardt, "Death by Free Choice: Modern Variations on an Antique Theme," in *Suicide and Euthanasia: Historical and Contemporary Themes,* ed. Baruch Brody (Dordrecht, Holland: Kluwer, 1989), 256.

14. Stephen L. Carter, *The Culture of Disbelief: How American Law and Politics Trivialize Religious Devotion* (New York: Basic, 1993), 11.

15. James M. Gustafson and Stanley H. Hauerwas, "Editorial," *The Journal of Medicine and Philosophy* 4 (December 1979): 346.

16. Cited in Gene Edward Veith, Jr., *Postmodern Times: A Christian Guide to Contemporary Thought and Culture* (Wheaton, Ill.: Crossway, 1994), 60.

17. James Hitchcock, "Competing Ethical Systems," *Faculty Dialogue* (Winter 1984–85): 34.

18. Engelhardt, *Foundations of Bioethics,* 12.

19. Ibid., 14.

20. Stout, *Ethics After Babel,* 120.

21. "Believers in God Are a Big Majority in U.S. Poll Says," *Nashville Banner,* 18 May 1993.

22. "Is There a Religious Revival Brewing?" *PRRC Emerging Trends* 15, Princeton Religion Research Center (April 1993): 1–5.

23. Engelhardt, *Bioethics and Secular Humanism,* 35, claims that "most of the fully secularized will find in their circumstances a comfortable ultimate meaninglessness, not a loss of meaning" in a secularized culture. "Comfortable ultimate meaninglessness" is an oxymoron. The explosion of philosophical and moral theories, not to mention the recent revival of ancient pagan religions, mitigates against the notion that comfort may be experienced simultaneously with ultimate meaninglessness.

24. D. Elton Trueblood, "Intellectual Integrity," *Faculty Dialogue* (Winter 1984–85): 49.

25. Stout, *Ethics After Babel,* 163.

26. Martin E. Marty, "Medical Ethics and Theology: The Accounting of the Generations," *Second Opinion* 17 (April 1992): 73. For discussion of each of these

and other ethicists, see Allen Verhey and Stephen E. Lammers, eds., *Theological Voices in Medical Ethics* (Grand Rapids: Eerdmans, 1993).

27. Leon Kass, "Practicing Ethics: Where's the Action?" *Hastings Center Report* 20, (August 1990), 6–7, cited in Ron P. Hamel, "On Barnard Haring: Construing Medical Ethics Theologically," in Verhey and Lammers, *Theological Voices in Medical Ethics,* 213.

28. Carl F.H. Henry, "Secularization," in *In Search of a National Morality: A Manifesto for Evangelicals and Catholics,* ed. William Bentley Ball (Grand Rapids and San Francisco: Baker and Ignatius, 1992), 23.

29. Stephen E. Lammers and Allen Verhey, eds., *On Moral Medicine: Theological Perspectives in Medical Ethics* (Grand Rapids: Eerdmans, 1987), ix.

30. *Summary Reflection Statement,* Genetics, Religion and Ethics Project, The Institute of Religion and Baylor College of Medicine, The Texas Medical Center, Houston, Texas (Houston: The Institute of Religion, 1 June 1992), 2.

16

Postmodernism: A Declaration of Bankruptcy

Kathryn R. Ludwigson

Only within the last two decades has the word postmodernism appeared as a label to identify the prevailing philosophy of the late twentieth century. The word "postmodernism," however, does not reveal anything about the intellectual content of that philosophy. The word merely states that this worldview follows modernism chronologically, thus announcing the demise of modernism. Not introducing something new, it is simply a declaration of the bankruptcy of modernism.

Postmodernism declares that the basic belief of modernism—trust in human reason to lead to truth—is no longer tenable. Modernism with its rationalistic base has been the dominant philosophy of Western culture since the seventeenth century. From the time of Christ until the seventeenth century, the traditional Western view was *theocentric/logocentric,* believing that God the Logos had revealed truth in Christ, in the Scriptures, and in nature and that words actually represent and connect with the things we talk about. God Himself was with the man in the Garden of Eden when words were first used. Thus, the Christian worldview believes the universe to be patterned by God who gave us minds—though not absolute like His—but sufficiently capable of grasping real meaning inherent in experience: revelation from God was the ultimate source of truth. Evangelicals still hold this view.

Kathryn R. Ludwigson is Professor of Literature at Toccoa Falls College in Toccoa Falls, Georgia.

Even before Christianity, the classical Greek world claimed this to be a meaning-laden universe, its meaning to be available by reason and intuition according to Plato, to be available by reason and logic according to Aristotle.

But in the seventeenth century, Descartes' radical disjuncture of revelation and reason led away from the prevailing theocentric worldview and initiated trust solely in human sense-preempted reason — a strictly *anthropocentric* worldview — later known as naturalism, humanism, or modernism. Reason, thus, freed from God, became master of human destiny; sense-preempted reason had all the answers — at least eventually! The scientific method of modernism — observation and experimentation — exemplified the right use of reason: what is "out there"/the real/the sensible particulars are fixed and give valid objectivity. As Bertrand Russell put it, "What science cannot tell us, mankind cannot know."[1]

Postmodernists, however, say such faith in scientific objectivity is an impossibility. There is no such thing as objective knowledge/reality; science reveals no "facts," no truth; we have only linguistic constructs. There is no reality "out there": the world is a fiction.

Thus — as so aptly expressed by the title of an essay by Wilhelm Wurzer, "Postmodernism's Short Letter, Philosophy's Long Farewell," in one fell swoop postmodernism wipes out all previous philosophies — Platonic epistemology with its trust in intuition and reason, Aristotelian trust in logic and reason, Christianity's trust in revelation and reason, and modernism's trust in sense-preempted reason. What is left? Only the *word* itself; nothing "out there" to write about, even no self, only the word.

But how then did language originate? Human beings playing word games with each other, enjoying a playful itinerary of words only, answer the postmodernists, for the imposition of meaning on a thing is really only an illusion, nothing more than an interpretation of some other thing. This in turn will be seen only as an interpretation as well: not mirrors (re)presenting reality as the modernists had said, but a labyrinth of mirrors reflecting neither the outer world of nature nor the inner world of subjectivity, reflecting only endless circularity — an *ex-centric* worldview. There are no facts, remember; the world is an illusion. Derrida, the most popular exponent of postmodernism, has said: "There is nothing outside the text; all is textual play with no connection with original truth."[2]

"Reality," thus, is formed by the powers of language/the word. As an example, notice the slippery use of the word "free":

"I'm free." TGIF day—free from the week's work.
"I'm free." Single person—not married.
"I'm free." Divorcée—marriage was a bondage.
"I'm free from pain"—I don't have any.
"He's free with his money"—liberal, generous.
"A free translation"—not literal nor exact.
"Free verse"—not using traditional poetic structures.
"Free admission"—doesn't cost any money.
"Free from slavery"—emancipation.

Another—rather humorous—demonstration of deconstruction: a new computer owner wanted to sue the manufacturer because the computer used language that was not politically correct; he said that the computer called him an *in*valid (invalid!!!)

By demonstrating in this manner how words "de-construct," the postmodernists shredded the modernists' belief in reason's ability to (re)present by words the reality "out there."

So, postmodernists concentrate on how to express—or celebrate the destruction of old forms—their apprehension of a meaningless, irrational world of incoherent particulars. Hence, the incoherent, garbled gobbledegook of contemporary literature, the random collage of art and music, the subjective/ egocentric/nonjudgmental educational system with its attendant reader's response, the dismissal of a traditional morality and the accompanying rising violence, and the alarming collapse of traditional jurisprudence. Let's take a deeper look.

Manifestations of Postmodernism in Our Society

Contemporary fiction writers and playwrights have littered the literary landscape with the seeds of postmodern influence and philosophy. Notice an early manifestation from Ionesco's *The Bald Soprano:*

Mr. Smith: Dogs have fleas, dogs have fleas.
Mrs. Martin: Cactus, coccys! crocus! cockaded! cockroach!
Mrs. Smith: Incasker, you incask us.
Mr. Martin: I'd rather lay an egg in a box than go and steal an ox.
Mrs. Martin (opening her mouth very wide): Ah! oh! ah! oh! Let me gnash my teeth.
Mr. Smith: Crocodile!
Mr. Martin: Let's go and slap Ulysses.[3]

Or take a look at John Barth's short story "Title" in his anthology of postmodern pieces, *Lost in the Funhouse:*

> Beginning in the middle, past the middle, nearer three-quarters done, waiting for the end. Consider how dreadful so far: passionless, abstraction, pro, dis. And it will get worse. Can we possibly continue?
>
> Plot and theme notions vitiated by this hour of the world but as yet not successfully succeeded. Conflict, complication, no climax. The worst is to come. Everything leads to nothing: future tense; past tense; present tense. Perfect. The final question is, Can nothing be made meaningful? Isn't that the final question? If not, the end is at hand. Literally, as it were. Can't stand any more of this.
>
> I think she comes. The story of our life. This is the final test. Try to fill the blank. Only hope is to fill the blank. Efface what can't be faced or else fill the blank. With words or more words, otherwise I'll fill in the blank with this noun here in my prepositional object. Yes, she already said that. And I think. What now. Everything's been said already, over and over; I'm as sick of this as you are; there's nothing to say. Say nothing.
>
> What's new? Nothing.[4]

Notice the willful randomness of language, its ambiguity, its "cheap, narrative collage" — unreadable fiction. As someone has said about this sort of literature: "One feels like a baffled child watching lunatics."

Or observe another early manifestation of the postmodern "philosophy" in Ionesco's drama *Chairs.* Two old people have hired an orator to deliver to an audience — which isn't there! — a message that will save the world, which the old man has spent his lifetime in writing. When the orator arrives, we discover that he is deaf and dumb.

> [He turns around again, towards the invisible crowd on the stage, and points with his finger to what he has written on the blackboard.]
> ORATOR: Mmm, Mmm, Guene, Gou, Mmm, Mmm, Mmm, Mmm. [Then, not satisfied, with abrupt gestures, he wipes out the chalk letters, and replaces them with others, among which we can make out, still in large capitals.]
> AADIEU ADIEU APA[5]

As he exits from the stage, the drama ends—significantly, I think!—with the words: "The main door is wide open onto darkness." I use the word "significantly" to point out that even those who deny a God-given universe laden with inherent meaning recognize that they are in the dark. "The message of the play is an antimessage," according to Rosette Lamont, "an ontological void";[6] as Ionesco himself told Claude Bonnefoy, it is about the absence of people, the absence of God, the absence of living meaning, metaphysical emptiness.[7]

We would be remiss if we did not mention what is perhaps the ultimate dramatic expression of postmodernism's belief in nothingness—Samuel Beckett's ultimate drama, untitled of course. It has two acts. But in the first act the curtain rises on a bare stage; there are no actors. It runs for half an hour, still no actors. And in the second act, the curtain doesn't rise at all.

T.S. Eliot's short lyric "The Hollow Men" was a very early recognition of where we now are.

> We are the hollow men
> We are the stuffed men
> Leaning together
> Headpieces filled with straw. Alas!
> Our dried voices, when
> We whisper together
> Are quiet and meaningless
> As wind in dry grass
> Or rats' feet over broken glass
> In our dry cellar.[8]

Consider postmodernism's influence on art: it is an expression of complete autonomy, an insistent banality which is nothing more than an "absurd conglomeration of debris." No longer does art represent the external world.

Consider postmodernism's radical effect on art criticism:

> For the sense in which a work of art has no content is no different from the sense in which the world has no content. Both are. Both need no justification; nor could they possibly have any.[9]

Further, consider postmodernism's influence on music—the atonal, dissonant, even silent, perpetual variation, and sheer noise of contemporary mindless "music" with its non-resolution — "a rock band that sounds like a lawn mower with a beat." Or consider John Cage's "prepared" pianos jangling with inserted household items, a percussion orchestra of pots and pans — anarchic harmony and happenings — or his silent piano piece *4'33''* where he sits for the designated time on a piano bench with the keyboard closed. As Solzhenitsyn has written:

> If visitors from outer space were to pick up our music over the airwaves, how could they ever guess that earthlings once had a Bach, a Beethoven, and a Schubert, now abandoned as out of date and obsolete?[10]

What about postmodernism's effect on education? Consider the new strategy of outcome-based education to deemphasize content in favor of programs of experience and growth, to replace formal classroom instruction with informal group activity sessions. Or a high school teacher's stating that what her students say in class is just as important as what she says. Or a literature professor in a state university telling his class that since words do not really communicate, they were, therefore, pursuing nonsense.

The collapse of traditional morality and the rise in violence, attacks, shakedowns, and robberies in the nation's public schools every day are indicators of the social effects of philosophical change. Even without instruction in the "philosophy" of postmodernism, our young people have caught its horrendous message "blowing in the wind": the absurdity, the nausea of life. Their natural — and logical — reaction is to "live it up," or why live at all.

The closing lyrics of Nirvana's pop hit "Smells Like Teen Spirit" were eerily prophetic not only of lead singer and Generation X antihero Kurt Cobain's recent suicide, but representative of the malaise of his generation: "I found it hard, it was hard to find, oh well, whatever, nevermind." Unable to any longer gain meaning from living it up, Cobain sadly chose to not live at all — the ultimate "nevermind" statement.[11]

Or as Squeaky Fromme explained to her captors when she tried to assassinate President Gerald Ford in 1975: "If you have no philosophy, you don't have any rules." And that insight had been previously expressed by French existentialist Jean Paul Sartre in his drama *Flies*. Orestes, having just killed his mother and his stepfather, is boasting to the populace:

You see me, men of Argos, you understand that my crime is wholly mine; I claim it as my own, for all to know; it is my glory, my life's work, and you can neither punish me nor pity me.[12]

Finally, consider the enthusiastic embracing of postmodernism by our law schools embracing the concept of "popular sovereignty."

Popular sovereignty as a motif emphasizing the energy and moral authority of will (and willful desire) rather than the constraints of a common moral order to which the will was bound to submit has "become the view emphasized today at most major law schools." "Law is stripped of any moral anchoring" and "political institutions thus become the forum for the triumph of the will."

But despite all the risks, this liberation from the myth of "truth" (whether understood as grounded in God or in reason), clears the way for a new, Godless kind of "civil religion" or "constitutional faith;" and it is this prospect that Mr. Levinson and his colleagues find so captivating. . . .

If there are no permanent moral truths, then moral "truth" becomes whatever history temporarily proclaims predominant.

. . . history in our time is hurtling toward disintegration of all the old verities that once held us together. . . .

. . . this book should be for all of us an alarm bell ringing in the night. Something ominous is afoot in the teaching of the law of this land.[13]

Why Postmodernism Came into Existence

And now *why* has postmodernism come into existence? What are the provocative causes? Though there were earlier harbingers of the demise of modernism, postmodernism — by that name — has been declaring bankruptcy of the old order for the past twenty years. But why? A number of reasons have been suggested.

1. The failure of sense-preempted reason as held by modernists to understand what quantum theory and microphysics have discovered: how can an electron travel two or more different directions simultaneously or move from one orbit to another without traveling the space between them? To try to find absolute truth is pointless.

Thus, we have the postulates of Heidegger's "Being," Jasper's "final experience," Sartre's authenticity (to mention but a few modern attempts)—none of which regained meaningfulness in life; none have led to truth. Hence, the change from classical physics provoked postmodernism's emphasis on noncontinuity, noncausality, and nonlocality.

2. The conviction that (post)modern people can have a revelation of their own and not be dependent upon antiquated traditional expressions, not be forced into traditional forms which stifle individuality. To be relieved of a sense of cosmic purpose, freed from God-controlled system of rights and wrongs, is exhilarating freedom, releasing the creativity of the individual, shoring up an eroded sense of the autonomous self. Not locked into merely mirroring nature, postmodernists can create their own unique realm of infinite possibilities and can never be duplicated.

3. The loss of faith in modernism's belief in evolutionary progressivism, painfully evidenced in the mass slaughters of the twentieth century. Derrida himself was a victim of anti-Semitism during the Nazi era.

4. The belief that cause and effect are illusory, intrinsically suspicious, hence the lack of sequence of plot in postmodernism's fiction.

5. Two world wars, the death of 66,000,000 Russians in the Communist regime, and the extermination of so many Jews in the German Holocaust. The blankness of the postmodernists is a way of staving off anxieties produced by the unexpected for which there is seemingly no resolution.

6. A reaction to the dominance of a mechanistic/commercialized/technological culture, which dehumanizes human beings, wresting power from human beings and investing it in the things.

7. The desire to give up the idea of truth as something to which they are responsible.

8. The desire to express philosophically a multicentered cultural pluralism.

Criticism of the Postmodern Position

And what is the answer to all of this? Let us consider several.

1. *Non-Sense.* Postmodernists said it themselves in denying the ability of the *senses* to convey truth. "We are at one of those historic junctures where we can only wonder," comments Charles Newman, "how our common sense was beaten out of us."[14]

2. *Contradiction!* Their statement that all concepts are illusory affirms a trustworthy, prior knowledge. Also, if words no longer com-

municate meaning, why do postmodernists continue to publish? And if there is nothing to know, how do they know there is nothing?

Obviously, the postmodernist's theory about our being trapped by the word itself in a language game is an example of metaphysical truth standing outside language: to deny truth is at once and the same time to assert another truth. Total nihilism is an incoherent position.

And though postmodernists lock humans into a "prison-house of language," as Neitzsche earlier stated, with no objective reality of language to express, they do not address the question as to the origin of language. Derrida, for instance, sidesteps the question of origin, declaring that language seems to have been "always already" everywhere.

3. *Ignoring a Universal Moral Law.* There is a law written in all of our hearts, one that crosses different civilizations and different ages, stating that we ought to behave in a certain way. Why would we be complaining about violence, sexual deviation, crime, if there is no universal morality? The law of God is written in our hearts (Rom. 2:15). They had the knowledge of God but "did not think it worthwhile to retain the knowledge of God, he gave them over to a depraved mind" (Rom. 1:28, NIV).

4. *Freedom from Responsibility.* If postmodernism insists on the demolition of the remaining remnants of traditional theocentricity and of modernism's anthropocentricity—an ahistorical stance—then it has an obligation to show how its own narcissistic position of responsibility to no one is an enhancement of civilization. As it stands, its position absolves everyone of responsibility, even begetting an unrestricted licentiousness; it is in reality "permanent revolution" such as Foucalt's postmodernism advocates. The end of that road is national suicide.

5. *Dementia.* "Depriving oneself of notions like rationality, objectivity, scientific method, rules of logic, is voluntarily to choose dementia since it is abandoning the only touchstone we have left to discriminate dementia from normality,"[15] writes Bruno Latour. "By doing away with rationality, no reality is left. . . . There is no longer any possibility of distinguishing . . . between witchcraft and science. Everything is equal. All the cows are equally gray."[16]

6. *Relative Pluralism.* Does anything that any individual "cooks up" go? Yes, says postmodernism. No, say evangelicalism and classical philosophy. Around 2,500 years ago Protagoras wrote that man is the measure of all things. However, "Not a single ancient Greek

philosophy ever once defended Protagorean relativity."[17] Socrates and his pupil Plato declared truth was absolute—something people lived up to, not some concept they created. And if, as postmodernism asserts, life is a patternless, meaningless, created fiction, then why don't postmodernists reverse this notion and impose order and coherence in their works?

Confirmation of the Bankruptcy of Modernism by the Greats

A significant number of contemporary observers have seen the great emperor of postmodernism, and he indeed has no clothes: Kathleen Agena: "The reason for the malaise is no integrating world view; the enlightenment has been undone";[18] Harvey Cox: "The liberal era has drawn to a close";[19] Maurice Valency: "We have come to the end of 'an art that does not heal' ";[20] Ihab Hassen: "Without some radiancy, wonder, wisdom, we all risk, in this postmodern clime, to become barren";[21] Wallace Stevens: "for the listener, who listens in the snow/And, nothing himself, beholds/Nothing that is not there the Nothing that is";[22] Charles Newman: "its [postmodernism] dirty little secret is that Demystification does not finally alleviate their human or aesthetic problems, but seems only to deepen and further conceal them";[23] Zbigniew Brzezinski: "a community which partakes of no shared absolute certainties . . . is a community threatened by dissolution."[24]

Even three of the prominent postmodernists—Rorty, Fish, and Derrida—have backed off from being identified with an extreme nihilism. Derrida, for instance, responded:

> Deconstructing academic and political discourse doesn't mean simply destroying the norms or pushing these norms to utter chaos. I'm not in favor of that sort of thing.[25]

All that he meant to do, he affirmed, was to demonstrate the *finiteness* of the human intellect, its inability to gain the *absolute* by itself—"experiencing the impossible."

"Great!" exclaims the evangelical. "Of course, we should always be humble, acknowledging our finiteness." *But* evangelicals add that God has revealed *absolutes* in the Bible and through Jesus Christ, has written His law in our hearts, and has given us rational ability to see and to understand His eternal power and divine nature, "so that men are without excuse" (Rom. 1:20).

What Can We Do About Postmodernism?

Gertrude Himmelfarb in her book, *Looking into the Abyss,* states that we will outlive postmodernism, just as we have outlived other isms.[26] This too shall pass. However, postmodernism has destroyed the very apparatus of criticism. As evangelicals we opt out and reaffirm a theocentric/logocentric world, accepting the Word that became flesh and dwelt among us, whose glory we beheld as that of the only begotten of the Father, full of grace and truth (cf. John 1:14).

More diligently, more fervently, more prayerfully than ever before we need to keep preaching the truth of the Scriptures, inspired by God and suitable for instruction, correction, and reproof (cf. 2 Tim. 3:16). We must show the flaws of the postmodernist "thinking." Recognize the lies of Lucifer in the Garden: "You will be like God" (Gen. 3:5). We have to diligently catechize our children, young people, and adults so that they really know what they believe. And we must make use of the plethora of multimedia available in our increasingly video-dependent culture.[27] The medium may not be the message, but for the MTV generation and beyond the medium must be one that rivals the vehicles of delivery in the popular culture.

In summary, the Apostle Paul's admonishment is ever the more relevant in dealing with the postmodern context: "when they will not endure sound doctrine" . . . then "hold fast the form of sound words" (2 Tim. 4:3; 1:13, KJV).

NOTES

1. As quoted by Huston Smith, *Beyond the Post-Modern Mind,* 2nd ed. (Wheaton, Ill.: Theosophical/Quest, 1989), 163.

2. Jacques Derrida, *Prophets of Extremity* (Berkeley, Calif.: Univ. of California Press, 1985), 3.

3. Eugene Ionesco, *The Bald Soprano* in *Four Plays* (New York: Grove, 1958), 40.

4. John Barth, *Lost in the Funhouse* (New York: Doubleday, 1988), 105.

5. Ionesco, *Four Plays,* 160.

6. Rosette C. Lamont, ed. *Ionesco: A Collection of Critical Essays* (Englewood Cliffs, N.J.: Prentice-Hall, 1958), 96.

7. Lamont, *Ionesco,* 69.

8. T.S. Eliot, "The Hollow Men," in *The Complete Poems and Plays* (New York: Harcourt, 1971), 56.

9. Susan Sontag, "On Style," in *Against Interpretation* (New York: Duell, 1966), 36.

10. Aleksandr Solzhenitsyn, "The Relentless Cult of Novelty and How It Wrecked the Century," *New York Times Book Review* 2 (February 1993), 3.

11. Kurt Cobain, "Smells Like Teen Spirit," in Nirvana, *Nevermind* (Geffen,

compact disc, 1991).

12. Jean Paul Sartre, *Flies,* in *No Exit and Three Other Plays* (Evanston, Ill.: Northwestern Univ. Press, 1955), 11.

13. Thomas Prangle, "Post-Modernist Thought," review of Stanford Levinson's *Constitutional Faith, Wall Street Journal* (January 1989).

14. Charles Newman, *The Post-Modern Aura* (Evanston, Ill.: Northwestern Univ. Press, 1985), 11.

15. Bruno Latour, "Clothing the Naked Truth," in *Dismantling Truth,* ed. Hilary Lawson and Lisa Appignanesi (New York: St. Martin's, 1989), 101.

16. Ibid., 106.

17. David Glidden, *Los Angeles Times* (26 March 1989).

18. Kathleen Agena, "The Return of Enchantment," *New York Times Magazine* (27 November 1983).

19. Harvey Cox, *Religion in the Secular City* (New York: Simon & Schuster, 1984), 268.

20. Maurice Valency, *The End of the World* (New York: Schocken, 1980), back cover.

21. Ihab Hassen, *The Postmodern Turn* (Columbus, Ohio: Ohio State Univ. Press, 1987), 230.

22. Wallace Stevens, "The Snow Man," in *Collected Poems* (New York: Random House, 1982).

23. Newman, *Postmodern Aura,* 197.

24. Zbigniew Brzezinski, *Out of Control* (New York: Scribner's, 1993), 113.

25. Jacques Derrida, "Interview" in *Wall Street Journal* (27 July 1993).

26. Gertrude Himmelfarb, *Looking into the Abyss* (New York: Knopf, 1994), 161.

27. For more insight into this issue, see chapter 18 by William E. Brown, "Theology in a Postmodern Culture: Implications of a Video-Dependent Society."

17

Newman Revisited: The Idea of a University in Postmodern America

C. Richard Wells

Wherever discussion turns to matters of higher education, the name John Henry Newman will surely appear. His treatise *The Idea of a University* was the first and remains the most definitive philosophy of higher education ever produced. A contemporary characterized the work as "the perfect handling of a theory"; others have ranked it with Aristotle's *Nicomachean Ethics* as the most valuable of all works on the purposes and aims of education.[1] Newman's contributions, of course, extend far beyond educational philosophy. He was a theologian and historian. He was also a poet, a preacher, a novelist, a reformer of sorts, and above all, a churchman. But as Newman later reminisced, "from first to last, education . . . has been my line."[2] And *The Idea of a University* — "perhaps the most timeless of his books and certainly the most intellectually accessible to readers of every religious faith and of none"[3] — is his legacy to higher education.

Oddly, while the higher education cognoscenti in the United States (we shall confine ourselves to this country) hold Newman in high esteem, almost reverentially so, they do not seem to take him seriously. Like the Pharisees — "Abraham's children" who do not "the deeds of Abraham" (John 8:39, NASB) — many in higher education honor the memory of Newman without engaging his mind.

C. Richard Wells is Associate Professor of Divinity at Beeson Divinity School of Samford University in Birmingham, Alabama.

He has become something of a museum piece, valuable as an artifact is valuable, for sentimental rather than for substantive reasons.

We say "oddly" because Newman was in some very important ways a century ahead of himself, almost the first postmodern. He seemed to anticipate the implications and the end of modernity before modernity ever got underway. Moreover, the crises in higher education which precipitated his discourses on the nature of the university were foreshadowings of the contemporary crises.

From Oxford to Dublin

John Henry Newman was born February 21, 1801 in London. He died August 11, 1890 in Birmingham.[4] His life thus spanned almost the entire intellectual sea change which was the nineteenth century. The first child of a fairly prosperous English family, Newman was brought up "an ordinary member of the Church of England,"[5] but experienced a conversion to evangelical principles — "a great change of thought" he described it[6] — in 1816, the year he matriculated at Trinity College, Oxford. Newman spent most of the next twenty-nine years, until 1845, defending the doctrines and principles of Anglican Christianity, usually within the context of the university, meaning (of course) Oxford. He was elected a Fellow of Oriel in 1822, and appointed Tutor four years later. In 1828, Newman assumed the vicarage of St. Mary's, a post he held until 1843. As the university church in Oxford, St. Mary's gave Newman a platform to publish his views, in some sense even required him to do so. He was the university preacher.

The pulpit of St. Mary's and his Oxford connection firmly established Newman in the role for which, besides the *Idea*, he is most well-known. During an extended Mediterranean holiday Newman got word of the Irish Church Reform Bill which greatly diminished the privileged position of Anglicans in predominantly Catholic Ireland. Shortly afterward came news that Thomas Arnold, an old Oxford colleague and now headmaster of Rugby, had proposed sweeping church reforms in order to stave off a threatened Parliamentary disestablishment. The threat of disestablishment mattered much less to Newman than the "reforms"; and he later reported a sense of urgency: "I had fierce thoughts against the Liberals," he wrote, and "I began to think that I had a mission."[7]

Upon his return, Newman formed a society, together with several Oxford colleagues, for the purpose of "rousing the clergy"[8] to restore the ancient faith now (Newman believed) fading in England.[9] Members of the "Oxford Movement" published a series of "Tracts for the Times" from September 1833 until February 1841 when (Newman's) Tract 90 set off a firestorm of protest.

Newman undertook the so-called "Tractarian" controversy in defense of Oxford and Anglicanism. He ended retaining Oxford ideals, but also by persuading himself that the Roman Church was the only truly catholic church. Tract 90, in fact, brought censure for Newman on grounds that he had opened the door to Catholic teaching in the church and in the university.[10] The censure led to Newman's resignation from the Oxford Movement;[11] and by the end of the year, whether owing to the censure or not, Newman was clearly rethinking the Catholic position. Four years later, on October 8, 1845, Newman summoned Father Dominic Barbieri to his room at Littlemore and was that night received into the Roman Catholic communion.

But Newman remained every bit an educator. In Rome the next year, Newman felt himself drawn to the Oratorian Rule, a privately supported community of secular priests. Little more than two years after his conversion, Newman was in Birmingham as Superior of the (only) English Oratory, with which he was to be associated for the rest of his life. The work of the Oratory included pastoral work, as well as scholarly labors, and both theological and adult education. Bishop Ullathorne of Birmingham, at first skeptical that an assembly of converts could form a proper Catholic community, later (1864) praised the Oratory for its educational endeavors, which included a "school for the education of the higher classes."[12] As an Oratorian, as in most of his life's work, Newman was first an educator.

Newman's reputation in higher education derives, however, neither from his work as an Oratorian nor his career as an Oxford don. It derives from a short-lived and ill-fated experiment, a blip on the timeline of his personal history. In April 1851, the Archbishop of Armagh, Paul Cullen, wrote to ask Newman whether he might offer suggestions of administration and faculty to staff a proposed Catholic university in Dublin, and incidentally "if you could spare time to give us a few lectures in education, you would be rendering good service to religion in Ireland."[13] Though hesitant at first, by midsummer Newman had agreed and set about preparing the discourses that fall. By all accounts, Newman agonized over this preparation, principally because he did not know his audience. Nevertheless, the lectures commenced on Monday, May 10, 1852, continuing on successive Mondays until June 7. Newman then published (but did not deliver) four other discourses together with the first five in February 1853, as *The Idea of a University*. Not only had Newman agreed to deliver lectures on university education, however, he had agreed to serve as president (rector) of the new Catholic University of Ireland. He would divide his time between Dublin and the Oratory in Birmingham. He wanted, he said, "to do as much work for the University as possible with *as little absence as possible* from this place [the Oratory]."[14]

The Catholic university proposal was itself the result of a tortured division within the Irish Catholic community. In the spring of 1845, Sir Robert Peel had proposed a series of educational reform measures aimed at conciliating the Irish Catholic majority who, despite legal protections were, for all intents and purposes, excluded from a university education. Catholics had been eligible to try for degrees at Trinity College (Dublin) since 1794, and provisions had been in place since that time for a Catholic college at Dublin. But no Catholic college was founded, and while Catholic students could pursue degrees legally, they often found it well-nigh impossible as a practical matter, and could not in any case accept scholarships or positions of trust without a formal act of apostasy to the Anglican communion. As a gesture of conciliation, Peel had proposed the founding of nonsectarian "Queen's Colleges," with no religious tests and no religious instruction except as provided by the sects themselves. The Irish hierarchy and laity were divided over this form of "mixed education," to which the Catholic university was, in fact, an alternative.

Newman thus had good reason to be anxious about his lectures, not to mention his presidency. He was to oversee an institution supported by some Catholics, opposed by others, and to some degree doubted in the minds of all. It lacked the most fundamental right of any institution of higher learning—to grant degrees! He must start "from scratch," and he must do so with divided time and energy, as a converted Catholic, and as an Englishman when the Irish seemed naturally to distrust anything or anyone English. And these were only the most obvious difficulties.

A child could predict the result. Newman served as rector of the university for (precisely) seven years, most of them years of frustration. The university itself managed to survive only until 1882 (the medical school until 1908), suffering for all its brief life from vacillating support and (somewhat relatedly) its inability to secure a Government charter.

For all that, Newman worked out his vision of the university to a surprisingly high degree. He innovated with curricula and scheduling.

He made appointments that brought the school notoriety. He established (well ahead of his time) schemes of governance that empowered the faculty and he worked diligently, though with only scant visible success, to redefine the role of professor and tutor so as to create a mentoring relationship between instructors and students. One can only guess what might have been had Newman worked under more salubrious conditions.

The First Postmodern?

In some respects, this chapter represents one interpreter's "guess." If the venture of an Irish Catholic university failed, we are left to ponder why Newman's "idea" of a university succeeded. But more, we are left to ask whether the "idea" has any relevance in a postmodern culture. The question is not an easy one even to address coherently, let alone to answer. The cultural distance between postmodern America and Newman's England and Ireland, the Tractarians' parochial debates over religious tests at Oxford, and Newman's peculiar Catholic slant on higher education is nearly overwhelming. Yet Newman's philosophy of higher education endures.

One explanation of its endurance is that Newman maintained a strident critical detachment from his own culture. Robert Pattison argues that in the terms interpreters generally employ to assess his contributions, Newman was unquestionably a failure. The conventional wisdom that credits him with leadership of the Oxford movement, with reviving English Catholicism, with being a modern-day Athanasius, or with prophesying the collapse of liberalism, is simply fallacious. On all counts, Newman was a failure. He should be numbered "among the Victorian greats," Pattison suggests, "because, though lacking in any single distinction or success, his various failures collectively comprise a major career."[15]

Far from making Newman irrelevant to contemporary culture, however (Pattison concludes) Newman's dissent from modern liberalism has "utilitarian as well as aesthetic value."[16]

> The great virtue of Newman's critique of liberalism is that it exists at all. That there should be one consistent view of the world opposed to liberalism root and branch, sharing none of its premises and despising all of its works is an inestimable benefit, for no one more than the liberal himself. Without some honest and unforgiving voice such as Newman's, the liberal would be lost in a labyrinth of his own ideology. He

would smugly assume that the paradoxical tenets of his creed are what Jefferson assured him they were, self-evident truths.[17]

It is in this sense that we dare to call Newman a "postmodern." For if anything holds together the various expressions of post-modernist thought, it is "the realization that there has been a funda-mental shift within modern western culture."[18] If modernist culture "stressed the autonomous nature of the individual and his/her ability to construct a coherent whole to life through the use of the scientific method and rational thinking. . . . The postmodernist perspective has challenged most of [those] core assumptions."[19] Whatever else may be said of Newman, he challenged those assumptions as well.

We do well to reiterate the point that Pattison makes. Newman's critique of modernist culture was not the work of a closet sympathiz-er, a collaborator, or an unwitting participant. There was nothing paradoxical about his assessment of modernist ideology. As few have ever been able to do, Newman stood aloof from his culture. His judgment arose from a different paradigm, a different worldview, than that of his own (and our own) culture. Yet, Newman would not have welcomed the suggestion that he was "premodern" or "anti-modern" as moderns typically use such terms. He was a rationalist, but not in the Enlightenment sense. He was open-minded, but not in the liberal relativistic sense. Newman early on embraced Darwin's evolutionary hypothesis, for example, as a suitable accounting for human physiolo-gy. Though not an "evolutionist" in a philosophical or metaphysical sense, Newman considered belief or disbelief in the scientific theory of evolution irrelevant to religious orthodoxy as such.[20]

It is just this curious tension between Newman's critique of liber-alism and his open-minded rationalism that makes his philosophy of higher education so richly suggestive for the postmodern. In *The Idea of a University* this tension appears in the full unfolding of a single principle, which on the one hand stands in utter opposition to heresy, to error, to liberalism, and which on the other hand, grows, adapts, and develops. In the *Idea,* Newman called it (for lack of better terms, he said) "knowledge" or "philosophy." It is at once dogmatic and relativistic, circumscribed and expansive. And the "idea" of a univer-sity, that is, the nature and the rationale of a university, Newman declared, is: "That it is a place of *teaching* universal *knowledge.*"[21] There is much in Newman's famous statement of the "idea" of a university that bears on the contemporary higher education enterprise.[22] Yet, to say it again, it is this tension between the critique of liberalism and rationalism that forms the core of Newman's philosophy. Newman's relevance for higher education stands or falls here.

The Critique of Liberalism

Apart from the tension to which we have referred, Newman's critique of liberalism would render him an extremely unlikely candidate for the title of "first postmodernist." His pleadings seem at times the product of an inexhaustible nostalgia; at other times, quite frankly, they seem the rantings of a crank. Even his most enthusiastic admirers admit that Newman could be irascible, often entering a fray just because, as Patton is supposed to have said of war: "God, I love it!" And he could bite the proverbial hand that fed him; giving no quarter even to his allies. First impressions and temperament notwithstanding, however, Newman's critique of liberalism was, for him, deadly serious intellectual (and ultimately social) business.

The seriousness of the liberal challenge derived from Newman's confidence in the power of *ideas* to create and sustain values and behavior. Liberalism was indifference to dogma; or, positively, the doctrine that beliefs are (nothing more than) social conventions. In the liberal view, beliefs served a cultural function, but they played no substantive role in human affairs. They changed from time to time and place to place, and they could be embraced or dispensed with promiscuously and without consequence. Such was the spirit of modernity which Newman saw taking shape before his eyes. Everything relative, everything historically and culturally conditioned, nothing absolute, everything up for grabs. For Newman, nothing could be more dangerous; for the idea that ideas don't matter, itself mattered profoundly!

The power of ideas to shape behavior dominated Newman's thinking. In his first book, for example, Newman interpreted the great Arian controversy and its aftermath in terms of the outworking of first principles. What many called a "dispute over a diphthong"[23] became for Newman not only an ecclesiastical and theological crisis of the first magnitude, but a change point in Western cultural history. Modernism, Newman thought, was only Arianism *recidivous*.[24] The principle is reflected supremely, of course, in the *Idea;* even in the form of Newman's argument. Newman begins with his statement of the *Idea:* "The view taken of a university in these discussions is the following: That it is a place of teaching universal *knowledge.*"[25]

Then Newman carefully worked out the implications of his

"view." It was crucial for Newman to begin with the idea, for in theology, as he believed in all of life's aspects, ideas or first principles determine outcomes.

Even to an uninitiated reader, Newman's confidence in the power of ideas would suggest that his "idea" of a university — that the university "is a place for *teaching* universal *knowledge*" — employs terms laden with the freight of Newman's own first principles. And indeed, it is precisely Newman's understanding of "teaching" and "knowledge" that makes the idea of the university relevant in postmodern culture. The relevance is especially apparent in Newman's proposal that university is a place for *teaching*, that is, not for research.

> The nature of the case and the history of philosophy combine to recommend to us a division of labor between Academies and Universities. To discover and to teach are distinct functions; they are distinct gifts, and are not commonly found united in the same person.[26]

The division to which Newman refers has insinuated itself with vigor into the most recent conversations taking place in higher education. From Carnegie Reports throughout the decade of the 1980s, to proposals for new ways of defining scholarship that reward good teaching, to critical discussions of the German university paradigm, these conversations support a growing realization that research and teaching often work at cross purposes, and that, as Newman argued, the first principle of the university is to *teach*. It remains to be seen how the tension now so keenly felt will resolve itself in the postmodern milieu; but for a variety of reasons the teaching role of the university will likely demand more and more attention.

In terms of postmodernity itself, however, Newman's concept of *knowledge* has even greater relevance than his concept of teaching. The liberal culture which Newman repudiated, and which now participates in the decay of modernity, embraces a philosophy of knowledge that Newman found untenable and which postmodern culture finds increasingly unsatisfactory. Much of Newman's argument in the nine discourses which form the core of the *Idea,* concerns the nature and place of *knowledge* in the university and in the wider culture. While we might choose any number of points in his argument, we shall confine ourselves to Newman's two main assertions about knowledge: (1) knowledge is its own end; and (2) theology is a branch of knowledge.

Knowledge Its Own End

"Knowledge its own end" represents Newman's most mature answer to one of "the two great controversies [of] the first half of the nineteenth century . . . the *uses* of a liberal education and . . . whether a university was to be religiously exclusive."[27] English Reform movements in higher education during this period tended to focus on one controversy or the other, sometimes both; and of the two, the former seems to have occupied Newman more fully. In any case, the *utility* of university education, the use that was to be made of it, was a subject of intense debate throughout the period of Newman's life, as it is once again today.

In the early years of the nineteenth century (1808–1811), the *Edinburgh Review* "fiercely lampooned the undergraduate curriculum at British universities as having lost touch with reality and therefore as not being able to prepare young men for the real world."[28] In the *Idea,* Newman alluded to the crisis created by these attacks. A "storm broke over the University [Oxford] from the North" he said;[29] the "Edinburgh Reviewers protested that no good could come of a system which was not based upon the principle of Utility."[30] Newman cited approvingly the defense of Oxford education by John Davison (Fellow of Oriel). In an essay on "Professional" (read "utilitarian") education Davison had argued (1) that "a Liberal Education is something far higher, even in the scale of Utility, than what is commonly called a Useful Education" and (2) that "[liberal education] is necessary or useful for the purposes even of that Professional Education which commonly engrosses the title of Useful."[31]

Newman himself defended Oxford education against the utilitarian movement in 1841. In January of that year Sir Robert Peel delivered a speech at the dedication of a public library in Tamworth which had excluded divinity texts from its collection. Taking advantage of his setting, and seizing a political moment (he anticipated election as Prime Minister), Peel extolled the virtues of practical, or "useful" knowledge. Utilitarian subjects, he said, would break down the social divisions engendered by sectarian claims and party interests. Science would ennoble character and enrich culture. Newman responded with seven withering letters to *The Times* which Robert Pattison described as Newman's "most public indictment of modern civilization."[32] Newman repudiated Peel's implicit claim that modern culture must dispense with religion in order to flourish and that theological and philosophical discussions must give place to science. The intractability of human nature, Newman countered, ensures that science will contribute nothing to culture without metaphysics. As Davison had put it decades earlier, "liberal" knowledge was essential to any "usefulness" education might have.

In the *Idea*, Newman argued, not that liberal knowledge had no usefulness, but that the pursuit of knowledge must not settle for merely "useful" ends. He wrote

> that alone is liberal knowledge, which stands on its own pre-
> tensions, which is independent of sequel, expects no comple-
> ment, refuses to be *informed* (as it is called) by any end, or
> absorbed into any art, in order duly to present itself to our
> contemplation.[33]

Liberal knowledge certainly has utility, but not for forming char-
acter or teaching professional skill. In one of the most celebrated passages in the *Idea*, Newman insisted that liberal education

> makes not the Christian, not the Catholic, but the gentleman.
> It is well to be a gentleman, it is well to have a cultivated
> intellect, a delicate taste, a candid, equitable, dispassionate
> mind, a noble and courteous bearing in the conduct of life —
> these are the connatural qualities of a large knowledge; they
> are the objects of a University.[34]

Liberal education is the "cultivation of the intellect, as such, and its object is nothing more or less than intellectual excellence."[35]

The *cultural* developments which underlie these passages have significant contemporary analogies. Newman himself placed his argu-
ment for the trained intellect in the context of an emerging periodical media, "an evil which is forced upon us in every railway carriage, in every coffee-room or *table-d'hote,* in every mixed company."[36] The "necessities of periodical literature, now so much in request" requires views on every subject from "half-formed and superficial intel-
lects."[37] The postmodern analogy, of course, is television, which af-
fects Newman's judgment only in degree, not in kind. Whole bodies of research confirm the worst fears of thoughtful laypersons that television subverts the educational process. Television homogenizes culture, steals time from intellectually stimulating activities, de-
grades personal investment in relationships, and distorts perspective. Much more than in Newman's age, higher education today must seek to establish what Newman called its "authority," that is, the cultural

authority of an intellectual life "safe from the excesses and vagaries of individuals."[38] Newman did not hold out much hope of success for the university in this venture; nor, perhaps, should we. But the increasing fragmentation of television-generated mass culture gives an air of urgency to the effort.

Theology a Branch of Knowledge

Newman had every reason to begin his lectures on the nature of the university by defending the right of theology to join the "empire" of all the sciences.[39] He no doubt wished to avert any suspicion of his Catholic fidelity. He also knew full well the desire of Irish Catholics for a university that would—unlike the Queen's Colleges—teach church dogma. And, of course, Archbishop Cullen would be present in the audience.

But Newman had a far more compelling reason; namely, his life-long opposition to liberalism. In Newman's mind, liberalism undermined the most fundamental principle of liberal education: Knowledge is whole; it is all of a piece, having its sole source in the Creator. The modern liberal disavowal of doctrine—that is, assertions of knowledge about God—in Newman's view simultaneously eviscerated the university. A university "professes to teach universal knowledge," Newman declared.[40] To exclude the knowledge of God from "universal knowledge" was logically inconsistent with that purpose.

> As to the range of University teaching, certainly the very name of University is inconsistent with restrictions of any kind. . . . Is it, then, logically consistent in a seat of learning to call itself a University, and to exclude Theology from the number of its studies?[41]

At no point perhaps does the difference between Newman's cultural context and ours stand out more starkly. In 1852, Irish Catholics assumed that something like "theology" should be taught in a *Catholic* university. A university of the church should presumably propagate the church's faith. In late twentieth-century America, most university educators, and probably for that matter almost everyone else, assume that something like "theology" should not be taught in any university (at least secular ones, if at all!). Newman would say that both generation's assumptions are wrong; for while the two assumptions are diametrically opposed, the rationale underlying each assumption is precisely the same: Religious instruction serves no purpose in the university curriculum except to advance sectarian interests.

In Discourse III, Newman was at pains to make clear to his partisan audience—and we can imagine they experienced a bit of shock when he did so—that theology is not Catholicism. Nor is it "remarks upon the physical world viewed religiously," what we might call philosophical naturalism. Nor is theology polemics, or generic Christianity, or even "an acquaintance with the Scriptures." Theology, said Newman, is simply "the Science of God, or the truths we know about God put into a system."[42] In short, Newman challenged the assumptions of his nineteenth-century hearers, and of his twentieth-century readers, that religious teaching is nothing more than indoctrination.

Newman issued the challenge in order to affirm the integrity of the *other* sciences in the university curriculum (how strange it sounds to our ears!), but also to affirm the integrity of theology in the curriculum. In several passages, Newman professes an enormous respect for the differences between the disciplines. Yet, he declares, while the disciplines have their peculiar methods, subject matters, and parameters, the differences must not devolve into separate identities.

> This I conceive to be the advantage of a seat of universal learning. . . . An assemblage of learned men, zealous for their own sciences, and rivals of each other, are brought, by familiar intercourse and for the sake of intellectual peace, to adjust together the claims and relations of their respective subjects of investigation. They learn to respect, to consult, to aid each other. Thus is created a pure and clear atmosphere of thought, which the student also breathes, though in his own case he only pursues a few sciences out of the multitude. He profits by an intellectual tradition, which is independent of particular teachers, which guides him in his choice of subjects, and duly interprets for him those which he chooses.[43]

Newman's worst fears about isolationist tendencies of the separate disciplines, and about the exclusion of theology from the university curriculum, are today realized. Faculty often do not speak to one another, even within departments on the same campus. The grammarians have no dealings with the literary specialists, nor the microeconomists with the macro. The modern university is really a multiversity, an assemblage of scholar ly fragments connected only by the colorless, tasteless, odorless paste of public relations material, not by the ideals of "universal knowledge." And even to mention the absence of religious instruction is to belabor a point.

From Newman's perspective, the absence of religious study must be felt with special acuteness, and in some ways even explains the fragmentation of university teaching. The sciences all (including theology) are aspects of one subject matter, given by God; and they are all thus "severally incomplete in their relation to the things themselves" so that "they at once need and subserve each other."[44] As aspects of only one subject matter, "[the sciences] differ in importance; and according to their importance will be their influence, not only on the mass of knowledge to which they all converge and contribute, but on each other."[45] To exclude any branch of knowledge from study, is to distort all, and knowledge itself. To exclude "theology," which "meets us with a profession and a proffer of the highest truths of which the human mind is capable,"[46] is to introduce the greatest possible distortion of human knowledge.

The magnitude of the distortion derives not only from the loss of the religious thematic itself, but from the inevitable intrusion of the remaining sciences into theology's province.

> I observe, then, that, if you drop any science out of the circle of knowledge, you cannot keep its place vacant for it; that science is forgotten; the other sciences close up, or, in other words, they exceed their proper bounds, and intrude where they have no right. . . . The case is the same with the subject-matter of Theology.[47]

This principle helps to explain the fragmentation of the university curriculum, of course. In the absence of theology, other sciences constitute themselves "the sole exponent of all things in heaven and earth . . . encroaching on territory not [their] own, and undertaking problems which [they have] no instruments to solve." But worse, "they would be sure to teach wrongly, where they had no mission to teach at all."[48] Modernity did exclude theology from its universities, of course; and the dangers Newman foresaw constitute a large substantial proportion of the contemporary crisis in higher education.

The collapse of modernity brings with it, however, at least the potential for change. Amidst the pluriformity of American culture, and despite a deeply imbedded legal and political tradition separating church (read "anything religious") and state (read "anything public"), the place of "theology" in the university is tenuous at best. Yet, as David Tracy has recently observed, postmodernity implies a "turn to the other," an engagement with subjects, views, perspectives, and ideas heretofore taboo under the modernist hegemony.[49] Like the collapse of the Soviet Union, the collapse of modernity opens doors. All sorts of visitors may enter, some more desirable than others, but religion at least walks among them. To cite Tracy again, if there "is a postmodernity it, too, is likely to be deeply ambiguous."[50] Yet the "others" not accounted for

> by the grand narrative of the dominant culture — return with full-force to unmask the evolutionary narrative of modernity as ultimately an alibi-story, not a plausible reading of our human history together. Part of that return of otherness . . . is the return of biblical Judaism and Christianity to undo the complacencies of modernity.[51]

If the university is a place for teaching universal knowledge, then "the university is at the very least obliged to pay attention to [the religious] dimension of its subject matter."[52] As George Marsden puts it, "I think it is fair to ask whether it is consistent with the vision of contemporary universities to discriminate against religiously informed views, when all sorts of other advocacy and intellectual inquiry are tolerated."[53]

Just maybe the postmodernist "turn to the other" will encourage higher education to that end. George Marsden at any rate suggests Christian activism "for universities to apply their professions of pluralism more consistently."[54] But Marsden is not sanguine about the possibilities for recovering the soul of the university, in light of which he proposes another strategy: "Christians should concentrate on building distinctively Christian institutions that will provide alternatives to secular colleges and universities."[55] In the last analysis, perhaps the distinctively Christian university is the only hope for realizing Newman's idea of a university where students are helped to think whole.

Christian Rationalism and the Development of Ideas

When Newman was received into the Catholic communion in 1845, he was completing *An Essay on the Development of Christian Doctrine,* a book over which he had labored painfully for almost a year, and over which he had brooded for a dozen. As it turned out, the book also crystallized disquieting thoughts he had had since 1839 about the theological justification for Anglicanism. The *Essay* was the proverbial "straw that broke the camel's back." Two days before Father Barbieri's visit to Newman at Littlemore, Newman wrote an "Advertisement" for the book, to which he added a "Postscript" testifying (in the third person) that "when he got some way in the printing, he recognized in himself a conviction of the truth of the conclusion to which the discussion leads."[56]

The role of the *Essay* in the development of Newman's own ecclesiology represents precisely the thesis of the book itself. Newman had argued that the core teachings of Scripture are formed and transformed in the consciousness of the Christian community over time, by a process of intellectual struggle.

> It is characteristic of our minds that they cannot take an object in, which is submitted to them simply and integrally. We conceive by means of definition or description; whole objects do not create in the intellect whole ideas; but are, to use a mathematical phrase, thrown into a series, into a number of statements, strengthening, interpreting, correcting each other, and with more or less exactness, approximating, as they accumulate, to a perfect image.[57]

The *Essay* had contributed to this "process of development in ideas"[58] at work in Newman's own life, even as it described the inevitable dynamic of "development" historically.

We have suggested that Newman's relevance for contemporary higher education derives from the peculiar juxtaposition of his critique of liberalism with his version of Christian rationalism. Newman's concept of development focuses that juxtaposition for us with special clarity. When translated into the dialect of higher education, the principle of development (Christian rationalism) offers both counterpoint and complement to the principle of dogmatics (critique of liberalism). Thus, on the one hand, Newman could vigorously affirm the quest for "universal knowledge" in his critique of liberalism. On the other hand, he could just as vigorously affirm academic freedom, scientific inquiry, theorizing, and the like, as essential to the task of unfolding ideas.

Obviously, Newman's concept of development is crucial to his emphasis on teaching.[59] Early in his career at Oxford, Newman argued strenuously in favor of the tutorial against the lecture method of pedagogy. He believed the former eminently better suited for real education which is not, as he said later in the *Idea,* a "smattering of a hundred things or a memory for detail," but "a philosophical or comprehensive view."[60] In one dramatic passage in the *Idea,* Newman goes so far as to declare that, if forced to choose

> between a so-called University, which dispensed with residence and tutorial superintendence, and gave its degrees to any person who passed an examination in a wide range of subjects, and a University which had no professors or examinations at all, but merely brought a number of young men together for three or four years, and then sent them away. . . . I have no hesitation in giving preference to that University which did nothing, over that which exacted of its members an acquaintance with every science under the sun.[61]

The engagement of minds, the give and take of discourse, in short, *the development of ideas,* would do far more to enlarge the mind and fit students "for their secular duties."[62]

Newman's principle of development has even more profound implications, however, for the postmodernist versus the modernist view of knowledge. In modernist, Enlightenment thinking, knowledge is accessible to reason more or less directly: "if we think clearly enough and with sufficient diligence we can come to the truth."[63] But postmodernist thinking — in varying ways and degrees, of course — does not accept that comfortable proposition. Nor would Newman, for whom truth emerges from the tortuous engagement of minds over time, not from postulates and formulae.

Newman exhibits these postmodern sympathies in one particularly striking passage from the *Essay.* In answer to the possible objection that his concept of development in *doctrine* ignores the givenness of *Scripture,* Newman replies:

> ideas are in the writer and reader of the revelation, not the inspired text itself; and the question is whether those ideas which the letter conveys from writer to reader, reach the reader at once in their completeness and accuracy on his first perception of them, or whether they open out in his intellect and grow to perfection in the course of time.[64]

The "question" is rhetorical, of course; Newman assumes that "ideas . . . open out" in the intellect and "grow to perfection." What is striking is that, for Newman, the Scriptures provided (as it were) the raw material for knowledge, not knowledge itself, at least not complete knowledge.

It would be fascinating to explore the affinities of this passage with certain postmodern epistemologies, but that belongs to another essay. We shall confine ourselves to one implication of this passage (and of the principle of "development" it represents) for higher education in postmodern culture. In doing so, we shall make use of a significant recent critique of Newman.

The critique is by David Kelsey, in his highly acclaimed analysis of the contemporary debate in theological education, *Between Athens and Berlin.*[65] Kelsey examines Newman and the *Idea* among several representatives of the "Athens" and the "Berlin" models of education, and as "an enormously influential classic in the controversial literature about the nature and purposes of higher education."[66] Despite his appreciation for Newman's achievement, Kelsey takes him to task for a theory "that is entirely abstracted from the concrete cultural setting of the values judged to characterize intellectual excellence and deemed worthy of cultivating for their own sake."[67]

Kelsey cites several passages from the *Idea* to the effect that human rationality is "the power of viewing many things at once as one whole, of referring them severally to their true place in the universal system, and of understanding their respective values, and determining their mutual dependence."[68] All the passages reflect Newman's first principle of development; but, for Kelsey they also reflect a peculiar view of personhood: (1) that which is "specifically human . . . is the capacity to know by contemplation"; and (2) "institutional realities [i.e., structures of social power] have no intrinsic bearing on what it is to be a human person."[69] For Newman, liberal education makes the "gentleman."[70] For Kelsey, "gentleman" suggests a privileged social status enjoyed by Newman and the few like him, then and now, with sufficient means to cultivate knowledge for its own sake.

If Kelsey means to charge Newman with an arid intellectualism that defines education as leisurely occupation with reading and thinking, then his critique falls short. Despite his emphasis on the cultivation of the intellect, Newman never detached education from real life concerns. In an extended discussion in Discourse VII, Newman stressed that knowledge is useful precisely *because* it is its own end:

"as health ought to precede labor of the body, and as a healthy man can do what an unhealthy man cannot do . . . so in like manner general culture of the mind is the best aid to professional and scientific activity, and educated men can do what illiterate cannot." The educated person will be able to take up "any one of the sciences or callings . . . for which he has a taste or special talent, with an ease, a grace, a versatility, and a success, to which another is a stranger."[71]

On the other hand, if Kelsey means to charge Newman with a culturally conditioned frame-of-reference, he has a case. The social context of university education in the late twentieth century differs profoundly from that of the mid-nineteenth. Expectations about who should attend college, relaxed admission policies, funding that expands the population of prospective students, growing occupational and professional demands for an educated workforce, the clamor of various interest groups both for access to, and a voice in, the higher education establishment—all these factors and many more have radically altered the cultural significance of higher education over the last century and a half. We can perhaps understand, if not excuse, Newman's "innocent theorizing" that failed adequately to account for the role played by social place and human agency—gender, ethnicity, religion, socioeconomic status, ideology, and the like—in the university today.[72] Newman was far too abstract and idealistic to serve as a paradigm for postmodern higher education.

At another level, however, a meta-theory level if you will, perhaps Newman yet does have a contribution to make. Newman's critique of liberalism, as we have argued, rested on his confidence in the power of ideas and on his commitment to universal truth. Hence his insistence that theology belongs in the "empire" of all the sciences. On the other hand, his vision of Christian rationalism rested on the principle of development. Ideas are never perceived full-blown. They must constantly undergo refinement, interpretation, correction, and application as they pass through times and cultures. Kelsey is surely right to attend to the voices of contemporary culture; and (we think) Newman would agree. They contribute to the "process of development in ideas."

Higher education in postmodern America has an opportunity to appropriate Newman's tension of "dogma" and "development" more fully than in any age since Newman wrote *The Idea of a University*. It is still very much an open question whether universities, especially secular ones, can re-deploy theological or metaphysical resources in their curricula ("dogma"), and whether they can take account of disparate claims ("development") without becoming killing fields in the culture wars. Newman himself called the university enterprise a "risk." That it is, but one surely worth taking.

NOTES

1. Martin J. Svaglic, "Introduction," in John Henry Newman, *The Idea of a University: Defined and Illustrated in Nine Discourses Delivered to the Catholics of Dublin in Occasional Lectures and Essays Addressed to the Members of the Catholic University,* ed. with intro. and notes by Martin J. Svaglic (Notre Dame, Ind.: Univ. of Notre Dame Press, 1982, [1873, 1899]), vii. Newman's work hereafter referred to as *Idea.*

2. Newman's Journal, January 1863, cited in A. Dwight Culler, *The Imperial Intellect: A Study of Newman's Educational Ideal* (New Haven: Yale Univ. Press, 1955), 244.

3. Svaglic, "Introduction," vii.

4. The preeminent Newman biography is Ian T. Kerr, *John Henry Newman: A Biography* (New York: Oxford Univ. Press, 1988). The most accessible definitive biography is Charles S. Dessain, *John Henry Newman,* 2nd ed. (Stanford, Calif.: Stanford Univ. Press, 1966, 1977). A useful concise treatment is Brian Martin, *John Henry Newman: His Life and Work* (Mahwah, N.J.: Paulist, 1990). Interested readers are also referred to Newman's autobiographical *Apologia pro Vita Sua,* available in several editions, and giving details of his life to 1845 when he converted to Roman Catholicism. Many of Newman's other works also contain autobiographical accounts.

5. Kerr, *Newman,* 3.

6. John H. Newman, *Apologia pro Vita Sua,* intro. by Philip Hughes (1864; reprint, Garden City, N.Y.: Doubleday, 1956), 127.

7. Ibid., 151.

8. Kerr, *Newman,* 81.

9. Kerr, *Newman,* 86.

10. Actually, Newman, *Apologia,* 188, had only argued that the "Articles [of the Church of England] do not oppose Catholic teaching; they but partially oppose Roman dogma; they for the most part, oppose the dominant errors of Rome."

11. Ibid., 197.

12. Ibid., 437–40.

13. Dublin University Correspondence, cited in Culler, *Imperial Intellect,* 131.

14. Cited in Culler, *Imperial Intellect,* 132.

15. Robert Pattison, *The Great Dissent: John Henry Newman and the Liberal Heresy* (Oxford: Oxford Univ. Press, 1991), 49.

16. Ibid., 211.

17. Ibid., 215.

18. Craig Van Gelder, "Postmodernism as an Emerging Worldview," *Calvin Theological Journal* 26 (1991): 413.

19. Ibid.

20. John H. Newman, *The Letters and Diaries of John Henry Newman,* ed. and intro. by Ian T. Kerr and Thomas Gorman (Oxford: Clarendon, 1976– 1988), 21:394–96.

21. Newman, *Idea,* xxxvii.

22. Interested readers should consult Jaroslav Pelikan's recent monograph for a thorough analysis of the higher education crisis in light of Newman. Cf. *The Idea of a University: A Reexamination* (New Haven: Yale Univ. Press, 1991).

23. Whether the Son was of the same essence *(homoousios)* of the Father, or only of like nature *(homoiousios)*.

24. John H. Newman, *The Arians of the Fourth Century* (1833; reprint, London: Longmans Green, 1895).

25. Newman, *Idea*, xxxvii.

26. Ibid, xl.

27. P.C. Dale, "Newman's *The Idea of a University:* The Dangers of a University Education," *Victorian Studies* 16 (1972): 5. Cf. also Newman, *Idea*, 2.

28. Pelikan, *Idea of a University*, 33.

29. Newman, *Idea*, 118.

30. Ibid., 121.

31. Ibid., 128.

32. Pattison, *Great Dissent*, 177. The letters were later published under the title *The Tamworth Reading Room.*

33. Newman, *Idea*, 81.

34. Ibid., 91.

35. Ibid., 92.

36. Ibid., xliii.

37. Ibid., xlv.

38. Ibid., xlvii.

39. Ibid., 345.

40. Ibid., 14.

41. Ibid., 15.

42. Ibid., 45–46.

43. Ibid., 76.

44. Ibid., 38.

45. Ibid., 35.

46. Ibid., 50.

47. Ibid., 55.

48. Ibid.

49. David Tracy, "Theology and the Many Faces of Post-modernity," *Theology Today* 51 (April 1994): 108.

50. Ibid., 107.

51. Ibid., 108.

52. Pelikan, *Idea of a University*, 39.

53. George M. Marsden, "The Soul of the American University," *Faculty Dialogue* 15 (Fall 1991): 116.

54. Ibid., 114.

55. Ibid., 117.

56. John H. Newman, *An Essay on the Development of Christian Doctrine*, 6th ed. (1845, 1878; reprint, Notre Dame, Ind.: Univ. of Notre Dame Press, 1989), xi.

57. Ibid., 55.

58. Ibid., 33.

59. Philip C. Rule, "Growth the Only Evidence for Life," in *John Henry Newman: Theology and Reform*, ed. Michael E. Allsopp and Ronald R. Burke (New York:

Garland, 1992), 100–103.

60. Newman, *Idea,* 109.

61. Ibid., 109–10.

62. Ibid., 110.

63. Mark S. McLeod, "Making God Dance: Postmodern Theorizing and the Christian College," *Christian Scholar's Review* 21/3 (1992): 277.

64. Newman, *Essay,* 56.

65. David Kelsey, *Between Athens and Berlin: The Theological Education Debate* (Grand Rapids: Eerdmans, 1993).

66. Ibid., 30.

67. Ibid., 42.

68. Newman, *Idea,* 103. Cf. also pp. 105, 114. Cited in Kelsey, *Between Athens and Berlin,* 44.

69. Kelsey, *Between Athens and Berlin,* 45.

70. Newman, *Idea,* 91; see above.

71. Ibid., 125.

72. Kelsey, *Between Athens and Berlin,* 46–47.

18

Theology in a Postmodern Culture: Implications of a Video-Dependent Society

William E. Brown

The restlessness so much a part of today's Western societies evidences more than the "end of the millennium blues." The cause is much deeper and broader: the modern world is moribund and with its approaching demise patrons have little time to mourn its passing. The assumptions of modernity, endemic in Western culture since the Enlightenment, are being laid to rest by the new weird order designated as postmodernism.

Postmodernism in Context

The era preceding modernism, usually identified as the "premodern" period, was marked by a devotion to realism. The premodern world saw a unity in truth and experience and cherished continuity. Exemplified by the classic philosophers and artists, premodern thinkers sought to discover fundamental truths in order to conform values and behavior to ultimate reality.

The gradual development of the premodern into the modern extended the unified view of life, but built upon the axioms of eighteenth-century thinking. Human reason was exalted as the unique means by which all of reality could be understood. Science and the quest for objective knowledge provided an optimistic hope for the future. Natural and moral evils were the result of the fact-value confusion present in anachronistic ignorance and superstition, most

---

William E. Brown is President of Bryan College in Dayton, Tennessee.

easily epitomized by religion, particularly Christianity. God was an unnecessary hypothesis to the modern mind which craved scientific certainty and moral autonomy.

In the world of literature and art, the assumption of unity was more implied than explicit. T.S. Eliot's *Wasteland* or the works of Picasso typified the modern approach to life and the world. Picasso's famous quips, "There is no abstract art. You must always start with something," and "Art is the lie that enables us to realize the truth," reflect such a modernist perspective.

In the extremes of the contemporary postmodern scheme, the search for unity has been abandoned. The postmodern mind "rejects modernism's uncritical faith in human reason and science to know the basic structure of reality together with modernism's faith in the idea of some sort of human moral and social progress."[1] Postmodern thinking is not a monolithic school of thought; rather, it is a mood informed by a method; a montage of images, experiences, and ideas. The postmodern is in some ways a rejection of the modern and in other ways a perversion of the modern mind-set.[2]

Key Elements of Postmodernism

In the public square, the premodern period was dominated by a combination of dogma, faith, and metaphysical assumptions. The primacy of modernity was scientific knowledge. The primacy of postmodern culture is technology, particularly information technology. The visual imagery of television has aided and abetted the rise of postmodern culture, at least at the popular level of experience. While many argue over television *content,* the television *experience* is by far the most defining influence with regard to the development of popular postmodern thinking.

How has a video-dependent culture absorbed the heart and soul of the postmodern? Three key characteristics of postmodern culture illustrate the parallel between the two phenomena.

Philosophical Solipsism

The underpinnings of postmodern society are much deeper and older than most acknowledge. Postmodern thinking is in many ways a rebirth of the nihilistic emphases of Nietzsche, who is sometimes referred to as the "fountainhead of postmodernism." At the fringes, philosophy in postmodern culture unravels before it can even get started. This is due in part to a return to the Nietzschean emphasis on subjective knowing. For Nietzsche, all knowledge is perspective.

There are no "facts," only interpretations from one's own perspective and will. Vattimo summarizes Nietzsche's attacked rationality whenever it was found.

> The project of nihilism is to unmask all systems of reason of persuasion, and to show that logic—the very basis of rational metaphysical thought—is in fact only a kind of rhetoric. All thought that pretends to discover truth is but an expression of the will to power—even to domination—of those making the truth-claims over those who are being addressed by them.[3]

In this scheme of thought, all life is subjective and the distinctions between truth and falsehood, essence and appearance, fact and interpretation, are dissolved. What matters is not whether a belief is true, but whether it is "life-affirming," that is, capable of providing feelings of power or freedom. Rorty claims that this approach began two centuries ago, when "the idea that truth was made rather than found began to take hold in Europe."[4]

Historical Abbreviation
In the postmodern world, history tends to flatten out at the level of contemporaneity.[5] The centers of history are so multiplied, the perspectives of history are so challenged, and the language of history is so disputed, that a "universal history" is not possible. "The dissolution of history," Vattimo adds, "means first and foremost the breakdown of its unity."[6] Michel Foucault attempted to delegitimize the present by isolating it from the past. Madan Sarup notes, "Unlike the historian who traces a line of inevitability, Foucault breaks off the past from the present and, by demonstrating the foreignness of the past, relativizes and undercuts the legitimacy of the present."[7]

Further, as argued by Heidegger and later Gehlen, a technological society becomes "non-historical." Progress becomes so expected that it represents no progress at all. New developments become increasingly less "new" and society becomes fixated (and bored) with technology. For the individual, the present becomes all that exists and all that matters.

Political Fragmentation
From a global perspective, the political landscape of the past was drawn by the conflicts which determined boundaries and the right to rule. In the premodern period, wars were the wars of kings and

princes who attempted to expand their borders or protect their economic strength and territories.

As the modern period began, *guerres de rois* gradually developed into conflicts between nations. The political scheme was defined by territorial borders (nation states). After WWI, the world, while still maintaining political boundaries, was divided ideologically. Democracy, fascism, and communism clashed in WWII, eliminating fascism as a major player and established the ideological fault line between democracy and communism.

With the dismantling of communism, the expected dominance of Western democracy has not occurred; rather, the more basic divisions among civilizations are highlighted. In the postmodern era, political fragmentation defines the world scene. No longer is the question, Whose side are you on? but rather, What are you? Ideas have given way to battle over ethnicity and origin. The war between civilizations has begun.

The cold war "victory," rather than providing a boost toward peace and unity, advances the postmodern move toward fragmentation and conflict. Old battles are resurfacing. Those with a common heritage band together to fight those who are different by nature, thus, for example, the depth of animosity between the Muslim Bosnians and the Orthodox Serbs. Even in our country, the designations "Irish-American" or "German-American," because of a common European background, do not conjure up the spirit of dissension as do "Latin-American" or "African-American."[8] The result is a restless world torn apart intellectually, socially, and spiritually. The tide of great ideas has ebbed and what remains are shallow puddles scattered across the beach.

Postmodernism and Popular Culture

At the popular level, society displays an ever-increasing addiction to postmodern themes. Anything can be juxtaposed to anything else. Everything takes place in the present. There is no meaning, no purpose. Everything is a joke that is not funny. There is a spirit of apathy, even meanness about life. It is Foucault, Derrida, shopping malls, television channel surfing, Monty Python, Beavis and Butthead, and David Letterman. One writer observes, "Postmodern artists do not limit themselves to a single all-encompassing theme. Idols of postmodernism such as Michael Jackson and Madonna reject a single, confining identity, and transform themselves into different roles, and possess a fluid identity."[9]

Television and Postmodern Thinking

No feature of modern culture so dominates life and thought as does television. The medium heavily influences all but the smallest minority of people, therefore, at no time in history has there existed such a level playing field with regard to information and entertainment. Culturally, television is the great equalizer. The socially high and mighty watch the same programs as the socially low and powerless. Television is the consolation prize for being poor.

Television is not science, it is technology. We are confronted with "the paradox of ultramodern technologies as simultaneously a prison house and a pleasure palace."[10] The postmodern dominance on technolgy is both "Orwellian and hopelessly utopian."[11]

In a practical sense, the thinking involved in watching television is radically different from that which is necessary in verbal communication (reading, speaking, listening). The gap between that which is visual and that which is verbal is profound, differing not only in degree but in kind. Gavriel Salomon notes, "Pictures need to be recognized, words need to be understood."[12] Neil Postman adds, "Pictures present the world as objects, language presents the world as ideas."[13]

The most extreme effect is seen on children. Winn summarizes, "As the child takes in television words and images hour after hour, day after day, with little of the mental effort that forming his own thoughts and feelings and molding them into words would require, as he *relaxes* year after year, a pattern emphasizing nonverbal cognition becomes established."[14] The result is deficiency in the ability to read intelligently, communicate clearly, and reason morally. This lack of cognitive ability resulting from early video-dependency is strangely akin to the willful activities fostered by certain postmodern assumptions.

Moral arguments and epistemological considerations have no place in a world of television. True, false, good, bad are the stuff of language and ideas, not visual images. In a video-dependent society, moral decisions are emotive not rational, not based on reasons or principles but on existential ecstasy or terror. The result is an increasing inability to discuss significant issues in a meaningful way. Whereas political debates of the past were distinguished by cogent argumentation and sophisticated ideas, current debates are limited to two-minute responses and five-second sound bites.

The visual does not supplement language, it displaces it. Unlike reading which requires an enormous amount of intellectual participation, television traps the brain into a passive dependency. Over thirty years ago, Bruno Bettelheim noted, "Television captures the imagination but does not liberate it. A good book at once stimulates and frees the mind."[15]

Moral and creative reasoning aside, the implications of devaluing verbal communication cut at the heart of a biblical worldview. God has chosen language as an integral mode of self-revelation. If the verbal is no longer important, where does that leave Scripture? The close tie between language and God is reflected by Nietzsche who complained, "I fear we are not getting rid of God because we still believe in grammar."[16]

Television and History

Television is responsible for the dehistoricization of experience. Historical events can be "experienced" at any time as long as they are recorded on film. The images of the past can be frozen in time and thawed out at the whim of a viewer. In this way, everything is the eternal present. Visual images immobilize a moment and remove it from the context. History is meaningless. Decontextualized facts become useless fodder for Trivial Pursuit™ or "Jeopardy!"

Trivialization

Everything that appears on television is trivialized. On the same screen we can surf through death in the Balkans, a ball game in Chicago, a mystery filmed fifty years ago (with most of the actors now dead), a cartoon, and a commercial for laxatives, all within a few seconds. The juxtaposition of these images is an incredible phenomenon, but one which we have come to expect with a shrug and a yawn. Sociologist Mark Crispin Miller notes:

> Repeatedly subjected to TV's small jolts, we become incapable of outright shock or intense arousal, lapsing into a constant, dull anxiety wherein we can hardly sense the difference between a famine and a case of body odor. The television montage bolsters our inability to differentiate, its spectacle of endless metamorphosis merely making all images seem as insignificant as any single image seen for hours.[17]

Theological Responses

While the reaction to postmodernism has been mixed, evangelicals are poised to meet the challenges of this new spirit of the times. The postmodern denial of objective truth does not necessarily portend the abandonment of the search for truth. Bottum reminds us that there is much overlap between the premodern and postmodern mind. "Though they disagree on whether God exists, premoderns and postmoderns share the major premise that knowing requires His existence."[18]

The demise of modernism in its many forms foreshadows hope for the future. The tyranny of secular thinking, once overthrown, can only provide greater opportunities for the message of Christ. Diogenes Allen claims, "The end of the modern world means that Christianity is liberated from the narrow, constricting, asphyxiating stranglehold of the modern world."[19]

The more extreme types of philosophical postmodernism will go the way of all flashes. They have, in the words of Thomas Oden, "the smell of death."[20] The popular addiction to video imagery, however, may present the greatest challenge to practical theologians and ministers. In a culture where "life is something you do when there is nothing good on television," the ironic trivialization of ultimate concerns must be confronted with the message of Christ.

The challenges posed by a postmodern, video-dependent culture require Christians to respond in a manner that clearly demonstrates an ability to "understand the times." Broadly speaking, two key elements are necessary to address some of the most influential aspects of popular postmodernism.

First, *Christianity must be presented in the broadest terms possible.* Christians can no longer assume a common acceptance of, or even understanding of, a basic Christian worldview. With the breakup of the traditional North American ethical structure, there are few shared values. For this reason, the Christian worldview must be set in the context of the world of worldviews in order to highlight the similarities and differences among them.

In the postmodern mind-set, the alternative to a Christian worldview is becoming less a defined worldview than it is an escape from worldview thinking altogether. God has crafted the human mind and spirit to respond to order and unity. For this reason, postmodern fragmentation creates despair, alienation, and restlessness. The breadth of Christianity, at least to the human mind, is compelling and addresses both the intellectual and spiritual dimensions of postmodern restlessness.

Christians must never forget that truth is essentially *Christus Nexus,* Christ at the center. The historical and theological significance of the life, death, and resurrection of Jesus Christ constitute *the* message of Christianity (1 Cor. 2:2; 15:2-8). The centrality of Christ forces the issue in confrontations with other worldviews and allows no measure of compromise or syncretism on the essentials.

At the same time, Christians must recognize disparate elements of truth which arise in a society untethered from the truth. Western culture is rapidly becoming more like Athens than Jerusalem, and the points of contact for the Gospel are far different from those of even fifteen years ago. Knowledge of our culture, creativity, and discernment are features of Christian proclamation that must regain prominence among communicators of Christian truth (Acts 17:16-34; 1 Cor. 9:19-23).

Social issues, whether abortion, AIDS, or crime, must be viewed as symptoms of much deeper problems which cannot be solved by more counseling, condoms, or convictions. The ethical dimensions of the message of Christ cannot be neglected. In spite of the fact that a video-dependent society is ethically desensitized, the latent morality present through general revelation remains. The themes of sin, repentance, and redemption at both the individual and national levels must be clearly communicated.

Second, *Christianity must emphasize the unifying dimension of Christ.* The dissolution of ideologies presents a great opportunity for Christianity. Battles among ethnic groups reflect the inability of individuals to think beyond the lowest common denominator. Ideas have given way to issues of ethnic origin and social allegiance. The vicious and senseless conflicts characterizing the current world scene evidence a world gone mad with hatred and fear. It is no betrayal to the cause of Christ to resist any and every form of bigotry and oppression.

The oneness feature of Christianity provides the unifying ideal in a world of increasing social and personal fragmentation. In Christ, "there is neither Jew nor Greek, slave nor free, male nor female" (Gal. 3:28, NIV). Whether black or white, Bosnian or Serb, Irish Catholic or Irish Protestant, the Gospel of Christ strikes at the heart of those influences which tear at peace and justice.

The end of the modern world signals new opportunities and new challenges for the church. The growing reliance on technology at the personal level, particularly evident in the bloated number of cable television channels available, computer "on-line communities," and the fascination with virtual reality, raises the specter of losing a generation to isolated, self-indulgent activities so easily associated with the postmodern mindset. In spite of hi-tech weirdness (or maybe because of it), the task of the church remains the same and takes on new dimensions: to proclaim Christ so that we may present every person complete in Him (cf. Col. 1:28).

NOTES

1. Jay M. Van Hook, "Christianity and the Challenge of Postmodern Philosophy" (Unpublished paper, 1990), 4.

2. It may be surprising that some feel postmodernism is a part of the modern, not a rejection of it. Lyotard claims that postmodernism "is not modernism at its end but in the nascent state, and this state is constant" (Jean Francois Lyotard, *The Postmodern Condition: A Report on Knowledge,* trans. Geoff Bennington and Brian Massumi [Minneapolis: Univ. of Minnesota Press, 1984], 81). The point is that the postmodern is defined by and needs the modern in order to exist.

3. Giannimi Vattimo, *The End of Modernity: Nihilism and Hermeneutics in Postmodern Culture,* trans. and intro. by Jon R. Snyder (Baltimore: Johns Hopkins Univ. Press, 1988), 6.

4. Richard Rorty, *Contingency, Irony, and Solidarity* (Cambridge: Cambridge Univ. Press, 1989), 3.

5. Vattimo, *End of Modernity,* 10.

6. Ibid., 8.

7. Madan Sarup, *An Introductory Guide to Post-Structuralism and Postmodernism,* 2nd ed. (Athens, Ga.: Univ. of Georgia Press, 1988), 58.

8. Samuel P. Huntington, "The Clash of Civilizations?" *Foreign Affairs* 72/3 (Summer 1993): 22–49.

9. Luis Britto-Garcia, "Critiques of Modernity: Avant-garde, Counterculture, Revolution," *The South Atlantic Quarterly* 92/3 (Summer 1993): 515.

10. Arthur Kroker, Marylouise Kroker, and David Cook, "Panic USA: Hypermodernism as America's Postmodernism," *Social Problems* 37/4 (November 1990): 443.

11. Ibid.

12. Gavriel Salomon, *Interaction of Media, Cognition and Learning* (San Francisco: Jossey-Bass, 1979), 36.

13. Neil Postman, *Amusing Ourselves to Death* (New York: Viking/ Penguin, 1985), 72.

14. Marie Winn, *The Plug-In Drug* (New York: Viking, 1977), 47.

15. Bruno Bettelheim, "Parents vs. Television," *Redbook,* November 1963. See also many of his other works where he describes the crucial role played by reading, particularly, *The Uses of Enchantment: The Meaning and Importance of Fairy Tales* (New York: Vintage, 1975).

16. For a discussion of Nietzsche on this point, see Alasdair MacIntyre, *Three Rival Versions of Moral Enquiry* (Notre Dame, Ind.: Univ. of Notre Dame Press, 1990), 98.

17. Mark Crispin Miller, *Boxed In: The Culture of TV* (Evanston, Ill.: Northwestern Univ. Press, 1988), 324.

18. J. Bottum, "Christians and Postmoderns," *First Things* 40 (February 1994): 29.

19. Diogenes Allen, "The End of the Modern World," *Christian Scholar's Review* 22/4 (June 1993): 340.

20. Thomas C. Oden, *Two Worlds: Notes on the Death of Modernity in America and Russia* (Downers Grove, Ill.: InterVarsity, 1992), 42. He refers specifically to those associated with literary and philosophical deconstructionism such as Derrida and Foucault. He, in fact, calls them "ultramodernists."

19

Postmodernism:
The Apologetic Imperative

John A. Sims

Twenty-five years ago sociologist Peter Berger told of a priest working in a slum section of a European city who when asked why he was doing it, replied: "so that the rumor of God may not disappear completely."[1] Berger's story, of course, was to point up the fact that the processes of modern secularization had so eroded modern belief in transcendence that belief in God had virtually been reduced to a rumor. The traditional Judeo-Christian view of reality was, at the time, quickly fading and was not expected to survive.

The forces of continuity and discontinuity are, of course, always at work in the shaping of society and religion. Much has changed, but much has also remained the same since Berger's assessment of the impact of modern secularization upon the Christian religion. It is difficult to delineate all the differences between the modern and postmodern outlook, but certain changes seem quite obvious. At the heart of the postmodern *geist* is a shifting sense of how to think about reality and how it can be known and/or experienced. From the seventeenth century onward science grew up like Jack's beanstalk, overshadowing all other forms of human knowledge and understanding. The Enlightenment represented the attempt of society to find a common vision of the goal toward which society should be moving. What emerged was a vision that centered in an optimism toward reasoned

---

John A. Sims is Professor of Religion at Lee College in Cleveland, Tennessee.

critical thought as the key to understanding reality and using that knowledge for the good of humanity—particularly the reasoned thought of the scientific method and the practical application of science through technology. Moderns generally accepted the Enlightenment understanding of knowledge, limiting rationality to that which is evident to the senses, self-evident, or incorrigible statements that cannot be reasonably doubted. The effect was to make rational science and technology the answer to virtually all human problems. There was little, if any, place in scientific knowledge for emotion, mystery, intuitive imagination, or the fulfillment of desires that science deemed unreal or illusory. Modern science tended to bracket the discussion of meanings, purposes, qualities, and invisible realities. The tragic irony of the modern *geist* was that its science and technology gave the Western world the highest standard of living it had ever known, but produced the greatest emptiness of the human soul.

Modern science's inability to satisfy the spiritual needs of those who placed too much trust in its methods, or dispel the cynicism of those who now criticize its results, does not mean that postmoderns are not ready to give up the fruits of the scientific enterprise by returning to some idyllic prescientific era. That kind of discontinuity is neither possible nor desirable. Contrary to what some suggest, postmoderns have not washed their hands of science and technology. But it is a fact of our time that more and more do wish to return to spiritual roots and have consequently questioned the ability of science to know the fullness of reality that was presumed in the modern era. Postmoderns have returned in large numbers to romanticism's glorification of emotion and irrationality as well as the romantics' esteem for the wisdom of nature and native cultures. The postmodern *geist* is definitely proving to be more open to what is perceived as divine reality and religious experience. Barriers to belief in supernatural and spiritual realities have crumbled like the Berlin Wall and the atheistic ideology that supported it. University of Chicago church historian and cultural analyst Martin Marty recently noted that the word *spiritual,* a word that had essentially lost its meaning and relevance in the modern culture, is now back. And it is back with a vengeance.

Underlying Assumptions of Postmodernism

It is generally agreed that postmodernism does not represent a clear-cut aesthetic or philosophical ideology. It is, therefore, difficult and somewhat dangerous to generalize about the meaning of the term. The desire to be postmodern has seemingly outpaced the ability of postmoderns to articulate exactly what they are all about. But there do seem to be key assumptions that underlie the movement that provide some understanding of the postmodern attitude toward religion. There is, to be sure, a deep suspicion of and discontinuity with modern forms of knowledge/rationality that purport to account for the way we are but are used instead as forms of power to oppress the abuse. Michel Foucault and Richard Rorty are prime perpetrators of this kind of suspicion. Both propound a relativistic and pragmatic perspective that denies that any overarching theory can be "true" or any practice "good" for everyone. Both advocate forms of nihilism in which deference is given to "the way the world looks to us" over any claim to absolute truth or goodness. Foucault argues that "truth" is always defined by those who possess power and is under the control of some "regime of truth." Reason is not some kind of innocent arbiter, but the accomplice of repression.[2] Rorty shares Foucault's suspicion of the theoretical foundations and the Enlightenment tendency to globalize discourse. The better option, he insists, is to simply ask tough questions and encourage conversation. Philosophers, Rorty thinks, have often modeled themselves after scientists — or rather, after an inaccurate picture of scientists. It would be better, he suggests, for them to think of themselves as being poets or novelists.

> Western literature is not trying to "get somewhere"; we do not worry whether Shakespeare is "closer to the truth" than Aeschylus, or if James Joyce is closer than Shakespeare. So philosophy — or the enterprise that will follow when philosophy comes to an end — should not look for progress or "the truth" but should find ways to encourage the widest and most open discussion — for its own sake.[3]

As Rorty concludes:

> There is nothing deep down inside us except what we have put there ourselves, no criterion that we have not created in the course of creating a practice, no standard of rationality that is not an appeal to such a criterion, no rigorous argumentation that is not obedience to our own conventions.[4]

The logic of such relativism, of course, is not only that there are no objective truths or moral standards to live by today, but that there can be no objective interpretation of the past—either in history, law, or politics. What texts say or authors intended, is irrelevant. All that really matters is what we think about what they wrote and whether or not it fits the current interpretation of what is socially and politically correct. This means that we are entirely free to revise the past and understand the present in light of values that have been shaped by the relativities of our own time and place. The good cannot be equated with what is true for there is no objective truth.

Postmoderns tend to reject "overviews" and "controlling viewpoints" in favor of particularly and pluralistic points of view. The suspicion is that "overviews" always tend to control and oppress. Nobody really has the controlling viewpoint although many make that claim in order to use its power to control and manipulate others. Postmoderns also challenge the Enlightenment assumption of human progress. It is a naive notion, they contend, that cannot give a realistic account of human events and experiences.

Huston Smith, a leading authority on world religions, recently noted that religion has always turned on belief in the existence of hierarchies, even if they were collapsed into a this worldly base in the modern era. But postmoderns, he notes, want nothing to do with hierarchy or, for that matter, any worldview. The rationale is that "if a worldview is taken to be an object report on the way the world is it will be privileged over the way the world looks from other angles of vision."[5] Absolute and changeless positions tend to marginalize alternative perspectives and those who subscribe to them. Postmoderns have a special aversion to hierarchies because they regard them as being fraught with racist, masculine, and ethnocentric interest. In place of worldviews and hierarchies they favor a kaleidoscopic vision of reality which offers an endless variety of forms. "Beyond these endlessly shifting gestalts," Smith notes, "there is nothing. Reality is amorphous."[6] The reality that is perceived draws its meaning from social contexts and practices that have no universal essence. There is no fixed "world," only our "view" of it—meanings that are embedded in particular backgrounds and contexts. It is never politically acceptable to posit any objective report of the way the world is for that would undermine the relativism and pluralism that the view assumes.

The epistemology that underlies this view of things, Smith suggests, is holism.

The epistemology that banishes the world is commonly called holism. Theoretical holism argues for the organic character of thought: concepts cannot be understood in isolation; their meaning derives from the theoretical systems in which they are embedded. Practical holism goes on from there to argue that, because thinking invariably proceeds in social contexts and against a backdrop of social practices, meaning derives from — roots down into and draws its life from — those backgrounds and contexts. In considering an idea, not only must we take into account the conceptual gestalt of which it is a part; we must also consider Wittgenstein's "forms of life," and Heidegger's historical horizons and ways of being-in-the-world, whose "micro-practices" (Foucault) give those gestalts their final meaning.[7]

It seems safe to conclude then that the postmodern climate is one that advocates particularity, pluralism, organicism, and enhanced nature, and more acceptance of nonsensory perception than moderns dared acknowledge. But the irony in the new situation is that while postmoderns are more open to spiritual reality and cosmic meaning than moderns, they have no place to plant their spiritual feet. What Francis Schaeffer said about moderns, "that they have both feet firmly planted in mid-air," is even truer for postmoderns.[8] They neither trust biblical revelation or the methods of modern science as the basis for a universal paradigm of rationality or meaning. The holistic vision of postmoderns is, in fact, not for universal rational explanation at all, but for the validity of multiple perspectives and experiences. Descartes' God of metaphysical theism, whose primary function was to provide a paradigm for universal explanation, has definitely yielded to Pascal's God of personal experience.

The New Apologetic Imperative:
An Evangelical Proposal

A generation ago Bernard Ramm offered an assessment of the apologetic task that seems particularly pertinent to the postmodern situation. In his *Varieties of Christian Apologetics* Ramm described apologetics as "the strategy of setting forth the truthfulness of the Christian faith and its right to the claim of the knowledge of God."[9]

The crucial question for apologetics has always been one of method or strategy. How should Christians set forth the logic of what they believe? In the postmodern context the discussion about method has focused primarily on the question of (1) whether Christians should defend the faith on the terms of some "publicly acceptable" criteria of truth, or (2) maintain their claims on the basis of the internal logic of the Christian faith.

Contemporary theologians David Tracy and Gordon Kaufman have been in the vanguard of those who argue that theology must have public, not private or parochial foundations, while George Lindbeck and Hans Frei have advocated the view that the primary task of Christian theology is one of self-description. William Placher interprets the latter perspective to mean that "Christians may seek common ground with particular non-Christians for particular reasons, but they do not assume that theology needs to defend its case according to criteria acceptable to all rational persons. They rather doubt," he adds, "that there are such criteria."[10] In this view the Christian faith ought to be commended and justified from the perspective of its own self-understanding, not in terms of some universal criteria for reasonableness or cultural quest for the ultimate meaning.

Christian Truth-Claims

Two obvious questions have to be broached with regard to the growing interest in this perspective. The most important one, of course, for the evangelical is whether or not it can be adequately reconciled with Christian truth-claims. The other concern has to do with the viability of such a strategy. Is an apologetic strategy built on a unique self-descriptive narrative to be preferred over one that attempts to ground faith in more rational universal forms of understanding? With regard to the latter question, it seems obvious that the postmodern ethos favors a strategy that emphasizes the unique claims of the Christian faith over one that builds on classical rational foundations. The possibility of making wider connections is stronger for those who emphasize Christian particularity. The contemporary *geist* definitely favors concrete modes of understanding and communication. Evangelical Christians today live in a cultural situation that actually encourages them to remain true to their own "story." They are certainly under no cultural obligation to sustain the now implausible modern mentality that postmoderns feel they have moved beyond. Defending against the claim that scientific rationality represents the only legitimate method of inquiry into reality, for example, is an intellectual burden that evangelicals no longer have to bear.

Perhaps more than at any time in their history, Christians find a cultural openness to their particularity and to their claim that they offer a true alternative vision. The postmodern imperative is for Christians to be willing to unapologetically say, "we don't look at things that way" and "neither do we live our lives" or "run our institutions" according to the common cultural patterns. When the church shapes its mission and its message according to the needs, desires, and concerns of the culture, as defined by the culture itself, it invariably distorts its own faith. The time has come for evangelical Christians to break free from the constraints of the universal form of rationality imposed by the Enlightenment and return to the unique wisdom of their own faith.

Something is obviously wrong when those who find themselves dissatisfied with secular modernity in the Christian West repeatedly turn East, or to some New Age quest for a mythic past as an alternative to modernism. Too often Christianity has been overlooked as the viable alternative to modernism because it has been an unwary bedfellow. Christians must overcome their fear of being labeled obscurantists and again embrace their own spirituality and understanding of truth. Placher is right to maintain that "Christians must remain faithful to their own vision of things for reasons internal to Christian faith, and if, in some contexts, that means intellectual isolation, so be it."[11] In the postmodern situation, however, there is less likelihood than ever that this will happen.

Arguing that the claims of the faith are true for those within the Christian tradition does not preclude Christians from arguing that these claims are also true for those outside their tradition which, of course, entails some criteria of intelligibility. The Christian claim to unique content does not preclude the Christian from maintaining that there is a God-given rationality common to all right-thinking persons whereby truth can be distinguished from error. Evangelicals may differ with modernists about the content of truth/reality (i.e., material truth), but they insist that formal principles of reason are necessary if truth is to be distinguished from error (i.e., formal truth). Otherwise, it would not be possible to distinguish true faith from gobbledygook. To disavow the existence of all rational principles is to destroy the necessary union of faith and truth that makes it possible to construct a Christian apologetic.

The Place of Reason
The other side of this coin, of course, is that while reason can help us detect the truth it cannot manufacture it. Truth/reality is always

superior to the logic which establishes it. Apologetics can prepare the heart for faith, but it cannot produce it. Faith is a gift from God that must be surrendered to and lived out as a matter of personal choice. It is the Holy Spirit, not logic, that finally seals Christian faith to the heart. It is in some ways fortunate that the postmodern apologist lives in an atmosphere that is more open to spiritual realities than was generally possible under the more rationalistic modern paradigm. The reality that most postmoderns stand ready to recognize is not a rational, cerebral, logical truth that can only be grasped through science or philosophy. They have been disillusioned and disappointed enough by the fruits of this kind of knowledge. What most postmoderns desire is a personal and transforming experience of reality. In their hope for the reality that can be known as a redeeming presence and not simply as a grand interpretive scheme, postmoderns seem much closer to the kingdom of truth than those in the Enlightenment tradition who put their whole trust in the canons of science and philosophy.

The Place of the Holy Spirit

Hopefully, Christian apologists in the postmodern era will discover anew how necessary the Holy Spirit is in the apologetical task. For only the Holy Spirit knows how to sort through the diverse cultural baggage, illuminating evidence that may have little to do with the rational paradigm of classical foundationalism, and convince non-Christians and half-believers alike of the singular truth of Christian faith. In an exceptionally well-done article on postmodern apologetics, David Clark pointed out that apologetics in Africa or Asia, or to any postmodern, will surely look different than it does to a modern who has been influenced by a restricted form of Enlightenment reasoning. "Shedding this straitjacket," Clark notes, "gives freedom to include as one piece of a broad reasoning process for the faith other evidence like a dream, a religious encounter, or a personal miracle experience."[12] The success of Pentecostals and charismatics in reaching the Third World is a case study of no small significance in demonstrating how those who have no interest in domesticating the Holy Spirit can experience phenomenal success in pluralistic situations.[13]

Donald Bloesch is correct in his contention that in their zeal to establish points of contact with the world evangelicals have allowed the truth of revelation to be determined by human reason rather than "letting the Bible impress its own truth upon the human mind through the power of the Holy Spirit."[14] The truth of revelation,

Bloesch notes, "cannot be placed under human control or subject to human verification . . . [but] remains God's own possession."[15] Calvin put the matter in proper perspective in the *Institutes* in noting that, "God alone is a sufficient witness of himself in his own word, so also the word will never gain credit in the hearts of men 'till it be confirmed by the internal testimony of the Holy Spirit."[16] This is, of course, true in any situation. But it would seem to be particularly so in the pluralistic settings faced by contemporary Christians.

There are different ways of thinking about the essential relationship of one's self to faith. There are those, probably a minority, who understand the relationship to be fundamentally one of knowing. The way to reality is through knowledge; the self is changed through knowing—an "intellectual conversion" as it were. The new self is thus constituted by what we think we know. Others believe that one is not changed by knowledge as much as by one's own actions, by what one wills and acts upon. The self is really defined by its free decisions. This existentialist perspective emphasizes "will" and "choice" over reason. Outcomes are determined by the quality of one's choices, much as the nature of one's life is largely determined by the quality of critical choices such as marriage or career. There is also an imaginative/feeling perspective that sees "feeling" and "imagining" as a more integrating key to the whole of reality than either "knowing" or "willing." Friedrich Schleiermacher is remembered for this particular understanding.[17]

In more recent times, however, there has been a renewed emphasis upon the historical approach to reality and the way in which the self is constituted through the narrative form. Those who advocate "narrative" or "story" over more rational or existential forms of explanation see it as a genre particularly suited for expressing the truth/reality of the Christian faith. It is preferred because it is a more personal, concrete form of expression that invites others to share in the story that has formed their community of faith. George Lindbeck argues that for those who are steeped in religious texts, as Christianity is, "no world is more real than the ones they (i.e. the texts) create. A scriptural world is thus able to absorb the universe. It supplies the interpretive framework within which believers seek to live their lives and understand reality."[18]

The Place of Biblical Narrative

Hans Frei, a narrative theologian at Yale, argued against starting with our experiences and thought patterns as modern persons and then demanding that the biblical stories fit into the modern criteria for truthfulness. Frei believed that the Christian must start with the biblical world, "allowing the biblical narratives to define what is real, so that our lives have meaning to the extent that we fit them into that framework."[19] The intent is to "truthfully" describe how the world looks from a Christian perspective, however unsystematically it may appear, as the basis for human conversation. Whatever connections can be made with those from other perspectives have to be drawn from common thought patterns and life experiences, not from predetermined universal rules or assumptions. This view assumes that the common ground that conversation partners find with each other is more personal and community based than the universal patterns that were assumed to be normative by those in the liberal Enlightenment tradition. This so-called "ad hoc" approach to apologetics does rightly assume that apologetics is more like an art, requiring intellectual creativity, than it is a neatly defined science.[20]

A narrative approach to apologetic theology, however, should not be construed to mean that the message of Scripture is incoherent. Charles Wood notes that even though there is a rich diversity of forms within the scriptural witness, the narrative framework provides a coherent means of relating to the whole.

> When one regards the biblical canon as a whole, the centrality to it of a narrative element is difficult to overlook: not only the chronological sweep of the whole, from creation to new creation . . . but also the way the large narrative portions interweave, and provide a context for the remaining materials so that they, too, have a place in the ongoing story, while these other materials — parables, hymns, prayers, summaries, theological expositions — serve in different ways to enable readers to get hold of the story and to live their way into it.[21]

The use of narrative is particularly effective as a means of conversing with those outside the Western intellectual tradition. If Christians are to be involved in meaningful conversations with Asians, Africans, and Latin Americans (where Christianity is growing the fastest), where the standards of "Western culture" are peripheral, they must talk more in terms of a living and personal God whose greatness lies in humility and suffering love — not one whose image is that of power and arbitrary will.[22] The narrative form best facilitates that purpose.

The primary concern that most evangelicals have with narrative theology is its susceptibility to subjectivist and relativistic interpretation. But evangelicals are perfectly capable of doing good narrative theology in a manner that is consistent with their own theological commitments. A faithful attempt to see the world in the light of the Bible, rather than the other way around, would seem to be a most promising opportunity in a postmodern situation. The opportunity to share through the life, cross, and resurrection of Jesus of Nazareth how God, in the power and presence of the Holy Spirit, is with us now is all that any evangelical could ask for. To remain faithful to the biblical witness, evangelicals must indeed continue to insist upon the "truth question." But the Gospel truth that postmoderns need to hear is not that God is "for us" in some abstract impersonal way, but that in Jesus of Nazareth God is personally with us in the community of faith.

There is no need to cave in to a postmodern relativism that denies that one perspective can be "truer" than another. Evangelicals must stand by their convictions that the biblical narratives refer to a reality outside the text and that what the narratives describe are not simply "history-like," but real history. The pragmatists that say it is enough that the narratives work in one's life will not do. Workability has its benefits, but it matters little if Christianity will work if it is, in fact, not true. An acceptable narrative theology must have historical rootedness. There may be a great deal of mythopoetic language in Scripture that is very similar to the kind of dramatic, figurative language found throughout the ancient world. But evangelicals cannot allow Scripture to be reduced to pious fiction, regardless of how "realistic" one may claim that it is. Princeton theologian Migliore observes:

> Historical study of the Bible reminds us that the narrative of the Bible refers to the realities outside the text. The central narrative is not to be construed as mere construct of the imagination of the community of faith. If the Gospels refer to the living God acting and suffering in Christ for our salvation, if the story they tell is not simply pious fiction, then historical study can never be irrelevant for Christian faith. The faith of the church does not stand or fall with the accuracy of every detail of the gospel story . . . but faith does stand or fall with the truthfulness of the gospel betrayal of the central events of the ministry, death, and resurrection of Christ. It matters to faith whether Jesus really befriended sinners, blessed the poor, and gave his life willingly for others.[23]

Theologians like Carl Henry, Donald Bloesch, and Daniel Migliore are to be commended for insisting that narrative theology cannot give up cognitivity (i.e., preserving some intelligible basis for truth claims outside the narrative itself).[24] There has to be some basis for choosing the Christian story over that of other stories if the impasse of conceptual relativism is to be overcome. On the other hand, what the narratives offer is not so much a set of reasoned propositions as a means of integrating biblical "wisdom" into human thought and experience.

Biblical Truth as Wisdom

Philosophers and cultural analysts have noted for some time the deleterious consequences that our Western culture has suffered in aiming at knowledge rather than wisdom. Mary Midgley and Nicolas Maxwell are among those who persuasively argue that we have been grossly misdirected in giving precedence to narrow specializations of knowledge over a wisdom that promotes human wholeness. Because this distorted aim wastes our intellectual powers, Maxwell concludes, it "has played a serious part in distorting our lives."[25] "Thinking out how to live," Midgley contends, "is a more basic and urgent use of the human intellect than the discovery of any fact whatsoever, and the considerations it reveals ought to guide us in our search for knowledge, as they ought in every other project we pursue."[26] In light of the direction that our Western culture has taken in modern times it is easy to agree with so much that Midgley and Maxwell have to say and applaud their efforts to encourage a return to a wisdom that is concerned with human wholeness. Their efforts, however, are not driven by a commitment to biblical wisdom, but by a pragmatic and humanistic agenda.

Edward Farley and David Ford, on the other hand, are Christian theologians who have a special interest in biblical wisdom as a more ideal norm for theological education and a useful integrating concept for apologetic theology. Farley wonders out loud, perhaps partly in jest, how "something born in the migrations of an ancient, nomadic, and tribal people, and at the scene of a crucified Jew and the fiery tongues of Pentecost ends up with classrooms, degrees, libraries, universities, Sunday schools, and teaching elders?"[27] Farley does not mean to suggest that the Judeo-Christian faith resists what he calls "ordered learning." A tradition of ordered learning, he notes, was evident in Judaism in the study of the Torah, special teachers (rabbis), and designated places (the synagogue). The early Christian community did nothing to repudiate the teaching tradition. On the contrary, the term "rabbi" was applied to Jesus Himself. What we find in Judaism and in early Christianity, however, was not some worldview built in coherent schemes, empirical knowledge, and propositional information. The kind of reality/truth that early Christians struggled to better understand was much more akin to what the Scriptures refer to as "wisdom." Farley is convinced that "ordered learning" today would be more biblical and effective if more attention could be placed on learning as *paideia* (i.e., the culturing of human beings in arete or virtue) and *wisdom* rather than the fragile and fragmented forms of knowledge coming out of the Hellenistic and Enlightenment tradition.[28]

Cambridge theologian David Ford argues that what Christians have to commend and defend in a postmodern world is the wisdom of Christ and the Cross. It is the Cross that truly constitutes the self and rightly relates the self to faith. This is the wisdom that stands in judgment on all forms of human knowledge and action. The wisdom of the Cross likewise provides a radical critique of all cultures and traditions — including the Christian tradition. It does not focus on the claims of the Christian religion, the Christian tradition, or Christian culture in any of its relativized forms. It focuses solely on Jesus Christ and the wisdom of His Cross. It delimits, as no other perspective can, what is to be commended and defended as Christian faith (1 Cor. 2:2). But it also provides the coherent link between Christ and the rest of the Christian story.

Throughout the narrative of Scripture, wisdom provides an effective and meaningful means of integrating faith with truth/reality. As Ford points out, wisdom allows more room for particularity than the modern preference for grand overviews, systematic integrations, and perspectives that homogenize people, places, and knowledge. Wisdom allows for diversity without fragmentation. It does not restrict itself to specialists or to those with formal education. Wisdom stretches the mind in all directions — God, the cosmos, history, religion, spirituality, society, self — and wrestles with radical questions such as death, suffering, evil, sin, weakness, foolishness, and redemption. It draws one into conflicts, commitments, and mysteries. It deals with life as it is lived and with the big questions about the origin, meaning, and destiny of life. Wisdom integrates and unites the intellectual/imaginative/emotional as well as the practical/institutional/social in ways that modern forms of knowledge and rationale cannot. Wisdom is never simply a matter of knowing but also being and doing. It does not disconnect the mystical from the intellectual or the institutional/organizational dimensions of life. It recognizes that there is mystery in meaning and meaning in mystery — both the coherences and incoherences of life. Most importantly, however, it is not an amorphous concept. It carries specific Christian content. It specifically means living in relation to God in love, praise, prayer, and social justice. And it proclaims and defends "Christ crucified" as the eternal "wisdom of God" and the essence of the Christian Gospel (1 Cor. 1:23-24, NIV).[29]

The Limits of Human Reason and Natural Theology

Wise apologists have always recognized the limits of human reason in defending Christian reality. Martin Luther warned that "we must not defend the faith until it collapses." C.S. Lewis issued a similar warning about the danger of putting too much trust in one's own arguments.

> I have found that nothing is more dangerous to one's own faith than the work of an apologist. No doctrine of that faith seems to me so spectral, so unreal as one that I have just successfully defended in a public debate. For a moment, you see, it has seemed to rest on oneself: as a result, when you go away from the debate, it seems no stronger than that weak pillar. That is why we apologists take our lives in our hands and can be saved only by falling back continually from the web of our own arguments, as from our intellectual counters, into the Reality — from Christian apologetics into Christ Himself.[30]

Karl Barth disavowed any dependence of faith upon natural theology or reasoned forms of apologetics, but he had no argument against biblical wisdom as the basis for a true knowledge of God. "Biblical wisdom," he noted, "is not a sacrificing of the intellect, a closing of the eyes, but an opening of the eyes to the living God who has been revealed in Jesus Christ. Wisdom is not a suspension of knowledge but the basis for a true knowledge of God."[31] In his *Church Dogmatics*, Placher argues, Barth was opening a "universe of disclosure" in order to "describe the world from a Christian that could draw what persuasive power it has from the coherence and richness of the whole."[32]

Evangelicals have always been at odds with some of Reinhold Niebuhr's theological methods and conclusions, but they should have no problem with his basic contention that the wisdom of the Gospel provides a truer, more realistic, understanding of the mysteries of human life than any alternative perspective. Drawing from the Apostle Paul, Niebuhr asserts that "what seems foolish from the standpoint of the world's wisdom, the message of the cross, becomes in the eyes of faith the key which unlocks the mysteries of life and makes sense of it."[33] Christians can always find some common ground in pluralistic situations for "there [will always be] a yearning for the true, the more ultimate, the unknown God beyond and above all the known gods of idolatry. It was at this point," Niebuhr says, "that Paul found a point of contact between the gospel and the religious yearnings of mankind. These religious yearnings do not yield a gospel. But they delineate the dimension of the human situation which makes the message of the gospel relevant."[34]

Following Pascal, Niebuhr asserts that the only alternative to delving into the mysteries of the faith is to forever remain a mystery to oneself. Apart from the Christian faith, human nature itself remains a great mystery. Any interpretation of life which "denies the boundless character of the human spirit, which rises above and beyond all finite limitations to confront and feel itself confronted by the divine," or which, "denies that man is a creature of nature, subject to its necessities and bound by its limits, (and virtually all views do one or the other) gives a false picture of the stature of man."[35] Another mystery that the Christian faith sees more clearly, more coherently, than any alternative view, Niebuhr insists, is the "mystery of sin." Modern culture's understanding of the evil in man fails to do justice to the tragic and perplexing aspect of the human problem. "Purely sociological and historical explanations of the rise of evil," Niebuhr asserts, "do not touch the depth of the mystery at all."[36] Then too, Niebuhr notes, there is the mystery of death. The only way that modern culture can resolve this mystery into meaning is to affirm that the historical process itself can guarantee the ultimate fulfillment of all legitimate human desires. Apart from complete despair and cynicism, the only cultural alternative is to see history as redemptive, as utopia in the making. Postmoderns, however, have seen through this hiatus and assert that there is no evidence that history produces this kind of effect. The most truly meaning-bearing answer, Niebuhr argues, is that

> we end our life in frustration not only because "our reach is beyond our grasp," i.e., because we are finite creatures with

more than finite conceptions of an ultimate consummation of life, but because we are sinners who constantly introduce positive evil into the operations of divine providence.

The answer of Christian faith to this problem is belief in "the forgiveness of sin and life everlasting." We believe that only a power greater than our own can complete our incomplete life, and only a divine mercy can heal us of our evil. Significantly St. Paul adds this expression of Christian hope immediately to his confession that we see through a glass darkly. We see through a glass darkly now, "but then" we shall "see face to face." Now we "know in part" but "then" we shall know even as we are known (cf. 1 Cor. 13:12). This Christian hope makes it possible to look at the perplexities and mysteries of life without too much fear.[37]

Is it possible to live in a pluralistic world in which it is claimed that there is no rational way to determine what, if anything, is true and still affirm that the best reason for being a Christian is because "it is true"? Evangelicals must boldly affirm that there are solid grounds for doing so. The wisdom of faith still provides more substantial reasons for Christian commitment than "personal preference" or some weak pragmatic appeal to the "usefulness" of faith. "When some postmodern asks me 'why should I go to church,' " Diogenes Allen says, "I still have the audacity to tell them 'because Christianity is true.' "[38] When Christians know the intellectual strength of Christian claims, Allen argues, they can live persuaded of its truth with their minds as well as their hearts.

Scripture attests to the fact that God has placed real structures in the created order that bear witness to His purposes for creation. Reality (truth) is not something we simply choose to create, or something socially imposed, but that which has been divinely ordered. If it is imprudent to abandon the truth that God has historically revealed in Jesus Christ, it is foolish as well to abandon the orders of creation. The language of faith does have real ontological status. The Christian can rest assured that his or her hope is as certain as the resurrected Christ. While Christians fulfill their calling to bear witness to a way of being and doing in the world that is grounded in the life, death, and resurrection of Jesus Christ, they can also rest assured that their faith has the support of what the late E.J. Carnell called "systematic consistency."[39] God has so tempered truth together that the whole person can be harmoniously related both to the universe over and against him and to the totality of his own person within.

As an expert in the philosophy of science, Allen notes that the postmodern situation has opened fresh apologetic opportunities in the area of cosmology. Contrary to what most moderns assumed, postmoderns now know that the status of the universe and our place in it has not been settled. The scientific and philosophical assumptions that prevailed in the modern era had the effect of producing serious skepticism about faith in a supernatural God, but new developments in science and philosophy support the view that the idea of God is precisely the reality that can best answer the great cosmological questions. The conviction among growing numbers of scientists and philosophers today is that God is the best possible answer to the key questions of: (1) Why does the universe have the kind of order that it has? and (2) Why does the universe exist at all?[40] Skeptics should be aware, Allen points out, that the truth issue is more than an intellectual matter. What is at stake is the heart, as well as the mind. If the universe is what is ultimate, not God, then we are all left to suffer the frustration of our deepest needs and desires which this universe obviously can never satisfy.[41]

It is an opportune time as well for Christians to demonstrate the practical value of their faith. Postmoderns have discovered that all knowledge is not inherently good, that there is no necessary connection between knowledge and its beneficial use. Society's greatest fears stem from the devastating potential of an expanded knowledge — such as medical technology, weapons for mass destruction, or environmental problems. Christianity is still the best possible hope for maintaining the legitimate worth of persons and for dealing with the social and moral issues that lie ahead. A Christian view of persons and things is our best prospect for restraining and controlling the fruits of our knowledge. It would indeed be foolish to discredit and abandon civilization's most viable hope. The strength of the Christian apologetic is not simply that it is rationally compelling, but that it shows everything else to be inadequate.

Wisdom in Quest of Responsibility

A case has been made for an apologetic strategy in the postmodern mileau that does not appeal to classical foundationalism, but to the uniqueness of Christian wisdom. The community of faith has its own story to tell. There are good reasons for adopting a narrative theology as the most promising means of commending and justifying Christian belief, provided that the "narrative" not be interpreted in ways that would rob the story of its essential truth content. The advantage of narrative theology is that it is personal, concrete, and uniquely applicable to real life. It lifts up the indispensability of Scripture in relating one, by the power of the Holy Spirit, to the living God that is revealed in Jesus Christ.

The burden of narrative theology, however, must always be to maintain its focus on Christ and the Cross as the "wisdom" of God and the only means whereby one can be rightly related to God. To see Jesus Christ crucified as the "wisdom of God" is to bring all claims to truth and all beliefs and practices (religious and secular) under the judgment of the Cross.

Apologetic strategy, however, is about more than questions of truth. The logic of Christian faith is that wisdom must be wedded to responsibility. An ultimate frame of meaning, an overarching wisdom that gives meaning to history and the human condition, is a wonderful thing. But there must be a willingness to act upon what one knows. The Christian life is not just about responsibility to one's self, or to the integrity of one's own community of faith, but responsibility to others.[42] The problem is not simply how to make the Christian faith credible to the world, but for Christians to live consistently and coherently under their own claims of love and justice. This is not a matter of the world setting the church's agenda, but of the church fulfilling its own. For the church to be the church it must be concerned to transform as much of this world, after the likeness of the homeland, as it possibly can. Reinhold Niebuhr once observed that there are two kinds of people: the "pure" and the "responsible." Niebuhr preferred the responsible. Evangelicals must do the same. What verifies Christian faith as much as its rational coherence is its power to motivate and sustain ethical action.

The self-giving agape love that has been revealed through the Cross is, by its very nature, a love that must be directed toward the good of others. Agape is the norm for social as well as personal existence. It is the norm for critiquing all secular and religious perspectives that pretend to altruism, absolute moral goodness, and divine sanction. Agape must not be confused with a mere feeling of benevolence toward others, just as the Cross must not become a symbol for sentimentality or passivity. Agape love, demonstrated through the Cross, functions as a protest against all forms of sinful self-interest. It is the ultimate standard for which we are to strive; it is also the power that enables the loving person to seek the good of others.

There are no easy solutions nor should there be any moral pretension to self-righteousness in the difficult arena where the struggle for truth and justice take place. It is beyond the scope of this chapter to flesh out the ethical obligations of a postmodern Christian community. But the one thing about which Christians ought to be certain is that they, like their Lord, have been called upon to be involved in their world. It will be part of the apologetic task for postmodern Christians to seriously reflect on the ecology of responsibility they have to the academy, other religious communities, and the wider society.

NOTES

1. Peter L. Berger, *A Rumor of Angels* (Garden City, N.Y.: Doubleday, 1969), 94.

2. William C. Placher, *Unapologetic Theology* (Louisville: Westminster/ John Knox, 1989), 94.

3. Ibid., 97.

4. Richard Rorty, *Consequences of Pragmatism* (Minneapolis: Univ. of Minnesota Press, 1982), xlii.

5. Huston Smith, "Postmodernism's Impact on the Study of Religion," *Journal of the American Academy of Religion* 57/4 (Winter 1990): 660.

6. Ibid.

7. Ibid., 661.

8. Charles Colson, *The Body: Being Light in Darkness* (Dallas: Word, 1992), 165.

9. Bernard Ramm, *Varieties of Christian Apologetics* (Grand Rapids: Baker, 1961), 13.

10. Placher, *Unapologetic Theology*, 18.

11. Ibid., 19.

12. David K. Clark, "Narrative Theology and Apologetics," *Journal of the Evangelical Theological Society* 36 (December 1993): 513.

13. For a recent analysis of this phenomenon, see, Harvey Cox, *Fire from Heaven: Pentecostalism, Spirituality and the Reshaping of Religion in the Twenty-First Century* (Redding, Mass.: Addison-Wesley, 1994).

14. Donald Bloesch, "Letting Scripture Speak for Itself," interview in *Academic Alert*, IVP's Book Bulletin for Professors 3/2 (Spring 1994): 1

15. Ibid.

16. John Calvin, *Institutes of the Christian Religion*, trans. Ford Lewis Battles, ed. John T. McNeil (Philadelphia: Westminster, 1960), 1.7.4.

17. Particularly see Friedrich Schleiermacher, *The Christian Faith*, ed. H.R. Mackintosh and J.S. Stewart (Philadelphia: Fortress, 1976).

18. George Lindbeck, *The Nature and Doctrine: Religion and Theology in a Postliberal Age* (Philadelphia: Westminster, 1984), 117.

19. Placher, *Unapologetic Theology*, 161.

20. See Hans Frei, "Eberhard Bush's Biography of Karl Barth," in H. Martin Rumscheidt, *Karl Barth in Review* (Allison Park, Pa.: Pickwick, 1981), 114; and William Werpehowski, "Ad hoc Apologetics," *Journal of Religion* 66 (1986): 282–301.

21. Charles Wood, *The Formation of Christian Understanding: An Essay in Theological Hermeneutics* (Philadelphia: Westminster, 1981), 100.

22. Placher, *Unapologetic Theology*, 160.

23. Daniel Migliore, *Faith Seeking Understanding* (Grand Rapids: Eerdmans, 1991), 49.

24. For Carl F.H. Henry's contribution to the discussion see his "Narrative Theology: An Evangelical Appraisal," *Trinity Journal* 8 (1987). Also, Hans Frei's "Response to 'Narrative Theology: An Evangelical Appraisal,' " *Trinity Journal* 8 (1987).

25. Nicholas Maxwell, *From Knowledge to Wisdom* (New York: Basil Blackwell, 1984), 47–64.

26. Mary Midgley, *Wisdom, Information, and Wonder: What Is Knowledge For?* (New York: Routledge, 1989), 21.

27. Edward Farley, *The Fragility of Knowledge* (Philadelphia: Fortress, 1988), 86.

28. This theme is explored in both *The Fragility of Knowledge* and Edward Farley, *Theologia* (Philadelphia: Fortress, 1983).

29. Ford makes a case for "wisdom" as a key integrating concept in "A Long Rumour of Wisdom: Redescribing Theology." An Inaugural Lecture delivered by David Ford as the newly appointed Regius Professor of Divinity in the University of Cambridge, 12 February 1992.

30. Walter Hooper, ed., *God in the Dock* (Grand Rapids: Eerdmans, 1970), 103.

31. Karl Barth, *Church Dogmatics*, vol. 2, part 1 (Edinburgh: T & T Clark, 1957), 423.

32. Placher, *Unapologetic Theology*, 135.

33. Robert McAfee Brown, ed., *The Essential Reinhold Niebuhr* (New Haven: Yale Univ. Press, 1986), 225. Several of Niebuhr's articles in this collection are pertinent to this discussion, particularly his "Coherence, Incoherence, and Christian Faith," "Mystery and Meaning," and "False Absolutes in Christian Interpretations of History."

34. Ibid., 231.

35. Ibid., 242–43.

36. Ibid., 246.

37. Ibid., 247.

38. Diogenes Allen, *Christian Belief in a Postmodern World: The Full Wealth of Conviction* (Louisville: Westminster/John Knox, 1989), 1.

39. "Systematic consistency," for Carnell, meant conformity to the law of non-contradiction and to all the external facts of experience.

40. Allen, *Christian Belief in a Postmodern World*, 3.

41. Ibid., 4.

42. Hauerwas argues that Christian ethics is about learning to live as a "peculiar people," a community of character. See Stanley Hauerwas and William Willimon, *Resident Aliens* (Nashville: Abingdon, 1989); and Stanley Hauerwas, *A Community of Character: Toward a Constructive Christian Social Ethic* (Notre Dame, Ind.: Notre Dame Univ. Press, 1981). Hauerwas is correct in maintaining that the Christian community must maintain its own unique character and live by its own agenda. True Christian character does have a persuasive power in the wider society. However, the internal logic of biblical faith is to reach out to the whole world. The Christian vision of reality includes the socially transforming and personal life-shaping power of the Gospel. Christians have to resist the temptation to privatize the Gospel narratives.

20

The Formal Foundation:
Toward an Evangelical Epistemology
in the Postmodern Context

Kelvin Jones

The Enlightenment, together with such historical transformations as the American and French revolutions and the indus-
trialization and urbanization of Europe and America, thrust
Western thought and culture into the modern era. In the last two
centuries the classical concept of truth[1] has been eroded by the tension between the earlier Enlightenment's ideal of a purely objective
rationalism and the later Enlightenment's focus upon the autonomous subjectivity of the individual. Much of modern theology, nineteenth-century liberalism most extensively, conformed to the Enlightenment's canons of epistemological objectivity, acquiesced to the
Enlightenment's separation of reason from both revelation and faith,
and reinterpreted faith according to modernity's focus upon the perceiving subject.[2]

The bifurcated epistemology by which Kant, followed in turn by
Schleiermacher and much of modern theology, attempted to correlate
faith and reason led to the ascendence of subjectivism[3] and secularism in Western thought and culture, and has culminated in the recent
fragmentation of modernity.[4] Modern Christian theology has suffered
a corresponding loss of consensus; pluralism is becoming, and is
often welcomed as, the lingua franca of theological as well as other
forums.[5]

Kelvin Jones is on the teaching faculty at Pinehaven Christian School in Pablo,
Montana.

Postmodernism, focusing upon the epistemic limitations and conditionedness of the individual, has emerged as essentially a protest against the epistemological ideals of the Enlightenment. In the words of one postmodern thinker, "Humpty-Dumpty is not going to be put back together again."[6] Indeed, the preeminent characteristic of postmodernity is its lack of consensus concerning the concept of truth.[7] The problem is usually set forth in one of two common-currency phrases, as many postmodernists dismiss either "a God's-eye view" or "an Archimedean point" of all knowledge as illusions left over from the age of Descartes.[8] Truth, and in parallel discussions the innate categories of reason, are seen as historically and linguistically conditioned social constructs, acquired through personal experience, which is predominantly relational rather than technical, subject-subject rather than subject-object interaction. In this way postmodernism, though it can be a helpful corrective of the unrealistic objectivism of the earlier Enlightenment, often abandons all hope of epistemological objectivity and descends quickly into conceptual relativism.[9]

The most evident initial response of Christian theology to postmodernism has been affirmative.[10] In this context evangelical theology is increasingly distinctive in its affirmation of the objectivity of truth and of the correspondence of revelation and reason as the ground of objective theological knowledge. A complete response to the epistemological concerns of postmodernism has not been fully offered by evangelicals, yet the basis of such a response is present in this volume. Together with Carl F.H. Henry, J.I. Packer, and Ronald Nash, we affirm that the Logos of God,[11] as the divine Agent in creation and providence, formally and correlatively orders the cosmos and human understanding and thus provides the ground of objective knowledge.[12] The Logos of the New Testament is the divine Mediator between God and humanity, not only cosmologically and, as incarnate in Jesus Christ, soteriologically, but epistemologically as well.[13] This correlation of ontology and epistemology through the Logos was integral to Western thought until the Enlightenment.[14] The later Enlightenment's rejection of the Logos as the ground of objective knowledge was integral to the Western turn to the subject, thus the loss of epistemological objectivity, the ascendence and dominance of subjectivism, the decline and fragmentation of modernity, and the current emergence of postmodernity's epistemological despair.

Human rationality in the image of God is ordered by the Logos of God to be formally correspondent with both the world God has created and with the general and special revelation He has provided. This correspondence of created reality, revelation, and reason is the ground of objective knowledge of oneself, the world, and the nature and will of God. The ordering of human reason by the Logos constitutes the formal structure of human rationality, which is distinct from the material content of an individual's thought processes and beliefs.[15] Henry's presuppositional apologetic, Packer's traditional affirmation of spiritual assurance, and Nash's appeal to basic beliefs have been considered elsewhere.[16] Time does not allow us to present our critique of evangelical presuppositionalism here; but we need to note, in all humility, that presuppositionalism misinterprets Romans 1:18-21 and similar texts, is logically invalid and apologetically weak, and confuses the ontic and noetic orders. Wolfhart Pannenberg has stated the point quite well.

> I do not deny that ultimately faith has its basis in the Word of God, assuming that the latter term is more precisely elucidated. But in fundamental theological discussion the basis cannot also be the starting point of its knowledge. It has been a common maxim since Aristotle that the ontic order and the noetic order do not always coincide. . . . theology has to tread a longer path before it can present God as the one we know.[17]

The Elements of the Formal Foundation

The rational dimension of the image of God in humanity is purely formal in nature. Henry has well observed that evangelical theology, by virtue of its affirmation of the Logos of God as the ground of objective knowledge, is best prepared and is responsible to delineate the categories of thought instilled in humanity by the Logos.[18] David Clark has recently argued that all apologetical dialogue appeals ultimately to "second level rational principles that believers and unbelievers hold in common" and that must be defended transcendentally, yet admits that to identify these formal principles "is a huge task."[19] The following is a brief, tentative proposal of the identity of the formal principles that constitute human rationality, the foundation of the noetic structure, and the innate ground of epistemological objectivity.

The biblical doctrine of creation provides the best explanation of *why* knowledge is possible;[20] this proposal is an attempt to explain *how* knowledge is possible. The epistemological proposal is grounded in the ontological assertion of creation; the ontological assertion is made rationally possible by the epistemological proposal. The ontological and epistemological aspects of the position are not welded together as are their counterparts in Henry's dyad of axioms, and they do not form a demonstrative proof of a superior worldview. Their efficacy is instead one of abductive complementarity: the biblical doctrine of creation provides a cogent explanation for this affirmation of a qualified epistemological objectivity; this particular epistemological formulation provides a cogent basis for the justification of the ontological affirmation. In combination they are preferable to alternative positions in their fulfillment of the criteria of consistency, correspondence, comprehensiveness, and viability.

The elements proposed below as constituting the rational order, or formal foundation, of human reason provide for the capability of the human mind to attain objective knowledge of reality, including knowledge of God. These formal principles are employed by the mind, for example, both in mundane activities such as driving a car and as the individual comes to know the truth of God that is available through general revelation.

The elements of the formal foundation are derived by abductive reasoning, that is, what Kant termed his transcendental method.[21] Abduction is necessary due to the formal nature and logical priority of the elements in reasoning; in order to determine them one considers what formal principles must be operative in order to account for the functioning of human reason. The delineation of this proposal proceeds from the following thesis statement.

The creation of humanity in the image of God, together with the ordering of creation by the same Creator according to formal principles corresponding to the noetic dimension of this image, is the ground of objective knowledge, including objective theological and hermeneutical knowledge. The adjective "objective" is not intended to denote a denial of either human finitude or fallibility, including the existential conditions of the acquisition and maintenance of knowledge, or an affirmation of absolute objectivity (which would require omniscience), but rather denotes the correspondence of mind and world and, therefore, of thought and object. This correspondence provides the ground but not the guarantee of objective knowledge.

The "formal principles" in this thesis are the *rationes aeternae* that originally subsist in the mind of God, and through His creative and providential will formally order creation and also constitute the formal foundation of the human noetic structure. These formal principles order human reason in such a way that they may, for the purpose of explanation, be thought of as the formal capabilities of human reason. As Aquinas explained this point, God has

> adorned the soul itself with intellectual light and imprinted on it the concepts of the first principles, which are, as it were, the sciences in embryo, just as He impressed on . . . physical things the seminal principles for producing their effects.[22]

The correlative ordering of both reality and reason by the Logos of God provides the formal correspondence between mind and world and, therefore, between thought and object. On this ground the mind is able to know truth, which is ultimately substantiated and personified in the nature/character of God, in the divine aseity, and the divine righteousness, respectively. The seven formal principles that order both reality and reason are: being, identity, abstraction, causation, spatiality, temporality, and morality.

The formal principles, instilled in creation by the Logos of God, are the ground of correspondence between the ontic and noetic orders. It is both demanding and necessary that in considering these formal principles, together with the support offered for them and the implications drawn from them, that we bear in mind the distinction between the ontological ground of the *rationes aeternae* and the epistemological process through which we come to an understanding of them. The points of support offered for a principle may, due to their abductive nature, give the appearance of circular reasoning. However, this appearance is attributable to the formal nature of the principles and to the necessity of employing them even in order to elucidate them. A high degree of interdependence is necessarily present among the formal principles, yet one can still distinguish legitimate interdependence from careless circularity.

The formal principle of *being* is first in order of priority and is the most basic of the principles. As an ordering principle of reality, this first element of the set ontically distinguishes real from nonexistent and noetically distinguishes truth from error. Apart from, prior to, and providing the ground for particular propositions concerning existence or nonexistence is the abstract, universal principle of being by which the mind differentiates between reality and nonreality. Aquinas affirmed the priority of this principle: in rational reflection, "what is first precipitated in the mind's conception is being. . . . it is the primary intelligible."[23] The human ability and corresponding responsibility to discern truth from error rests upon this principle, usually in cooperation with one or more other formal principles. On the basis of this principle we are able to assess the veracity of propositions concerning abstract entities as well; in this way we understand the principle of identity to be formally valid as well as materially objective (or as Henry would term it, ontologically grounded).

The principle of *identity,* with its concomitants such as disjunction, is the ground of ontic individuation and of the validity of logic. As is the principle of being, identity is an ordering principle necessary to coherent reality and inevitably presupposed in reason in that the denial thereof is self-defeating. The principle of identity is necessary to the concepts of individual, agent, and instrument, which are elements of ethical reasoning.

The principle of *abstraction* is the ground of relation and categorization within creation and of the innate human capability of logical, mathematical, and linguistic reasoning (thus providing for the objectivity of meaning in interpersonal communication). This principle is a sine qua non of reason, underlying the processes of relating objects, properties, concepts, conditions, and relations to one another. For example, the positing of "A is like B," the elementary school student's exercise of "circle the object which is not like the others," and advanced taxonomic analysis all presuppose the formal principle of abstraction, by which entities are related to or differentiated from one another according to qualities abstracted from each.

Nicholas Wolterstorff proposes that abstraction occurs "when, in listening to a musical work, I focus my attention on a certain limited range of the work's features and allow others to recede into the penumbra of my attention." Moreover,

> it may well be that what differentiates one science from others is that it deals with only a certain limited range of the properties of those entities which fall within the scope of that science's theories. If so, then abstraction is at the basis of our differentiation of sciences.[24]

The formal principle of abstraction is also the basis of symbolic communication, in which meaning is imparted to, retained by, and drawn from a symbol or set of symbols. This principle, then, is the ground of the objectivity of meaning[25] and of linguistic, interpersonal communication. Analogical predication involves compound abstraction, that is, defining by implication an abstract relation between two categorically separate instantiations of a property. The human ability to reason and communicate via analogical predication, together with the ability to define by abstraction the concept of transcendence, provides for the validity and objectivity of theological reflection and language.[26] Finally, the formal principle of abstraction is an element of that reasoning by which we engage in critical analysis of both the material content of and formal relations within our own thought.

The principle of *causation* both orders reality and is the ground of causal reasoning. Here again, the denial thereof is both rationally and volitionally self-defeating (of course, this is no obstacle to someone who is happy, or at least willing, to affirm an ultimately incoherent, unintelligible, and meaningless universe, but this and other forms of nihilism are not attractive options to those who regard viability as a criterion of worldviews). The principles of identity and causation are the most widely and easily recognized of the principles; they are essential to what is known as common sense (which should be distinguished here from common beliefs). Causation is necessary to the idea of purpose and to the concept of a teleologically ordered universe.

The principle of *spatiality* is reflected in the three-dimensional order of the physical universe and in the innate human ability to perceive and reason accordingly. The principle of *temporality* is reflected ontologically in the linear succession of present moments and epistemologically in the corresponding human perception. That these principles are constant to human consciousness makes them more difficult to identify as formal principles, because the natural inclination is to confuse, as Kant did, spatiality with space and temporality with time.[27] Spatiality is not space in the concrete sense but the ordering of the physical universe as spatial. It is only because the universe is so ordered that our perception of the external world consistently serves us well. It is because our minds possess the ability to order spatial perceptions in correspondence with the external world that we are able to find our way around. The formal principle of spatiality is essential to the efficacy of metric (e.g., geometric and trigonometric) reasoning and to the respectability of the engineering professions.

Similarly, it is because the universe is temporally ordered that our constant perception of temporal progression proves functional (we do not expect counterintuitive theories of spatial and temporal relations to transcend their theoretical status).[28] The formal principle of temporality is distinct from time in the specific or concrete sense. Fortunately, or rather providentially, our formal capability of temporal perception corresponds to the temporally ordered universe. A point of pragmatic support is that it simply works for us to understand ourselves and the external world as existing under the ordering principle of temporality. Temporality as a formal principle is essential to the concept of causality within the natural order, and to mathematics in that the concept of numbering is a temporally ordered activity.

The principle of *morality* is the ground of the ontic and noetic distinctions between good and evil and between right and wrong. The ontological ground of this principle as well as the preceding principles is the Logos of God. Apologetically, just as the concept of error, which few will consistently deny, presupposes the concept of truth, so the concept of evil, which few will consistently deny, presupposes the concept of good. As is true of the preceding six principles, the formal principle of morality is prior and necessary to specific ethical judgments.[29]

This proposal of the formal foundation, to the extent that it is accurate, implies that belief in God is not and need not be an innate, material element of the foundation of the noetic structure. The image of God in humanity includes, through the capabilities of the formal foundation, the ability and, therefore, the implicit responsibility to infer, even apart from special revelation, the eternal power and divine nature of the Creator.

Though belief in God is not innate, the disposition to believe in God is, and results from the volitional and affective as well as cognitive dimensions of the image of God. This disposition, however, is often overcome prior to regeneration by the corruption of the volitional dimension of the image and hindrance of the objectivity of the mind through sin. The disposition is liberated in the process of conversion through cognitive realignment with the biblical worldview and volitional desire for reconciliation with God. This liberation is accomplished through the convicting ministry of the Holy Spirit upon the heart.

Belief in God is formed through experience and draws upon all of the formal principles in the experience of and reflection upon general and special revelation. The inferential movement of Romans 1:18-21 from created reality to the transcendent Creator relies in an especially direct manner upon the principle of abstraction. The epistemic sufficiency of this account of human reason implies the superfluity of the doctrine of illumination as affirmed in the Augustinian tradition.

The challenges confronting this delineation of creation as the ground of ontic-noetic correspondence and thus of epistemological objectivity require the reiteration of the tentative nature of this proposal. We can be confident that the distinction between formal principles and material propositions within the noetic structure overcomes the impasse which besets conflicting claims to metaphysical presuppositions or properly basic beliefs. However, several questions remain.

Is each of the formal principles necessary, and tenable against criticism? Is this set of seven formal principles sufficient?

Is the position that these principles order both creation and human reason, yet are purely formal (and universal, in contrast to the material and specific points of reality, perceptions, and judgments that presuppose and reflect them), both accurate and tenable?

Can the necessarily high degree of interdependence present among these formal principles as basic to an objective epistemology be defended against the charge of circular reasoning?

These questions require further interaction with the relation between the ontic and noetic orders. Further research in this area should accordingly seek a fuller delineation of the creative and providential ordering of creation and human reason by the Logos of God.

The Formal Foundation in the Postmodern Context

The complementary proposals of Henry, Packer, and Nash posit the correspondence of revelation and reason as the ground of objective theological knowledge. We have concluded that this proposed correspondence does indeed provide a promising ground for objective theological knowledge that is consonant with postmodern attitudes toward the relation of faith and reason. The evangelical proposal may in this respect be better received by postmodernity than it was under the rigid epistemological canons of modernity, because it is largely cogent and preferable, especially in terms of its efficacy in providing a viable ground of epistemological objectivity that still acknowledges our human finitude and fallibility and our individual conditionedness.

The similar proposal of a formal foundation, which is preferably understood as a refinement rather than a rejection of the evangelical proposal, is also amenable to the mainstream of postmodern thought in that it acknowledges the distinction, overlooked by modernity, between our human potential for objective knowledge and the individual conditionedness which so easily ensnares us as we seek to understand life and to converse with one another. As noted above, the formal foundation provides the ground but not the guarantee of objective knowledge. Objectivity, in theology as well as in other areas of inquiry, is only attainable to relative degrees by finite, fallible, and volitionally corrupted humans—yet it remains a viable as well as a necessary ideal of our thought.[30]

The proposal of the purely formal nature of the foundation of human reason is also more consonant with postmodern than modern views in its acknowledgment of the complementarity of the epistemological and ontological aspects of the Christian worldview. Both aspects are justified abductively rather than asserted on the basis of an allegedly ahistorical, autonomous epistemological standpoint, and both are either explicit in or inferred from the Christian Scriptures. The position as a whole does not pretend to any demonstrative proof, but instead provides a coherent position that is supportive of and consistent with a vigorous affirmation of Christian faith, as well as defensibly correspondent with the whole of human experience. These qualities lend themselves to an apologetical approach that is more philosophically respectable now, in the postmodern context, than it was under the strictures of modernity.

The epistemological openness of this position allows for a stronger affirmation of the objectivity of revelation and the correspondence of revelation and reason than was acceptable to modernity, and avoids the unrealistic modern ideal of a detached, unconditioned, impersonal objectivism. It requires neither conformity to naturalistic or positivistic assumptions nor a leap of faith, but leads to an account of human experience that is cogent for both the believer and the one who does not affirm the biblical worldview.

This position affirms the responsibility of each individual to acknowledge the reality of God on the basis of the self-revelation of God and the epistemic proficiency of human reason, and correspondingly attributes non-acknowledgment to the corruption of the will by sin. This corruption includes progressive tendencies toward self-deception and denial of responsibility in the self-centered rejection of truth and reason. The atheist who relies upon reason to deny God inevitably, and culpably, resorts to formal inconsistency or material inaccuracy in some area—in the language of Romans 1, this is suppression of the truth in unrighteousness—in order to maintain the denial. The objectivity of this Christian position is qualified but not vitiated or marginalized by the finitude, fallibility, existential conditionedness, or sin-corrupted state of the individual. Here again, the enduring point of reference is the correspondence of revelation and reason: the self-revelation of God and the innate proficiency of human reason provide for objective theological knowledge and therefore bring us all to accountability before our Creator.

Conclusion

The proposals of Henry and Nash are open to improvement in the area of their presuppositionalism. A preferable proposal would affirm the purely formal nature of the rational dimension of the image of God in humanity. This formal character opens the proposal to what initially appears to be less assurance concerning the ground of objective theological knowledge than is provided by Henry's presuppositionalism or Nash's properly basic belief in God. However, this alternative proposal is more closely aligned with Romans 1:18-21 and with the important distinction between the formal principles of reason and the material propositions of the noetic structure.

This alternative proposal of a formal foundation also is preserved from the postmodern rejection of classical foundationalism, because the postmodern criticisms target either the foundational status of specific material propositions or beliefs or the unqualified universality of certain rationalistic ideas. In affirming the purely formal quality of the correspondent relation between revelation and reason, evangelical theology would be in an even better position to affirm and cogently formulate a correspondence of ontology and epistemology which modernity abandoned and postmodernity, if it will, could recover.

As Western thought and culture continue in the postmodern era, evangelical theology has the opportunity to present anew its understanding of the truth of God and of the ground of objective theological knowledge. The answer to the perennial question of Western thought and culture, "What is truth?" lies in the Logos, God incarnate in Jesus Christ, who is the transcendent ground of the correspondence of creation, revelation, and reason, and therefore of objective knowledge, including objective hermeneutical and theological knowledge.

NOTES

1. Implicit in the concept of truth is the question, to which this paper pertains, of knowledge. In Western thought and culture, truth has traditionally and primarily been understood as the quality of correspondence between a proposition and its referent (the major alternative views have been the coherence and pragmatic theories of truth). Aristotle posits that "to say of what is that it is not, or of what is not that it is, is false, while to say of what is that it is, and of what is not that it is not, is true." Aristotle, *Metaphysics* 4.7, trans. W.D. Ross, in *Great Books of the Western World* (Chicago: Encyclopaedia Brittanica, 1952), 8:349.

The underlying epistemological affirmation is, in the words of Thomas Aquinas, that *"Veritas est adaequatio rei et intellectus"* ("Truth is the adequation of thing and intellect"). Aquinas, *De Veritate* Q. 1, A. 1 (cf. *Summa theologica*, 1.16.1, and *Summa contra Gentiles,* 1.59), cited in A.N. Prior, "Correspondence Theory of Truth," in *The*

Encyclopedia of Philosophy, ed. Paul Edwards (New York: Macmillan, 1967), 1:224.

Secondary to this common, epistemological sense is the ethical sense of truth as the quality of a person who virtuously fulfills his or her created purpose, innate potential, or undertaken responsibilities. This ethical sense is consonant with the philosophical concept of beauty as teleological fulfillment.

Theologically, truth is ultimately substantiated and personified in the nature/character of God, in the divine aseity and the divine righteousness, respectively.

2. Harvey has observed that modern Protestant theology "may be regarded as a series of salvage operations, attempts to show how one can still believe in Jesus Christ and not violate an ideal of intellectual integrity" (Van Harvey, *The Historian and the Believer: The Morality of Historical Knowledge and Christian Belief* [New York: Macmillan, 1966], 104). Neo-orthodox theology recovered much of the content of traditional theology through its reassertion of the transcendence of God and the necessity of revelation, yet continued to conform to modernity in its method and interpretation of faith, and so did not recover the premodern confidence in the objectivity of theological knowledge.

3. "Subjectivism" here refers to the position that the personal, primarily affective rather than cognitive experiences and perceptions of the individual are normative in deciding matters of truth, meaning, and value. The intended contrast is with objectivism, the position that reality external to the individual subject is normative in determining truth, meaning (as distinct from significance), and value (per se, as distinct from the subject's values and evaluations).

4. Dilley observes: "Modern philosophizing recognizes no universals, no agreement as to facts, methods, or experiences. There are clearly many different views of facts, many proposed methods, many types of experience to be found. Philosophical fragmentation is the rule" (Frank B. Dilley, *Metaphysics and Religious Language* [New York: Columbia Univ. Press, 1964], 71). The poem "The Second Coming," composed earlier in this century by William B. Yeats (1865–1939), offers a precursor of this condition, reading in part: "Things fall apart; the centre cannot hold." See, *The Poems of W.B. Yeats: A New Edition,* ed. Richard J. Finneran (New York: Macmillan, 1924), 187.

5. See, for example, Craig M. Gay, "Plurality, Ambiguity, and Despair in Contemporary Theology," *Journal of the Evangelical Theological Society* 36 (1993): 209–27. Commenting rather pointedly on the pluralism regnant in American higher education, Yandell notes, "Students and faculty regularly tell one another that the objective truth is that there is no objective truth and that since no one's values are any better than anyone else's we ought to tolerate everyone's values, because of course tolerance is a better value than intolerance" (Keith Yandell, "How to Teach What You Don't Believe," *Christian Scholar's Review* 21 [1991]: 160).

Tracy writes that to read contemporary theology is to recognize "a radical pluralism, indeed, even an intense conflict of interpretation, from which there can often seem no honorable exit" (David Tracy, "Theological Method," in *Christian Theology: An Introduction to Its Traditions and Tasks,* 2nd ed., ed. Peter C. Hodgson and Robert H. King (Philadelphia: Fortress, 1985), 37.

Allen observes: "As we enter a postmodern or post-Enlightenment world many people, including theologians, are becoming distressed by the plurality of worldviews. Many have been driven to relativism by the collapse of the Enlightenment's confidence in the power of reason to provide foundations for our truth-claims and to achieve finality in our search for truth in the various disciplines" (Diogenes Allen, *Christian Belief in a Postmodern World: The Full Wealth of Conviction* [Louisville: Westminster/John Knox, 1989], 9).

6. Walter Truett Anderson, *Reality Isn't What It Used to Be: Theatrical Politics, Ready-to-Wear Religion, Global Myths, Primitive Chic, and Other Wonders of the Postmodern World* (San Francisco: HarperSan Francisco, 1990), x. Anderson predicts that the present seed of discontent with the assumptions of modernity is growing into a metaconflict about beliefs. He notes that the debate extends to such questions as whether the categories of reason are innate or are merely social constructs, which point is central to the evangelical proposal (p. 62).

7. Heller asks, "Should we explore the possibility that the absence of a dominating concept of truth is actually the manifestation of the dominating culture of the contemporary (post-modern) world?" (Agnes Heller, *A Philosophy of History in Fragments* [Cambridge, Mass.: Blackwell, 1993], 135). Rorty, proceeding from a radical historicism and a thorough pragmatism, presses even further in rejecting truth as a pretension of metaphysically oriented philosophy: "There is no such thing as 'the best explanation' of anything; there is just the explanation which best suits the purpose of some given explainer" (Richard Rorty, *Objectivity, Relativism, and Truth*, Philosophical Papers, 1 [Cambridge: Cambridge Univ. Press, 1991], 60).

8. Bernstein is representative of many postmodernists when he cites "the growing sense that there may be nothing—not God, Philosophy, Science, or Poetry—that satisfies our longing for ultimate foundations, for a fixed Archimedean point upon which we can secure our thought and action" (Richard J. Bernstein, *Beyond Objectivism and Relativism: Science, Hermeneutics and Praxis* [Philadelphia: Univ. of Pennsylvania, 1983], 230). He observes, though, that the epistemological and moral ideal, which would be realized in "dialogical communities that embrace all of humanity and in which reciprocal judgment, practical discourse, and rational persuasion flourish. . . . is still a telos, a telos deeply rooted in our human project" (p. 231).

9. Rorty advocates the abandonment of the search for some "metaphysical comfort" in life, for our thought and action have no a priori ground but are only culturally, that is, conversationally, developed. Rorty attempts to separate his position from relativism in the literal or consistent sense: "So the real issue is not between people who think one view is as good as another and people who do not. It is between those who think our culture, or purpose, or intuitions cannot be supported except conversationally, and people who still hope for other sorts of support (Richard Rorty, *Consequences of Pragmatism* [Minneapolis: Univ. of Minnesota Press, 1982], 182).

Sheila Davaney notes that one element of postmodernism is the view that "human beings are thoroughly cultural and social beings whose experience is shaped, molded, and literally constituted by the cultural and linguistic resources available in any given historical context" (Davaney, "Options in Post-Modern Theology," 197).

10. Diogenes Allen is representative of many who, though their individual perspectives, concerns, and approaches diverge quickly beyond this point of consensus, together affirm: "Rather than be disturbed by the recent displacement of foundationalism . . . Christian theologians ought to be glad to be rid of a thorn in its side since ancient times. They need not endorse irrationalism nor relativism but may rejoice that the contingency of the universe and the socially mediated character of

our knowledge undermine any foundationalist project and the narrow views of reason and rational grounds that have historically resulted from foundationalism" (Allen, *Christian Belief in a Postmodern World*, 152).

11. In this chapter the term "Logos" denotes the divine Logos, the Second Person of the Trinity; the term "logos" will denote the ordering principle referred to in philosophical discussion of cosmology and epistemology, without necessary reference to the Logos of Christian theism.

12. Carl F.H. Henry's position is set forth especially in *God, Revelation and Authority* (Dallas: Word, 1976–1983); and *Toward a Recovery of Christian Belief: The Rutherford Lectures, October 1989* (Wheaton, Ill.: Crossway, 1990). J.I. Packer's view is presented especially in *God Has Spoken* (Downers Grove, Ill.: InterVarsity, 1979); "The Adequacy of Human Language," in *Inerrancy,* ed. Norman Geisler (Grand Rapids: Zondervan, 1980); "God the Image-Maker," in *Christian Faith and Practice in the Modern World,* ed. Mark Noll and David Wells (Grand Rapids: Eerdmans, 1988). Ronald Nash's position is given especially in *Faith and Reason: Searching for a Rational Faith* (Grand Rapids: Zondervan, 1988); *The Word of God and the Mind of Man* (Grand Rapids: Zondervan, 1982); and *Worldviews in Conflict: Choosing Christianity in the World of Ideas* (Grand Rapids: Zondervan, 1992).

13. Packer rarely refers to the Logos as the ground of correspondence between mind and world or between revelation and reason; he emphasizes instead the closely related point of the intrinsic linguistic capability of humanity as created in the image of God. Henry and Nash note that in classical Greek philosophy the term *logos* was used to refer to the order and correlation of thought and reality. Though Hellenistic Judaism attempted to relate this concept to God, the Old Testament concepts of the Word of God and wisdom that is from God were the precursors of the New Testament concept of the Logos of God given in such passages as John 1:1-9 and Colossians 1:16-17.

Patristic theologians related human rationality and epistemological objectivity to the image of God instilled in humanity by the Logos. Augustine further held that the rational structure of the mind corresponds to the rational structure of the world because both correspond to the mind of God. He posited that the *rationes aeternae* that subsist in the mind of God also order created reality and are through divine illumination reflected in human rationality.

14. Henry, Packer, and Nash regard Kant as the most influential proponent of what became modernity's abandonment of the image of God in humanity as the basis of human rationality and point out that Kant did not provide an adequate explanation for the existence of the categories of reason he proposed in its place. Henry and Nash maintain that modernity's loss of objective knowledge and meaning are traceable directly to the ascendance of Kantian epistemology, and that recovery of the idea of humanity as created in the image of God is the best resolution of the loss of objectivity in Western thought and culture.

15. Henry describes this formal element as the precondition of thought, the underlying logical foundation or system of categorical principles which makes reasoning possible. Nash refers to this element as the a priori rationality common to humanity and notes with Henry that the law of noncontradiction and the conceptual distinction between truth and error are essential to rationality. He notes that Augustine suggested that the *rationes aeternae* include beauty, truth, goodness, number, square, and circle and that Gordon Clark tentatively regarded causality, unity, space,

time, substance, truth, and God as a priori categories of thought.

16. Kelvin Jones, "Revelation and Reason in the Theology of Carl F.H. Henry, James I. Packer, and Ronald H. Nash" (Ph.D. diss., The Southern Baptist Theological Seminary, 1994).

17. Wolfhart Pannenberg, *Systematic Theology,* trans. Geoffrey W. Bromiley (Grand Rapids: Eerdmans, 1991), 1:242, n. 141.

18. Henry, *God, Revelation and Authority,* 5:350.

19. David K. Clark, "Is Presuppositional Apologetics Rational?" *Bulletin of the Evangelical Philosophical Society* 16 (1993): 9–10.

20. The biblical doctrine of creation, specifically of the creation of humanity in the image of God, provides the most consistent, comprehensive, cogent, and viable explanation for the objective epistemology implicit in Scripture.

21. Immanuel Kant, *Critique of Pure Reason,* trans. Norman Kemp-Smith (New York: St. Martin's, 1965), B25.

22. Thomas Aquinas, *De veritate,* trans. R.W. Mulligan (Chicago: Regnery, 1952), 11.3.

23. Thomas Aquinas, *Summa theologica,* trans. English Dominican Fathers (New York: Benziger, 1948), 1:q. 5.

24. Nicholas Wolterstorff, *Reason within the Bounds of Religion Alone,* 2nd ed. (Grand Rapids: Eerdmans, 1984), 153, n. 28.

25. Royce Gruenler develops this point in *Meaning and Understanding: The Philosophical Framework for Biblical Interpretation,* Foundations of Contemporary Interpretation, vol. 2, series ed. Moises Silva (Grand Rapids: Zondervan, 1991), 168–75.

26. As Anselm prayerfully wrote so well, "Lord, I acknowledge and I thank You that You have created me in this Your image, in order that I may be mindful of You, may conceive of You, and love You." Anselm, *Proslogium,* trans. Sidney N. Deane (La Salle, Ill.: Open Court, 1962), 6 (translation modernized in this quotation).

27. Kant, *Critique of Pure Reason,* B37–73.

28. In this respect also the distinction between formal principles and material propositions is necessary. For example, theoretical physics, with which I am not well acquainted and which specializes in things too small or too far away for me to observe, has yet to woo me away from affirmation of such things as straight lines in space. I regard theoretical physics as still engaged in the scientific process of successively approximating the truth, and perhaps having backslidden from my perhaps naive affirmation of space as three-dimensional and linearly ordered. Yet this affirmation, though fundamental among my beliefs, is a material proposition, and is not an element of the formal foundation of my noetic structure. It is not easy to maintain the distinctions between spatiality and three-dimensional space or between temporality and linearly progressing time, because I find it virtually impossible to dwell upon the concept of otherwise-ordered space or time, to the point that I have wondered whether three-dimensionality is in fact necessary to any coherent definition of spatiality, or linearity is necessary to any coherent definition of temporality. However, I am very interested in maintaining the distinction and the overall proposal, so I will tolerate the difficulty of this point until I am persuaded differently.

29. This point is supported, against multiculturalism's strong tendency toward moral relativism, by James Q. Wilson, *The Moral Sense* (New York: Free Press, 1993).

30. This is a theme of Paul Helm, ed., *Objective Knowledge: A Christian Perspective* (Leicester, England: Inter-Varsity, 1987).

21

Evangelism
in a Postmodern World

James Emery White

Kenneth Myers has written that the "challenge of living with popular culture may well be as serious for modern Christians as persecution and plagues were for the saints of earlier centuries."[1] Perhaps the greatest cultural challenge facing Western Christianity, certainly in America, is the growing acceptance that we live in a postmodern, post-Christian world.[2] At its heart, postmodernity is the removal of all foundations. Truth, morality, interpretive frameworks, all are removed in a postmodern context. The challenges this cultural shift poses for Christendom are formidable indeed.

Evangelical Christianity has so emphasized confronting individual lives with the claims of the Gospel that it has often neglected the decisive need for a Christian engagement of contemporary culture. Yet individuals are often the product of their culture and, therefore, a divorce between an understanding of our current context and the enterprise of ministry is nothing less than folly.

Therefore the questions this chapter will attempt to answer are decisive: How does one evangelize a postmodern person? How does a church develop an evangelistic strategy for a post-Christian generation? The answers begin to be formed through an understanding of the dynamics of our postmodern world—a world that has rejected Enlightenment understandings of truth.

James Emery White is Pastor of Mecklenburg Community Church in Charlotte, North Carolina.

Three Processes of Modernity

What are the forces at work in contemporary American culture that are of particular relevance to the evangelistic task? Sociologist Peter Berger, among many others, has suggested three dominant sociological trends in contemporary American culture which have shaped current life and thought: secularization, pluralization, and privatization.[3]

Secularization. Secularization is the process by which "sectors of society and culture are removed from the domination of religious institutions and symbols."[4] Here is the process whereby the church is losing its influence as a shaper of life and thought in the wider social order.

The church was once the dominant institution in most communities. Today, morality and truth are more often the property of the media. For example, television may not tell us what to *think,* but it certainly tells us what to think *about.* Howard K. Smith, for years an ABC commentator, estimated that at least four-fifths of what the average citizen continued to learn about the world after leaving school came "filtered through observation" of a journalist.[5] The process of secularization has filtered out ideas and agendas from the public square that are religious in nature. Page Smith sarcastically remarks that in our day, "God is not a proper topic for conversation, but 'lesbian politics' is!"[6]

In regard to evangelistic concerns, the process of secularization makes the Christian faith seem less *real* than other concerns or ideologies. As one man commented to me recently about an aspect of the Christian faith, "That's fine for church, but not for the real world."

Privatization. The second mark of modernity is "individualization," or "privatization," which Berger defines as follows:

> Privatized religion is a matter of the "choice'" or "preference" of the individual or the nuclear family, ipso facto lacking in common binding quality . . . this religiosity is limited to specific enclaves of social life that may be effectively segregated from the secularized sectors of modern society.[7]

An interpreter of Berger, Os Guinness, has defined privatization as that "process by which modernization produces a cleavage between the public and the private spheres of life and focuses that private sphere as the special arena for the expansion of individual freedom and fulfillment."[8] The origin of this dynamic may very well have been the church's acceptance, during the seventeenth and eighteenth centuries, of the claim of science to the throne of public, factual truth.[9]

The practical dynamic of this stream of modernity is that one's personal faith is often suspended in relation to business, politics, or even marriage and the home. A compartmentalized faith is manifest with personal faith as one of many worlds or "pockets" of experience that make up the unrelated composite. This trend was seemingly evident to historian Theodore Roszak who, after traveling to America, remarked that Christian faith in America was one that was "socially irrelevant, even if privately engaging."[10] Perhaps this dynamic was most clearly demonstrated by the founder of the fast-food chain McDonald's, who was quoted as saying, "I believe in God, family, and McDonald's — and in the office, that order is reversed."[11]

For the evangelistic task, privatization can make the Christian faith merely a matter of personal preference.[12] Sociologist Robert Bellah interviewed a woman who captured the spirit well: "I believe in God. I'm not a religious fanatic. I can't remember the last time I went to church. My faith has carried me a long way. It's 'Sheilaism.' Just my own little voice."[13] As a result, faith is trivialized to the realm of mere personal opinion.

Pluralization. The final stream within modernity, according to Berger, is "pluralization," that "the man in the street is confronted with a wide variety of religious and other reality-defining agencies that compete for his allegiance or at least attention."[14] Again, Guinness offers a good interpretation of Berger's thought, writing that pluralization is that "process by which the number of options in the private sphere of modern society rapidly multiplies at all levels, especially at the level of world views, faith and ideologies."[15]

Berger speaks of the traditional role of religion as a "sacred canopy" covering the contemporary culture. Today that canopy is gone, replaced instead by millions of small tents.[16] For example, Barrett's *World Christian Encyclopedia* lists over 20,000 denominations, with over 2,000 in the United States alone.[17]

It should be noted that the process of pluralization means far more than a simple increase in the number of "faith options." Langdon Gilkey is correct when he observes that "many religions have always existed"; what is unique is a "new consciousness" that "entails a feeling of rough parity, as well as diversity, among religion. By parity I mean at least the presence of both truth and grace in other ways."[18] Harold O.J. Brown adds that by pluralism, we mean not only many and varying convictions, but "value pluralism, namely, that all convictions about values are of equal validity, which says in effect that no convictions about values have any validity."[19]

The result of this process is quite simply the devaluation of truth. For the evangelistic enterprise, this is an imposing challenge. To borrow from Lesslie Newbigin, evangelism is at its heart "truth to tell." Yet the sheer number of choices and competing ideologies suggests that no one perspective or religious persuasion has the inside track on truths about the spiritual realm.

To further complicate evangelistic efforts, this devaluation of truth has also fostered a "smorgasbord" mentality in regard to whatever construction of personal beliefs *are* present. Malise Ruthven calls the United States the "divine supermarket." The technical term is "syncretism," the "mix and match" mentality of pulling together different threads in various religions in order to create a personal religion that suits an individual taste. As a result, Christianity becomes simply one of many competing worldviews, no better or worse than another, which exists in the milieu of our society.[20]

The Four Marks of Modernity

If secularization, privatization, and pluralization are the three processes of modernity, what have been the results of these processes? In essence, these processes of the modern world have created what is now being called "post" modernity, that which has come after modernity.

Four characteristics have emerged from the processes of modernity that describe our current context: moral relativism, autonomous individualism, narcissistic hedonism, and reduction naturalism.[21]

Moral Relativism. The value of "moral relativism" states that what is moral is dictated by a particular situation in light of a particular culture or social location. The usual phraseology is "what is true for you is true for you, and what is true for me is true for me."

The breakdown of morals in our day is almost epidemic; recent studies indicate that lying is now a part of our culture, a trait of American character, and that one-third of all married men and women have had a least one affair.[22] Allan Bloom, in the introduction of his best-selling *The Closing of the American Mind,* writes that there "is one thing a professor can be absolutely certain of. Almost every student entering the university believes, or says he believes, that truth is relative."[23]

Autonomous Individualism. The value of "autonomous individualism" espouses that the individual person is autonomous in terms of destiny and accountability. Ultimate moral authority is self-generated. In the end, we answer to no one but ourselves. Our choices are ours alone, determined by our personal pleasure, and not by any higher moral authority. As Oden notes, the "key to 'hairesis' (root word for 'heresy') is the notion of choice—choosing for oneself, over against the apostolic tradition."[24]

Narcissistic Hedonism. In Greek mythology, Narcissus is the character who, upon passing his reflection in the water, became so enamored with himself that he lost thought, fell in the water, and drowned. The value of "narcissistic hedonism" is the classic "I, me, mine" mentality that places personal pleasure and fulfill ment at the forefront of concerns. The popular ethical expression of this mind-set is simply this: "if it makes you happy, and it doesn't hurt anyone else, then it's 'okay.' " The mainstream dissemination of this perspective is perhaps best seen in the plethora of Television talk shows that daily baptize relativity even as they dominate the airwaves with egoism.

Reductive Naturalism. "Reductive naturalism" is the value which states that what can be known is only that which can be empirically verified. In other words, what is real is that which can be seen, tasted, heard, smelled, or touched. If it cannot be examined in a tangible, scientific manner, then it is not simply unknowable, it is meaningless. The verdict such a view imposes on religious claims is self-evident.

The *trauma* of the postmodern world is that modernity and its offspring has failed to deliver on its promises. Rather than enhancing personal satisfaction and fulfillment, it has proven to be a barren wasteland. Moral relativism has led to a crisis in values; autonomous individualism has led to a lack of vision; narcissistic hedonism has created empty souls; and reductive naturalism has proven inadequate for human experience. Yet Christians have not responded as effectively as they might through the articulation of a compelling alternative, much less by understanding the new realities postmodernity places upon evangelism. It is to this question, then, that we now turn.

Yesterday's Evangelism and Today's Unchurched

Understanding the three streams of modernity and their impact on culture is an important beginning. But what of our friend who is not a Christian? Let's set up an imaginary line:

1	2	3	4	5	6	7	8	9	10

On one end of the scale, the "1," we have someone who is completely divorced from a relationship with or knowledge of Christ. On the other end of the scale, at the "10" mark, is the point in time when the process of evangelization results in that person coming to saving faith and knowledge in Christ as Lord and Savior. This extremely crude scale illustrates two important truths: first, that evangelism is both process and event, and second, that people can be at different points along the journey.

Let's begin with yesterday's nonbeliever, before the postmodern context, in terms of where they might be on our scale. Speaking in broad terms, where was the unsaved person of the 1950s?

Without taking time to defend the proposition, the typical nonbeliever of the 1950s more than likely had the following in their spiritual résumé: a belief in the deity of Christ; a belief that truth existed and that the Bible was trustworthy; a positive image of the church and its leaders; church background, knowledge, and experience that was relatively healthy; and a built-in sense of guilt or conviction when they violated the basic values of the Judeo-Christian heritage.

So on a scale of 1–10, they could easily be placed at around an "8."

1	2	3	4	5	6	7	8	9	10

This was why many of the evangelistic approaches of the 1950s *worked* in the 1950s. The top approaches of evangelical churches in that decade could fairly be summed up in four strategies: door-to-door visitation, revivals, Sunday School, and busing.

Door-to-door visitation was effective because people opened up their doors to ministers and other folk related to a church and would invite them into their home. Why? They had a positive image of the church and its leaders. They had in their history some experience with the church or Christianity that was relatively sound and positive.

Revivals were productive because people who needed Christ would actually *attend* them. Revivals were often a communitywide event, akin to the county fair. And because they were already sitting on an "8," a brief and passionate presentation of the Gospel through song and word would be enough to "bump" them over to a "10."

Sunday School was effective because individuals were willing to begin their exploration of a church through a small-group experience. Further, through "enrollment" campaigns, people would respond to a door-to-door visitation campaign for enrollment in Sunday School, and because of their cultural background, feel compelled to attend as a result.

Busing was nothing less than anointed for its time. But it depended on parents who would gladly send their children off on a bus without anything more than the church's supervision.

But what of our postmodern world? Sadly, few if any of the realities and assumptions upon which previous methodologies were built are still valid. It has been said of the Baby Busters, those born between 1963 and 1977, and the first generation to grow up in a postmodern context, that they lack even the *memory* of a hope-giving Gospel.[25]

Many people outside of the church struggle with the concept of Christ's deity. Many think Jesus Christ was a good man, perhaps, even a prophet, but not God in human form. Further, 72 percent of Americans deny the existence of absolute truth, and few have confidence in the historical accuracy or ethical authority of the Bible.[26]

Beyond intellectual concern, the current generation has seen scandals erode the church's image, and cite negative experiences in their church background as reason for their lack of involvement. Spiritual illiteracy has never been higher. Rather than conviction, a militant spirit toward ethical choices reigns supreme. The current view is that there should be no outside authority determining moral choices.

So where does the typical unchurched person of our day rest on our imaginary scale? One could theorize that they are about a "3."

| 1 | 2 | **3** | 4 | 5 | 6 | 7 | 8 | 9 | 10 |

The impact this has on evangelism should be readily seen. Think again of the four major approaches: Few churches attempt a bus ministry today, for most people are more cautious about letting their children go unattended to a religious event. The reality is that it is highly doubtful in our day of sexual scandal that many parents would allow their children to go unattended to a church, much less on a bus without their supervision.

Door-to-door visitation is outlawed in many areas and impossible in closed, guarded-gate communities. Few, if any, people enjoy an unannounced visitor knocking on their door. Revivals no longer have the cultural support they once enjoyed and have very few unsaved people in attendance. One-shot exposures to the Gospel might move someone from a "3" to a "5," which makes such a "harvest" approach problematic. Sunday School is finding that many seekers do not wish to begin their spiritual journey with an intimidating church-specific small-group experience. So today, the most common methods of reaching out to the modern world are at best irrelevant, and at worst offensive.

Evangelism in a Postmodern World

So how does one evangelize in a postmodern world? What would an effective church strategy incorporate? The following might provide some direction for the twenty-first century church, and as Stanley Grenz has suggested, allow us to "claim the postmodern context for Christ."[27]

1. Our Approach, Method, and Style Should Be Culturally Relevant

When Jesus spoke to the woman at the well, He talked of water. When He dialogued with fishermen, He discussed fishing. When He conversed with tax collectors, He spoke of money. The Apostle Paul, when confronted with Greek philosophers on Mars Hill, responded in like with a conversation rooted in Greek philosophy. His driving passion was to become all things to all men in order that he might save some (cf. 1 Cor. 9:22).

Effective churches will attempt to convey the message of the Gospel in a manner that is understandable to contemporary culture. The key to conveying the truth and the claims of Christ is building effective bridges of communication and understanding between believers and nonbelievers.

The criticism of contextualization is that theological compromise — almost by necessity — takes place. And certainly there are churches and leaders who have overstepped the biblical parameters in their zeal for relevance, but to dismiss the importance and need for contextualizing the *presentation* of the Gospel because of the risk of compromise is far from warranted or wise. Culture is not "neutral," as many critics are quick to point out, but neither do we find the presentation of the Gospel culture-free in the biblical materials.

Millard Erickson, building off of the insights of William E.

Hordern, offers a helpful distinction in the use of the terms "translation" versus "transformation." Every generation must "translate" the Gospel into its unique cultural context. This is very different than "transforming" the message of the Gospel, however, into something that was never intended by the biblical witness. Transformation of the message must be avoided at all costs. Translation, however, is necessary for a winsome and compelling presentation of the Gospel of Christ.[28]

Indeed, the translation of the Gospel into the forms of contemporary culture has been in the vanguard of every great evangelistic movement, beginning with the nontraditional methodology and culturally nuanced presentation of Jesus Himself. Luther translated the Bible into the common language of the people and used "drinking" songs for hymns; Ira Sankey used contemporary music (the "waltz") to draw crowds for Dwight L. Moody's crusades; and Billy Graham bravely went forth with his New York City crusade in the 1950s that crossed Protestant/Catholic lines.[29]

The Gospel has always been contextualized. In our modern world, method and style must be brought kicking and screaming into the twenty-first century or else we will lose our full potential for reaching the postmodern Generation X and beyond for Christ. While the message is timeless, the method is not, and we've confused traditionalism with orthodoxy far too long.

Too many churches operate on a 1950s American middle-class methodology and mind-set. But the culture of 1950s has obviously long since passed, and we can't use yesterday's tools in today's world and expect to build a church for tomorrow.

2. Relationships Must Be Built with Nonbelievers

The average nonbeliever is functionally insulated from the most common evangelistic approaches. As we noted above, they do not attend revivals. They are not appreciative of door-to-door visits. They do not see a "Jesus Loves You" bumper sticker and feel like pulling off to the side of the road and repenting.

They will be reached as believers intentionally build relationships with them and share a credible verbal witness. This is the most effective and impactive form of evangelism. It is as simple and profound as that.

The dilemma today is that few believers have active, healthy relationships with nonbelievers. The typical Christian cannot name three non-Christians they've shared a meal with in the last six months. We have withdrawn into holy huddles and Christian cliques. At times, in our politically and socially polarized environment, non-Christians are even viewed as the enemy.

But they are not the enemy, and the most effective means of evangelism is within the context of a personal relationship where the right to be heard has been won. Nothing is as powerful as a personal testimony and the visible difference of Jesus Christ in a life. In the postmodern world, we must recapture the idea that the kingdom of God is extended one person at a time.

3. Evangelism Should Be Understood as Process and Event — with a Renewed Emphasis on Process

Evangelism involves process *and* event. This is decisive for the modern church as the typical non-churched person is spiritually illiterate and far from able to comprehend (much less accept) the most elemental truths of the Christian faith. With this in mind, effective churches will create a context for the adoption process to take place in the lives of nonbelievers. The "event" of coming into a personal relationship with Christ as Lord and Savior is but the culmination of a spiritual pilgrimage as a "seeker."

As a result, effective churches will intentionally strive to cultivate and support this process. A context should be created in order to allow seekers to explore Christianity in a way that is conducive to the process leading to the "event." In essence, if the Gospel is indeed a scandal to the world, a safe place needs to be created for seekers to hear and explore a very unsafe message. The biblical basis for such an effort can be found in Jesus' parable of the sower (Matt. 13) and Paul's warning to the Corinthian church to be sensitive to nonbelievers in their worship (1 Cor. 14).

4. Maintain a Biblically Functioning Community

Jesus clearly maintained that there was a direct relationship between Christian unity and effective evangelism (John 13 and 17). He taught that the world's attention would be arrested if His followers would maintain relational unity. The postmodern Generation X, or the "Baby Busters," places a remarkably high value on community, and that holds great promise and opportunity for the church.

The dilemma is that community is seldom found within the contemporary church. Even if present, the unchurched do not perceive the church to offer much in that area. A recent survey of the unchurched in Charlotte, North Carolina, a city with over 600 churches, discovered that the second biggest reason for not attending church was perceived disunity within the churches. "Churches have too many problems," said one person, "and I've got enough problems in my life. I don't need to come to church and get more." Some put a different twist on it, saying "Churches are judgmental, inflexible and hypocritical toward people."[30]

Without unity, there cannot be growth. Without unity, we have little to offer the world that it does not already have. No church will be free of disagreement, but growing churches will handle it in the context of relational unity. Authenticity and genuine relationships will be decisive for the effective presentation of the Gospel. According to many observers of postmodern culture, "it is no longer enough to present the gospel's propositional truths. What will attract Xers, they say, is a strong, caring community of people who can be trusted."[31]

5. Apologetics Must Be Used—but Updated

The need for apologetics has never been greater, but the questions of the postmodern generation must be answered sensitively. No longer is the question "Is there a God?" but rather, "Which God?" The question is not "Was Jesus the Son of God?" but "How can I believe there's just one way to heaven?" "Is the Bible true?" has become "Is there truth?"

Current approaches to apologetics have been built from a certain set of presuppositions. To return to our evangelism scale, that group of people were on an "8." But they are no longer on an "8," but a "3," and this demands a radical change in our efforts. John R.W. Stott once commented to a small group that his classic book *Basic Christianity,* if written today, would have to be developed in an entirely different manner. When pressed as to a reason, he insightfully noted that he simply assumed a certain level of knowledge and belief that is not currently present. Postmodern apologetics will answer different questions and go back further to begin the conversation. Rather than begin with the truth and authority of Scripture, we now need to begin with the idea of truth itself.[32]

But it is not merely the questions that need changing, but the method and approach itself. Rather than telling people what to believe—a didactic approach—people must now be led to discover the truth for themselves through a more Socratic method. Leighton Ford is correct in encouraging younger evangelists to recapture the art of storytelling.[33]

6. Christianity Should Be Portrayed as Practical

The attention of many nonbelievers will not be initially arrested through truth, but through practical assistance. "Show me that it works," said one man, "and then we can talk about whether or not it's true." A twenty-one-year-old woman from Los Angeles writes, "Show me relevance. Help me deal with career decisions, morality, AIDS, dysfunctional families, substance abuse."[34] These are the questions of today's generation.

Again, this methodological shift could be misunderstood if not put in the context of an evangelistic strategy that remains firmly rooted in the proclamation of truth. The evangelistic move would be to demonstrate the practical relevance of the Bible to marriage, finances, and parenting. But rather than declare that it's truth because it works, we would maintain that it works because it is *true*. Therefore, practical relevance and application would be the doorway into the issue of truth in general.

7. A Vision of the Church's Mission Must Be Recaptured

There is little doubt that biblically, each church is called to a fourfold purpose: worship, ministry, discipleship, and evangelism. But the mission of the church is undeniably narrow: to seek and to save the lost (cf. Luke 19:10).

Surprisingly few people embrace this mission. Win Arn has estimated that 90 percent of all laypeople feel the mission of the church is to meet their needs, while only 10 percent feel that the church's mission is to win the world.

A renewed emphasis on this mission is what is behind many of the "seeker-targeted" churches. Simply put, seeker-sensitive churches target seekers. This approach has been sadly misunderstood and caricatured. Every church, consciously or not, has selected a primary "customer." For most churches, it is the "already convinced." One pastor informed me that his Baptist church could not grow any larger because there were no more Baptists in his area. Though this is an extreme, it betrays the underlying attitude of many churches and their leaders.

If this understanding of mission remains unaltered, then the cause of Christ for this generation will be greatly hindered. The reason is simple: the postmodern generation may very well be the most difficult generation in the history of Western civilization to reach with the Gospel. If we are unwilling to make the effort, or fail to even contend that the effort needs to be made, then failure is certain.

Frighteningly, this seems to be the prevailing mood. Most denominational statistics would report that over 90 percent of their church growth falls into two camps: biological and transfer. Biological growth is essentially "winning your own." The children of members and regular attenders become believers and follow in their parents' footsteps—a kind of "procreative evangelism," if you will. Transfer growth occurs as a result of a Christian moving into a new geographic area and joining a church, or a local believer deciding to change his or her church home.

Conclusion

Churches will have to continue celebrating both types of growth, but in terms of their own sense of mission, will need to make a conscious effort at prodigal growth and conversion growth. Prodigal growth is reaching those who have consciously given up on church, what we might term nominal Christians, but who may have a general belief in Christianity intact from their youth. Conversion growth is reaching those who are not interested in spiritual things, or who have rejected Christianity altogether.[35]

The church must respond to the social streams impacting contemporary society. This will require both informed and reformed methods of evangelism and apologetics. Our privatized, pluralized, and secularized postmodern world calls for the church to rethink its missionary and outreach strategies. New challenges open the door for new opportunities.

Charles Dickens wrote of a day that was "the best of times, it was the worst of times."[36] A similar sentiment could be shared about the postmodern world. Never has such a challenge been before us; never has the opportunity for making a difference been so great.

NOTES

1. Kenneth A. Myers, *All God's Children and Blue Suede Shoes: Christians and Popular Culture* (Westchester, Ill.: Crossway, 1989), xii.

2. On postmodern thought and culture, a number of books can be perused to varying degrees of satisfaction, such as the following: Gene Edward Veith, Jr., *Postmodern Times: A Christian Guide to Contemporary Thought and Culture* (Wheaton, Ill.: Crossway, 1994); Frederick B. Burnham, ed., *Postmodern Theology: Christian Faith in a Pluralist World* (New York: HarperCollins, 1989); David Ray Griffin, et al., *Varieties of Postmodern Theology* (Albany, N.Y.: State Univ. of New York Press, 1989).

3. Peter Berger, *The Sacred Canopy: Elements of a Sociological Theory of Religion* (Garden City, N.Y.: Anchor/Doubleday, 1969). Another treatment of these three

streams of modernity from a Christian perspective can be found in Andrew Walker, *Enemy Territory* (Lexington, Ky.: Bristol, 1991). An excellent analysis can also be found in Robert Wuthnow, *The Struggle for America's Soul: Evangelicals, Liberals, and Secularism* (Grand Rapids: Eerdmans, 1989).

4. Berger, *Sacred Canopy*, 107. See also David Martin, *A General Theory of Secularization* (Oxford: Blackwell, 1978); and Martin E. Marty, *The Modern Schism* (London: SCM, 1969).

5. Fred Fedler, *An Introduction to the Mass Media* (New York: Harcourt Brace Jovanovich, 1978), 8. On the impact of technology on contemporary culture, see O.B. Hardison, Jr., *Disappearing Through the Skylight: Culture and Technology in the Twentieth Century* (New York: Viking, 1989).

6. Page Smith, *Killing the Spirit: Higher Education in America* (New York: Viking, 1990), 5.

7. Berger, *Sacred Canopy*, 133–34; cf. Peter Berger, Brigitte Berger, and Hansfried Kellner, *The Homeless Mind* (Harmondsworth, Great Britain: Penguin, 1974), chap. 3.

8. Os Guinness, *The Gravedigger File: Papers on the Subversion of the Modern Church* (Downers Grove, Ill.: InterVarsity, 1983), 74; cf. Thomas Luckmann, *The Invisible Religion* (New York: Macmillan, 1967). Perhaps the best investigation into this dynamic of modernity was offered in Robert Bellah, et al., *Habits of the Heart: Individualism and Commitment in American Life* (San Francisco: Harper and Row, 1985). A recent chronicle of America's privatization of faith can be found in Phillip L. Berman, *The Search for Meaning: Americans Talk About What They Believe and Why* (New York: Ballantine, 1990).

9. On this, see the analysis offered by Lesslie Newbigin, *The Gospel in a Pluralist Society* (Grand Rapids: Eerdmans, 1990).

10. Theodore Roszak, *Where the Wasteland Ends* (Garden City, N.Y.: Anchor, 1973), 412.

11. Quoted in *Context* 15 (November 1981): 6.

12. As John Naisbitt and Patricia Aburdene note in *Megatrends 2000: Ten New Directions for the 1990's* (New York: William Morrow, 1990), for contemporary society, "Spirituality, Yes. Organized Religion, No" (p. 275). A similiar point is made by George Barna, *The Frog in the Kettle* (Ventura, Calif.: Regal, 1990), 41–42, 117.

13. Bellah, *Habits of the Heart*, 221.

14. Berger, *Sacred Canopy*, 127. The historical background to this stream of modernity is illuminated in Nathan O. Hatch, *The Democratization of American Christianity* (New Haven: Yale Univ. Press, 1989).

15. Guinness, *Gravedigger File*, 93.

16. Ibid., 94. The idea of religion as a canopy serves as the motif for Martin E. Marty's recent exploration of modern American religion, *Modern American Religion: The Irony of It All, 1893–1919* (Chicago: Univ. of Chicago Press, 1986), the first of four projected volumes on twentieth-century American religion.

17. David B. Barrett, *World Christian Encyclopedia: A Comparative Survey of Churches and Religions in the Modern World A.D. 1900–2000* (New York: Oxford Univ. Press, 1982).

18. Langdon Gilkey, *Through the Tempest: Theological Voyages in a Plural istic Culture* (Minneapolis: Fortress, 1991), 21.

19. Harold O.J. Brown, "Evangelicals and Social Ethics," in *Evangelical Affir-*

mations, ed. Kenneth S. Kantzer and Carl F.H. Henry (Grand Rapids: Zondervan/Academie, 1990), 279.

20. It should be noted that it is the process of pluralization which leads to the individuation which underlies the process of privatization. The reason for this is that inherent within pluralism is differentiation, and diversity inevitably leads toward individuation. On this, see Benton Johnson, "Modernity and Pluralism," in *Pushing the Faith: Proselytism and Civility in a Pluralistic World,* ed. Martin E. Marty and Frederick E. Greenspahn (New York: Crossroad, 1988), 14.

21. These four marks were first suggested to my thinking by Langdon Gilkey, *Naming the Whirlwind* (Indianapolis: Bobbs-Merrill, 1969); and most recently by Thomas C. Oden, *After Modernity . . . What? Agenda for Theology* (Grand Rapids: Zondervan/Academie, 1990).

22. See James Patterson and Peter Kim, *The Day America Told the Truth: What People Really Believe About Everything That Really Matters* (New York: Prentice-Hall, 1991).

23. Allan Bloom, *The Closing of the American Mind* (New York: Simon and Schuster, 1987), 25.

24. Oden, *After Modernity . . . What?* 74, 157.

25. See Andrés Tapia, "Reaching the First Post-Christian Generation," *Christianity Today,* 12 September 1994, 18.

26. George Barna, *Virtual America: The Barna Report for 1994–1995* (Ventura, Calif.: Regal, 1994), 82.

27. See Tapia, "Reaching the First Post-Christian Generation," 20.

28. See Millard J. Erickson, *Christian Theology,* one vol. ed. (Grand Rapids: Baker, 1983, 1984, 1985), 113–16.

29. On this, see the author's *Opening the Front Door* (Nashville: Convention, 1992).

30. Survey commissioned by Mecklenburg Community Church, Charlotte, North Carolina, performed by the Barna Research Group.

31. "Xers" refers to Generation X, the Baby Busters, born between 1963 and 1977, considered the first post-Christian generation. See Tapia, "Reaching the First Post-Christian Generation," 21. Insights into this generation can be found through Douglas Coupland, *Generation X: Tales for an Acclerated Culture* (New York: St. Martin's, 1991); Neil Howe and Bill Strauss, *13th Gen: Abort, Retry, Ignore, Fail* (New York: Vintage, 1991); and William Mahedy and Janet Bernardi, *A Generation Alone: Xers Making a Place in the World* (Downers Grove, Ill.: InterVarsity, 1993).

32. For a further discussion of this and other issues related to the topic of truth, see the author's *What Is Truth?* (Nashville: Broadman and Holman, 1994).

33. See Leighton Ford, *The Power of Story* (Downers Grove, Ill.: InterVarsity, 1994).

34. See Tapia, "Reaching the First Post-Christian Generation," 20.

35. See Eddie Gibbs, *In Name Only: Tackling the Problem of Nominal Christianity* (Wheaton, Ill.: Victor/BridgePoint, 1994).

36. Charles Dickens, *A Tale of Two Cities* (New York: Oxford Univ. Press, 1989), 1.

22

Proclamation
and the Postmodernist

Rick Gosnell

A great chasm exists between the church and contemporary society. The chasm reflects the church's inability to effectively communicate the Gospel message in today's culture. Our contention is that in order to evangelize those members of contemporary society who might be characterized as "postmodern" in their thinking, the church must evaluate its approach to ministry and mission in the twenty-first century.

This chapter will examine the methods of Christian proclamation in light of a postmodern paradigm. In particular, it will focus on the role of the laity in personal evangelism and offer some practical suggestions for preaching to postmodernists[1] in public worship.

The Postmodern Paradigm

Various scholars and writers offer diverse opinions regarding the emergence of the postmodern worldview.[2] Here we will utilize Hans Küng's helpful perspective on the postmodern worldview. Küng borrows from Thomas S. Kuhn and calls this transition phase a "paradigm change" in the wider context of society as a whole. A paradigm is a social construction of reality; it is a belief system that prevails in a certain community. Kuhn writes that when paradigms change, the world changes with them. Therefore, a major paradigm shift is constant with a leap into a new thought pattern — into a new worldview.[3]

Rick Gosnell is Pastor at Livingston First Baptist Church in Livingston, Alabama.

The modern (Enlightenment) paradigm is in transition to an emerging postmodern paradigm in which change occurs in the "entire constellation of beliefs, values, techniques, and so on, shared by the members of a given community."[4] An observable change is evident in the way people generally perceive themselves, society, the world, and ultimately God.

Küng insists that "postmodernity" is not a magic word that explains everything nor a polemical catchphrase, but a heuristic term.[5] "Postmodern" serves as a code for an epoch that has only just begun in this century, a period whose intrinsic value is acknowledged but has not quite been comprehended. Postmodernity is neither an apologetic for modernity nor a self-confident condemnation of it. The question of religion demonstrates, for Küng, that "modernity . . . is not — as it is for some reactionaries — a 'finished program' nor is it . . . an 'unfinished project,' rather, modernity is in transition, it is a paradigm that has grown old that must be built up anew."[6] Subsequently, we will use the word "postmodern" to designate a paradigm shift from the modern worldview. Some philosophical and ideological patterns once associated with the modern worldview have been reconsidered and reappropriated within a new paradigm, or a new worldview.

A Relativistic and Pluralistic Attitude

The postmodern worldview is relativistic — truth is relative. Jonathan Culler asserts, "As they [postmodern persons] see it, truth is either meaningless or arbitrary."[7] There is no place for universal reason in a postmodern world where all paradigms, or worldviews, are equal because each paradigm has its own logic.[8] Reason is also viewed as inconsistent with postmodern confidence in emotion, feeling, introspection, intuition, autonomy, creativity, imagination, fantasy, and contemplation.[9]

The relativist believes that there is an irreducible plurality of conceptual schemes. Furthermore, there is no substantive overarching framework or single meta language by which persons can "rationally adjudicate or univocally evaluate competing claims of alternative paradigms."[10] There is *nothing* that might be labeled the standard of rationality.

Religious truth is perceived as a "special kind of truth and not an eternal and perfect representation of cosmic reality."[11] The task of enforcing a single official reality construct is extremely difficult in the postmodern world. The polarization is a division between *different kinds* of beliefs, rather than between different beliefs.[12] What is true is defined by what persons believe.[13]

A Revised Interaction between the Text and the Reader

The first signal of an approaching doom for the modern era came in the 1930s in the form of an intellectual movement that came to be known as the New Criticism.[14] The New Criticism said to the reader, "The poem is yours. Read it. Read it *closely,* and find its meaning right there, in the poet's own words. . . . This meant staying close to the text—sometimes chewing through it word by word, thought by thought—rather than straying too far into history or biography."[15] Instructors in academia began to teach that there were several ways to interpret a literary work. Some of these methods, notably reader-response theory, located meaning in the experience of the reader. Meaning does not inhere in a text; it resides in the interaction between the text and reader. The modern objectification of the text has given way to a postmodern hermeneutical paradigm of understanding the text through participative dialogue.[16] One reads for the pleasure of the experience, not in pursuit of truth or knowledge.

The importance of the author is diminished in the postmodern. The demise of the author symbolizes a decline of responsibility and a protest against author(ity). Postmodernism privileges the text and elevates the reader. Readers are given the power to define and create textual meaning.[17] Since postmodernists diminish the importance of the author as a writer of texts, they spend little energy on discovering what the "author really meant."[18]

No Subject-Object Dichotomy

The emergence of a new postmodern paradigm is accompanied by the end of epistemologically centered philosophy. This new postmodern paradigm means the end of "the subject" and the "objective world."[19] The postmodern paradigm refuses to make distinctions and divisions between body and soul, the physical and the mental, reason and the irrational, the intellectual and the sensual, the self and the other, nature and culture, and reality and utopia.[20] All that modernity has set aside, including emotions, feelings, intuition, reflection, speculation, personal experience, custom, metaphysics, tradition, cosmology, magic, myth, religious sentiment, and mystical experience, takes on renewed importance in the postmodern paradigm.[21]

Postmodernists affirm the ontological continuity between the knowing human subject and the objective world which the human subject knows.[22] Because of their interest in the self as it relates to others, to nature, and to the world, they move beyond epistemology into ethics and advocate programs for personal transformation, solving the ecological problem, defusing the nuclear threat, and establishing world peace.[23] Postmodern thought provides support for the ecology, peace, feminist, and other emancipatory movements. Postmodernists are "societally conscious."[24] The "societally conscious" are pro-nature and post-materialist.

A Religious but Non-ecclesial Orientation

The postmodern paradigm reveals that most persons are not so much believers as they are "possessors of beliefs."[25] The adventures that matter to postmodernists are the adventures of the private life.[26] Their own personal insights and views are more important than those of organized religion. They are believers without belonging. A person does not have to go to church to be a good Christian. With their inner direction, they will not respond to shoulds, oughts, obligations, or appeals for long-term commitments.[27]

Noninstitutional religion is preferred as an alternative to modern, organized mainstream religions. Postmodernists are communal by choice; it appears that they either desire community or they do not desire community. For the postmodernist, religion is not equated with the local church. Religion has a meaning that transcends the individual and the local congregation.[28]

The shift in worldview from the modern to the postmodern paradigm challenges the church—as the people of God—to evaluate its methods of proclamation. The methods which were effective in reaching persons for Christ under the rubric of the modern paradigm may not be effective, or as effective, within that of its postmodern successor.

Methods and Tools of Personal Witness
in Light of a Postmodern Paradigm

Since postmodernists exhibit a non-ecclesial orientation, the role of the laity is extremely important in communicating the Christian message to them. George Hunter insists, "It is even more important to recover the apostolate of the laity than the apostolate of the clergy."[29] Hunter further points out, "The laity have a better opportunity than the clergy to reach undiscipled people. . . . Church laity have many more bridges to undiscipled people than church professionals could ever duplicate."[30]

Laity is a word derived from *laos,* a Greek word meaning people. Laity includes all people who believe and are committed to Jesus as Savior and Lord. The doctrine of the priesthood of all believers also means that every Christian is a minister. Findley Edge avows, "The doctrine of the priesthood of all believers means that the primary responsibility for God's ministry in the world rests upon the shoulders of the layperson and not upon the shoulders of the clergy."[31] Every believer is a servant in the priesthood of Christ. Robert Coleman asserts, "Whether one is considered clergy or laity makes no difference in the world of evangelism."[32] The church as a whole has been entrusted with the ministry of evangelization.

Lesslie Newbigin proposes a "declericalized" [lay] theology for contemporary culture.[33] According to Newbigin, "It is . . . important that all its [the church's] lay members be prepared and equipped to think out the relationship of their faith to their secular work."[34] The missionary encounter occurs in their secular work.

What methodology should be utilized by the laity in its outreach to undiscipled people? In the remainder of this section we will discuss the deductive and inductive models of Christian witness, the spiritual autobiography, and the personal testimony as tools for lay witnessing.

Deductive and Inductive Models of Christian Witness

The literature on evangelism offers two basic approaches to Christian witness: the deductive and the inductive. The deductive model takes many forms; however, it generally emphasizes three stages. First, the witness announces a general Gospel to another person. Second, the witness appeals to this person for an umbrella commitment to the general Gospel that has been shared. Third, it is presupposed that if the person accepts this general Gospel, he or she will later work out the implications of this commitment throughout his or her life.[35]

Deductive methodology is concerned primarily with the accurate proclamation of the Good News; its secondary concern is persuading non-Christians to become Christians; and its tertiary concern is to exhibit a Christian presence. The deductive method focuses primarily on the content of the Christian message to be shared.[36] It would tend to view the "gospel as a set of true propositions to be rationally presented and to be assented to intellectually."[37] Deductive evangelism is more geared to persons who are high in their receptivity to the Gospel's message. Chronological time *(chronos),* or a short-term propositional approach, tends to be emphasized in the deductive approach.

The inductive model begins with the particular and moves to the general.[38] George Hunter points out:

It [the inductive model] has four basic stages. (1) The witnesser discovers, or the person shares, some particular need for which the gospel is relevant. (2) The witnesser then shares a particular point or facet of the gospel that is relevant to the need. (3) The witnesser appeals to the person for a commitment — response to the facet that has been shared. (4) The witnesser knows that God will be involved in the process of evangelization.[39]

Inductive methodology accentuates presence, persuasion, and proclamation more or less in that order. Establishing credibility is crucial for those who prefer the inductive approach. Much of their persuading is done before the Gospel is ever verbally shared. The inductive method focuses more on context instead of content; the context will determine what is to be shared and when it will be shared. The inductive approach is concerned more with seasonal time *(kairos)* than chronological time *(chronos)*. Long-term relationship building is more important than a short-term propositional approach. The inductive approach is more geared toward persons who are low in their receptivity to the Gospel.[40]

George Hunter has refined the inductive approach into two operational models: an Inductive-Grace model and an Inductive-Mission model.[41] Hunter utilizes Maslow's hierarchy of needs which demonstrates a hierarchical understanding of human motivation. The following needs are identified and presented in order from lowest to highest: physiological, safety and security, love and belonging, esteem (self-esteem and esteem from others), self-realization, aesthetic, and worldview.[42]

The Inductive-Grace model is designed to approach human beings who are on the lower levels of Maslow's hierarchy. Perhaps they have some physiological needs which are unmet, or they feel unloved or unwanted. The grace model is operative when one encounters a person exhibiting behavior driven by a lower level need. Hunter sets forth the model in four stages:

(1) You establish a relationship of trust with the individual, and in the context of this established fellowship you discover or the person shares some need for which a facet of the gospel is relevant. (2) You then share and explain that facet of the gospel that is relevant to the need now driving this person. (3) You appeal to the person to open his being and to

receive this particular resource of the gospel at this particular point in his life. (4) You trust that if the person does respond, God will honor the process and the person will indeed taste the grace of God.[43]

The Inductive-Mission model is offered to those who are on the higher level of Maslow's hierarchy of needs and enables them to meet these motivational needs through service to others. The Inductive-Mission model operates in three stages. First, the witness shares with the undiscipled person a certain Christian cause involving the needs of a person, an environmental issue, or a political issue within the community. Second, the witness appeals to the undiscipled person to join the Christian cause and explains the reasons for engaging in such a cause. Third, the witness believes that if undiscipled persons participate in the Christian cause they will experience the kingdom of God and that experience will be in some way self-authenticating and lead them to faith in God.

Since postmodernists subscribe to a holistic approach to life in general—no dichotomy between the body and soul—they are more inclined to become involved in social action and social ministries advocated and supported by the church in its community. Postmodern people express very religious concerns such as the need for meaning and purpose in life, the need for significance, the need to make a contribution, and the need to be needed. They want to be involved in the needs of the community and contribute to the betterment of society. Because of the postmodernists' inclination toward social involvement and interest in social issues, the church which more actively and visibly practices holistic evangelism in the community will attract them, engage them in some ministries, and have opportunity to share with them the Gospel message.

The Spiritual Autobiography and Personal Testimony

Delos Miles defines the spiritual autobiography as a person's firsthand religious experience as it relates to the Gospel story.[44] The spiritual autobiography is an attempt to interpret, through narrative form, a deep religious experience in one's life story. The spiritual autobiography, however, does not focus merely on one moment of religious experience, but upon the broad spectrum of one's life story and how the religious aspect is interwoven within the whole. Miles observes that the autobiography has been utilized in evangelism from the earliest days of Christian history.[45] The autobiography has a prominent place in the witness of the church. Paul tells the story of his conversion three times on three different occasions. It is an effective way to present the Gospel story because it communicates with authority, variety, and interest from an incarnational stance.[46]

The personal testimony is a brief presentation of "one or two clips out of one's spiritual lifescript."[47] A testimony is an account of what someone experiences or sees. Michael Green observes that the personal testimony was an important tool of evangelism in the early church.[48]

In the testimony witnesses describe their lives before receiving Christ, how they received Him, and how receiving Christ has made their life meaningful. The testimony is a useful tool in evangelism for several reasons. First, every Christian has a testimony. Second, the testimony is always relevant and up-to-date. Third, the testimony gives the non-Christian firsthand information about the witness. Fourth, the personal testimony really communicates. It is intriguing, interesting, and opens up conversation. Fifth, it is a very natural thing to do; it is simple, everyone can do it. Sixth, it brings Christianity out of the expected area — out of the church building into the real world. It helps the non-Christian see Christ at work in someone else's life today.

When the appropriate moment for sharing their faith arrives, laypersons can share about God's love through the spiritual autobiography or the personal testimony. The postmodernist believes that life is a "matter of telling ourselves stories about life and this story making is not just about human life, but is human life."[49] Through the telling of stories persons give themselves identity.[50] Thomas Boomershine points out, "In the end of the resurrection narrative in Mark 16:1-8 each person is called to tell the story. . . . Telling the story is the calling of every follower of Jesus in daily life."[51] These personal stories about the Christian life have a tremendous impact when using the inductive method of personal witness — which occurs in the context of relationships between persons who live and work together. The stories about the good news of Christ's love are most meaningful when they are told by one person to another in a context of personal relationship.

Postmodernists will be open to hearing the stories of other persons because these stories give purpose and shape social existence. Because the postmodernist diminishes the role of the author and the importance of the individual, the spiritual autobiography and personal testimony can exalt God and not the person. Postmodern people are not anti-religious but anti-ecclesial; therefore, they may be open to the spiritual autobiography and personal testimony. Each of these tools may provide a point of contact or identification with the undiscipled person's life.

Methods of Proclamation in Worship

Public proclamation is another means by which the Christian message is communicated to postmodernists. The following methods of public proclamation are considered: deductive and inductive preaching, biblical preaching, stories in preaching, and calling for commitments.

The Deductive and Inductive Methods of Preaching

Here we will describe the deductive and inductive methods of preaching and draw some conclusions about which methodology is more appropriate for communicating with the postmodern generation.[52] The deductive and inductive methods of preaching are concerned primarily with the movement of thought.

The deductive method. Deductive reasoning moves from a general principle or truth to a particular application or experience. The deductive method of reasoning begins by "stating the thesis, breaking it down into points or sub-theses, explaining and illustrating these points, and applying them to the particular situation of the hearers."[53] The main point is presented first and then disaggregated into particulars. The major premise is accepted and authoritative and the rest of the sermon specifically supports that general premise.[54]

There are some general advantages to the deductive method of preaching. It begins with authority, and some people want authority. Deductive reasoning is appropriate if listeners are in agreement with the speaker and if the listeners accept the authority of the Bible, the church, and the preacher. In deductive preaching, however, there is no dialogue, no listening by the speaker, and no contributing by the hearer.

The inductive method. Inductive movement begins with the particulars of life experiences and points toward principles, concepts, and conclusions.[55] Induction is based upon cumulative examples and proceeds from specific instances to formulate a general principle. Examples are cumulative until a principle or generalization is reached.[56] Craddock insists, "The inductive process is fundamental to the American way of life. . . . Everyone lives inductively, not deductively."[57] People are concerned with specifics. For example, people are more concerned with the death of someone very close to them than the theological nature of mortality. In the parables Jesus did not make a call for faith in general, but in relation to a specific life situation. For Jesus, the subject matter was not the nature of God but the hearer's situation in light of God. The role of the listener is crucial in inductive movement. Craddock asserts, "Christian responsibilities are not . . . predicated upon the exhortations of a particular minister . . . but upon the intrinsic force of the hearer's own reflection."[58] The speaker seeks to lead rather than push. The speaker explores with the listeners before explaining what they have found. Inductive preaching is "a quest for discovery."[59] Inductive preaching lays out the evidence and the examples and postpones the conclusions until the listeners have a chance to weigh the evidence, think through the implications, and then come to the conclusion with the preacher at the end of the sermon. In fact, the hearer is allowed to complete the sermon. The sermon becomes part of the listener's experience.

The preacher, in the inductive method, serves as a "player-coach" or "group leader of an exploration party."[60] The preacher seeks to guide the listeners from where they are to where they need to be without any great show of authority or coercion. The listener is allowed to "assume a measure of authority in the process of reaching conclusions."[61] Instead of beginning with truths and proving those truths, the inductive preacher helps the listeners see the truth in such a way that they are "ready to accept, agree with, and respond to that truth at the end of the sermon."[62] The inductive method "invites the hearers to make a series of small discoveries about the biblical text building toward a larger 'So that's what this passage is saying to us!'"[63] Lewis claims, "We will never *convince* others with our preaching; we can only help them to convince themselves."[64]

The deductive method of preaching is too rational and seeks to prove what is determined to be true by the speaker. The major premise is accepted as authoritative by both the speaker and the listener. Postmodernists, however, will not accept the authority of the speaker; they protest against authority. Because truth is relative for them they may not accept the guidance from a perceived authority figure and prefer to reach their own conclusions. If the text is the authority then they will give their attention to its presentation. The deductive method does not allow for any dialogue between the speaker and the audience. The hearer is not allowed to contribute. The postmodern audience prefers participative dialogue with the text and

the sermon. Deductive preaching in which the propositional statements are supported by stories will be more appealing than the
deductive approach alone.

The inductive method of preaching will be appealing to the
postmodernist. The inductive approach does not begin with a principle, or doctrine, but with examples. The role of the listener is accen-
tuated in the inductive approach. The hearer is allowed to reflect,
through participative dialogue, on the sermon. There is no subject-
object dichotomy between the sermon and the hearer. The sermon is
not an object to be observed from a distance. The hearers are allowed
to make the sermon a part of their personal experience. The speaker
allows the hearers to weigh the evidence and reach their own conclusions. The sermon becomes part of the listener's experience. The inductive approach allows persons to convince themselves. The inductive method enables postmodern people to involve their emotions, feelings, introspection, intuition, creativity, imagination, fantasy, and contemplation to make the sermon relevant for themselves.
Meaning resides in the experience between the hearer and the
sermon.

Biblical Preaching

Herb Miller suggests that vital congregations use biblical preaching.[65]
According to Miller, a biblical sermon is one that contains a high
percentage of biblical content. Postmodernists are receptive to the
Bible as a text which involves them and a text with which they can
enter into genuine dialogue. The modern objective was to derive
from the biblical text historically accurate accounts about the persons, events, and religious understanding of the ancient times in
which the texts were produced and about which they spoke. The
modern agenda was to discover the original intent of the author.
Postmodernists, however, are interested in how the text can be personally meaningful to them today regardless of the original intent.

The communicator can preach from the creation accounts of Genesis and emphasize the relationship between humanity and the created order. Both humans and the environment were created by God
and were intended to exist in harmony. The communicator can
preach from the prophetic books of the Old Testament—such as
Isaiah, Jeremiah, Amos, and Micah—where justice is emphasized
inside both the religious and cultural spheres of existence. The communicator can preach from the Gospels and focus on the humanity of
Jesus. Postmodernists are interested in understanding how Jesus'

ethical lifestyle and holistic approach to life and ministry are applicable for them in today's world. The biblical stories take on renewed meaning in the context and life of the reader.

The Revelation of John can be appealing to the postmodern hearer. James Blevins offers a postmodern interpretation of the Book of Revelation.[66] Blevins illustrates the postmodern belief that meaning does not inhere in a text; it resides in the interaction between the text and reader. Blevins offers a fresh and exciting interpretation of the biblical text and suggests some contemporary applications for the twentieth century. The text is not objectified, but gives way to a postmodern hermeneutical paradigm of understanding the text through participative dialogue. Blevins portrays Revelation as a drama with seven acts. He presents within each act a contemporary interpretation of the apocalyptic events. Revelation 8:7 through 9:15 contains various apocalyptic plagues which Blevins reinterprets and for which he suggests a postmodern application. His interpretation of this section focuses upon two issues which are of vital concern to postmodernists: the environment and social justice. The text becomes the lens through which the person can see nature, human beings, and God. Through a dialogical encounter with the Revelation of John, as Blevins presents it, the reader and text are mutually transformed. The text is allowed to have multiple meanings and the reader is given opportunity for a new interpretation. Blevins' novel interpretation does not stress dogmatism, rather it stresses realities associated with contemporary, postmodern life.

Use Stories in Preaching

Postmodernists are interested in stories. Harvey Cox insists, "Postmodern theology will thrive on stories."[67] Boomershine claims:

> Story is a primary language of experience. Telling and listening to a story has the same structure as our experience. . . . The episodes of our lives take place one after another just like a story. One of the ways we know each other is by telling our stories. We live in stories.[68]

Stories allow the speaker to contemporize the Gospel message. Bruce Salmon points out:

> To speak of contemporizing then, is to speak of restorying the gospel. Propositional statements may be necessary for

theology, for exegesis, but they are not adequate for preaching. To say, "You are forgiven," or "God loves you," apart from the biblical story is almost meaningless. Similarly, to simply repeat the biblical story without making contact with our stories is not enough. But to connect the biblical events with the nitty-gritty happenings of our lives, ah, that is occasion for grace![69]

Good stories convey truth because they provide the auditor with a picture of reality. Stories are attractive because they somehow illumine the listener's own life. Stories allow persons to reflect upon their own stories and find answers to their own problems.[70]

Salmon observes that stories can be used in deductive, narrative, or inductive sermons to increase preaching effectiveness.[71] Stories may be used deductively as examples to demonstrate a truth, or they may be used inductively as illustrations to point analogically to a truth.[72] Preachers using the deductive approach can state a truth and then use a story as an example to support the general proposition. A narrative form of preaching would allow for the use of the spiritual autobiography as a sermonic device in which to communicate the good news of Christ's love. Preachers using the inductive approach can tell a story and some aspect of the story is used analogically to move the hearer to a new level of understanding.

Again, Salmon points out, "Stories may be able to teach, console, and persuade more effectively than any other form of communication. Stories can focus experience even more forcefully than actual events."[73] Good stories can be used to overcome the dichotomy between thought and feeling. Stories which deal with relational experiences can be utilized to stress the need for community service, social activities, holistic approaches to nature, and social action with respect to the responsibility for liberation, social justice, and ecological protection.

Calling for Commitments

Ronald J. Allen claims that inductive preaching works better when seeking to challenge persons.[74] The inductive sermon invites the listener to "identify sympathetically with the data of experience. The sermon brings these data into conversation and confrontation with appropriate theological resources."[75] Therefore, if communicators want to challenge postmodern people to make commitments, whatever they may be, they should preach inductively.

The objective of the commitment must be specific and, as we noted earlier, may best be related to specific hands-on tasks in social service and justice ministries. Postmodernists will commit to become actively engaged in projects which they support — environmental, justice, and service issues in the community. This preliminary commitment can, in turn, provide a believer with the opportunity to utilize the Inductive-Mission model of Christian witness. Through the efforts of the believer's witness and the work of the Holy Spirit, the postmodernist may eventually commit his or her life to Christ and the work of the kingdom. Contemporary believers must be patient when seeking responses from postmodernists.

Conclusion

The emergence of the postmodern paradigm indicates that people have lost faith in the philosophies and ideologies of the modern period. Diogenes Allen and Jerry Gill indicate that the emergence of the postmodern era creates an openness to faith.[76] Hunter points out, "Individuals who have lost faith in anything — a religion, a philosophy, a lover, a drug, a pipe dream, a utopian promise, or in themselves — tend to look for something new upon which to norm and inform their lives."[77] Changes in a person's life and thought patterns can open doors that stimulate an openness to previously screened out messages.

The laity will play a significant role in communicating the Gospel to a postmodernist society. The laity should use the Inductive-Mission model, the spiritual autobiography, and the personal testimony when witnessing to postmodernists. The inductive method of public proclamation, in which stories are utilized, will be more appealing to postmodernists than the deductive method. The postmodernists' willingness to hear the Gospel does not imply that they will necessarily receive it and become a part of the kingdom of God. This willingness, however, opens a door to communication that has been closed for decades.

NOTES

1. The term postmodernist is used as a synonym for "postmodern person" or anyone adhering to a postmodern worldview.

2. For various opinions see the following: Pauline Marie Rosenau, *Post- Modernism and the Social Sciences: Insights, Inroads, and Intrusions* (Princeton: Princeton Univ. Press, 1992), 5; Diogenes Allen, *Christian Belief in a Postmodern World: The Full Wealth of Conviction* (Louisville: Westminster/ John Knox, 1989), 4; Walter

Truett Anderson, *Reality Isn't What It Used to Be: Theatrical Politics, Ready-to-Wear Religion, Global Myths, Primitive Chic, and Other Wonders of the Postmodern World* (San Francisco: HarperCollins, 1990), 44; Andreas Muyssen, "Mapping the Postmodern," *New German Review* 33 (Fall 1984): 22–52; Todd Gitlin, "The Postmodern Predicament," *The Wilson Quarterly* 13 (Summer 1989): 73; Anthony Giddens, *The Consequences of Modernity* (Stanford: Stanford Univ. Press, 1990), 51; Matei Calinescu, *Five Faces of Modernity* (Durham, N.C.: Duke Univ. Press, 1987), 265; Philip Cooke, *Back to the Future* (London: Unwin Hyman, 1990), x; and Bryan S. Turner, "Periodization and Politics in the Postmodern," in *Theories of Modernity and Postmodernity,* ed. Bryan S. Turner (London: SAGE, 1990), 11.

3. Thomas S. Kuhn, *The Structure of Scientific Revolutions* (Chicago: Univ. of Chicago Press, 1970), 111.

4. Hans Küng, "The Reemergence of the Sacred: Transmitting Religious Traditions in a Post-Modern World," *Conservative Judaism* 40 (Summer 1988): 11.

5. Ibid., 10.

6. Ibid., 17.

7. Jonathan Culler, *On Deconstruction: Theory and Criticism after Structuralism* (Ithaca, N.Y.: Cornell Univ. Press, 1982), 22.

8. Rosenau, *Post-Modernism and the Social Sciences,* 128. See also Huston Smith, *Beyond the Post-Modern Mind* (Wheaton, Ill.: Theosophical, 1989), 233; idem, "Postmodernism's Impact on the Study of Religion," *Journal of the American Academy of Religion* 58 (1990): 660.

9. Rosenau, *Post-Modernism and the Social Sciences,* 129.

10. Richard J. Bernstein, *Beyond Objectivism and Relativism: Science, Hermeneutics, and Praxis* (Oxford: Blackwell, 1983), 8.

11. Anderson, *Reality Isn't What It Used to Be,* 8.

12. Ibid., 19.

13. Anderson cautions the reader concerning one negative effect of relativism and pluralism by stating that "once we let go of absolutes, nobody gets to have a position that is anything more than a position. Nobody gets to speak for God, nobody gets to speak for American values, nobody gets to speak for nature" (Anderson, *Reality Isn't What It Used to Be,* 183).

14. Ibid., 80.

15. Ibid., 81. See also Cooke, *Back to the Future,* 96. Cooke writes, "Knowledge derives from the interrogation of texts. . . ."

16. The hermeneutic for the postmodern person is one of a post-critical appropriation of texts which makes contemporary life meaningful and which fosters a sense of cultural unity over time—a second naivete.

17. Rosenau, *Post-Modernism and the Social Sciences,* 20–21.

18. Ibid., 32.

19. Gary Brent Madison, *The Hermeneutics of Postmodernity: Figures and Themes* (Bloomington, Ind.: Indiana Univ. Press, 1990), x. The objective world is one which is fully what it is in itself and which simply waits around for a cognizing subject to come along and form a mental representation of it.

20. Ibid., 61.

21. Gerald Graff, *Literature against Itself* (Chicago: Univ. of Chicago Press, 1979), 32–33. See also Axel O. Hirschman, "The Search for Paradigms as a Hindrance to Understanding," in *Interpretive Social Sciences: A Second Look,* ed. Paul

Rainbow and William M. Sullivan (Berkeley: Univ. of California Press, 1987).

22. Ted Peters, "Toward Postmodern Theology, Part 1," *Dialog* 24 (1985): 223.

23. David Ray Griffin, *God and Religion in the Postmodern World: Essays in Postmodern Theology* (Albany, N.Y.: State Univ. of New York Press, 1989), x. See also Wade Clark Roof, *A Generation of Seekers: The Spiritual Journeys of the Baby Boom Generation* (New York: HarperCollins, 1993), 22–23, 66.

24. This term is borrowed from Tex Sample, *U.S. Lifestyles and Mainline Churches: A Key to Reaching People in the 90's* (Louisville: Westminster/John Knox, 1990), 25–28. Sample describes various lifestyle groups within the United States. The "societally conscious," a subcategory within the Cultural Left, are deeply concerned about social issues. Conservation, consumer matters, environmental integrity, social justice, and peace issues are among the key interests of the "societally conscious." They believe in the integrity of nature, that it is not to be dominated but cooperated with, that it has a wisdom of its own, that the world really is one, and that in a materialistic society the nonmaterial dimensions of living are richer and more meaningful.

25. Anderson, *Reality Isn't What It Used to Be*, 9.

26. Gitlin, "The Postmodern Predicament," 75. See also Roof, *A Generation of Seekers*, 16.

27. Sample, *U.S. Lifestyles and Mainline Churches*, 32.

28. Robert N. Bellah et al., *Habits of the Heart: Individualism and Commitment in American Life* (Berkeley: Univ. of California Press, 1985), 226.

29. George Hunter, *How to Reach Secular People* (Nashville: Abingdon, 1992), 113.

30. Ibid., 114.

31. Findley B. Edge, *The Doctrine of the Laity* (Nashville: Convention, 1985), 45. See also Bill J. Leonard, "The Church and the Laity," *Review and Expositor* 85 (1988): 627.

32. Robert E. Coleman, "Theology of Evangelism," *Review and Expositor* 77 (1980): 478. See also Robert E. Coleman, *They Meet the Master: A Study Manual on the Personal Evangelism of Jesus* (Wilmore, Ky.: Asbury Theological Seminary, 1973), 8, where he insists that every Christian is to demonstrate the Gospel. For more on Coleman's position related to lay evangelism see Robert E. Coleman, "The Great Commission Life-Style," in *Evangelism on the Cutting Edge*, ed. Robert E. Coleman (Old Tappan, N.J.: Revell, 1986), 141.

33. Lesslie Newbigin, *Foolishness to the Greeks: The Gospel and Western Culture* (Grand Rapids: Eerdmans, 1986), 141. See also Carlyle Marney, *Priests to Each Other* (Valley Forge, Pa.: Judson, 1974), 14; and Dieter T. Hessel, *Social Ministry*, 2nd ed. (Louisville: Westminster/John Knox, 1992), 19. For another good source on the laity see Richard J. Mouw, *Called to Holy Worldliness* (Philadelphia: Fortress, 1980).

34. Ibid., 143.

35. Examples of this approach are: Continuing Witness Training (C.W.T.) and Witness Involvement Now (W.I.N.) of Southern Baptists, James Kennedy's Evangelism Explosion (E.E.), and Campus Crusade's Lay Institutes for Evangelism (L.I.F.E.).

36. Delos Miles, "A Wholesome and Intelligent Evangelism," *Faith and Mission* 2 (Spring 1985): 30.

37. Delos Miles, *Evangelism and Social Involvement* (Nashville: Broadman, 1986), 136.

38. For an excellent discussion of the inductive model of Christian witnessing see the following: Delos Miles, *Introduction to Evangelism* (Nashville: Broadman, 1983), 254–58; idem, "A Wholesome and Intelligent Evangelism," 29–31; idem, *Evangelism and Social Involvement,* 135–38; and George Hunter, *The Contagious Congregation: Frontiers in Evangelism and Church Growth* (Nashville: Abingdon, 1979), 45–51.

39. Hunter, *Contagious Congregation,* 45.

40. Several proponents of the inductive approach are: Ralph Neighbour, Wayne McDill, W. Oscar Thompson, Rebecca Manley Pippert, Jim Peterson, and Richard Stoll Armstrong. See these resources: Ralph W. Neighbour, Jr. and Cal Thomas, *Target-Group Evangelism* (Nashville: Broadman, 1975), 17–18; Wayne McDill, *Making Friends for Christ* (Nashville: Broadman, 1979), 68–87; W. Oscar Thompson, *Concentric Circles of Concern* (Nashville: Broadman, 1981), 13; Rebecca Manley Pippert, *Out of the Salt-Shaker and into the World* (Downers Grove, Ill.: InterVarsity, 1979), 127–51; Jim Peterson, *Evangelism as a Lifestyle* (Colorado Springs: NavPress, 1980), 42–43; idem, *Living Proof: Sharing the Gospel Naturally* (Colorado Springs: NavPress, 1989); Richard S. Armstrong, *Service Evangelism* (Philadelphia: Westminster, 1979), 51–69.

41. Hunter, *Contagious Congregation,* 45.

42. Hunter, *How to Reach Secular People,* 141. For Maslow's discussion on this topic see Abraham H. Maslow, *Motivation and Personality* (New York: Harper and Row, 1970), chaps. 3–4.

43. Hunter, *Contagious Congregation,* 47.

44. Miles, *Introduction to Evangelism,* 161.

45. Ibid., 162–63. Miles contends that the New Testament may be considered an evangelistic autobiography of the twelve apostles and Paul. The "we" sections of Acts (Acts 16:10; 20:5) may be considered evangelistic autobiographies.

46. Ibid., 163.

47. Green, *Evangelism in the Early Church,* 117. For more details on the personal testimony see Michael Green, *Evangelism through the Local Church: A Comprehensive Guide to All Aspects of Evangelism* (Nashville: Oliver-Nelson, 1992), 496–541; and G. William Schweer, *Personal Evangelism for Today* (Nashville: Broadman, 1988), 80–83.

48. Green, *Evangelism in the Early Church,* 206–7.

49. Anderson, *Reality Isn't What It Used to Be,* 102.

50. Madison, *Hermeneutic of Postmodernity,* 95–96.

51. Thomas E. Boomershine, *Story Journey: An Invitation to the Gospel as Storytelling* (Nashville: Abingdon, 1985), 194.

52. It is important to note that I am focusing completely upon the *method* of presenting the Gospel and not the content of the message.

53. Charles H. Kraft, *Communication Theory for Christian Witness* (Maryknoll, N.Y.: Orbis, 1991), 110.

54. H.C. Brown, Jr., Gordon Clinard, and Jesse J. Northcutt, *Steps to the Sermon: A Plan for Sermon Preparation* (Nashville: Broadman, 1963), 108.

55. Ralph L. Lewis and Gregg Lewis, *Inductive Preaching: Helping People Listen* (Westchester, Ill.: Crossway, 1983), 32, 43. See also Brown, Clinard, and Northcutt, *Steps to the Sermon,* 109. Brown, Clinard, and Northcutt explain that in the inductive method the thesis or general truth is presented after specific instances have been

presented one by one to lead up to the generalization. In the deductive order the thesis looks forward to the material that is to come; in the inductive order the thesis looks backward to the material already presented.

56. Ralph L. Lewis, *Persuasive Preaching Today* (Ann Arbor, Mich.: Litho-Crafters, 1979), 164.

57. Fred B. Craddock, *As One without Authority,* 3rd ed. (Nashville: Abingdon, 1989), 58, 60. See also Lewis, *Inductive Preaching,* 47.

58. Craddock, *As One without Authority,* 58.

59. Lewis and Lewis, *Inductive Preaching,* 32.

60. Ibid., 45.

61. Ralph L. Lewis, "Proclaiming the Gospel Inductively," *Review and Expositor* 84 (1987): 52.

62. Lewis and Lewis, *Inductive Preaching,* 81.

63. Thomas G. Long, *The Witness of Preaching* (Louisville: Westminster/ John Knox, 1989), 82.

64. Lewis and Lewis, *Inductive Preaching,* 106.

65. Herb Miller, *The Vital Congregation* (Nashville: Abingdon, 1990), 38. Miller defines a vital congregation as one which carries out the ministry of Jesus Christ by saying and doing what Jesus said and did. This ministry helps people (1) form a spiritual connection with God; (2) form a loving connection with other people; and (3) form a committed connection with great causes.

66. James L. Blevins, *Revelation as Drama* (Nashville: Broadman, 1984). See also James L. Blevins, *Revelation* (Atlanta: John Knox, 1984).

67. Harvey Cox, *Religion in the Secular City: Toward a Postmodern Theology* (New York: Simon and Schuster, 1984), 213.

68. Boomershine, *Story Journey,* 18.

69. Bruce C. Salmon, *Storytelling in Preaching: A Guide to the Theory and Practice* (Nashville: Broadman, 1988), 33–34. Salmon asserts that preaching should include both stories and explanations because the Gospel story raises questions which cannot be adequately answered solely by more stories.

70. Lewis and Lewis, *Inductive Preaching,* 160.

71. Salmon, *Storytelling in Preaching,* 48.

72. See James W. Cox, *Preaching* (San Francisco: Harper & Row, 1985), 207–15. Cox explains that examples are actual instances or cases that demonstrate a truth. Illustrations are comparisons of one thing to another. Illustrations are of the following types: explicit (simile and analogy), implied comparison (metaphor and allegory), and story (anecdote, a parable, or a fable).

73. Salmon, *Storytelling in Preaching,* 39.

74. Ronald J. Allen, "The Social Function of Language in Preaching," in *Preaching as a Social Act: Theology and Practice,* ed. Arthur Van Seters (Nashville: Abingdon, 1988), 178.

75. Ibid.

76. Jerry H. Gill, *On Knowing God: New Directions for the Future of Theology* (Philadelphia: Westminster, 1981), 14. See also Allen, *Christian Belief in a Postmodern World,* 19.

77. George Hunter, *To Spread the Power: Church Growth in the Wesleyan Spirit* (Nashville: Abingdon, 1988), 77.

23

So What Happens after Modernity?
A Postmodern Agenda
for Evangelical Theology

Thomas C. Oden

Although evangelicals tarry wistfully at the frazzled end of modernity, there is no cause for despair, demoralization, panic, or immobilized frustration. Believers are being invited by providence to remain open precisely to these emergent historical conditions. Even seeming retrogressions offer gracious possibilities, as was the case with Noah, the Babylonian captivity, and Jonah. Biblically viewed, this cultural disintegration is a providential judgment of sin and a grace-laden opportunity for listening to God.

Those well-instructed in classic Christian spiritual formation are better prepared than carnal humanists to understand that amid any cultural death, gracious gifts of providential guidance are being offered to humanity, and unsullied forms of the providential hedging of God in history are emerging so as to curb human folly and sin. Orthodox believers can continue to appreciate many technological, social, and economic achievements of modernity, even while soberly recognizing that their ideological underpinnings now face radical crisis.

As the smell of decaying modernity reeks through the air, postmodern Christian consciousness is emerging in the most unexpected places—universities, investigative journalism, psychological laboratories, rock music, physics research—often spanning all cultural bar-

Thomas C. Oden is Henry Anson Buttz Professor of Professor of Theology and Ethics at the Theological School and the Graduate School of Drew University in Madison, New Jersey.

riers, economic interests, and social locations. Evangelical soul care is rediscovering its identity amid this postmodern passage.

There is no single definitive expression of postmodern evangelical spirituality. I am seeking to describe a starburst of renewing forms of small-group spirituality rooted in evangelical memory. It is no narrow, monolithic, fixed entity, but a multi-colored splash of grace-enabled evangelical experimentalism.

If these whimpers echo the dying modern agony, what are the birth cries of postmodernity? History does not stand still. It is always confronting people of the evangelical communities with new constraints, emergent options, and impending requirements. The challenge today is not the same as in the days of Justin Martyr of Athanasius or Mother Theodora of the Desert of Wycliffe or Phoebe Palmer or Charles Finney.

The Trajectory toward Tomorrow: The New Christian Realism Grounded in Paleo-orthodox Social Values

Those made alive by the continuing vitalities of evangelical preaching, eucharist life, and classic Christian spiritual formation are now living in a decisive period of evangelical opportunity, a consequential moment of apostolic apologetics.

Long-set-aside possibilities and aptitudes for spiritual formation are at long last now viable which have had a prolonged history of being disdained by modernity. We are thinking here of sexual purity, covenant fidelity, the wonderful privilege of parenting, the rediscovery of providence in history, and the grace to reason morally out of the premise of revelation. We need not be driven to despair by the immediate pressures these postmodern anxieties thrust upon us, but rather grasp these options as opportunities for attesting God's own coming.

Since no finite mind can see into the future, it would be folly to pretend to make a program out of futurity, or to claim that some wished-for course of action is likely to become a future trend merely because it is a present tendency. Those who depict the present situation descriptively and then pretend to extrapolate these trends into enduring norms do not understand (as did classic Christian orthodoxy) the essential feature of human freedom, its infinite reversibility. Futurists who imagine that postmodernity is on a fixed or predictable trajectory have failed to grasp the simplest point about the indeterminacy of human freedom amid the constancy of grace.

Assuming the radical unpredictability of God-given, sin-drenched freedom, it is still possible to ponder likely directions of postmodern Gospel spirituality on the road ahead. Inheritors of evangelical soul care and spirituality are likely to be focusing major efforts on one-on-one relationships and on building families and primary communities of accountability. They will more likely be calling small scale intensive localities to take responsibility for their own futures, than turning their futures over to designer-elites who tend always to plan their own interest first into any projected social design. They will be more attentive to modest, incremental shifts toward proximate justice than hooked on supposed totally revolutionary redefinitions of the universal human order. This requires a scaling down of social planning and a scaling up of personal accountability.

Christ changes human history one by one. Christian realism seeks organic changes grounded in particular rooted social traditions, rather than pretenses of massive social engineering on the premise that no adequate neighborhoods, families, or communities of prayer ever previously existed.

Christian realism is more apt to invest confidence in personal, accountable communities than to look always toward macrocosms of central planning or bureaucratic solutions to ground-level local and domestic problems.

After-modern evangelical spirituality will be above all searching for the recovery of family stability, abiding marriages, and decent environments for the future of children. Christian realism will be looking for ways to benefit from the social experience of multiple generations, not merely from our own generation. We look especially to periods of proximate stability in ecumenical orthodoxy. We look to societies that have sought to live by eternal verities long before the devastations of terminal modernity.

The trajectory of postmodern reconstruction, in short, promises to be an organic approach to incremental change grounded in traditionally tested values formed less by abstract rationalistic schemes than by concrete historical experience. The new Christian realism will nurture the incremental increase of slow-growing human organisms, trustable relationships, long-term friendships, and covenant sexual fidelity, foregoing the illusory rhetoric of social mapmaking, human engineering, or cumbersome schemes of economic redistribution with which humanity has had such miserable historical experience over the last two centuries.

If something like that trajectory actually takes hold, by grace, it will hardly be a quick or easy passage. It may happen more out of economic pressures, political necessities, and moral revulsion (through which providence also works) than as a result of some idealistic, rationalistic blueprint on some social planner's tilted drawing board. The only thing reasonably certain about the future after modernity is that it will outlive our shrewdest probability estimates and scientific forecasts.

Salvageable Remnants of Modernity

It would be wrongheaded to infer that every aspect of modern consciousness is dead or that all social and political achievements of the last two centuries are lost. Modernity is not dead in the sense that all its repercussions and consequences are over, but in the sense that the ideological engine propelling the movement of modernity is broken down irreparably.

What then is redeemable about modernity? If modernity is in spirit dead, is it possible to speak of aspects of modern consciousness that are salvageable and worthy of emergency triage? Many ambiguous institutional residues, cultural souvenirs, and intellectual remnants of Christianity's passage through modernity are worth rescuing and preserving: much of modernity's poetry, artistic imagination, architecture, wonderful music, popular democratic processes, hard-won civil liberties, impressive medical breakthroughs, highly accessible computer data bases, high-tech marvel, and complex forms of market exchange.

Postmodern Christian families will continue to benefit from modernity's communication devices, fiber optics, and nuclear medicine. We have not seen the end of virtual reality or bar-coded plastic cards or bioengineering or hard rock. This is all modernity, and who would be so foolish as to suppose that it is either unambiguously evil or obsolete?

But can it save from sin, or render life meaningful, or heal guilt, or arrest boredom, or liberate from idolatry? It is foolish to claim too much. With each modern technological advance comes a heightened temptation to treat each limited good as if absolute and to use good technological means for evil moral ends. Only the consummate and unconditional source of all good is worthy of worship.

The apprehensions of orthodoxy are constantly being mitigated and calmed by the premise that the Holy Spirit has determined to continue enabling the liveliness of the body of Christ. Only on the falsely hypothesized premise of the default of the Holy Spirit (the least likely premise in the Christian understanding of history), could the called-out people come to nothing. Special forms and expressions of the church are constantly coming to nothing, but not the body of Christ being enabled by the Holy Spirit.

Idolatries Divested

Many fashions and styles of modernity have appeared, thrived, languished, and expired since the flourishing of Gregory the Great or Bonaventure. The death of once-modern Aristotelian scholasticism was already a fact by Calvin's time. The *via moderna* of nominalism died with the emergence of Descartes. The *via moderna* of Cartesian rationalism faded with the emergence of the empiricist tradition. Later the *via moderna* of Newtonian physics receded with the emergence of Einstein's physics and relativity theory and the advent of quantum mechanics. The once-confident premises of Victorian sexuality waned with the emergence of psychoanalysis.

Christian spirituality has lived through all of these changes, having accumulated many centuries of historical experience in dealing with various deaths of once emergent forms of modern consciousness. Only the historically illiterate imagine this recent passage of Enlightenment modernity to be the first or unprecedented or absolutely decisive one.

Our once proud individualistic forms of secular modernity are dying of their own self-chosen or corporately self-determined diseases: drug addictions, elective abortions, self-caused genital herpes, soaring suicide rates, and trigger-pulling urban muggers and killers. It is a self-destructive scene. It is wholly unconvincing to argue that these behaviors are absolutely predestined either by nature or nurture.

All these are, broadly speaking, self-selected, individually and socially self-chosen forms of damnation. Where many fathers have chosen to be absent, where the state has become a surrogate family, where many women voluntarily choose to have babies knowing the father would be absent, the kids do the suffering, not because they themselves have chosen it, but because others have chosen it for them. That is what we mean by the term "socially self-chosen" (as distinguished from individually self-chosen). The human tragedy would be much simpler if no one else suffered from our sins, and we suffered from no one else's sin. But that naïveté is not consistent with our social nature or with the Christian premise of the sociality of sin.

Meanwhile a postmodern civilization is struggling to be born.

Evangelically formed pilgrims traveling through the postmodern corridors of power who remember that sin pervades all human striving will not expect postmodernity to be without pride, sensuality, and perennial temptations to corruption. But we do have a right to expect that we can learn something useful from the moral tailspin of recent decades.

Those who willingly enslave themselves to passing idolatries should not be surprised when these alluring gods are found to have clay feet. When these beloved modern arrangements and systems die, the idolaters understandably grieve and feel angry and frustrated. Meanwhile, the grace-enabled soul can celebrate the passage through and beyond modernity, and remember the imperceptible providences of history whereby each dying historical formation is giving birth to new forms and refreshing occasions for living responsibly in relation to grace.

In each one-on-one meeting, evangelical soul care invites the dispossessed, displaced persons and wandering families of late modern times not to be afraid to enter the postmodern world, anymore than Paul feared going to Spain, or Whitefield feared entering the contentious villages of Hannoverian England, or Methodist circuit-rider Freeborn Garretson feared entering the uncertainties of the Illinois frontier, or Phoebe Palmer feared confronting the old world of British aristocrats or the new world of California miners. Each one of those crossings was analogous to our postmodern passage.

Through our finite losses, God makes way for ever new formations of the soul and the social process. Individuals and cultures come and go, but the faithfulness of God endures from everlasting to everlasting. Finite minds see the river of time from a particular vantage point in the stream, but God, as if from above in eternal simultaneity, sees the entire river in its whole extent, at every point synchronously. The One who meets us on the Last Day is quietly present already in the death of cultures as the judge of sin both corporately and individually chosen.

Life lived in Jesus Christ does not waste time resenting the inexorable fact that each culture like each person eventually dies. Sanctifying grace offers beleaguered cultural pilgrims the power and means of trusting fundamentally in the One who proffers us this ever-changing, forever-dying historical process. Some today are being spiritually formed by martyr-teachers from John Chrysostom to Dietrich Bonhoeffer. They are ready to take these steps, walking by faith not by sight.

The Unexpected Emergence
of Paleo-orthodoxy within Postmodernity

The very term and concept of "orthodoxy" emerged within the Christian tradition, rather than being borrowed and adapted from non-Christian sources. More recent orthodoxies (Freudian, Marxian, Darwinian, Keynesian, etc.) are viewed as orthodox by analogy with Christian orthodoxy with its historic succession of apostolic teaching.

Christian orthodoxy is textually defined by the apostolic testimony, as a fulfillment commentary on the Hebrew Bible. The term paleo- (old, seasoned) orthodoxy is employed to make clear that we are not talking about neo-orthodoxy, a particular movement within twentieth-century Protestant theology that actually was far more attached to the assumptions of modernity than is postmodern paleo-orthodoxy. Were it not for neo-orthodoxy as a popularly recognizable movement, the term paleo-orthodoxy would be an oxymoron. "Paleo" becomes a necessary prefix only because the term orthodoxy has been preempted and to some degree distorted by the modern (Bultmannian-Tillichian-Niebuhrian) theological tradition of neo-orthodoxy.

Christian orthodoxy in its ancient (paleo) ecumenical sense is summarily defined sacramentally by the baptismal formula (in the name of the Father, Son, and Holy Spirit), liturgically by the eucharistic event, and confessionally by the baptismal confession with its precisely remembered rule of faith as recalled in the Apostles', Nicene, and Athanasian Creeds, and their subsequent consensual interpretations. Under heretical attack, definitions emerged in the seven ancient worldwide councils and in other consensually received regional councils that have held fast through the changes of Protestant reform.

Orthodoxy is that sustained tradition that has steadily centered the consenting church in the primordially received interpretation of the apostolic witness. It means thinking within the boundaries of the ancient church consensus about the canonically received apostolic preaching so as to contextually apply that tradition to ever emergent cultural situations.

As Orthodox Judaism calls the Jewish tradition back to its classical rabbinic sources, and as Roman Catholic orthodoxy returns to the teaching tradition of the see of Rome, so does classical Christian teaching among Protestants call us back to the apostolic tradition as attested in Scripture, and reappropriated by the martyrs, saints, consensual preachers and writers of primitive Christianity.

The Paleo-orthodoxy Reading of Scripture and Tradition

The ancient consensual writers constantly warned hearers not to believe them if they spouted off contrary to Scripture. They frequently said in effect: if I happen to say something in a way that distorts the apostolic testimony that you have repeatedly heard in the services of worship where the Hebrew Bible and the Gospels and epistles are liturgically read—if that happens do not follow me, but Scripture as interpreted by the mind of the believing church.

There is nothing in the core tradition of orthodox hermeneutics that pits tradition against Scripture. Even the oral tradition that was so highly valued by Basil and others was never pitted against the written tradition of apostolic writings, but only received gratefully as a complement consistent with the written word. There is no way to validate or argue for the orthodox tradition without by reference to Scripture, since orthodoxy is nothing more or less than the ancient consensual tradition of exegesis. The canon of Holy Writ is the crucial criterion for all classic Christian interpretation.

Developing a Classic
Christian Critique of Modern Criticism

There is among "mod-surviving" evangelicals a flourishing critique of criticism, discontented with failed Enlightenment methods. This critique of methods of secular criticism is what we need to try to teach lay believers who are tempted to despair over the course of current events.

What's so skewed about conventional modern methods of investigation? They are ideologically tilted, antireligiously biased, and historically ignorant.

Discovering Premodern Roots

Central to their critique is the growing recognition that many views and analytical methods often thought to be modern are actually premodern in origin. The critique of criticism delights in revealing precisely how that which was assumed prematurely to be uniquely modern actually has a long history and is demonstrably grounded unawarely in ancient wisdoms. Unmasking the premodern roots of modernity is an endlessly entertaining game for postmodern classicists.

Some even erroneously think of criticism itself as if it were by definition strictly a modern phenomenon, as when modernity is described as itself the age of criticism, as if it had no premodern prototypes. Blinders have been installed by modern advocates to prevent us from seeing the patristic, medieval, Reformation lineage of modern ideas. This habit stands in perfect accord with the ideology and settled habits of modern chauvinism.

College courses in the history of psychology do not generally cover any texts or ideas before Wilhelm Wundt or Sigmund Freud, thus ignoring the fact that the dynamics of repression and behavior modification had been investigated in classical pastoral care for two millennia before Freud. Nor have the contributions to the theory and practice of the intensive group experience in eighteenth-century religious societies and covenant groups ever been appraised as a fit topic in Soc. 101. Nor has the impact of holiness revivalism on social change often been recognized by historians of the nineteenth century (excepting a few specialized historians of revivalism like Timothy Smith, Nathan Hatch, Donald Dayton, David Bebbington, and Mark Noll). Central to the classic Christian critique of modern criticism is simply pointing out the historic roots of methods falsely presumed to have been invented recently — since Rousseau, Feuerbach, Nietzsche, and Freud.

Unmasking the Pretentions of Hyper-modern Criticism

Postmodern evangelical spirituality is no longer willing to be infantalized and spoon-fed by faltering modern methods of supposedly disinterested criticism. Part of the delightful and intriguing game of postmodern neoclassic consciousness focuses upon puncturing the myth of modern superiority, the pretense of modern chauvinism that assumes the intrinsic inferiority of all premodern wisdoms.

Here are some potential harbingers of an emerging postmodern evangelical critique of modern criticism:

The critique of *modern psychotherapeutic* theories is occurring among evangelicals such as Stanton Jones, Gary Collins, Wayne Oates, and Archibald Hart. They are observing how pathetically ineffective psychotherapy has been over against spontaneous remission rates, thereby applying an empiricist-behaviorist grid to the assessment of psychotherapies, even as the counter-Enlightenment Protestant evangelicals themselves observed the behavioral consequences of speculative theories and tendentious opinions.

Sociology of knowledge seeks to show how social location determines the formation of ideas. The critique of *sociology of knowledge* is proceeding among evangelicals, who have learned to apply social location analysis to the sociologists. Evangelicals are now asking candidly about how knowledge elites driving hypermodern criticism can harbor persistent and often silent private and elitist interests that shape the outcomes of their supposedly impartial investigations. Postmodern evangelical spirituality of the sort found in Peter Berger, Ron Sider, Richard Mouw, Kwami Bediako of Ghana, and Rene Padilla of Argentina, does not hesitate in boldly using sociology of knowledge as a tool to investigate and disarm ideologically motivated advocates of particularly skewed social constructions of reality, even as the classic evangelical and orthodox Protestants themselves were critics of self-deception with regard to egoistic interests flying under the flag of idealistic rhetoric.

The task of *historical studies* must now be reassessed precisely amid the collapse of historical studies (this is already happening with Pannenberg, Wilkin, Braaten, and Jenson among Lutherans, and among others Anthony Thistelton, Gerald O'Collins, Richard B. Hays, and Ben Witherington III). Postmodern neoclassic historical research is as interested in the plain textual content analyses of Josephus, Eusebuis, Socrates, Scholasticus, Sozomen, Jeromen, Augustine, Theophylact, and Theodoret of Cyrus as in modern ideologically shaped (Marxist, psychoanalytic, ultrafeminist, or deconstructionist) mutations of revisionist historical criticism.

The postmodern evangelical critique of *hermeneutical criticism* (as seen in Peter Stuhlmacher, Martin Hengel, Eta Linnemann, and Brevard Childs) stands poised to speak of the normative canon and the plain sense of Scripture, resisting speculative fashions of redaction and form criticism and reader-response theories and socio-pragmatic contextualizations that tyrannize and nonchalantly rape the text. The best traditions of classic Protestant hermeneutics (such as those of Martin Chemnitz, Abraham Calovius, John Quenstedt, John Gerhard, Martin Bucer, John Owen, along with Edwards, Wesley, and Finney) were keen observers and critics of speculative historical approaches that violate the text. The classic evangelical hermeneutic trusts the apostolic primitive remembers more than contemporary ideologically motivated advocacy deconstructionists with wild imaginations.

Postmodern evangelical consciousness is less inclined than antimodern fundamentalism to cower and recoil from this methodological fray. It is more willing to play devil's advocate, enter the critical debate, and stand ready when necessary to announce that the emperor (in this case the uncritical knowledge elite) has no clothes. Modern academia, which imagined itself handsomely furnished with elaborate intellectual attire, elegant theories, and intricate methods of re-search, is within the postmodern environment feeling extremely vulner-able, ever more exposed, more than slightly unclad and unmasked.

In all these ways and more the trendy modes of criticism are being found susceptible to a telling postmodern orthodox critique of criticism. This opens the way for a deepened inquiry into the truth claims of classic Jewish and Christian texts, including those of the Orthodox, evangelical, and revivalist traditions of spiritual formation that are self-consciously shaped by the revelation of God in history. The postmodern ethos introduces us to a postcritical situation of opportunity in which it will be assumed that significant players will have broad proficiencies in modern critical methods precisely in order to rectify the limitations and personal hubris of those methods.

Does modern historical criticism represent a devastating chal-lenge to the principle of apostolicity? Briefly answered, no. When criticism is working well, so that an orthodox skepticism places in question the speculations of the historical critics, there is nothing to fear from solid historical inquiry into the tradition of transmission of apostolic testimony. There is only the task of improving historical inquiry and bringing it ever closer to the datum of the incarnate, risen Lord and His body, the church.

Neo-Oppression Analysis

Another case—dare we mention it? It is now time to speak up in college departments of religion and old-line seminaries for the long-suffering oppressed: evangelicals and pietists. A new form of oppres-sion analysis is required in our stuffy cubbyhole of academia, to show that the most marginalized and oppressed group in Protestant theo-logical education is currently least represented in its faculties: those who come from its evangelical and peitistic heartland. Those most maligned and humiliated and demeaned are believers who bear the unfair epithet of "fundy," like Jews who wore the star of David on their clothes in Germany in the 1930s.

Those who have the least voice in the academic caucus game—far less than ethnic minorities or officially designated oppressed groups—are evangelical students from the poor side of the exegetical tracks. I speak candidly of biblical believers who are assigned pariah roles in Scripture courses, those forced into a crisis of bad conscience by being required to conform in ideologically tilted social ethics courses, who are given bad grades because they have read George Ladd or taken Turretin seriously or have grown up loving the hymns of Fanny Crosby.

It is time for those who have patiently sat through repetitive courses in guilt to apply a specific social oppression analysis to the new oppressors: the tenured radicals who in syncretistic faculties reduplicate only themselves when new appointments are made; who are tolerant only of latitudinarians, who neither have nor seek any church constituency; who debunk the plain sense of Scripture, who never enter into a room with a Bible unless armed with two dozen commentaries that enable them to hold all decisions in a state of permanent suspension; who lack peer review because they do not know any colleagues in the guild different from themselves.

Among self-satisfied knowledge elites this postmodern critique of criticism will be caricatured as if it were precritical. Rather, we say postcritical. In my own case, it is far too late to be precritical if one has already spent most of one's life chasing rainbows of a supposed psychoanalytic, sociological, and historical criticism based on the premises of modern chauvinism (that newer is always better, older worse). That can no longer be precritical which follows after assimilating ten generations of Enlightenment ideology, empiricist investigation, and idealistic speculation.

If it is thought precritical merely to take seriously sources of wisdom that emerged before a modern period which is deceptively dubbed "the age of criticism," then in that sense all devout Jews, Muslims, and Christians join in the delight in being precritical—but note how self-incriminating that narcissistic premise is to the integrity of modern criticism, if it supposes that one is able only to use sources of one's own historical period. If that is what criticism amounts to, let us be spared it.

My experience as a countercultural radical taught me not to trust anyone over 30. My tardy learning is teaching me that it may be increasingly difficult in divinity to trust any writer under 300.

Some Postmodern Paleo-orthodox Writers:
A Preliminary List

The writers who have or who are currently undertaking this classic Christian critique of criticism are remarkably dispersed among varied traditions, as seen in this partial list, leading off in each case with young men and women writers:

Eastern Orthodox: Vigen Guroian, John Breck, Thomas Hopko, Leonid Kishkovsky, Stanley Harakas, John D. Zizioulas, Kallistos Ware, and Vladimir Lossky.

Roman Catholics: Paul Mankowski, Eleanor Stump, George

Weigle, Russell Hittinger, Richard John Neuhaus, Paul Vitz, Michael Novak, Tom Howard, Germain Grisez, Joseph Ratzinger, Han Urs von Balthasar, and Malcolm Muggeridge.

Anglican: Alister McGrath, John Milbank, Robert Webber, Phillip Turner, John Stott, and Lesslie Newbiggin.

Reformed: James Davison Hunter, Michael Horton, Mark Noll, Elizabeth Achtemeier, Alvin Plantinga, George Marsden, Nicholas Wolterstorff, Donald Bloesch, Brevard Childs, Max Stackhouse, and Thomas Torrance.

Baptists: Stanley Grenz, David S. Dockery, David Wells, Nathan Hatch, Timothy George, D.A. Carson, and Clark Pinnock.

Wesleyans: David Hay, William Abraham, Ben Witherington III, Roberta Bondi, Geoffrey Wainwright, David Steinmetz, and those inimitable jokers of postmodern classic Christian criticism: Stanley Hauerwas and Will Willimon.

This mélange has varied characters of different sorts and warts, but what they have in common is that all have survived the death of modernity ever more deeply committed to the renewal of time-tested evangelical spiritual disciplines. Each of these writers has already produced a significant bibliography. This list is much healthier than the few souls that could be named in *Agenda for Theology* in 1979 as faint premonitions of postmodern orthodoxy.[1] Then it was a cloud the size of a man's hand; now it is misting; in a decade it will shower; someday there may be a hurricane.

The Young Fogeys

What is happening today is a profound rediscovery of the texts and wisdom of the long-overlooked classic pastoral tradition. For young evangelicals this means especially the neglected biblical interpretation of the Eastern church fathers of the earliest Christian centuries. These rediscoverers are the young fogeys of the postmodern world.

What is happening amid this historical situation is a joyous return to the sacred texts of Christian Scripture and the consensual exegetical guides of the formative period of its canonization and interpretation. Young "mod-surpassing" evangelicals are those who, having entered in good faith into the disciplines of modernity, and having become disillusioned with its illusions, are again studying the Word of God made known in history as attested by prophetic and apostolic witnesses whose testimonies have become perennial texts for this worldwide, multicultural, multigenerational remembering and celebrating community.

Our intention in these pages has not been merely to repeat a tired, innocuous truism that an old generation is perishing and a new generation being born. What is much harder is to designate precisely how the community of faith is negotiating a passing of a former massive cultural ascendancy, and how the ancient testimony of the body of Christ is connecting with the emergence of a new culture.

What is now clear is that a worldview is ebbing, perhaps not wholly extinct yet, but numb in emergent vitality, and only awaiting a lingering expiration process of failed ideologies: autonomous individualism, narcissistic hedonism, reductive naturalism, and absolute moral relativism. Others may call that world something other than terminal modernity, but it seems there is no better way of naming it.

In describing the trek from liberal Protestant modernity to a postmodern classic reappropriation of the patristic exegesis and evangelical soul care, my own autobiographical journey is being described in part. After spending more than half my adult life as an avid advocate and defender of modernity (from Marx through Nietzsche and Freud to Bultmann, with stops along the way with Fritz Perls, Carl Rogers, Alexander Lowen, Martin Heidegger, and Eric Berne), what has changed for me is the steady slow growth toward consensual ancient classic Christianity with its proximate continuity, catholicity, and apostolicity. This has elicited for me a growing resistance of faddism, novelty, heresy, anarchism, antinomianism, pretensions of discontinuity, revolutionary bravado, and nonhistorical idealism.

Did my Ph.D. teach me moral courage? That would really be stretching it. Yale may have tried, but either it didn't take or this grad student didn't notice. Now, if asked to offer a single gift of insight to my reader, it would be to seek the ground of moral courage and intellectual freedom. For Christians that ground lies in the resurrection of Christ, the willingness to die daily, and trust God beyond the gods.

This study was originally conceived as the first half of a more detailed argument on the present church crisis which included an expanded study of:

- the gentle duty of compassionate admonition,
- the apostolic practice of pastoral counsel,
- confidentiality in confession,
- the right of the laity to absolution,
- the binding and mending of table fellowship,
- the restorative intent of communion discipline,
- and the value of communion discipline for the political order

Readers who wish to pursue further these subjects may consult that discussion.[2] The remaining half of the argument as earlier conceived may be found in *Corrective Love: The Administration of Communion Discipline*.[3]

To young fogeys, we close with this expression of hope: Center yourself in the text of the primitive apostolic witness. Listen to Scripture *with* the historic church. You will then be more ready to receive the empowerment of the Spirit to hold fast to the oneness, holiness, catholicity, and apostolicity of the community of faith amid any cultural contingency. Thus prepared, the Holy Spirit will give you new freedom to resist accommodating to systems of syncretistic secularizing spirituality that have already miserably failed.

Avoid the chief temptation of the believer in the jaded liberal culture: to be too easily intimidated by a modern consciousness already desperately on the defensive. Do not slide unawarely down the slippery slope of overestimating the vitality of the prevailing local fad. Do not dance down the primrose path of accommodation to a modernity now collapsing.

Finally, we plead the aesthetic beauty of retrogression, not to twentieth-century fundamentalism, not to American revivalism of the nineteenth-century, not to the eighteenth-century pietism, nor to the seventeenth-century Protestant orthodox scholasticism, or to sixteenth-century classic Reformation teaching, but to the future through the route of classic Christian exegesis of the first five centuries, the ancient ecumenical tradition to whom all Christians — Catholic, Protestant, and Liberal — have a right to appeal.

NOTES

1. Thomas C. Oden, *Agenda for Theology: Recovering Christian Roots* (San Francisco: Harper and Row, 1979).

2. Much of this material, including chapters 2 and 23 in this volume, can be found in a different and expanded form in Thomas C. Oden, *Requiem: A Lament in Three Movements* (Nashville; Abingdon, 1995).

3. Thomas C. Oden, *Corrective Love: The Administration of Communion Discipline* (St. Louis: Concordia, 1995).

RESOURCES FOR FURTHER STUDY

· ·

Aeschliman, Gordon. *Global Trends*. Downers Grove, Ill.: InterVarsity, 1990.

Allen, Diogenes. *Christian Belief in a Postmodern World: The Full Wealth of Conviction*. Louisville: Westminster/John Knox, 1989.

Alston, William. *Perceiving God: The Epistemology of Religious Experience*. Ithaca, N.Y.: Cornell Univ. Press, 1991.

Anderson, Leith. *A Church for the 21st Century*. Minneapolis: Bethany, 1992.

Anderson, Walter Truett. *Reality Isn't What It Used to Be: Theatrical Politics, Ready-to-Wear Religion, Global Myths, Primitive Chic, and Other Wonders of the Postmodern World*. San Francisco: HarperCollins, 1990.

Barna, George. *The Frog in the Kettle: What Christians Need to Know about Life in the Year 2000*. Ventura, Calif.: Regal, 1990.

Berger, Peter. *The Homeless Mind: Modernization and Consciouslessness*. New York: Vintage, 1973.

Bernstein, Richard J. *Beyond Objectivism and Relativism: Science, Hermeneutics and Praxis*. Philadelphia: Univ. of Pennsylvania, 1983.

Carson, D.A. *The Gagging of God.* Grand Rapids: Zondervan, forthcoming.

Cobb, John B. "Two Types of Postmodernism: Deconstruction and Process." *Theology Today* 47 (1990): 149–58.

Colson, Charles. *The Body.* Dallas: Word, 1992.

Conner, Steven. *Postmodernist Culture: An Introduction to Theories of the Contemporary.* Oxford: Blackwell, 1989.

Coupland, Douglas. *Life After God.* New York: Simon and Schuster/Pocket, 1994.

Derrida, Jacques. *Writing and Difference.* Chicago: Univ. of Chicago, 1978.

Dockery, David S. *Biblical Interpretation Then and Now.* Grand Rapids: Baker, 1992.

Ellis, John. *Against Deconstruction.* Princeton: Princeton Univ. Press, 1989.

Erickson, Millard J. *Evangelical Interpretation.* Grand Rapids: Baker, 1993.

Feyerabend, Paul. *Against Method.* London: Thretford, 1975.

Finger, Thomas. "Modernity, Postmodernity—What in the World Are They?" *Transformation* 10 (October–December 1993): 20–26.

Fish, Stanley. *Is There a Text in This Class? The Authority of Interpretative Communities.* Cambridge: Harvard Univ. Press, 1980.

Gitlin, Todd. "The Postmodern Predicament." *Wilson Quarterly* 13 (Summer 1989): 67–76.

Grenz, Stanley J. *A Theology for the Community of God.* Nashville: Broadman and Holman, 1994.

Griffin, David Ray, William A. Beardslee, and Joe Holland, eds. *Varieties of Postmodern Theology.* Albany, N.Y.: State Univ. of New York Press, 1989.

Guinness, Os. *Dining with the Devil: The Metachurch Movement Flirts with Modernity.* Grand Rapids: Baker, 1993.

Hardison, O.B., Jr. *Disappearing Through the Skylight: Culture and Technology in the Twentieth Century.* New York: Viking, 1989.

Harvey, David. *The Condition of Postmodernity.* Cambridge, Mass.: Blackwell, 1989.

Hauerwas, Stanley. *After Christendom?* Nashville: Abingdon, 1992.

Hirsch, David. *The Deconstruction of Literature.* Hanover, N.H.: Brown Univ. Press, 1991.

Hunter, George. *How to Reach Secular People.* Nashville: Abingdon, 1992.

Jencks, Charles. *The Language of Postmodern Architecture.* London: Academy Enterprises, 1984.

Kroker, Arthur. *Panic Encyclopedia: The Definitive Guide to the Postmodern Scene.* New York: St. Martin's, 1989.

Kroker, Arthur, and David Cook. *The Postmodern Scene: Excremental Culture and Hyper-Aesthetics.* New York: St. Martin's, 1986.

Lindbeck, George A. *The Nature of Doctrine: Religion and Theology in a Postliberal Age.* Philadelphia: Westminster, 1989.

Lundin, Roger. *The Culture of Interpretation: Christian Faith and the Postmodern World.* Grand Rapids: Eerdmans, 1993.

Lyotard, Jean-Francois. *The Postmodern Condition: A Report on Knowledge.* "Theory and History of Literature," Vol. 10. Translated by Geoff Bennington and Brian Massumi. Minneapolis: Univ. of Minnesota Press, 1984.

MacIntyre, Alasdair. *After Virtue.* Notre Dame, Ind.: Univ. of Notre Dame Press, 1984.

Mahedy, William, and Janet Bernardi. *A Generation Alone: Xers Making a Place in the World.* Downers Grove, Ill.: InterVarsity, 1994.

McGrath, Alister E. *Intellectuals Don't Need God and Other Myths.* Grand Rapids: Zondervan, 1993.

McKeever, Kerry. "How to Avoid Speaking About God: Poststructuralist Philosophers and Biblical Hermeneutics." *Journal of Literature and Theology* 6 (1992): 228–38.

McKnight, Edgar V. *Post-modern Use of the Bible: The Emergence of Reader-Oriented Criticism.* Nashville: Abingdon, 1988.

Murphy, Nancy, and James William McClendon, Jr. "Distinguishing Modern and Postmodern Theologies." *Modern Theology* 5 (1989): 191–214.

Myers, Kenneth. *All God's Children and Blue Suede Shoes: Christians and Popular Culture.* Wheaton, Ill.: Crossway, 1989.

Oden, Thomas C. *After Modernity . . . What? Agenda for Theology.* Grand Rapids: Zondervan/Academie, 1990.

———. *Two Worlds: Notes on the Death of Modernity in America and Russia.* Downers Grove, Ill.: InterVarsity, 1992.

Percy, Walker. *Lost in the Cosmos: The Last Self-Help Book.* New York: Farrar, Straus & Giroux, 1983.

Placher, William C. *Unapologetic Theology: A Christian Voice in a Pluralistic Conversation.* Louisville: Westminster/John Knox, 1989.

Postman, Neil. *Technopoly: The Surrender of Culture to Technology.* New York: Vintage, 1993.

Raschke, Carl A. "Fire and Roses: Toward Authentic Postmodern Religious Thinking." *Journal of the American Academy of Religion* 58 (1990): 671–89.

Rorty, Richard. *Objectivity, Relativism, and Truth.* New York: Cambridge, 1991.

Russell-Jones, Iwan. "The Contemporary Text: Media and Preaching— 'Losing My Religion' on MTV." *Journal of Preachers* 15:4 (1992): 36–39.

Schlesinger, Arthur M. *The Disuniting of America*. New York: Norton, 1992.

Smith, Huston. *Beyond the Postmodern Mind*. Wheaton, Ill.: Theosophical, 1989.

Stiver, Dan. "Much Ado about Athens and Jerusalem: The Implications of Postmodernism for Faith." *Review and Expositor* 91 (1994): 85–102.

Stout, Jeffrey. *The Flight from Authority: Religion, Morality, and the Quest for Autonomy*. Notre Dame, Ind.: Univ. of Notre Dame Press, 1981.

Tapia, Andres. "Reaching the First Post-Christian Generation." *Christianity Today*, 12 September 1994, 18–23.

Taylor, Mark C. *Erring: A Postmodern A/Theology*. Chicago: Univ. of Chicago Press, 1984.

Timmerman, John H., and Donald R. Hettinga, eds. *In the World: Reading and Writing as a Christian*. Grand Rapids: Baker, 1987.

Tracy, David. *Plurality and Ambiguity: Hermeneutics, Religion, Hope*. San Francisco: Harper and Row, 1987.

Van Gelder, Craig. "Postmodernism as an Emerging World View." *Calvin Theological Journal* 26 (1991): 412–17.

Veith, Gene Edward, Jr. *Postmodern Times: A Christian Guide to Contemporary Thought and Culture*. Wheaton, Ill.: Crossway, 1994.

Walhout, Clarence, and Leland Ryken. *Contemporary Literary Theory: A Christian Appraisal*. Grand Rapids: Eerdmans, 1991.

Walsh, Brian J., and J. Richard Middleton. *The Transforming Vision: Shaping a Christian World View*. Downers Grove: Ill.: InterVarsity, 1984.

————. *Truth Is Stranger Than It Used to Be*. Downers Grove, Ill.: InterVarsity, 1995.

Wells, David F. *No Place for Truth: Or, Whatever Happened to Evangelical Theology?* Grand Rapids: Eerdmans, 1993.

————. *God in the Wasteland.* Grand Rapids: Eerdmans, 1994.

White, James Emery. *What Is Truth?* Nashville: Broadman and Holman, 1994.

SELECTED NAME INDEX

Englehardt, H., Jr. **269, 279**
Eribon, D. **85**
Erickson, M. **16, 18, 127, 366, 373**

F
Farley, E. **335–36, 343**
Farrar, F. **169**
Fedler, F. **372**
Fish, S. **35, 40, 145, 218, 243, 252–53, 290**
Ford, D. **335–36**
Ford, L. **369, 373**
Foucalt, M. **26, 35, 72–73, 85–87, 93, 103, 241, 245, 316–17, 326, 328**
Frei, H. **77, 329, 332, 342**
Freud, S. **27, 33**
Fuchs, E. **231**

G
Gadamer, H. **54, 66, 102, 208, 231–32, 241, 247, 253**
Garrett, J. **66**
Gay, C. **355**
Geertz, C. **77**
Geisler, N. **127, 263, 266, 357**
George, T. **404**
Gibbs, E. **373**
Gilkey, L. **35, 51, 372–73**
Gill, J. **104–31, 241, 243, 251, 387, 391**
Girard, R. **66**
Graham, B. **368**
Green, M. **381, 390**
Greimas, A. **188**
Grenz, S. **78–81, 87, 102, 147, 404**
Griffin, D. **16, 18, 34–35, 39–40, 43, 51, 76, 86, 102, 246, 252, 389**
Groff, W. **235**
Gruenler, R. **215, 358**
Guinness, O. **360, 372**
Guroian, D. **403**
Gustafson, J. **272, 276, 279**

H

Habermas, J. 71–72, 85, 91
Hagner, D. 204
Harakas, S. 403
Hart, A. 400
Harvey, D. 85
Harvey, V. 355
Hasel, G. 214
Hassen, I 71, 85
Hatch, N. 47, 400, 404
Hauerwas, S. 272, 276, 279, 343, 404
Hays, R. 179–80, 189, 401
Heidegger, M. 127, 208, 218, 232, 294, 316, 328
Heil, J. 237
Helm, P. 358
Helminiak, D. 103
Hemingway, L. 27
Hendricks, H. 134
Henry, C. 276, 280, 335, 343, 345–47, 349, 352, 354, 357–58, 373
Hick, J. 106, 258–59, 265
Hill, A. 145
Hirschman, A. 388
Hobbes, T. 27
Hodge, C. 170
Hodgson, P. 252, 355
Holland, J. 37, 51
Holmer, P. 87
Hooper, W. 343
Houston, W. 145
Howard, T. 404
Hume, D. 27
Hunter, G. 18, 377–79, 387, 389, 391
Hunter, J. 47, 404
Husserl, E. 208

I

Iannone, M. 169–70, 172
Ingleby, J. 103
Iser, W. 218

Z

SCRIPTURE INDEX

David S. Dockery is president of Union University in Jackson, Tennessee. Prior to this post he served as associate professor of New Testament theology at Southern Baptist Theological Seminary, Lexington, Kentucky. Dockery is author or editor of several books, including *Biblical Interpretation Then and Now: Contemporary Hermeneutics in the Light of the Early Church; New Testament Criticism and Interpretation;* and *Christian Scripture: An Evangelical Perspective on Inspiration, Authority, and Interpretation.* His Ph.D. degree is from the University of Texas, Arlington.